Alf McCreary

Behind the Headlines

An Autobiography

50 YEARS IN JOURNALISM

COLOURPOINT BOOKS

Dedicated to
Hilary-Anne Beck McCreary

Published 2013 by Colourpoint Books
an imprint of Colourpoint Creative Ltd
Colourpoint House, Jubilee Business Park
21 Jubilee Road, Newtownards, BT23 4YH
Tel: 028 9182 6339
Fax: 028 9182 1900
E-mail: info@colourpoint.co.uk
Web: www.colourpoint.co.uk

First Edition
First Impression

A catalogue record for this book is available from the British Library.

Designed by April Sky Design, Newtownards
Tel: 028 9182 7195
Web: www.aprilsky.co.uk

Printed by W&G Baird Ltd, Antrim

ISBN 978-1-78073-054-7

Front cover: Harrison Photography

CONTENTS

"Nothing is more highly to be prized than the value of each day."

Johann Wolfgang von Goethe

FOREWORD

L AST YEAR I had an e-mail from Facebook, telling me that 57 people were waiting to be my 'friends'. Are you kidding me?

Call me old fashioned but, for me, that's not what friends are all about. A friend is someone with whom you have a lot in common, someone whom you really like, whose conversation is interesting and whose company you enjoy. Someone with whom you have a shared history. Someone… like Alf McCreary.

Alf and I have been friends for around fifty years and, trust me, he is one of the good guys.

We hooked up shortly after arriving at Queen's, two scholarship boys from the country, wide eyed and clueless. We soon dived in the deep end, relishing the opportunity to follow our passions… Alf in hockey, me in music. There was a great 'can do' attitude amongst our intake. There were a bunch of us, Catholic, Protestant it didn't matter a damn, who threw ourselves into University life with gusto. We were like kids who got let loose in the toy shop. Within a few years Alf was editor of *Gown*, the Queen's newspaper, and I was running The Glee Club. Happy days! As Alf relates in the book, many of that gang went on to become movers and shakers, not only in Northern Ireland, but internationally.

Alf's career path after University is an object lesson in the combination of talent and hard work bringing success. As a journalist, through the dark days he brought an even-handedness to his reporting which was by no means the norm back then. That wasn't easy. Alf is a man of integrity and this was a hallmark of his work during his days at the *Belfast Telegraph*, for example. He was never content to toe a party line.

When Alf returned to QUB to handle public relations, I remember thinking, "What a perfect gig!" It was a match made in Heaven!

As a writer, Alf has been a great and a valued chronicler of Northern Ireland life. His craftsmanship is never less than superbly professional but, for me, what shines through always is his humanity, never more so than in this book. It's a great read, simple as that.

OK Alf... I now think it's your round!

Phil Coulter

 A LF MCCREARY DETAILS his personal odyssey with disarming courage and a searing honesty. In part his story is a social history of the *mores* of Northern Ireland in the second half of the twentieth century.

The narrative is stamped by acute observation and an ear for anecdote which provides a revealing and often humorous insight on many of the leading public figures of the time.

The humanity which surfaces in reflections on politics and related violence at home, and accounts of obscene poverty in the Third World, is conveyed with the passion of an award-winning journalist who ranks among the outstanding descriptive writers of his generation.

From a humble boyhood in Bessbrook to carefree days as a student at Queen's and some challenging times as a high-profile member of the university's staff, from a life in the media observing Northern Ireland's darkest days to sharing confidences with leaders of Church and State, from dining at high table to surviving on subsistence rations in hunger-stricken Africa – this is an autobiography that is never less than fascinating and compels the reader's attention.

Roy Lilley
Former Editor of the Belfast Telegraph 1974–92
and Editorial Director 1992–98

PREFACE

Philip Guedalla, the lawyer, writer and wit, once noted that "The preface is the most important part of the book. Even reviewers read a preface."

That may be so, but I am also attracted to the comment from George Bernard Shaw that "The man who writes about himself and his own time, is the only man who writes about all people and about all time."

There is indeed a universality about every autobiography because it deals essentially with human nature which changes little down the ages. However, it is also salutary to remember that a memoir is not necessarily a definitive account of what happened. It is what the author remembers about what he or she believes took place.

A friend of mine said recently that writing an autobiography is a bit like pulling a rope from a hedge. Once you start tugging, you never know what is in there.

So it was in this spirit of discovery and adventure that I began tugging some time ago on the long rope of my own life. It proved to be a surprising, self-revealing and at times a deeply-emotional experience. What appears in print is entirely my responsibility, and I hope that you will find my journey as interesting, challenging and surprising as I have done.

Alf McCreary
26 September 2013

CHAPTER ONE

The Model Village

I WAS BORN out of wedlock in the small South Armagh village of Bessbrook during the Second World War, when the German forces of Adolf Hitler were on the rampage across Europe. Soon after my birth, I was wrapped in a blanket and placed in a drawer, because there was no cot available. From this inauspicious beginning – the exact circumstances of which I did not know of until many years later – the only way for me was to progress upwards…

My teenage mother, Lena McCreary, was deeply affected by my birth, because of the then stigma of being an unmarried mother. Much later on, she told me of the guilt she felt in those days and of being confined to a back room in the family home almost until the birth. It must have been an ordeal for her, and I felt sad for her when she finally told me about it.

However, I don't think she ever fully realised, until she was virtually on her deathbed, that I too suffered emotionally from being born out of wedlock, and that it took me a very long time to come to terms with the perceived shame of not having parents who were married – in other words, of being 'illegitimate' – as if any baby or adult can ever be an 'illegitimate' human being.

I don't believe that Lena ever came to terms with it herself, and she carried the sense of social stigma for the rest of her days, even though she was later happily married to a local man and they had five children of their own. We all retain a vivid memory of her strong character and some of her quirkiness.

My father, Norman Leitch, who was twenty-two when I was born, offered to marry Lena, but my maternal grandmother, Minnie McCreary thought that he was not good enough for her daughter, though I never discovered why. Perhaps it was because there was a strict hierarchy in the village, starting with the mill managers and then the doctor, clergy and schoolteachers, and ultimately reaching down to the mill workers, the labourers and the unemployed.

Norman was young, uneducated and without a job, because he refused to work in the mill. So his lowly social status may have added to Lena's 'disgrace' of having an 'illegitimate' child. Norman himself may have been deeply hurt by the rejection by my grandmother after offering to do what was regarded as the 'right thing' in those days. Maybe she thought that they were not suited for each other, and that they were much too young to get married, but she never shared her thoughts with me about this, and I was too young and shy to ask her about it.

My father later left the village to make his career in England and he ended up as a very rich man. I believe that my grandmother's rejection of him spurred him on to make his own way in life and to show 'the McCrearys' what he could do, and I respect him for that. Norman was a charmer but also an able businessman, who wrote two booklets about his native Bessbrook, which he loved. Not surprisingly I was not mentioned in either of them. He called them *Paddy's Progress*, which in many ways was the story of his own life.

My grandmother Minnie McCreary, née Brown, was a strong but highly-strung woman who died from a heart attack when I was 16, and unfortunately I never really got to know her well, even while I was being brought up in her house. Her main contribution to my life, apart from deciding that my father was not good enough for her daughter, was to give me my Christian name. One day she went down to the local registry office and simply named me 'Alf' – not 'Alfred' which is my formal name on legal documents, but 'Alf', which I have always used personally and professionally. Nobody in the family ever knew why she did this, but it is a reminder that so much of our lives are already shaped for us, before we have the ability to put forward our own views.

With the benefit of hindsight, I sometimes think that my grandmother's decision not to allow my parents to marry had unexpected benefits for me, as my father was a strong character with whom I might not have lived easily, and he had to carve out his own path in life.

However, there was pain in my own journey, particularly in my teenage years. My grandfather, Tommy McCreary, who adopted me and became my guardian, was my hero. There had been talk among old aunts about having me adopted by strangers, such was the self-righteous shame that they so quickly felt second-hand about my mother's predicament.

A young girl who was 'in trouble' in those days was really in trouble. Over sixty years later Lena told me, almost as an aside, that she had never wanted me to be adopted, but that two local families had shown a willingness to do so. It was only a couple of days later that the shock of what she had told me sank in, and I began to realise that in September 1940 she was powerless to prevent me from being adopted by an outside family.

It must have been a heart-breaking situation for her, and for the other pregnant and unmarried young girls during those harsh times when there was little or no sympathy for one-parent families. However my grandfather, who had the final say, would have none of it, and he took me in as one of his own. I always loved and respected him for doing that.

It took me years to realise how lucky I was to have been reared by a warmly supportive maternal family, in which my kindly Aunt Jean became a surrogate mother. My charismatic Uncle Bill, who was only a few years older than me, became a protective big brother with whom I have remained close for a lifetime, and we have had many an escapade together. Sometimes I wonder, if I had been less fortunate as a young child born out of wedlock, would I have ended up in one of those notorious industrial schools or similar institutions in Ireland, where children were so vulnerable to the savagery – and in many cases the sexual perversions – of those who were supposed to protect them?

Today it is difficult to convey to people the sense of unwarranted shame that was felt by my mother and me because of my 'illegitimate' birth. In modern life one parent families are commonplace, and many couples decide to marry nowadays only after their children are already born. Nevertheless it was a huge struggle to overcome this perceived early 'handicap' of illegitimacy in the Northern Ireland of the Forties. Nor was it easy for a young boy to understand the background when he was told that the girl whom he had been reared to accept as his 'sister' was in reality his mother.

This was nobody's fault. It was the way rural Irish society behaved in those days, in trying to deal with a situation for which no-one had any simple answers. When at the age of five, I saw my mother abruptly leave the family home, to marry another man from the village without keeping me with her (and she was probably not encouraged to do so by her new husband), the scene etched itself sharply in my memory, where it remains to this day. At that stage I was too young to understand why she had decided to leave me behind, and it was only later that I was old enough to try to understand how she must have felt.

Sadly, the normally strong link between a mother and her first-born child was never securely forged in our case, nor, to our mutual regret, was the relationship ever completely healed. Lena was proud of my own family and my career achievements, and I grew to appreciate her courage, if not her bluntness, particularly in her old age when she suffered from ill-health.

I tried many times to think my way into Lena's early trauma, but we talked rarely of such things. Unfortunately it is only the people living through such challenges who know just how painful they have been. I also always recognised my mother's good points – she was handsome and well-read and she had been pretty in her youth. She had a flair for colour, design and craftwork, and she could be agreeably convivial when she wanted to be, especially at a family party. She could also be gruff and direct, and more than once too often.

Yet at times, in her own way, she was sensitive and caring. Despite all the missed opportunities, I still think of her often. Sadly, I know that even if she were still alive today, we could not obliterate or deal properly with the past. Her death at the age of eighty-four a few years ago released both of us from a circle that never could quite be closed.

I am also aware that none of us were able to change the past. I realise that other young people were worse off than me in those difficult times, and that my early experiences helped to make me what I am today, with the help of so many other people. If I apply the law of unexpected consequences, I could conclude that most of the important things in my life have worked out for the best, even though some of them may not have seemed like doing so at the time.

Such introspection at the start of an autobiography may seem to some an unnecessary intrusion into the privacy of people now long dead. It is not intended to be so, nor an exercise in self-justification. Nor is it a lack of respect for those concerned, nor do I wish to hurt any members of my wider family.

However, it is a recognition that much of our character is formed in early childhood and that our innate courage and grit are tested by such deep emotional challenges. In such a situation the child grows into adult emotional maturity and survives, or bends under a burden that can become crippling.

During my professional career as a writer and journalist, I have conducted many interviews in depth, and I have often noted how a dysfunctional or difficult parent/child relationship can form emotional roadblocks than can obstruct young people on their journey to adulthood and even into old age. Many people with a 'normal' childhood find this very hard to understand. Others with a similar experience to mine will recognise it immediately.

It is my hope that in overcoming these emotional obstacles in my own life, there is reassurance for other young people who feel betrayed or emotionally vulnerable. There can be a way out, and with the benefit of a good family and friends in the early, formative years, there can be an upward path of self-reliance and of learning to overcome the obstacles in life. It is also a huge bonus if you are fortunate enough to share a happy and secure family life of your own in adult years, as I have done.

Having now unburdened myself of some of my emotional baggage, it is ironic – if not paradoxical – to record that my early childhood seemed relatively carefree. The angst came afterwards – in early childhood you can be innocently happy without having to think about it.

My journey has involved many dimensions, and the major part of my life has been spent away from Bessbrook. That journey has taken me from my native village to the nearby grammar school in Newry, then to Queen's University in Belfast as the first of my family to study there, then into daily journalism with the *Belfast Telegraph*, and also around the world to fulfil my writing ambition, to meet some remarkable people, and to report on some exceptional situations.

However, it is best to begin at the start, and my journey began a long time ago amid the hills, fields and lakes in the rural beauty of South Armagh…

§

I was brought up in the 'model village' of Bessbrook, which had been established by the Richardsons, a Quaker family who came from Warwickshire to County Armagh in the reign of King James I. Later, in the mid-nineteenth century, the family took over an already-established linen business in the Bessbrook area, and developed it beyond all recognition. This was something of which I was unaware until many years afterwards, because a small boy in every era measures the history of his home heath only in terms of the number of fish he has caught, or the runs scored at cricket, as well as the goals in football. The economic origins of the village never crossed my mind in those days, and the historical Bessbrook seemed to belong to another planet. It was only much later on that I realised why shrewd businessmen had seen the manufacturing potential of a village which had a good supply of water for driving mill machinery, as well as a plentiful supply of cheap labour.

A textile trade was carried on in Bessbrook as early as 1760 by a family called Pollock, and they sold it to Joseph Nicholson and Sons in 1802. The business and its property were bought in 1845 by the Richardsons, and John Grubb Richardson was the sole owner from 1863 to 1878, when it became the property of the Bessbrook Spinning Company Ltd, though the Richardsons retained a significant influence over the company. The economic conditions were favourable for linen manufacture in mid-eighteenth century Ireland, with industrial grants for the establishment of bleach greens.

It was John Grubb Richardson in particular who made his mark on Bessbrook, and his strong Quaker principles of temperance and non-violence led him to establish the 'model village' without pawnshops, police or public houses. The police came to Bessbrook in due course, and although the village remains without public houses to this day, there were always flourishing pubs in the adjacent village of Camlough, and one at the nearby Millvale.

In its own right, Bessbrook was an early practical experiment in temperance social reform and certainly in its early years it deserved the title of a 'model village', based as it was in a locality of different religions and political outlooks. It also produced some of the finest linen in the world, including tablecloths that graced the liner *Queen Mary* on her maiden and subsequent Atlantic voyages, and other linens which were used in the Savoy Hotel in London and other high-class establishments across the world.

Apart from the economic benefits of a large workforce and good water power, Richardson's deep religious motivation was also a driving force. In today's secular world, there is such suspicion about religion-based philanthropy, but Richardson was a man of his times and the people of Bessbrook had little choice but to back his vision and to accept his religious motivation if they wanted to have a secure living. Remarkably, Richardson's social experiment began just when the deaths due to the Irish potato famine were decimating the Irish population in so many parts of the island. The prospect of a steady job, food and affordable housing must have appeared like a heaven-sent opportunity to anyone living in the Ireland of 1845. Richardson's industrial plans were soon flourishing, and so too was his social experiment of a 'model village'. From the nucleus of a small green, the village and its housing expanded rapidly.

When I lived in Bessbrook, the villagers had a good working knowledge of its history, but for them it was primarily a place where they could earn a living. In my early childhood I had obviously no idea of these connections with the Richardsons or the fact that Bessbrook was a 'model village'. That is not to imply, of course, that it had all 'model people'. The village no doubt had its quota of bullies, drunks, criminals and wife-beaters, as well as its God-fearing citizens, who were trying to lead blameless lives, or as much as any human being can earnestly aspire to.

However, in another sense Bessbrook was indeed a 'model village', one where an unusual social experiment in harmonious community living had succeeded to a surprising extent, and where generations of its inhabitants had been given a secure job in the bosom of their family, at a time when many thousands of Irish people had to emigrate to earn a living. For much of my life I took these achievements of the 'model village' for granted. It was only later on that I realised the rich heritage I had been bequeathed, as well as the privilege of living within that close-knit community before the decline of the linen industry and the pace of change which altered Bessbrook utterly, and forever.

All these observations were gained only with hindsight, and in the far distant days of the Forties, my first memories of Bessbrook as a child were those of looking out of our front window at Wakefield Terrace and seeing American GIs taking up positions beside telegraph poles and behind walls in preparation for the Normandy D-Day landings. The Second World War, which was then raging, was well beyond my infant consciousness, but it was only later that I came to realise that when I first went to school, the concentration camps at Auschwitz and elsewhere were only being discovered. I was also aware much later that the Allied victory over Germany was a close-run thing, particularly during the perilous early days of the struggle.

If Hitler's forces had triumphed, my life story and those of my generation in Ireland would have been very different indeed. It is still unnerving to realise that as a young child I was alive at the same time as Adolf Hitler and all the other demons of the Third Reich, as well as Stalin and Mussolini. However, I was not to know then that I would spend most of my journalistic life in Belfast, reporting on the decades of some of the worst violence in Europe since the Second World War, as well as in post-conflict Vietnam and Cambodia, and the long terrorist wars in Sri Lanka and the Sudan.

Fortunately, however, most of my early boyhood memories were of a village which gave me a deep sense of belonging, as well as the shared values of people living as a community before the new technology of communication, and particularly of television, destroyed the provincialism and relative innocence of those early days. Bessbrook gave me not only a home, but also solid values for life. These included the importance of hard work, lasting friendships, and the initiative to get out and try my luck in the bigger world as soon as the opportunity presented itself. In the meantime, there was much to enjoy and to learn from, in the life of the village.

CHAPTER TWO

Life and Death

WHILE THE BESSBROOK which I knew as a boy was a 'model village' in concept, its population had, as I have said, all the virtues and shortcomings of any community of human beings. Most people were not well off materially, but Bessbrook in the post-war days from 1945 still had a rich community life. It was economically dependent on the success of the local linen mill, but it was also centred on the shared institutions which had their origin in the Quaker concepts of the Richardson family.

In my boyhood I knew no other world, and I grew up among people who taught me much that was to stay with me throughout my lifetime. Later, I left Bessbrook to go to university, only occasionally to return to visit my family. Nevertheless, the old cliché is true – you can take the boy out of the village, but you cannot take the village entirely out of the boy.

One of my lasting memories of Bessbrook was its vibrant community life. People lived in neat rows of houses and there was a neighbourly spirit, long before the days when television, mobile phones and the other marvels of modern communications created a world where, paradoxically, many people no longer know how to communicate in the same way to one another as human beings. In the village I knew all my neighbours in Wakefield Terrace and as a boy I was welcomed into their homes.

At the top end of Wakefield Terrace were the Livingstones, including Wesley who was an outstanding singer in a village which was full of musical talent. Many a Saturday night the best singers used to gather around the 'Big Tree' just outside my bedroom in Wakefield Terrace and welcome in the Sabbath Day in cross-community harmony.

Next door on the downward slope of Wakefield Terrace, and beyond the McCrearys' house on the far side from Livingstones, were the Cosgroves, who were Catholics – but I did not know what that meant. I only knew that Eileen Cosgrove was a friendly, pretty girl much older than me, and that she took me for walks as a toddler.

Our neighbours beyond the Cosgroves were the Browns, and beyond them lived the Bradleys and the McColls. Throughout my adult life, I occasionally met Marie McColl, who married a charming man called Joe Moore, and she kept me informed about many of the people I had known in the village. They included her sister Betty, who married the Reverend Alfred Skuce, the local Methodist minister. There weren't many other people called 'Alfred' in my life at that time, so I remember him particularly well, as a quiet and friendly man with a Southern Irish accent.

Across the street from the McColls lived my 'Aunt Maria' Bell – who was my grandmother's sister – and her husband Geordie. Every November approaching Remembrance Sunday, Aunt Maria went through agonies as she relived with even more intensity the traumatic death of two of her sons Albert and David during the Second World War. The village Cenotaph was only a few yards across the Square from Aunt Maria's house, but it might as well have been permanently in her front room, such was her endless suffering. Even as a child, I remember her weeping and distraught in the period just before Remembrance Day, though I could not understand why she was behaving in that way. Our Presbyterian minister, the Reverend Sidney Carser, said it had been two of the worst days of his life, when he had had to walk down the village to Aunt Maria's house to comfort her and Uncle Geordie, after they received official confirmation that their sons had been killed. As a boy I knew little about the Second World War, but I realised from the suffering of Aunt Maria and some of the stories of the older men in the village that it must have been a terrible series of events.

In the decade or so after the end of the Second World War, life in the village seemed altogether normal to me, with opportunities for fun and enjoyment. Two doors up from Aunt Maria and her endless trauma was the terraced house of an old lady called 'Issy' Burns, who had a confectionary store. She was probably called Isobel, but I could not get my child's tongue around her full Christian name.

I have vivid memories of going into 'Issy's' small shop in the front room of her house, where she would come out from the kitchen to serve a small boy with a precious penny clutched firmly in his tiny sweating hand. The shop had many delights, including strips of liquorice, maybe even liquorice allsorts, jars of brandy balls and bulls' eyes, and other confections which made it hard for a child to choose even one of them.

"Have you anything for a penny?" I would ask, and Miss Burns would wait patiently for the almost interminable time it took for me to make my mind up. Eventually, and with difficulty, I would make my choice and Miss Burns would pour the sweets from a tin ladle into a thin paper bag which I would clutch close to my chest on my short walk back to 5 Wakefield Terrace. That was my idea of heaven.

Those were the days of innocent pleasures, and even in later childhood and early youth there was no mention of drugs of any kind. To us 'glue' was something which you used to stick pieces of paper together, and 'ecstasy' was a frame of mind when your favourite football team won the FA Cup. Of course there were misdemeanours, such as pinching apples from local orchards or tying black string to the letterboxes of old people's houses and torturing them with incessant knocking on their doors from a safe distance – every time they answered the knock there was nobody on the door step. Such behaviour seems silly now, and one's heart goes out in retrospect to the older people in the village whose orchards were raided, and others who were plagued by phantom 'door-knockers'. However, such misdemeanours seem innocent by today's standards, with the modern form of 'recreational rioting'.

By contrast, our village pastimes were overwhelmingly ordinary, like learning how to ride a bike. Just across from our house was an ornate but hideous brick structure known as 'The Fountain', which gave its name to Fountain Street. It was at the centre of a square, and it was here that I first learned to balance properly while riding a bike, before crashing down the hill into somebody's doorway, and falling off. This was no surprise, as I was riding an ancient machine borrowed from my Aunt Lizzie, another one of my grandmother's sisters. It was so old that it was known as 'an upstairs model', because of its high handlebars. The brakes were dodgy, and so were the tyres, but it was the only bike I had access to, and it was free. It was not until much later that my family could afford to buy me a proper new bike to cycle into Newry to attend the grammar school, and back again. The model was a glittering Raleigh, with shiny black and gold trims, and I loved it dearly.

On the far side of Charlemont Square was a grocer's shop owned by Fred Bell, who always wore a long brown overall, which was at that time the hallmark of the provision trade. He was probably a good grocer, but he was an even better public speaker. He had the grand title of FNL Bell JP, and every year at our annual church business meeting and social evening he stood up to propose the vote of thanks to the ladies who had made the tea. I was amazed at his eloquence and in my early tongue-tied teens, I could not imagine how he had the aplomb to speak that way, and without using notes. It took me many years to understand that such apparently magical accomplishments are not as difficult as they seem, provided you know how to do it, and that you never take such skills for granted.

Two doors up from Fred Bell's was a chip shop owned by Jimmy Chambers, who was also the local postmaster. The food was served by a village character called Barney Larkin, whose chatter was even more memorable than the fish and chips, which were a luxury in those days. Jimmy was a small and ebullient man whose main claim to fame was that he had played soccer for an English First Division team, and had also won many soccer caps by playing for Northern Ireland. His Post Office was a focal point for the village, and he had taken over from an earlier postmaster called Barney O'Neill, whom I recall as a gentle and elderly man.

Next to the chip shop was another business owned by two eccentric old gentlemen called Jackson, who wore half-length grocer's aprons. They seemed so desperately old to me that I could never understand how they could rush about so energetically. I thought that they were lucky to be even able to stand up at all.

Next to Jackson's shop was Collins' butchers, which was owned by a Catholic family. I don't remember how I knew that, but I sensed that it was important to realise that they were Catholics, though I could not understand why this could be of importance to anybody. One night I was wakened in my bedroom by a loud banging in Fountain Square. I saw a crowd of people waving Union Jacks and beating loudly on tar barrels which just happened to be on the site, because road contractors had been working there during the day. I was told afterwards that the noisy crowd was celebrating a rare election victory by a local Unionist politician.

Our house at Wakefield Terrace was a plain, two-story dwelling. The bedrooms were upstairs, and mine was on the corner where I had a sweeping vista of Fountain Square and the village war memorial. There was an indoor toilet on the ground floor at the back, but the house had no bathroom, which was typical of its time. However there was a kitchen/scullery, and I remember my grandmother washing clothes by hand, with the aid of a scrubbing board, and then wringing them laboriously through a mangle. I used to help her sometimes, and I soon realised just how laborious it was.

The living-room was also at ground level, and there was a tiny hall which opened onto Fountain Square. This provided us with a grandstand view of all the public processions in the village, big and small. Every July the Orangemen would march past on their Somme Commemoration parade, and then turn right abruptly past our front door to pay their respects as they passed the Cenotaph. One year Great-Uncle Albert, who had a permanently bad leg because of a war wound, was in charge of the parade and as he passed our house, he gave the order, "Caps aff" rather than, "Remove headgear". We were all greatly embarrassed that he had not shown more panache on such an important occasion.

Fountain Square was also the focus of much less important activities, which were nevertheless memorable in the life of the village. Every day a local woman, whose family reared pigs, came round the houses, pushing a small wheeled cart into which families emptied buckets of household swill. This helped to feed the pigs, and also kept the small houses free from smelly food and other refuse.

One afternoon I went to watch a pig being slaughtered, and I recoiled at the screams of the poor animal as it was being dragged out to its doom. A man called Short hit the pig on the head with a big sledgehammer, and as it slumped to its knees he expertly cut its throat. This was a shocking experience for a small boy to witness, and while it did not make me become a vegetarian, I was made aware that everything had its price. I figured out that, in providing the ingredients for the traditional Ulster fry of bacon and eggs, the hen had played a part, but the pig had been totally committed.

Life and death in the animal world became a commonplace experience in a village where people reared their own pigs and poultry, and where men and boys went out to shoot pigeons and trap rabbits as a means of providing food for a large family. Many years later I marvelled at the fact that pigeon and rabbit had become a delicacy in smart restaurants, when, for us, these were relatively humble foodstuffs to help to stave off hunger.

Horses also played an important role in the village, but for transport and not for food. I recall watching a funeral, and the hearse with ornate glass windows was drawn by black horses with high, sweeping plumes. Funerals were awesome and personal in a village where everyone knew everyone else. One night we were told that an old man from the village had just died, and a few of my friends and other boys gathered outside his house to pay our respects. At that stage, I knew that death was a very serious thing which would inevitably happen to everyone, but I hoped that it would not come to me for a very, very, very long time.

Possibly I had a childhood fear of hell and damnation which was increased by a series of deaths among my grandmother's siblings, and at regular intervals. The Browns had weak hearts, and coronary attacks killed them all, one by one. Among them was Uncle Willie, a cheery little individual whose limp did not prevent him from working as a hoist-man in a grain store in nearby Newry. Many a time, on my way to and from school, I watched him steer the grain bags from the crane, safely into the loft. I wondered how a man with such a bad limp could be so strong and supple, especially at his age.

Another distant relative, my Great-Uncle George, worked as a gardener for better-off local residents, and shortly after tea-time one summer evening he dropped dead in one of their gardens. His dead body was carried home on a door, because there was no stretcher available. I remember my sense of shock that such a big, strong and jovial man could die in an instant, and on a lovely night among his vegetable plots, when all the scented flowers were in blossom around him.

I recall how one evening in springtime I watched the funeral of a former soldier who had lived in Fountain Square. When they took the coffin out of his small house, a lone piper in a green jacket and saffron kilt walked slowly ahead of the funeral procession, and the plaintive wail of 'Oft in the Stilly Night' wafted over the village. Even today, when I hear that beautiful melody played on the bagpipes, the memory of the ex-soldier's funeral comes back to me.

There was high drama too when animals, as well as people, suddenly died or got into big trouble. One day a large horse was grazing near a swamp and found itself trapped in the clinging, down-sucking mud. As it slowly began to sink from sight, a group of men rushed around frantically with ropes and harnesses, and slowly pulled the terrified animal to safety. By the time that the rescue operation had been completed successfully, the whole village population seemed to be looking on. In those days before television, our drama was real and home-made.

I also remember a horse-drawn cart going around the village with people selling milk from the local farms to villagers, who collected it in big jugs. There was also a local greengrocer called James Kernohan who sold his fresh produce from a cart and assured his customers that his potatoes were all so outstanding that they were 'balls of flour' – even if they weren't always quite that good. It was such a far cry from the bland and cellophaned packets of potatoes in the supermarkets of today.

It was important to keep the main street of the village in good repair, and there was always immense excitement on the rare occasions when the 'tar men' came into view. The boiling liquid had a pungent, unforgettable smell, and once it was poured along the street and covered by lorry-loads of stone chips, a steam-roller came cranking along laboriously and noisily, with its clouds of billowing smoke and hissing eccentricities.

Long afterwards, as a journalist with the *Belfast Telegraph*, I wrote a story about two old men from South Derry who used to go to the seaside at Portrush on summer days when, they told me, "the tar was melting on the roads". When my article was published in the newspaper, one of our well-read compositors asked me, "Was that quote true, or did you make it up?" I retorted indignantly, "Of course I didn't make it up, why do you ask?" He replied, "There is no offence meant, but in some of John Steinbeck's writing he mentions the same phenomenon, of old men always claiming that on summer days the tar melted on the roads." I seem to recall that the tar melted on the roads around Bessbrook every summer during my boyhood, but probably not as often as I like to imagine. Perhaps I too have become like a bit of an old character from a Steinbeck novel!

During my boyhood and early life in Bessbrook, we were looked after by the National Health Service. Of course, I had no idea then that health care cost anything. It was only later on – after my many visits to Africa, India, Latin-America and other parts of the developing world, where in some areas, health care is virtually non-existent – that I appreciated the privileges we enjoyed and continue to enjoy under the NHS, despite all its challenges.

In my early years, the asthma I suffered from was severe, and one night I was so badly affected that my grandmother Minnie McCreary had to call for the local physician, Dr Robinson. He was a much-liked and respected doctor, but punctuality was not his greatest virtue. In fact he seemed to live his life at least an hour behind everybody else! However, he eventually arrived at our home in Wakefield Terrace that night, to find me wheezing greatly and fighting for breath. He gave me a foul-tasting spray to inhale, but even before I used it, I began to feel better, just because Dr Robinson was in the room with me. He belonged to that generation of family doctors whose bedside manner was as potent as the medicines they prescribed, and sometimes more so.

One of my favourite writers is Laurie Lee and in his evocative memoir, *Cider with Rosie*, he describes the Christmas season in his native village of Slad, which always reminds me of my own Bessbrook. I am not sure when I discovered the magic of Christmas. It may have been the moment when I pressed my nose against the window of Jowell's shop, which was two doors away from my house, and watched in wonder as a large Santa Claus beamed at me through the frost-flecked glass. It was probably only a model Santa in those days, but to me, he seemed excitingly authentic. When, in later childhood, someone told me the truth about the 'real' Santa, it was one of the big disappointments of my life, but one of the many delights of having children and grandchildren is being able to relive the magic of Santa and of Christmas through their eyes.

The Christmas of my boyhood was a community event, particularly in terms of the carol singing. Every Christmas morning a large group of villagers rose up very early and slowly walked around the village streets, singing carols. I have a clear memory of joining a school friend, George McMurray and his sisters, Meta and Eleanor, in the Harland Hall at the bottom of the village and how we slowly worked our way round the squares and the back streets, up through the heart of Bessbrook past the Technical School, further up the hill to Abbey View, opposite the Roman Catholic chapel, and finally to the tiny Methodist Church, where the minister conducted a short religious service.

The crocodile of carollers was led through the village by the local undertaker, George Preston, and as boys, we always thought it hilariously funny to associate him with the song 'I'll Walk Beside You'. On Christmas morning George usually walked in front of us with a big torch, which he shone at the upstairs windows of many of the houses which we passed. Some people slept on, at that unearthly hour, but others raised their bedroom blinds and gave us an encouraging wave. At that early time, with the bright moon lightening our walk, it really felt as if we were on a special pilgrimage and that we were celebrating, like the angels and the shepherds of the Gospels, the 'Birth of the Christ-child'.

These were the days long before Advent carol services became as commonplace as they are today (to the point almost of boredom), and childhood nativity plays were unheard of. The only carols I remember were those which we sang as we tramped around Bessbrook early on Christmas morning, or when Christmas Day fell on a Sunday and we sang in our own church. Throughout my life I have retained a deep affection for Christmas carols, and every time I am in Boston in New England, I pay homage to the statue of the former Episcopalian minister Phillips Brooks who wrote 'O Little Town in Bethlehem'. Similarly, when I visit St Columb's Church of Ireland Cathedral in Derry, I am conscious that it was Cecil Frances Alexander, the wife of a former Bishop of Derry, who wrote 'Once In Royal David's City'. We must have sung these, and many other carols, in our Christmas morning meander around Bessbrook. Once that was over, the rest of the day was predictable.

In my earliest memories, the Christmas stocking was the great delight. The anticipation began when I hung up a large sock on the mantelpiece over the fire on Christmas Eve. I never knew whose sock or stocking it was – perhaps my grandfather's – but it was certainly not mine, which was far too small. On Christmas morning there was always wonderment as I nervously took down the sock from the mantelpiece. There was never much in it, compared to the stockings of today. There was an apple or maybe an orange, and a pencil and rubber, and a few coins carefully wrapped in tissue paper, and sometimes a small bar of chocolate. However I looked on this as a treasure-trove, and above all, it had been filled by Santa Claus himself!

It seemed incredible that such a large man as Santa had been able to squeeze down that narrow chimney without leaving soot on the linoleum, and then squeeze back up again to his sleigh with the reindeers waiting for him above the roof of Ferguson's house, just across the road. Perhaps he was already flying back over the rooftops to his home in Santa Land, having filled the stockings of all the children in the world. How could he possibly do that, I thought, and still keep smiling and stay full of energy? One year I was convinced that I actually saw him, cheerily waving good-bye to me as his sleigh disappeared into the morning sky. This was magic indeed.

Christmas lunch was just as predictable as the rest of the day. In my Aunt Jean's, where my grandfather and I lived and shared a bedroom after my grandmother's death, the Christmas lunch always consisted of turkey and the traditional trimmings, including Brussel sprouts. These were a delicacy for my Uncle Dave, but their heavy smell hung over the house for the rest of the day. One year I nearly missed the Christmas lunch altogether. I was working as a student postman and delivering mail all over the village and the surrounding district. It was hard work to pedal the big red Post Office bike, and also to balance the heavy sack of letters and parcels on my back and on the handlebar, as I travelled up and down hills and lanes, avoiding angry dogs and wayward cattle or sheep.

The Christmas morning sorting and delivery in the post office was easier because the mail was light. Nevertheless I had to set off on my big red bike and finish the job as quickly as possible. Unfortunately, or perhaps fortunately, each stop on my delivery route was accompanied by a glass of sherry or beer from villagers, whose hospitality I could not possibly refuse. Many people also gave me a half-crown tip, so as I tippled on and pocketed the tips, my large ex-Army coat became bogged down by the coins, and soaked by the driving rain. Somehow, I steered the red bike through the wind and rain and arrived tired but elated at my home. I staggered in cheerfully, only to realise that I had kept everyone waiting, and they were not amused. Worse still, I was full of Christmas cheer and sherry, and they were not. However after a quick bath, I reappeared at the lunch table for one of the most memorable Christmas lunches I can remember. Hunger is always a good sauce.

Christmas lights have always had an attraction for me, possibly because the only decorated tree in our village was bolted to the balcony of the local Institute, known to most people as the 'town hall'. There were no other seasonal lights in the village due to the post-war scarcity of everything, so the illuminated tree at the town hall was a major part of our Christmas celebrations.

One year I remember cleaning my Aunt Lizzie's backyard, which was a considerable chore for the sixpence, or 'tanner', which she paid me to do it. I then bought a bar of chocolate peppermint cream with part of the proceeds, and carefully hoarded my treasure for the rest of the day until the early evening dusk when a throng of other villagers gathered to watch the local squire 'Master Jack' Richardson switch on the Christmas tree lights at the town hall. I remember his reedy voice carrying across the crowd from the balcony in the thin cold air, and I cannot recall a word he said, but I knew that when the lights were switched on, in their sparse but dazzling beauty amid the winter darkness, the Christmas celebrations had really begun.

Winter fuel was particularly important at Christmas. I remember one year a coal man bringing a full bag to our house and emptying it into the little coal cellar under the stairs. My grandmother asked him to bring in another one, and he obliged willingly even though the coal was wet and heavy, and he was covered in grime and sweat. My grandmother paid him immediately, and as she carefully counted the coins and placed them into his grimy hand, she thanked him profusely for the extra bag. He replied, with a lisp which I thought was very funny "That's all right, missus. One bag of coal is no good to anybody in the mouth of Clismas."

It was all part of the mutual concern and care which people had for each other in the village, but with the increasing years, that spirit of Christmas seems to have diminished, with endless carols in supermarkets and Christmas 'sales' early in December, and even earlier of late. The speed of communication and travel, the traffic jams and airport queues, and the endless television coverage as well as rampant commercialism has made it more difficult to keep Christmas special, particularly as a religious celebration of seasonal goodwill rather than a mid-winter pagan festival.

Despite all this, and my years of Christmas celebrations in many places, there is still a little of the magic of my Christmas childhood which is embedded deeply in my heart and soul. It may be awakened by the timeless depth of a Bible reading about the Incarnation, or the overwhelming beauty of superb music such as Handel's *Messiah*, or the excitement in the eyes of a grandchild opening a Christmas present. On those occasions, in my far mind's eye, I still see Santa Claus waving to me in my childhood bedroom in Bessbrook, as he soared over the roof of Ferguson's house and sped off under the stars with his reindeer and sleigh to his home in Santa Land. The Bessbrook boy has long left the village, but a part of that Christmas magic still lives on in the boy, and it probably always will.

Bessbrook village centre – with 5 Wakefield Terrace on the right.

CHAPTER THREE

Family Matters

IT IS DIFFICULT to know precisely what I learned, and from whom, as I grew up in the village of Bessbrook. There were many influences ranging from school and the sports field, from the church to village societies, and most of all from my home and my adopting family.

My Aunt Jean who lived to be over ninety, was invariably thoughtful and loving, and I had a deep affection and admiration for her until the day she died, and afterwards. She was always supportive in my educational and personal development, and even as a first-year student at Queen's University, she helped me prepare for my matriculation examinations in Latin to gain entry to the Honours School in Modern History.

Jean also kept closely in touch with my career, and she read the *Belfast Telegraph* every night. She could therefore tell me, sometimes weeks afterwards, her opinion on what I had written. Like her father, she became profoundly deaf in her old age, but she remained remarkably well-informed about, and interested in, current affairs.

Jean was the gentle matriarch of the wider family. She kept a list of everyone's birthdays and posted off cards each year, with meticulous accuracy. At her funeral in Bessbrook Presbyterian Church, I was privileged to deliver a tribute. I noted that although she was neither rich nor famous in the world's eyes, she was indeed rich in her warmth, and famous for her kindness and hospitality. So she was indeed rich and famous, in the best way possible.

My Aunt Jean's husband was a Welshman called Denzil Jones who was a soldier during the Second World War, and they married shortly after the war ended. They spent part of their honeymoon in the Irish Republic, and they brought me back a beautiful toy motorbike, complete with a rider and his life-like plastic face. It was a rare and wonderful present for a small boy during the austerity of the post-war years, and it was typical of their kindness towards me.

Denzil Jones, whom I called Uncle Dave, was a man of fixed views, who always dressed neatly and retained his soldierly bearing, right to his final days. He rarely talked about the war, but one evening he told me about lying hidden in the jungle in Burma with his colleagues, and silently watching a large group of Japanese soldiers, who greatly outnumbered them, slowly filing past through the thick foliage. He also told me how the Japanese had stopped briefly, and how he had watched the moonlight glint off a sword of an enemy officer. After what seemed to be an eternity, the Japanese moved on, and Uncle Dave and his colleagues escaped an almost certain death, or the horrors of a Japanese prisoner-of-war camp. Such details from someone so close in our family brought home to me the reality of war.

My Uncle Bill, my mother's younger brother, was another major influence throughout my life. He was only sixteen years older than me – a gap which seemed enormous in the early days, but one which shortened most agreeably as we grew older. Bill was a handsome young man with enormous charm, a sharp brain and good sporting ability. He was my childhood hero, and it was he who gave me a lifelong introduction to soccer. He was a member of the Bessbrook Strollers football team which won the Irish Junior Cup in 1945 – a considerable feat for a team from a small South Armagh village.

Uncle Bill was also in the local flute band, and it seems that when he did not know how to play a tune on parade, he whistled it anyway. He originally worked on an oil lorry which delivered supplies to rural South Armagh. Cross-border smuggling had been rife there during the war years, and almost at any other time when a profit could be made by dodging the customs men on either side of the border. South Armagh was long known as 'bandit country' and for good reason.

During one of my early assignments as a *Belfast Telegraph* reporter, I interviewed in Crossmaglen the local Nationalist MP Eddie Richardson, who had a quote for every situation, real and imaginary. As a parting gift he gave me a bottle of poteen, an alcoholic liquid with a kick like a mule and one which was highly illegal to produce, because of the dangers to health. I was aware of the illegality, and I asked Eddie what I would do if the police stopped me and found the bottle of poteen in my possession. He replied, "Tell them that you are rubbing it into your bad knee!" Shortly after leaving Eddie, I was indeed stopped by the police and then – very fortunately for me – waved on after they had checked my driving licence. The bottle of poteen in the boot remained my secret.

This was in the days before the Troubles, so it is not hard to imagine the skulduggery and danger that enveloped South Armagh later on in the midst of a bitter campaign between the Provisional IRA and the security forces. However during the time Uncle Bill was working on the oil lorry, the only danger in South Armagh was from being stopped by customs men.

Later on Bill became a policeman. On a visit to see him in Belfast when he was stationed in Donegall Pass, I marvelled that he could simply step out in the street and stop all the traffic with one wave of his hand, just like the policeman in the Percy French song about the Mountains of Mourne. That seemed to me to be power indeed. Later on Bill took me on a walk past a beautiful building situated behind lush green lawns in a leafy suburb of Belfast. "What's that place called?" I asked in my childish innocence. He replied "That's Queen's University, and some of the most beautiful girls in the world go there." I had no idea that a country boy like me could, or ever would, go to a place like Queen's University, because, to my knowledge, no-one from my village in Bessbrook had ever done such a thing. Fortunately, many years later, I won a scholarship to Queen's, and I learned about all the attractions of the University, and its beautiful young ladies, for myself.

When I was in my mid-teens Uncle Bill, with his charming wife Eileen, emigrated to America, and I was heartbroken because I thought that I would never see him again. In those days, long before air travel became so cheap and available, it was extremely difficult for families separated by vast distances to see loved ones again.

Bill, however, kept closely in touch and he had a profound effect on my education. When I was about fourteen, my grandparents sat me down at the breakfast table and told me that I could no longer attend grammar school, because they could not afford to pay the travel costs.

This was because my grandfather had retired from his job as a civil servant, and they were living on his small pension. Naturally I was stunned at the news, because I was aware of other young people who also had their education cut short because of family financial difficulties, and I knew that this seemed to be happening to me.

However, Uncle Bill came to the rescue. He sent enough money regularly to help us over the financial crisis, and I was therefore able to finish my grammar school education. In no other period of my life was 'money from America' so important.

Meanwhile, Uncle Bill was forced to take a series of back-breaking jobs in America (including furniture removal), but he eventually prospered in the food business and ended up as head of catering with Trans World Airlines at their headquarters in JFK airport in New York. This development meant that Bill had access to all the top restaurants in the city, and in my post-student days when I was able to afford the air fare from Dublin to America, I experienced some of the most famous restaurants and clubs in New York, and also the stimulation of mixing with the Irish-American community who were among the movers and shakers in that wonderful city, which I loved instantly and still do. On my first night in New York Bill took me to a pub in Manhattan where the Irish-American customers knew more Irish songs than I did. On the same night Bill drove me down Fifth Avenue, and I sat open-mouthed as we stopped at traffic lights and had to listen to a full-scale row between a middle aged couple in a car in the next lane. Bill laughed and said to me "Alf, welcome to New York!"

My first experience of motoring in America was tricky. Up in the Pocono Mountains in Pennsylvania, I was driving a borrowed vehicle, and trying to master the automatic transmission as well as the intricacies of left-hand drive. "How am I doing?" I asked Bill anxiously. He replied "Alf, you're doin' real good. There is only one slight detail, if you don't mind me mentioning it. You're driving on the wrong side of the road." This was typical of Bill's laconic sense of humour.

He was always on hand to welcome me to New York, and even to bail me out when my money ran short, in the days before credit cards were invented. On one occasion, he sent me the cash to fly me back from Albuquerque to New York, and another time when I flew in from Guatemala after completing a Third World assignment which began several months earlier in India, Bill was there to guide me through Customs and Immigration and to help me avoid the queues. He was wearing my late grandfather's gold watch and chain, and I felt that even in New York at the end of a long and gruelling world trip, the warmth of my family was all around me. Bill McCreary was technically my uncle, but he was the best big brother I could ever have had.

He had an older brother called Jimmy, who was a shadowy figure in my childhood, and tragically he died in his early twenties from tuberculosis. For a long time, I never appreciated the trauma that Jimmy's death had on the rest of the family, and I sometimes think that because of the relatively short age gap between Uncle Bill and myself, I became a kind of younger brother to him. I know that he missed Jimmy terribly, though he rarely talked about it.

My grandfather Tommy McCreary was a small stout man, who usually wore a soft hat to hide his bald head. He always dressed in a three-piece suit, with his beloved gold watch and chain draped across his ample stomach. Every night at 6 pm he would check his watch against the chimes of Big Ben in London, which were transmitted on radio by the BBC Home Service. We always listened to this as we had supper in our kitchen. One evening in January 1953, my grandfather turned on 'the wireless' to hear the day's news, and we were told that the *Princess Victoria* ferry had gone down in a violent storm off the Irish coast, on her way from Stranraer to Larne, with the loss of 133 lives. I can still remember the shocked silence, as we listened and tried to take in the magnitude of the tragedy.

Many years later, when I was writing a book on the history of Larne Harbour, I researched all the details of this tragic loss of life and I also talked to the relatives of some of those who had died. The slow, agonising death of those people did not bear thinking about, and my detailed history of that episode did not lessen my lifelong fear of drowning at sea.

In the early Fifties, radio was one of the main sources of information, long before the modern 24/7 media when a story is dissected, kicked around and moved on so much that the initial shock of the bulletin soon wears off. In those days as I have said, my grandfather kept up with the latest news, and every day he read the *Belfast Telegraph* and the *Daily Mail* thoroughly. Even in his old age he was always well-informed about current affairs, and when I came home on certain weekends from Queen's University, we invariably discussed the latest headlines.

Perhaps, however, 'discussed' is a somewhat grandiose term, because my grandfather was profoundly deaf. We shared the same bedroom, and he was an early riser. If I asked him "What time is it?" he would reply, "Oh, it's raining outside", because he hadn't heard my question properly and he would just try to guess what I had been asking him. Despite his hearing difficulties, we communicated well enough, and his hearing improved dramatically after he had had a few drinks.

His favourite tipple was Tuborg Gold beer with a shot of Powers' whiskey, and he was able to handle this formidable alcoholic combination well into his old age. One night when we were in the Carrickdale Hotel near Dundalk, he told me about his service in the First World War with the Royal Irish Fusiliers. He joined up only because his younger brother Sandy had lied about his age and had joined the Royal Irish Fusiliers some months previously. In doing this, Sandy had caused great distress to his mother.

So, in order to obtain Sandy's discharge, my grandfather took his place. He never told me about the legalities of this, and I am sure that the details were blurred by the chaos of war. By all accounts my grandfather was not a keen soldier. He told me about the day when Lord Carson reviewed the troops at Clandeboye near Bangor before they embarked on troopships for the slaughter of the battlefields in Flanders. He said that when the word spread through the tents that Carson was on the site, the boys from County Armagh stayed put and refused to go out to see him. "To hell with Carson!" they said. Disillusion with the war was already setting in.

Tommy McCreary served as a stretcher-bearer during the Battle of the Somme, when more than 2,000 men from the 36th (Ulster) Division were killed on the first day of the hostilities. Like most old soldiers from the First World War, he rarely talked about his experiences, most probably because of the horrors they had experienced. My grandfather must have witnessed great suffering during his time as a stretcher-bearer in the muddy brutality in Flanders. He once told my Aunt Jean of witnessing the amputation of a soldier's leg without an anaesthetic. Whiskey was the only palliative they could offer the patient.

However one evening he did tell me about being billeted in a French chateau and sleeping there in his combat uniform between clean silk sheets which became badly soiled by the mud on his boots and military leggings. He never explained why he slept in his uniform and I can only guess that he was moving quickly in transit with his unit across the battlefields area, and that there was no time or opportunity for the niceties of civilisation such as showers, or even a water supply, despite the splendid setting of a French chateau.

My grandfather also told me about being captured by the Germans and being forced to work in a salt mine. I cannot remember how that episode ended, or how long he remained a prisoner of war, but given that he had been at the Somme in 1916, he may well have been incarcerated by the Germans for up to three years by the time the war ended. During the war he also 'borrowed' from somewhere an elaborate German pipe made of ornately decorated porcelain, and I could imagine him having put up his feet somewhere in Germany as he puffed on his war trophy.

When he told me these stories, I was in my early twenties. Unfortunately I did not realise then how important it was from a family point of view to encourage him to tell me more about his adventures during the war.

Tommy McCreary was a stalwart of the Royal British Legion for most of his life. He wore his war medals every Remembrance Sunday, for as long as his strength enabled him to take part in the Legion parade. When he died, my mother gave me these medals of his, and I had them carefully framed. They have pride of place in my living room, and after the Remembrance Services each November, I place a fresh poppy on the war medals of Fusilier Thomas McCreary, No 14499, of the Royal Irish Fusiliers.

After the First World War, my grandfather went back to his home village of Glenanne in South Armagh, not far from Bessbrook. His father had been a labourer, but Tommy McCreary did better for himself and became a civil servant. He worked for the Social Security Department, and in my later childhood I knew that he helped people to 'sign on' at the 'buroo' office in Newry. He had beautiful copper-plate writing, of which he was very proud, and he turned it into his own art form.

My grandfather was an Orangeman, but not in the sense that he was a bigoted 'Williamite'. He told me that he had joined the Orange

Order because it was the only Protestant 'youth club' in the rural locality where he grew up. He talked to me about all-night soirees in the Orange Hall, and about playing the fiddle for Irish dances. He also played the harmonica and the 'Jew's Harp'. He had a life-long love of Irish traditional music. In his early days he lived in an Ireland united under British rule, and the cultural distinctions were less rigid than today.

Many of my grandfather's drinking pals were Roman Catholics, and he regularly travelled to the Crossmaglen 'buroo' office to sign on the local men. Most of these would have been staunch Irish Republicans, but this did not matter to Tommy McCreary. Nor did they care that he was an Orangeman. After they had signed on, they all went off with my grandfather to the local pub in Crossmaglen. Drink was always a great leveller in rural Ulster.

Tommy McCreary was a staunch Presbyterian who cleaned and polished his black shoes every Saturday night to wear to church the next day. Sunday was the Lord's Day, and it was a day of rest, and therefore certainly not for polishing shoes. My grandfather was a God-fearing man, who listened to the entire broadcast of Handel's *Messiah* every year in the run-up to Christmas, and although he lived a Christian life, without fuss or ostentation, he was also worldly-wise, and he liked his occasional tipple at the weekends.

On certain Sunday afternoons he would set off for Newry, from thence to Warrenpoint by steam train, and eventually over to Omeath in the Irish Republic by boat with large numbers of other passengers. The attraction was not the beautiful scenery of Carlingford Lough, but the fact that the pubs were open over there on a Sunday, unlike the situation in the North, where the Lord's Day was rigidly observed. Following several hours of drinking, the sturdy but not steady Northerners returned in the open boats, and many of them staggered up the stony beach at Warrenpoint and into the arms of the waiting customs men, who confiscated the smuggled gifts which the drinkers were trying to bring home to their irate wives as peace offerings.

No-one ever seemed to query the lack of logic in such behaviour, because the would-be smugglers were inevitably apprehended. Nor did anyone query the wisdom of crossing the often choppy lough in an open boat. There was drink to be had in Omeath on a Sunday, and to the sober Northerners, that was logic enough to embark on the short but potentially perilous sea crossing.

My grandfather was a law-abiding wee man. So one occasion when he took me to Omeath to buy me a watch from the Free State, where such goods were cheaper, he was worrying about how he would smuggle it across.

As he finished his Tuborg beer and chaser of Powers' whiskey in an Omeath pub, he asked me what he should do. I said that one way to smuggle across the watch was to lay it flat on his bald head and hide it with his soft hat. He agreed that this was a splendid idea.

I then owned my first car – a Morris Mini – and I suggested that I would drive the both of us to the customs post on the border and, in the unlikely event of an official asking us if we had anything to declare, I would pretend that we had nothing to smuggle. The plan seemed foolproof, and as I drove down the road towards Newry at around sixty miles an hour, my grandfather and I became involved in an animated conversation, which became ever more incomprehensible due to his deafness.

In no time at all I was approaching the outskirts of Newry, and it was only then that I realised that I had driven right through the customs post with my smuggled watch lying flat on my grandfather's bald head. It was one of those days when the customs men had decided to stay indoors, totally unaware that my grandfather and I were making good time, in more ways than one, on our journey home. He, of course, had forgotten altogether about smuggling the watch across the border on his bald head, and I had to remind him about it, once we had reached Newry. He took off his hat and proudly presented the watch to me, and I felt that we had managed our time very well indeed on that memorable afternoon.

My grandfather became more eccentric as he grew older. He smoked heavily, and he was afraid of developing cancer. So to avoid this, he used to light up a cigarette which he had punctured in several places with a safety pin in order to let the 'tar' escape before he inhaled the smoke into his lungs. I never found out the medical benefits of doing this – if there were any, that is – but my grandfather believed in taking those precautions, and the very fact of doing so gave him peace of mind.

Tommy McCreary was a man of few words. Yet when he spoke, people listened to him. One of his great phrases was, "don't worry, it won't signify", and he was rarely bothered by anything. However, I recall one occasion when his jaunty aplomb was temporarily punctured from on high.

It was on the afternoon of Aunt Lizzie's funeral, and after the burial the entire family gathered to have tea in her large kitchen. Protestant funerals were solemn occasions, and while everyone munched their ham salad, there was very little conversation. At a certain point, however, one of the ladies appeared with a large kettle of boiling tea and she asked my grandfather, "Uncle Tommy, do you want a refill?"

He replied "I do indeed", and held out his cup. Whereupon she started to pour the tea from the heavy kettle, but she was aiming from over my grandfather's shoulder. Unfortunately, her aim was poor. She missed the cup entirely, and mistakenly poured the boiling tea all over my grandfather's crotch. He sprang up instantly with the pain and yelled at the mortified young woman. "Daughter dear, you've scalded me, and my lad and all!" His indignation, like the pain, was very apparent, but the rest of the mourners around the table pretended not to notice, while also trying desperately not to laugh out loud.

I was a bit taken aback that my normally gently-spoken grandfather had complained loudly about somebody scalding 'his lad', and with so many ladies present, but I also knew that he must have been in great discomfort, and I realised that he was a real man in more ways that I had imagined.

My grandfather's brother Sandy was of similar build to him, and even more hard of hearing. They were fond of one another, and they visited each other regularly. However each meeting usually became an amicable shouting match, because they found it so difficult to hear one another. After my students days at Queen's I decided to take them, as a treat, to the Ulster Folk Museum near Belfast, which contained among its many exhibits some examples of nineteenth century rural houses. They enjoyed themselves, but they were not over-impressed, which became clear when my grandfather remarked to me, "Sure we were brought up in houses like that." In his own way he would give me a new definition of the term 'living history'.

Uncle Sandy, as we called him, was always full of good advice and when my grandfather told him that he intended to sail to New York in a trans-Atlantic liner – this was in the Fifties – Sandy replied, "I sailed to America years ago, Tommy, and I advise you to sit in the middle of the boat. It can be hard going when the sea gets rough."

Sandy was a 'born again' Christian and he used to preach the Gospel wherever he could. He always carried religious tracts wherever he went, and every time he met me he would press a couple of these into my hand, with the solemn advice to, "let the Man Above take charge of your life". I was too embarrassed to say anything to him, and I would never have dreamed of refusing his offering. Like my grandfather, he was a decent man, and he was greatly respected by the entire family.

In my early teens I was invited to act as an usher at Uncle Sandy's daughter's wedding in Dungannon, and I understood that I was required to wear morning dress. So I hired the trousers and the jacket with tails, and set off for Dungannon by train. I was careful however to tuck the tails into my jacket so that they would be hidden by my raincoat.

When I arrived in Dungannon, I realised to my horror that there had been a misunderstanding, and that I was the only one at the wedding wearing morning dress. It was bad enough to witness the stares of the guests, as this totally over-dressed usher brought them to their pews. It was even worse at the reception afterwards, because I was afraid that the guests would mistake me for the head waiter, and ask me to take their orders.

Uncle Sandy was younger than my grandfather but they had other brothers. I remember my family talking about an 'Uncle Jemmy' who lived in Glasgow. One of the other Scottish relatives was Jackie McCreary, a talented footballer who captained Derry City in 1949 when they won the Irish Senior Cup for the first time. I was only a boy then, but I knew that this was a great achievement.

As my grandfather grew older, he became even more mellow. He slept a great deal during the day, and snored loudly in his sleep, both day and night. He loved nature, and he was always telling me about the beauty of the wildlife and the plants all around us. This is something which I inherited from him, and I am glad that my children all love the natural world as well. There was so much my grandfather taught me, that it was only in recent years that I began to realise how fortunate I was to have known him.

As he moved into his eighties, my grandfather slowed up physically, of course. Despite his deafness, he was always great company. He was a contented man, who had no regrets or burningly unfulfilled ambitions. In some ways he had had a hard life. He came from a poor rural background, he had served on the battlefields of France, he had raised a family on a small salary during the depression, he lost a son to TB at an early age, and he had taken a new grandson into his household when others in the wider family had suggested giving the baby away to adoptive parents. Tommy McCreary was a member of that tough generation of Ulstermen who lived through difficult times, but had learned just to get on with it, and he knew how to enjoy life. He was never well off financially, but in his loyalty and affections, he was a truly rich man.

My grandfather died peacefully at the age of eighty-four, and there was a big funeral for him in Bessbrook. Shortly before we closed the coffin, my mother and I paused to have a last look at him. She said to me, "I've kept a lock of his hair. He was such a special wee man." She said it in a way that made me aware how emotional and caring she really was. This was a side of herself which she rarely allowed me to see, but I knew that she and I had both deeply loved Tommy McCreary, the wee man in the coffin. He had played such a truly pivotal part in our lives at a time when we had few benefactors anywhere, and his love and generosity had made all the difference to both of us. We owed him so much, in our different ways, and his death ended an important chapter for all of us.

CHAPTER FOUR

On and Off the Rails

IN THE 'MODEL VILLAGE' of Bessbrook in the late 1940s and 1950s there was a myriad of delights for inquisitive small boys, both on and off the rails.

One of the attractions was the Bessbrook–Newry tramway which had been opened in October 1885, and was only the second hydroelectric tramway in Ireland. Its purpose was to transport coal and flax from the canal quays in Newry, in order to provide power and raw material for linen manufacture in Bessbrook. In return, the tram transported the finished products including damask, towels and sheets to Newry on the first stage of their journey for export.

During their journeys between Bessbrook and Newry, the trams passed under the large Craigmore Viaduct which still carries the railway lines from Belfast to Dublin. I remember illegally walking across the top of that viaduct with my pals on several occasions, and often admiring the arches from a distance, especially when a beautiful blue steam locomotive hauled the Enterprise along the track.

Many years later, when carrying out research for a book on the history of Belfast Harbour, I discovered that William Dargan, the famous Irish railway contractor, had built the Craigmore Viaduct, which had been designed by Sir John MacNeill. Dargan's contracting company had also played a major role in digging out the mud from Belfast Harbour in the early nineteenth century to make it a hugely successful port. He deposited the 'spoil' in the Victoria Channel where it formed Dargan's Island. Later this was re-named Queen's Island, in honour of Queen

Victoria's visit to Belfast in 1849, and this is where the famous Olympic Class liners, including *Titanic*, were built.

Ten Bessbrook–Newry trams ran daily under the Craigmore Viaduct, and each could haul around 100 tons of goods, as well as a full load of passengers. I remember the distinctive appearance of the passenger wagons and the exciting bustle associated with the tram. It was all part of the normal daily life of the village, and I still recall the hard, wooden seats. It was always an adventure to ride along the scenic narrow gauge line to the town of Newry, which had so many other attractions, including the bustling weekly market.

The tram also brought workers from Newry to the Bessbrook mill every morning, and back home in the evening. The Bessbrook villagers called the others 'Newry neuks', though I did not know what that meant, while the Newry people described the Bessbrook workers as 'Oul jam and bread'. This was a jibe because the Bessbrook workers could afford jam, as well as butter, on their bread during meal breaks. It was also an indication that both sets of workers were badly off.

Colourful nicknames were common in the linen mill and in the village. These were given to 'characters' who had been mill workers and were later pensioners, well-known to everyone.

One man with an annoying, high-pitched voice was called 'Squealer'; another with a big mouth was 'Rubbergub'; and a young fellow who walked for miles on his own was 'Long Distance'. A man with blonde hair was called 'White' Tom Black, because there were several other 'Blacks' in a village with differently-coloured family names, including the 'Pinks' and the 'Greens'. There was also a man who complained about suffering from "a horse's stomach", but it was said that he had 'shell shock' from his time in active service during the First World War.

Back on the tracks, the Bessbrook–Newry tram continued to operate for over sixty years, but it was closed down in 1948. This was partly due to competition from road transport, and partly a reflection on the diminishing importance of linen manufacture in the post-war era. One of the redundant passenger wagons was bought by the Sisters of Mercy Convent in Bessbrook, where it was used as a summer house, minus the wheels and buffers. The rebuilt Number 2 Power Car was bought by a Manchester company which used it as a cricket pavilion for visiting teams. In 1955 it was handed over to Belfast Corporation, and it is now on view in the Ulster Folk and Transport Museum in Cultra. Many years later I took two of my grandchildren, Molly and Thomas McCreary, to the museum to look at the tram which was such a part of my boyhood.

The tram was an integral part of the operation of the linen mill. This was a big, ugly building, like many of the textile mills of the period, but it was a distinctive landmark in Bessbrook. I would hear its hooter summoning people to their work every weekday morning: one blast at 7.15 am, one at 7.45 am and a final blast for the foot-draggers ten minutes later. The workers filed in through several gates which were then closed. The latecomers were locked out, and suffered the loss of half a day's pay, which was a significant sum in those hard times.

My mother and Aunt Jean, and some of my friends who had worked in the mill, told me later that there was a good atmosphere of banter and work sharing amid often harsh conditions, with low pay. The Richardsons were hard-headed businessmen as well as philanthropists. It was widely believed then that the prevalence of TB in the Bessbrook area was partly caused by the damp working conditions in parts of the mill.

One of my most abiding memories was of a huge illuminated sign erected on top of the mill in 1945 to celebrate VE Day, the end of the Second World War in Europe. Even though I rarely set foot in the linen mill itself, the nearby mill pond and grounds were part of my myriad of delights. The pond was a source of hydro-electricity for the mill, but it also had numerous recreational attractions. It became a thick skating rink in the big frost of 1947, which was talked about for many years afterwards, and in the summertime, we swam to a little island at one end to look out for the eggs in the swans' nests. When George Bernard Shaw visited the village, he reputedly remarked that the swans looked as if they were bored out of their minds – which they probably were.

I learned to swim in the pond by doing a 'dog-paddle' across to the island and back again. My swimming has scarcely improved since then, though the warm waters of places like the Mediterranean and Indian Ocean later on were much more agreeable than the smelly and dirty mill pond. I was aware that swimming was dangerous, and that the dark waters of this otherwise exciting place also masked human tragedy, with at least one suicide there in my early years.

For a village of its size, Bessbrook had perhaps more than its share of tragedies, including the suicides at different times of our physician Dr Robinson, and the Reverend Rodgers, the Church of Ireland rector. These deaths were especially shocking because both men were regarded as pillars of our small village society.

On a happier note, however, the big 'Pond Field' was a great place for football and cricket. We could not afford proper goal-posts, but we threw down our jackets which were just as effective. It was here that I learned my first lesson about standing up for justice, when captaining a Boy Scouts team against a local eleven. Their captain Bertie Weir tackled our boys crudely and painfully and I warned him to stop. He ignored me and carried on with his bullying. I challenged him once again to stop, but he yelled back, "What are you going to do about it?"

This was the point of no return. Much to my own amazement, I stepped forward and hit him so hard on the jaw that he landed on his back. He threatened to hit me in retaliation, but eventually after much bluster, he decided not to do so, and the game continued in relative peace. This all happened in the heat of the moment, and I never held a grudge against Bertie, who had his own struggles in life. I have not hit anyone in anger since then, but I learned a valuable lesson about standing up to bullies which I was able to draw upon in later life, including on one occasion in my dealings with an overbearing news editor.

Those were days of innocent youth, when my pastimes included fishing for tiddler 'spricks', collecting chestnuts along the Crow's Walk, playing cricket and football, dodging the rain, and going for long walks with my family and friends. There were no television sets, mobile phones, iPads or the other double-edged attractions of our technological age, so we had to make our own amusement.

A favourite walk of mine with Morris Brown, Graham McAleer and a few other local boys was the leisurely trek to Camlough Lake and the beautiful surrounding countryside. We would rib each other mercilessly, and talk incessantly about everything from football to the prettiest girl we had seen in the previous week. We also had a standard joke of going to the Florentine café in Newry and ordering "one chip and three forks" because we were chronically short of cash. Sometimes we would also talk about our latest foray to the Savoy cinema in Newry, which was not remotely as salubrious as its name – though not actually a flea-pit. In the Savoy cinema we watched some of the memorable movies of the Fifties, and it was here that I fell in love with exotic blonde actresses such as Kim Novak and Doris Day.

An alternative cinema was the tin hut 'Hibs Hall', on top of a large hill on the outskirts of Bessbrook village, just past the Convent. There we would watch breathlessly most of the movies of derring-do Westerns, and skulduggery of all kinds, when baddies fought against the goodies but nobody's hat came off.

Another favourite walk in Bessbrook was through the tree-lined grounds surrounding 'The Woodhouse', which was the seat of the local squire, 'Master Jack' Richardson. I recall my mother and Aunt Jean taking me there as a toddler, and most vividly in autumn when the ground was thick with fallen leaves. Later on, I often walked to The Woodhouse with the local lads, and occasionally we plucked up courage to tip-toe across the trim lawns and peep in through the window, hoping that no-one would see us.

Many years later, as an established writer, I was invited to officially 'open' the same Woodhouse, which had then been developed into housing apartments. It was an enjoyable ceremony to which I invited my boyhood friends who had nervously peeped through those same windows with me so long ago, and we all knew that we would not have been allowed inside as village boys in the heyday of the Richardsons.

In fact the only member of the family I ever met was 'Master Jack' himself, who in 1969 gave me a signed copy of the 1945 *History of Bessbrook*, which I still prize highly.

The Woodhouse was also part of the larger estate, which contained Deramore (now spelt 'Derrymore') House, an elegant eighteenth century thatched cottage where the Act of Union was drafted in 1800, to become law the following year. This important piece of legislation abolished the Irish Parliament, and helped to create the United Kingdom. Deramore House was built between 1776 and 1787 by Isaac Corry, who was the MP for Newry in the Irish Parliament for over twenty-five years. Corry sold the house in 1810 when he moved to Dublin. The entire demesne, with some 140,000 trees, was later bought by the Richardson family who donated it to the National Trust in 1952, and it is now open to the public.

Deramore House was closed when I lived in Bessbrook, and not surprisingly its historical significance passed me by completely. I was more interested in the normal pursuits of an energetic country boy. Little did I know then that those happy times would end, as life in the village changed, and the linen mill slowly declined.

§

In the meantime, however, the heartbeat of the village was centred in the local Institute or 'Town Hall' which had been built by the Richardsons in 1886–87 as a place for recreation and self-improvement. The philosophy of the Richardsons and the motto in the Town Hall, were encapsulated by a large mural inside the building. It stated: "In essentials, Unity, in non-essentials, Liberty; in all things, Charity." This quotation has been wrongly attributed to St Augustine, and also modified by many people including a sixteenth century Catholic Bishop in Italy and a seventeenth century Lutheran pastor in Germany. Whatever its origin, the quotation always impressed me as a worthy, if not always practical, motto for any society.

The Bessbrook Institute, to give it its formal name, had a library which was much less popular than the darts room and billiards and snooker tables. I never developed the knack of playing these games which were so important to other people. I also discovered that the atmosphere in the snooker and billiards room, during big competitions, was as sacred as the inside of a cathedral, with a silent reverence which was broken only by applause for a fine shot.

The Town Hall was used for many functions, including church socials, guest-teas, and dances. I remember the early days of the show bands, with a group called 'The Downbeats', led by called Eber Clarke, with its star saxophonist Norman Vance. The atmosphere was not that of a 'Ballroom of Romance', but Bessbrook had many good dancers, including the diminutive Billy Meek, whom my mother – no mean dancer herself – rated as one of the best in the village. The high-ceilinged building was also large enough for badminton, which was played to a good standard, including exhibition matches.

Bowling was hugely popular, among mostly older men who took this sport seriously as they walked on the well-kept green in College Square. Many younger men played hand-ball in two large alleys adjacent to the Town Hall. One of the stars was 'Stiddy' Thompson, whose hands were as tough as a squash racquet, as he propelled the small, hard ball into every corner of the alley.

My friends and I, though much less skilled at this specialised pastime, spent happy hours at the handball game. One of the troubles, however, was keeping the ball in the alleys, and far too often we trooped round to knock on the door of Billy Elliott and his wife, the caretakers of the Town Hall, to ask: "Can we please have our ball back?" It was a miracle that neither of them were driven to strangle us for our endless interruptions of their busy life in looking after the large building.

Table tennis was also popular, and one of the best players was Kenny Morrow, who could return shots to the table from a vast distance, and with maddening regularity. However my most vivid memory is of the night of 6 February 1958, when the games were suddenly stilled and the bats were laid down silently. We had just heard about the Munich disaster in which an aeroplane carrying the Manchester United team and officials, as well as supporters and sports reporters, had crashed, with the loss of twenty-three lives. The victims included several of the famous 'Busby Babes', such as Duncan Edwards. For those of us who played soccer and knew the names of all the leading players of the day – and particularly those who belonged to Matt Busby's Manchester United – it was like hearing about deaths in the family.

The shadow of death also hung over another sport, which had been extremely successful in Bessbrook. A local team had won the Provincial Towns Rugby Cup on four consecutive seasons, from 1885–88. This was a considerable achievement for a small village, which also produced several international players. However the sport died out, partly because one of the players called McGaffin received fatal injuries in one of the games. I read the details on his headstone in the local graveyard where I was cutting the hedges for my Great-Uncle Davy, the sexton of the Presbyterian Church, for the princely sum of seven shillings and sixpence.

Work like this was a financial boon, because I had very little money, and I was always on the look-out for employment. One year I was taken on by a farmer called Alderdice to gather potatoes from the drills in the fields. It was backbreaking work, but I was glad to get it. I still remember the farmer picking me out from a queue of hopefuls, with the words: "I'll take that big fella with the white hands". He paid me ten shillings for the day's work, plus a free lunch of bacon, cabbage and potatoes, washed down by buttermilk, which was really 'bitter' milk. My mother told me to make sure that I gave value for money in my work, and I always tried to do so, whether it was cutting hedges, gathering potatoes, working as a bus conductor or postman in my student days, or writing hundreds of thousands of words later on for newspaper editors and book publishers.

The manual employment gave me a regard for those who earn their living through hard labour. This also developed in me a work ethic which proved invaluable in my later writing career, in which hard graft is as important as inspiration or a flair for the written word.

Religion, or more accurately going to church, was an important part of my early life. By accident of birth, I became a Presbyterian, and I have remained a member of that church all my life. Like most children of the day, I had no say in the matter, and I was despatched to Sunday school each week, followed by morning service in Bessbrook Presbyterian Church with my grandfather, who attended regularly. The local church was established on Boxing Day 1854, and a new 'Meeting House' was opened two years later, and extended in 1865 and 1876. The first minister there was the Reverend Thomas Cromie, who remained in Bessbrook for over fifty years, until his death in 1906. The minister in my time was the Reverend Sydney Carser, a saintly man who had spent his early life working in the Belfast shipyard.

Every Sunday morning, the service started behind time because Mr Carser was consistently late, and I never could work out why, because the Manse was only a short distance away. Once in the pulpit, however, Sydney Carser soon hit his stride. I cannot remember his preaching, apart from the rare occasions when he became worked up about his sermon, raised his voice, and thumped his fist on the side of the pulpit. What he said was less important than what he did, however. He was a kindly man with a big, beaming smile and thick rimmed glasses, and he was well known for his home visitations. During these, the best china and food were set out to entertain 'the minister'. He must have had a continual battle to keep his weight down, but we never heard about this particular struggle with the flesh. Mr Carser was respected on all sides, and even as a child I sensed that he was a good man, though I could not explain why. Children often have an unerring instinct about older people, for better or worse.

Sunday School was a world unto itself. My first memory was of a junior class taught by Anson Chapman. He was an insurance man, and a fine tenor whose party piece at annual socials was to sing 'Good-bye' from the musical, *The White Horse Inn*. At Sunday School Mr Chapman taught us the nineteenth century children's hymn by Philip Bliss which contains the lines: "God is always near me, Hearing what I say, Knowing all my thoughts and deeds, All my work and play." This was an alarming prospect for a small boy, especially as I was told at home that God had a big black book and that my name would be written in it if I did anything wrong. No doubt it was an effective way of dealing with a naughty youngster, but I am surprised in retrospect that this did not make me an atheist for life.

As we grew older, we had to take our Sunday School lessons seriously, and once a year we were subjected to an oral examination by one of the elders from nearby Presbyterian churches, who were mostly farmers. Each year, apart from one, I had a 100 percent success, like most of the other pupils. Once, however, I had ten marks deducted for not knowing one detail about the Crucifixion, and I felt that my life was a failure at that moment. Overall, we were given a good grounding in the Scriptures, but I regret to say that I forgot most of what I had learned by rote. It took much longer to apply those rules to the sterner business of life.

Despite the solemn atmosphere of the Sunday School examinations, which were held in the church itself, there was also irreverent horse-play. My fellow conspirator and life-long friend, Geoffrey Martin spent part of one afternoon finding out how far he could spit from the balcony to the ground floor of the church. By good judgement, or sheer bad luck, one of his juicier spits landed on the head of the very worthy Clerk of Session, Willie Stewart, who was walking up the stairs to the gallery. I thought that this was extremely bad form, but nevertheless hilarious, though I was too scared to laugh out loud. I cannot remember any repercussions from such misbehaviour, possibly because Willie Stewart had other things on his mind, as well as on his head.

The Presbyterian Church was set on a hill overlooking the village. Lower down was the Church of Ireland building with its distinctive spire. I was rarely in that church, apart from attending special services with the Boy Scouts, but I always thought – probably unfairly – that the Anglicans in Bessbrook looked on themselves as a cut above the

Presbyterians. The Methodist Church was situated near the centre of the village, and I only went to services there after carol singing on Christmas mornings. In those days, unlike now, inter-church services simply did not take place, and each denomination kept to its own. This applied also to the smaller congregations, including the Society of Friends. They worshipped in a building at Deramore – possibly because the Richardsons, who had built Bessbrook, were strong members of that denomination.

The Roman Catholic chapel was within a short walking distance of the main Protestant churches, but in all my time in Bessbrook, I never entered the building. This was not a conscious bias against Catholicism – it never simply occurred to me to do so. The nearest we had to ecumenism, in those days when the word had not been invented, was to watch the Reverend Carser involved in long conversations in the village square with the Roman Catholic priest. I never could figure out why they did this: did they enjoy talking to one another, or were they also making a symbolic point in public about the importance of good community relations?

Bessbrook had a mixed population, and although I was never aware of any discrimination either way, there was a subtle social apartness of which I became more conscious later on. I used to think that many of my boyhood friends were Catholics, but I was wrong. A few neighbouring children were Catholics, and we played football, and shared other childhood games.

However we were educated in Protestant or Catholic primary schools, and never the twain did meet *en masse*. I was conscious, however, that some Catholics behaved a bit differently at times from Protestants. For example, I once watched (through a gap in the wall of the Pond Field) a parade of Hibernians making their way along the road after morning Mass in the Catholic Chapel. Each man and woman on parade was wearing a green collarette, but I knew that my grandfather always wore an Orange one when he was marching with his Lodge. I did not understand then why normal grown-ups would do such things, and I still don't quite understand why adults from either community in Northern Ireland need to wear bits of coloured cloth around their necks to show the world what they believe in.

This is partly because I was brought up to assume that the majority of people lived as peacefully as we did. In the housing estate where I lived in my teens, our next door neighbour was a member of a Hibernian band, and he practised his drumming so loudly that we could hear it every time he played. However none of us complained, for fear of offending our Catholic neighbours, and they were equally courteous to us.

I was aware of the Convent on the hill just above our church, because they rang bells at prayer times around noon. However, I never had any reason to go in there. It was remote from my daily life, except for one occasion when I had to deliver a Post Office telegram to one of the nuns. I walked up to the big front door, with the buff envelope in my hand, and rang the bell nervously because I did not know what to expect. I had never met a nun before. After a long wait, I heard footsteps coming to the door, and it was opened by a pretty young woman with a nun's dress, hood and white cowl. I silently handed her the buff envelope containing the telegram.

Telegrams often contained bad news, so she drew in her breath as she read the name on the envelope, and then she exclaimed in relief, "Oh, thank God – it's for somebody else!" I suddenly realised that nuns were human beings, just like me.

I never knew the exact religious make-up of the village, nor did I see any reason to find out. Certainly there must have been cultural differences at a time when religious practice was strict, but on the whole, we got on well together, and Bessbrook gave me a broad religious and cultural outlook which I have retained all my life. Little did any of us know then, however, that within a few decades Northern Ireland would be engulfed in appalling sectarian violence and that at Kingsmills, near Bessbrook, ten innocent men would be murdered in cold blood by Republican extremists, simply because they were Protestants.

In stark contrast, one of my warmest memories of my Catholic contemporaries was when I played football for a religiously-mixed youth team called Evergreen. We took part in a knock-out competition in Newry, where it was said that the 'gate money' was going into a fund for building a new Roman Catholic chapel. That did not worry me. The most important thing was to win the competition, which we did. I was the Evergreen goalkeeper, and I was impressed by the skill of the young man between the opposite goalposts. After the game, I told him,

"You played a blinder. What's your name?" He replied, "Pat Jennings", and he went on to become an outstanding goalkeeper for Tottenham Hotspur, Arsenal and Northern Ireland. In his prime he was, without doubt, one of the best goalkeepers in the world.

Decades later, I visited Pat at Highbury, the then Arsenal headquarters, to write his profile for the *Belfast Telegraph*. Because of our previous connections in Newry, he invited me to his home, where he gave me signed pictures for my children. When I handed one to my son Mark back in Belfast, he said enthusiastically, "That's terrific Dad – and you even got his autograph. Did he ask for yours?" That was a young boy's hero worship of his Dad, and I felt really flattered.

Looking back on my early days in Bessbrook, I realise that I learned much about life there, apart from my formal education at school. The 'model village' gave me a sense of belonging to a vibrant and religiously mixed community, a love of nature and the outdoors, and a wide knowledge of sport which is always an international passport to share conversations with strangers of a like mind. I also learned to be part of a team, as well as sometimes being a loner, and I was made aware that there was a God to worship, though I did not think greatly about it then, nor did I worry about the ways in which other people worshipped Him.

Without realising it, I was being made aware of some of the most important qualities in life, such as loyalty, hard work, sportsmanship, humour, courage, initiative, fair play, a sense of right and wrong, and how to get on with people. These were standards which I carried, almost unconsciously, into my adult life, and tried to live by, though often imperfectly. I am by no means a model person, but I have always owed a great deal to the 'model village' of Bessbrook.

CHAPTER FIVE

Learning the Hard Way

Ｍy formal education began in Bessbrook Public Elementary School in August 1945. On my first day I met my friend Geoff Martin, who still tells me that we walked hand in hand down the main street of the village. I cannot remember walking 'hand in hand', but he and I have remained close through our long careers – mine in journalism and his in local and national student politics, and later in the Eighties and Nineties as a senior figure in the European Commission, where he opened the EC Office in Belfast and served for several years as Head of the EC Office in London.

Our careers overlapped, and we met frequently. Geoff has a layer of extrovert bonhomie, though he can be tough-minded when required. However, he also has a deep sense of loyalty, and a strong streak of sentimentality. This is most often expressed in his unwavering affection for his roots, which he always says are planted in South Armagh. He is a good friend to me, and it was a bonus when we discovered, only in our sixties, that we are second cousins.

My first memory of the infants' school in 1945 was of being taught to knit. Maybe it had something to do with the austerity of the war years, and with teaching us to be self-reliant. Sadly, however, I never got the hang of knitting, and the scarf I produced had more curves on it than a dog's hind leg. That was bad enough, but it was even worse when I lost marks overall for my poor knitting skills.

This was at the end of the Second World War, when large parts of continental Europe were still in turmoil, and Northern Ireland was beginning to adjust uneasily to the new peace. Naturally I had no idea of what was happening beyond Bessbrook. It was only much later that I became aware that the Second World War had ended only a short time earlier, in the spring of 1945. Just a few months before I had first gone to nursery school, the Allied troops had liberated the remaining notorious concentration camps throughout Germany.

Life in my infants' school was not as enjoyable as it is for children today. There was a strict atmosphere, and my two teachers were firm, though kinder than the men who taught in the boys' school next door. My teachers were physically 'Little and Large': Mrs Bell, the wife of the local rent collector Billy Bell, was as thin as a pencil, but her colleague Mrs Skuce was a big woman in every way. The classes were taught in a room where you could read the large clock on the Town Hall, just across the park. I remember the agonising minutes when I watched the hands of that clock slowly move to the time for our break, which meant that I could go to the toilet without having to put up my hand nervously and ask the teacher's permission to do so. As a result, I trained myself to develop one of the strongest bladders in Ireland.

There was a large number of children for only two teachers, and sometimes we were assisted by senior pupils. I remember a pretty older girl in nursery trying to teach me 'long' addition across three columns of figures, but I could not understand it. After several failed attempts, I was summarily sent back down back to the baby infants' class. No explanation was given to me, nor – as far as I know – to my grandfather or my Aunt Jean. Those were the days when parents or guardians did not argue with teachers.

Primary school, the next stage of my education, was basically a battle for survival. The conditions, compared to today, were Dickensian, and this was not surprising because the Bessbrook Public Elementary Schools actually were established by the Richardsons in Dickens' day! The toilets in the boys' school were primitive, and they were the cockpit for many fierce bare-knuckle fights. The boys were released into the playground at specific times, during which we would run around madly until the break ended, and we were then summoned back into the classroom. This was in order to clear the playground for the girls from the school next door. The boys and girls, who were educated in adjacent sections of the same building, never met outside.

Our lunch was taken in the playground, and it is hard to remember what we had to eat. We had to bring our own 'piece', though we did get an ample supply of school milk. I never felt deprived or hungry, but it is possible that some of my colleagues were malnourished. In my home I have a picture of our assembled class which was taken in the late Forties, and few of the boys looked well-off.

Though the conditions in the school were hard, we could tolerate this because we were not aware of anything better. Physical punishment was routine, and I remember keeping my head down in fear when one pupil, who today would be classed as 'special needs', was beaten around the room by an irate teacher for failing to understand what he was being taught.

The headmaster was a fearsome individual called James Darragh, who was nicknamed Jemmy. He was a small, tweedy man with a grey moustache, and he was often covered in chalk dust. He was a strict disciplinarian, and I was frightened of him. However, I knew that there was no point in complaining about it at home, because teachers were all-powerful in their own domain.

Though physical abuse was frequent in the boys' school, there was no evidence, or even a hint, of sexual abuse, and I am convinced that this never took place. However I now understand why children who complained of sexual abuse by clergy in institutions run by the Roman Catholic Church throughout Ireland at that time were afraid to complain to their parents about this. They knew that nobody would believe them.

It is difficult to know whether Jemmy Darragh was a good teacher or not. His cane was a frayed billiard cue, with straggly lumps of wood at the end, which made the beating more painful. One day he punished the entire class for leaving the playground and for rushing down past the traffic to the nearby 'Boiler Hill' to play football. When we returned, he lined everyone up for punishment, including his favourite pupil, Gordon Breasley. Gordon was a gifted boy with whom I became friendly, and I was devastated later on, when he died during his teens as the result of a motor accident.

I sometimes wonder if James Darragh was any more fearsome than some of the other school principals of his day. Though he was prone to caning pupils, he was not deliberately spiteful, cruel or unfair. Certainly the stories I heard later on about the terror in some of the schools run by Roman Catholic clergy at that time made me think that there might have been places worse than Bessbrook Boys' School, with all its drawbacks.

In those days our horizons were limited. One of the great treats was the annual Sunday School Trip. We would assemble around 8.30 am on a summer's day at Bessbrook Presbyterian Church, and march down to Charlemont Square (which had been named after one of the local gentry, though this meant nothing to us). We then travelled by road to Newry where we embarked on the steam train for Warrenpoint. This was a great, clanking mechanical monster, emitting steam, hot water and noise, and driven by a man in a shiny peaked cap, while another man with a blackened faced shovelled coal into a huge fire which heated the boiler to produce the power.

This was like being in Heaven, for a small boy, and as the train clicked and clanked its way along the line, with soot flying and soiling one's Sunday-best (and only) suit, the delights of 'The Point' lay ahead. These included a packed lunch, with bottles of lemonade which were a rarity for everyone in those days. We had our meal in a local church hall, and there was also ample time to wander around Warrenpoint, and to sample the even rarer ice cream or admire the scenic view across the Lough to Omeath and Carlingford on the other side. They sat snugly within the Republic of Ireland, which seemed so remote. I always loved the view across Carlingford Lough, but I disliked the stony beach which was always Warrenpoint's main drawback as a tourist resort.

All too soon, it was time to start going back towards Bessbrook, and the 'wee trip' would be over for another year. However there was a consolation for those boys who attended a weekly meeting run by a local evangelist called Johnny Qua. These were good opportunities to meet our friends, though the meetings were meant to be all about Bible readings and prayers. One night Mr Qua prayed for a long time, and asked the Lord to heal his bad back. I was surprised by this, because I thought that the village doctor would know more about bad backs than God, but I deduced that if Johnny Qua believed that God was all-powerful, he must have been sure that He could make his back better too!

The main attraction of these meetings was the annual reward of Johnny Qua's 'excursion' to Rostrevor, which was even further away than Warrenpoint. We went there by road, and the first stop was at a little shop, just across from the Great Northern Hotel, which was itself an upmarket tourist attraction in Rostrevor, and has long since closed. At the roadside shop we bought sweets and lemonade, which were considerable treats during those austere post-war years. Then we would climb the steep, wooded hill to look at the Cloughmore Stone, a huge geological relic of the Ice Age, which was known to us simply as 'the Big Stone'.

After our brief exposure to this solid treasure, we went to a clearing in the trees called 'Fiddlers' Green', and there we wrestled, played 'tig' or football, and frolicked until it was time to go home. When we reached Bessbrook, we all formed a circle in the main square, and after Johnny Qua had removed his hat, we all sang self-consciously; "Praise God from whom all blessings flow, praise Him all creatures here below/Praise Him above, ye Heavenly host, praise Father, Son and Holy Ghost." I rarely hear the Presbyterian Doxology sung nowadays, but when I do, it always reminds me of Johnny Qua's 'Wee Excursion'.

Following our annual excursions to Warrenpoint and Rostrevor, our world would shrink back to our village and classroom, where Jemmy Darragh, to his credit, tried to widen our horizons through learning. We were made to memorise all the woollen towns of England, and other geographical wonders of the wider world, though this did not make much sense to us, at the time.

However, it was a relief to take part in singing classes. As ever, Mr Darragh had detailed plans in place to make sure that they would work. He would write the words of 'The Minstrel Boy' or 'Linden Lea' on the big blackboard. We would copy these laboriously in our jotters, and then learn them by heart. The next day we would be lined up, with smaller boys in front of the bigger boys at the back. We would carefully learn the music, and then we would sing. Those boys, including myself, who were not singing loudly or tunefully enough would soon discover Jemmy Darragh's forefinger hovering menacingly in front of their mouth, or sometimes inside it, to make them open wider. Miraculously it all seemed to work, and the choir usually sang rather well. I have had a lifelong love of good music and I always listen with affection to the words of 'The Minstrel Boy' and 'Linden Lea'.

In the primary school, I did much better at English grammar and composition than at mathematics. Jemmy hammered the grammar into me, but I was able to handle it without too much trouble. Many years later, when I was a television critic for the *Belfast Telegraph*, a primary school teacher said to me that she used to cut out my weekly column and pin it on the blackboard for her pupils to parse. I told her that if she handed one of my television columns to me at that very moment, I would probably not be able to parse it myself!

Most boys in Bessbrook finished their basic primary education and then went on to the technical college, or took up a trade, or worked in the linen mill. Jemmy Darragh must have been extremely frustrated at the limited prospects for his pupils, and even more so when the less bright remained unemployed and hung around street corners.

Around the age of eleven, a decision was made for me by Darragh which proved to be one of the most important of my life. One day he asked the class, "How many boys want to prepare for the Eleven plus examination?" I did not know what this meant, but when several of my pals including Stanley Aulds and Jim Archer put up their hands, I did the same.

Darragh looked at me and said, "McCreary, I'm not sure you'll make it. But I'll try you anyway." When I went home, I told my grandfather and my Aunt Jean what had happened. Although they had very little idea about the Eleven plus examination either, they gave me permission to try it, even though it meant taking extra lessons after normal school time.

The Eleven plus examination had resulted from the 1947 Education Act in Northern Ireland, which itself originated from the 1944 Education Act in Britain. This gave all young people who had passed the Eleven plus or 'Qualifying Examination' an opportunity to enter a grammar school. In most cases, the fees were paid by the local education authority. If successful, a pupil could aspire to university education, and if he or she gained the right grades in the A level examinations, the fees would also be paid.

In retrospect, the 1947 Education Act was one of the most revolutionary pieces of legislation in the history of Northern Ireland. It empowered entire generations of young people to prepare for a professional career, and to play a pivotal role in the political, social and business life of their native province.

There is a direct link between the 1947 Education Act and the mobilisation of a young Catholic generation who campaigned successfully for Civil Rights from the late Sixties onwards and later for totally equality of opportunity for all citizens of the State, irrespective of their religious or social background. The late Father Denis Faul, a Dungannon priest who strongly supported the civil rights movement, once told a journalist colleague of mine, "The Eleven plus was the greatest act of Catholic emancipation in the twentieth century."

All of this was a far cry from the young boys like me who were preparing for an examination in 1950–51, which had only been introduced a few years earlier. It must also have been experimental for Jemmy Darragh, as a teacher, and we must have been among the first classes he prepared for the examination.

The Qualifying Exams were taken over several days at different times of the school year. I found them difficult, and I thought that I might not pass. On the morning that the results were due in the post, we waited expectantly in the kitchen at 5 Wakefield Terrace in Bessbrook. The brown envelope with the Education Authority's postmark duly arrived, but it was addressed to my grandfather who was my official guardian, and not to me.

For some reason, I thought that this meant I had failed, but when my grandfather read the letter he said "Son, you've passed, well done!" My heart leapt. I knew that I would be going to Newry Grammar School, if we could afford it, and not to Bessbrook 'Tech' or to a trade apprenticeship or into the linen mill. My educational adventure had already started.

I left Bessbrook Boys' School that June with few regrets, and hardly a backward look, except to remember occasionally the harsh times and Jemmy Darragh's cane, as well as the good times on the football field and in the school playground.

However I now realise what I owe to Mr Darragh. He gave me a good basic education, particularly in composition and English grammar, and he steered me successfully through the Eleven plus and opened a whole new educational world for me. I just wish that he had spared us from so much of his cane.

My first few days at Newry Grammar School were a shock. The Bessbrook schools had been small, and therefore familiar. However in

Newry there were lots of classrooms, a great deal of noise and bustle, with children shouting, racing along corridors with big, awkward schoolbags, and brushing past or colliding with one another. There were bells that rang to tell you it was time to change classrooms, there were teachers in black cloaks which made them seem like a race apart, and there were bigger boys who would give you a boot up the backside if you were not careful.

Incredibly, there were also girls. In Bessbrook the girls were next door to my classroom but we never saw them. In Newry the girls were right beside me, and that was altogether different. They were dressed in long brown uniforms with thick brown tights, and they did not quite look the way I expected girls to be, because they were so muffled up.

However when we went to dancing classes everything changed. We learned the fox-trot, the waltz, the Moonlight Saunter, and even 'the Gay Gordons', which was something very different to what it would mean today. The girls lined up on one side of the school canteen, with its permanent odour of boiled cabbage, and the boys on the other.

When the teacher told us to pick a partner, the boys – being as stupid and unfeeling as only boys can be – headed straight for the prettiest girls. I learned only later, in places far away from Newry Grammar School, that the prettiest girls are not always the nicest people, and that other girls are much more attractive in different ways.

At Newry Grammar School the teachers had a profound influence on all of us, for better or worse. Good teachers could instil in us a love for their subject, but a bad teacher could put you off for life. My Latin teacher was a fierce character, and as a result I came to loathe Classics.

My history teacher Johnny Spence was a peppery little man with a reddish-purple face, and he also took no prisoners. He regularly told us that "Civil servants are not civil", and he was famous for his malapropisms. He would lecture us about "The Charge of the Calvary", rather than the 'Cavalry', and we had to keep a straight face beneath his stern gaze, though we were squirming helplessly inside. However I was to be grateful to Mr Spence in my senior classes at Newry Grammar School where his expert tuition in history helped me to win a scholarship to Queen's University.

Our algebra teacher was a big friendly man called Paddy Shellard, and he tried hard to help me to understand the intricacies of his subject, without success. Miss Hood was a wispy, dreamy lady who attempted to teach me French, and so did a genial but authoritative man called Walter Moore. They must have had some success, and although my French is limited, I found it useful as a last resort on my later travels, especially in places like French-speaking Africa, and the Far East.

Mr Dalzell, nicknamed 'Duck', taught geography, and I wish I had paid more attention to him. Mr Livingstone, inevitably called 'Livvy' taught chemistry, but this subject always remained a mystery to me, and I disliked the pungent smells in the laboratory.

The headmaster James Greenlees was an awesome figure who occasionally taught physics as well as running the school. He had a short fuse, and in the classroom he sometimes hurled a solid wooden duster at a pupil who exasperated him.

He also walked around the school jingling his keys, which was always a fair warning for us to scramble out of his way. One day I was struggling with big crates on 'milk duty' when I heard the keys jingling along the nearby corridor. I could not escape in time. Mr Greenlees swept round the corner like a gowned emperor and yelled at me "Get off the face of the earth boy, off the face of the earth!" He swept past without further ado, and left me standing speechless. In my later years at school, I came to know James Greenlees much better, and I realised that he was a good man who cared deeply about his school and his pupils.

Sadly, my early years in Newry Grammar School were not happy, partly because I had been told in the worst possible way that I was 'illegitimate', and at that stage, it really mattered to me.

One night in Bessbrook I told several of my pals that I was going home early because my 'father' Tommy McCreary did not want me to stay out late. Then a bumptious boy said to me with a sneer "He's not your father. He's your grandfather, and you are a bastard." Children can be immensely cruel and he had said it deliberately to hurt me. I hated being called a bastard, because this was a term of abuse, and I was innocent. I pretended not to notice the deliberate barb, but this upstart had hurt me deeply.

I was unable to talk about this to anybody, and certainly not to my grandfather or my Aunt Jean. So I kept it to myself, though I was not happy about it. I could not understand why I was called a 'bastard' through no fault of my own, and the hurt seeped in to me, to the point where I began to lose self-confidence at an age when this is important to any young person.

However there was no counselling in those days, and I had to get on with it. It was a crossroads at which some other children might have let their heads drop, and sought refuge in drugs or other forms of anti-social behaviour.

In my case, two things helped me to regain my self-esteem. One was sport and the other was writing. I had always been quite good at sport, thanks to my upbringing in Bessbrook, and at Newry Grammar School I soon made my mark as a hockey player.

The school did not cater for rugby or soccer, so there was no other choice. I started out as a centre-forward for one of the junior hockey teams, but eventually I was drafted into goal by the sports teacher EF Agnew, known to us as 'EFA'. He later went to Campbell College, a rugby school, where he trained a generation of good hockey players who later knocked Newry Grammar out of the Schools Cup, to my great regret.

At Newry I eventually succeeded the outstanding goalkeeper George Compston, when he left the school, and I went on to win caps for the Ulster Schools side, and was picked for the final 'trials' for the Irish schools team. I remember travelling to Dublin with my ungainly 'pads' and hockey gear, only to discover that the trials game had been called off due to a waterlogged pitch.

The 'sitting' goalie was Wesley Griffiths from King's Hospital School in Dublin, and he was automatically chosen again for international duty. I remember the disappointment of trudging back from the non-trial at Londonbridge Road in Dublin, and without the prospect of ever winning an Irish schools cap. In my teens these things were very important. So I did what I always did in those days of challenge – I tightened my belt, kept my mouth shut, and got on with it.

The hockey at Newry Grammar had other hidden advantages, however. Being a regular on the First XI, I could travel with the team to Belfast to play against RBAI and Campbell College. It also meant that I could have lunch in a Belfast restaurant, which was a big deal for a country boy, and I could also sneak in with my hockey companions to watch a 'naughty' French film in a cinema near the Great Northern Railway terminus in Great Victoria Street.

My hockey career also gave me the opportunity to travel to Dublin a number of times, when I played for Ulster Schools against Leinster Schools. After the match we were taken to Lansdowne Road in Dublin to watch an international rugby match between Ireland and Wales. It was totally different from soccer or hockey which I had been used to, and Dublin itself was exciting for me. It was like a foreign land, and full of people with strange accents. I am not sure that I have really come to terms with Dublin since then.

The opportunity to travel regularly outside Bessbrook and Newry widened my awareness of life beyond the bubble of my early school days. Yet even in Newry Grammar School things were changing. One day Mr Greenlees came into our classroom and told each of us what we were going to study during our senior years at the school.

His decisions were based partly on the result of the Junior Certificate examination, in which I had clearly better marks in arts subjects than in science. Not surprisingly he told me that I would take arts for Senior Level examinations. Once again my educational future was being determined by a teacher who decided my future for me.

However, James Greenlees was absolutely right in his choice for me. There was also the added bonus that I would be able to study more closely with the senior English teacher Miss Ethel Meneely, who more than anyone else gave me the confidence and self-esteem which I needed. It was she who guided my steps in a direction that would ultimately lead to a career in writing, and which would take me not only away from Bessbrook and Newry, but also carry me around the world much later on.

Miss Meneely had three outstanding qualities as a teacher. She was able to transmit her deep love of English literature, she could instil self-confidence in a pupil, and she could inspire you to work even harder.

On a one-to-one basis Miss Meneely was a good teacher. Under her watchful eye, I read and wrote about many of the major figures in English literature, including Milton, Keats, Wordsworth, Shelley, Byron, Coleridge, Hazlitt, and Gerard Manley Hopkins.

Some of the quotations from the great writers have stayed with me for a lifetime, and the older I get, the more I appreciate their insight and wisdom. However it would be wrong to suggest that my reading and love of English literature began in Newry Grammar School.

As a young boy I read avidly adventure stories, like *Treasure Island*, a copy of which was Christmas present from my grandmother and which I have kept to this day, and I devoured all the comics such as *The Dandy* and *The Beano*, with their larger than life characters like Desperate Dan, and the runner Alf Tupper who broke world records in athletics, and all on a diet of fish and chips!

Because there was little or no television available, reading was one of the best ways to escape into other worlds of knowledge and adventure. However it was my mother, an avid reader, who gradually introduced me to 'grown-up' literature,

So I read everything I could find, including all the short stories of W Somerset Maugham and Tolstoy, novels by AJ Cronin, large chunks of Dickens and all kinds of books which showed me how life was lived in the big world outside. I remember reading Richard Llewellyn's 1939 novel *How Green Was My Valley*, in which I discovered what was then called 'the facts of life'. I was surprised at how it all worked, but I thought that it was an ingenious arrangement, and presumably very enjoyable.

Miss Meneely added to my knowledge of English literature by lending me books and poems which were not on our prescribed course. They included the poems of TS Eliot, with his masterly account in *The Journey of the Magi*, and Edward FitzGerald's translation of the *Rubayait of Omar Khayam*, with its memorable lines "The Moving Finger writes, and, having writ, Moves on: nor all thy Piety nor Wit: Shall lure it back to cancel half a Line, Nor all thy Tears wash out a Word of it..."

Under Miss Meneely's tuition, I was constantly encouraged and intellectually stretched. One day she said to me, "You write so fluently. If you can maintain this standard, there's no knowing where you might end up." I did not understand the implications of what she was saying, but I was grateful for her compliment.

Many years later I met Ethel Meneely at an Ulster Orchestra concert. It was shortly after the publication of one of my books, and she said to me, "That's the best thing you have written so far." To me, that was praise beyond my imagination, coming from a woman who had taught me so much. Before I could thank her properly, she had moved off. I made a point of writing to thank her for all she had done for me, but I kept postponing it because of the pressure of other things. Tragically, she died soon afterwards and my letter of thanks was never written. I have often thought about this, with sadness, but perhaps Ethel Meneely did not seek or need my thanks. She already knew that all her considerable efforts on my behalf had not been in vain.

In my latter years, the atmosphere improved greatly for me in Newry Grammar School. The frantic strategies for survival of my early years had developed into a greater self-confidence, whereby I knew that, with hard work and some good fortune, there was a distinct possibility that I might win a scholarship to Queen's. In my final years, I studied English, History and Geography at A Level, and I gained an average mark of over sixty percent in all three, which ensured that I would receive funding from the local education authority.

I had learned from Miss Meneely that Miranda's words in Shakespeare's *The Tempest*, "O brave New World, That has such people in it" was the sadly ironic observation of an innocent and vulnerable young girl. I knew that in going to Queen's University in 1959, I was entering into my own 'brave new world', but I hoped that by then that I had already learned enough about life to keep my eyes wide open, and to look after myself.

Bessbrook Public Elementary School

CHAPTER SIX

Brave New World

WHEN I WENT up to Queen's University in October 1959 to read for an Arts degree, it was the beginning of one of the happiest years of my life. Within a few months I had fitted in to the hectic pace at Queen's, which seemed impressively cosmopolitan to a country boy like me. I had found and settled in to my student digs; I had made it immediately into the First XI in the Queen's men's hockey club and I was playing with and against Irish internationals; I was dating a lovely girl called Jean Russell who was then Miss Northern Ireland, and I passed my first year examinations and gained entry into the university's Honours School of Modern History.

However at the end of that euphoric year, another kind of reality kicked in. My relationship with Jean had ended, my scholarship money had run out, and I had to take a summer job as a bus conductor in Great Yarmouth, that tacky English holiday resort on the Norfolk coast. I was also apprehensive about the prospect of entering the Honours History class at Queen's at the start of my second year, because the level of scholarship and hard work seemed so daunting. I knew only too well that I had to pass my exams to stay at Queen's and to qualify for a continuing scholarship, so my survival instinct kept me on track in my formal education. I was also still greatly dependent on financial support from my grandfather, who gave me £50 each term from his meagre old-age pension. Yet despite the drawbacks of that dismal summer of 1960 in Great Yarmouth, my first year at university remains in my memory as one of the high periods of my life.

My formal education during my first year was a blur. I studied history and geography, with geology making up the requisite trio of subjects. History and geography were reassuringly familiar, but geology was a nightmare, and I still don't know how I passed my first year examinations. Perhaps it was the whispered assistance of friends at the 'practical' exams in the Great Hall which helped to pull me through.

The Queen's staff seemed to belong to another planet. I had no idea that Professor JC Beckett who lectured me in first year was an eminent authority in Irish history, or that Professor Estyn Evans was a distinguished international geographer. Nor did I realise that Professor Michael Roberts, who told us the murderously fascinating story of Rasputin and the Russian Royal family, was also a world expert in Swedish history.

The lectures were merely something you attended between playing hockey, drinking coffee in the students' union, chatting up people in the library, and generally learning to grow up. However it was my informal education in the university of life that taught me so much in my first year at Queen's. This included the most basic skills of opening a bank account, learning to mix with a wide variety of new people, and eking out my money to pay for basic expenses.

The university population was much smaller in those days, with just over 3,000 students. It was also a much smaller campus, which was concentrated around the beautiful Sir Charles Lanyon building set apart in gracious lawns along University Road. There was also a communal familiarity that flourished within a small student body in relatively confined spaces. Most important of all, for those like myself who attended Queen's in this era, this was the first time in Northern Ireland's history that the university gave an entire generation of Protestant and Roman Catholic students the opportunity to meet, study and relax together in a non-threatening atmosphere – although I was not conscious of this at the time, because religion was not important to most of us then.

Looking back, however, I am now aware that Queen's was an island of bridge-building in a province where the school education system at primary and secondary levels was overwhelmingly segregated between Protestants and Catholics. Significantly, my contemporaries were mostly scholarship students from both main communities, and they later formed the cadre of professional leaders, writers, politicians and others who were prominent in Northern Ireland society – I will mention some of these later on.

I remain proud of the key role which Queen's played in breaking down the educational and community barriers and giving us the kind of broad, liberal education which had not been available to most of our parents and grandparents, who could not afford to go to university. The tragedy was that this integrated education had not started early enough in the history of the province to prevent the horrors of the Troubles that occurred from the late Sixties onwards.

There were several ways of making your name at Queen's in the late Fifties and early Sixties: either through outstanding scholarship, which ruled me out, or through student politics and debate, which scared me stiff, or through sport, which was my strong suit. Having played hockey at Newry to inter-provincial schoolboy level, I was drafted in to the Queen's senior team in my first week by Bob Poots, an Irish international whom I had known well at Newry Grammar School. My role was to deputise briefly for the injured regular goalkeeper David Kernohan, a talented player who had represented Irish Schools during his time at Campbell College, and who became a friend of mine. Fortunately, I managed to keep my place on the First XI and won a University 'Blue' sporting award at the end of my first year.

These sporting achievements may seem trivial to outsiders, but they helped me to gain in confidence and to have an 'identity' around the campus. As in Newry Grammar School earlier, I learned yet again that people respected you for what you achieved, irrespective of your family background. Success in hockey also enabled me to travel to Germany for the first time, in 1960, with the combined Queen's University's men and women's teams, where we took part in an international tournament in Essen.

I remember one hard fought game, in which our men's team defeated a crack side from West Berlin, and the match was broadcast live on German radio. This was a far cry from my hockey games in the Newry Grammar School's hen-run pitch only a year earlier. I had travelled far not only in hockey terms but also, more importantly, in terms of experiencing life in Germany only fifteen years or so after the end of the Second World War.

Several years later I was fortunate enough to play for the British

Universities team against the West German Universities in the first international of its kind between the two countries. The game was scheduled to take place in Munich, and on the afternoon before the game some of our players who were sightseeing in that lovely city became involved in a row with German civilians about queuing for a bus. An elderly German tried to thump our guys with his umbrella, but the row seemed to peter out. However that evening the Munich police interrupted dinner at our hotel and took several of our colleagues away for 'questioning'. In the end the British Ambassador had to interrupt his evening at the local Opera House to secure the release of our players, so that the match could take place the next day. We defeated the West German team heavily, which gave us much satisfaction, but I was very much aware that Anglo-German relations were in need of great repair, so soon after the War.

That German experience also opened my eyes to the immense attraction of international travel, but at that stage I had no thoughts about journalism. The student newspaper, *Gown*, seemed to be a closed shop, and it was far outside my world. Little did I think then that, several years later, I would end up as the editor of *Gown*, on my way to a professional career in journalism.

Another important source of informal learning for me in those years was Belfast itself. I had visited it briefly around the age of eleven with my Uncle Bill, and later at sixteen with a school friend from Bessbrook who had relatives in the city. I discovered in my first year at Queen's, when I was nineteen, that Belfast was an even more exciting city than I had realised. The old Smithfield of the late Fifties and early Sixties was a treasured emporium of second-hand books, vinyl records and all kinds of ancient, fascinating and mostly irrelevant objects. The city was full of people with a distinct and sometimes harsh but attractive accent, which was so different to that of my own soft-spoken people in South Armagh.

There were lots of cars, trolley-buses, people scurrying to and from work, and a threadbare little man who solemnly coaxed thin tunes from a saw, while earning a pittance from passers-by at the City Hall. There were countless smoky pubs – not that I could afford to go to many – but the nearest to the university was the Queen's Bar. One day the entire male population of the Union crowded into the same bar to watch a much-publicised drinking contest between two students who had even less money than sense. The great face-off soon petered out disappointingly, due to lack of cash and stamina!

Opposite the Queen's Bar was the earthy but often crowded Italian cafe which everybody dubbed 'Smokey Joe's', and which was one of the few places where we could have an affordable meal on special occasions. There were exciting dance halls everywhere, including Romano's, the Plaza, the faraway Floral Hall and many others, but the Queen's hop on a Saturday night was the best of all of them. The big test of success with the opposite sex, however, was to bring a girl from the hop in the sweaty Students' Union to the smoochy atmosphere of the darkened drill hall, which was normally used for training by the students' Officer Training Corps.

Many a male ego was diminished by not being able to persuade a partner to come across to the drill hall, and from there, to be allowed to leave her 'home' – or more realistically, to her bus or train. Those who went further did not talk about it, and we all knew that those who talked about it had never gone further. I remember leaving one young girl 'home' to a relative's house at the respectable hour of 11.30 pm, only to be given a rollicking on the doorstep by her tipsy uncle, for being late. She was mortified, and I felt sorry for her. All the women at the Queen's hops were beautiful, of course, but sometimes these occasions would have the air of a cattle market about them, especially when the girls had to walk past the steady gaze of the men who were sizing them up in the McMordie Hall in the Students' Union, as they went on their way to the dance floor.

On other nights we made our own amusement, and often in the Glee Club run by Phil Coulter, who later became a professional song-writer, soloist, band-leader, and also a good friend of mine. Coulter was one of those talented Derry people who have music in their blood. However, he also had the persuasive ability to harness a large range of students to perform in his Glee Club, including some people whom he told me later "had everything but talent". Phil also had the nerve to chat up national pop stars like Helen Shapiro, who was singing at the Grand Opera House, and persuading her to perform in front of the astonished but appreciative Glee Club audience.

Coulter was studying for a music degree, but half way through he joined the professional music business. His many achievements include writing Eurovision Song Contest hits, Hollywood film scores, Celtic music in its many forms, and the rugby anthem, 'Ireland's Call'. However his biggest achievement of all was in re-inventing himself continually to achieve long-term survival in the tough music business. Throughout it all he has remained modest, and loyal to his friends. I can still remember fondly his antics at the Glee Club, whose ambiance so neatly personified the buzz, ingenuity, fun, camaraderie and sheer unexpectedness of life at Queen's in my early days.

Inevitably my first year at university wound to an end. I remember standing anxiously in the historic quadrangle in early June 1960, waiting for my first year results – and breathing a huge sigh of relief when they were posted on the notice board. My successful application to the Modern History School meant that I would be embarking on a course where there would be no examinations until my finals three years later. This would create formidable academic challenges when these finals duly took place, but it meant at least that my university scholarship and therefore my financial situation would be secure. That was the most important factor of all for me.

As I have said, part of my summer holidays that year was spent on the buses in Great Yarmouth, which was hard work with not much pay. Geoff Martin and I shared rooms in a smelly digs where the male proprietor would waken me every morning by wiping a dishcloth over my face! Martin frequently avoided this fate by dating a young lady early in the morning in a local graveyard, but I had no such luck. Great Yarmouth was full of holidaymakers who boarded the buses in droves at rush hour, and asked for "two tickets to t'pier", as I fumbled with my ticket machine and tried to stem the human tide. Sometimes when the theatres and pubs emptied on a wet night, it was so bad that the bus driver would put out the lights and the student conductors such as myself would lie flat the big seats along the back, so that no-one could see us. Disgracefully, we all pretended that our bus was out of service.

One of the few consolations on our days off was going to the theatre, where national pop stars like Lonnie Donegan and Billy Fury were performing. Unfortunately in one sense, I was most fond of the big jazz bands like Duke Ellington and Count Basie, and, apart from Bill Haley and the Comets, I never fully appreciated the new rock era sensations including The Beatles and the Rolling Stones.

My Great Yarmouth venture ended with much needed money in my pocket and I returned to Belfast to start my second year at Queen's. By that stage so much had changed for me, however. The novelty of the student hops had diminished somewhat, I had already won my coveted hockey 'Blue', and the stern challenge of the Honours History School was about to begin.

I also had to pass my matriculation Latin examination to stay in the School, which wasn't easy, and then fit in to the very different demands of the Modern History department. Compared to my history lessons with my teacher Johnny Spence in Newry Grammar School, however, this was not discipline at all. Spence had taught us how to swot, and his canny knack of neatly summarising the entire history course had helped me to achieve the high mark of eighty-four percent in my A Level exams.

At Queen's, however, I was virtually on my own, apart from attending lectures and weekly or fortnightly tutorials. My university teachers required an essay now and again, but for the most part there was no direct pressure on me to work. Therefore it was easy to drift back to the old habits of drinking too much coffee in the Students' Union, and finding excuses not to work too hard. Another major drawback for me at this stage of my university career was the lack of yearly exams, so that there were no annual targets during the three year course. Perhaps they were trying to teach us the need for self-discipline and for setting our own targets, but the history course was so wide ranging that I spent far too much time in running to try to catch up.

My struggle to keep up with the increased demands of scholarship came at the same time as my personal life was throwing up other big challenges. Decent student accommodation was scarce and it was largely beyond my means – with the result that I shared mostly dismal, grotty flats with various other students who were also broke much of the time. In one of the worst flats, three of us – all strapping young heterosexual males – had to sleep together in one large double bed for a few weeks, because the landlord was too stingy to provide another two mattresses. We were resilient enough to make the best of it, because we had no alternative.

Those were also years of just trying to survive, and it was all part of our student routine. Despite the fleeting romances and other attractions of university life, a student's existence at that time was far from 'romantic'. When I walk past some of my former student accommodation in the Queen's area today, I smile knowingly to myself – but I also wince at the memory of how awful it really was.

The challenging business of growing up in the Belfast of the early Sixties was however incidental to my formal education, which was central to my time at Queen's. I had to study European history from the Middle Ages onwards, as well as British, Colonial and American history, and also Irish history in even more detail. Gradually I discovered that history was not about dates, but about politics and people as well as economics and religion – and, above all, about power.

It was a tall order to obtain a good honours degree, but I persisted doggedly throughout the course. My companions in the small classes of the Honours School included Austin Currie, who went on to become a leading member of the Social Democratic and Labour Party and a candidate in an Irish Presidential election. I always liked and respected Austin and he did not get half enough credit later on for his work for civil rights and for civilising the politics of Ireland, north and south.

My other colleagues in the Modern History Honours included Ronnie Spence, who became a senior civil servant, and Harry Uprichard, who was eventually elected as Moderator of the Presbyterian Church, as well as Eddie Orr, who became a senior executive in the United Kingdom with the Renault car company. Queen's was that kind of place where your 'ordinary' class mates ended up with important roles much later on in their careers. My contemporaries, or near contemporaries, at Queen's also included Seamus Heaney, Stewart Parker, Bernadette Devlin, Eamonn McCann, Robin Eames, Oliver Napier, John Taylor, Ian Brick, David Fell, Gerry Loughran, Des Rea, Brian Mawhinney, John Dunlop, Cahal Daly and many others who had a high public profile in later years and who made a noticeable contribution, for better or worse depending on one's point of view, to the life of Northern Ireland or further afield.

It was also a time for meeting people who would become lifelong friends, and who would all make their own mark. They included Brian and Dorothy Gordon, Joyce and Barney McCaughey, Hilary and Howard McNally, Charlie and Rosemary Wilson, Carol and Terry Stewart and many others from undergraduate and early post-graduate days. I am aware that it is dangerous to make lists, and that the names of some of my friends will have slipped from my memory temporarily, and I apologise to them in advance!

One advantage of studying at Queen's in those days was the helpfulness of the staff of the History Department. One of my early lecturers was Michael Barnes, a most exotic character, who seemed to me to have dropped in straight from Mars rather than the Oxbridge College where he had gained his degree. He used to lecture us about 'The Whigs' in English history, but I found my attention wandering as I watched him slide his long curling fingers through his sparse, greasy hair amid thick clouds of cigarette smoke. Everybody seemed to smoke everywhere in those days.

I had never met anyone like the rumpled and erudite Barnes, but he turned out to be a good friend, always ready to help, and I appreciated his kindness in meeting all of us immediately at the end of our gruelling finals, when we gathered for a drink in the Botanic Inn. Michael also went on to become the visionary Director of the Belfast Festival at Queen's in one of the darkest periods of the Troubles. He was able to bring superstars like Michael Palin to Belfast, and I recall one of his Festivals, which attracted to a greatly troubled city world-famous ensembles like the National Theatre, the Royal Ballet and the Moscow Radio Symphony Orchestra – and all within the space of three weeks. Queen's and the Ulster public owe a great debt to this man, who was in my view never fully appreciated by the University and others for what he had done, and who tragically died so young.

Professor Lewis Warren, another historian, also became a good friend. During a big freeze in the early Sixties, when there was no Saturday hockey being played for weeks, I plucked up the courage to tell Warren that I was floundering in parts of the history course. I asked him for advice, and promised that I would try my best to take it in. Over the next few weeks, I wrote him a series of essays and he began to teach me the importance of writing with brevity, but also with authority. I remember how he said to me, "The more simple things seem, the more complex they may be beneath the surface." I have often thought of his advice during my writing career, and I owe him a great deal.

Lewis wrote an international bestseller about the English monarch King John, and he told me gleefully about how a Los Angeles policewoman had stuffed his paperback down her blouse as she was called off in a speeding squad car off to try to deal with a shoot-out. One of the wayward bullets was deflected by Warren's thick paper book which was nestling safely against her chest, and this helped to save her life! Lewis and I remained friendly after I graduated, and I was greatly saddened by his untimely death from cancer. He was both a scholar and a gentleman, who typified the very best of the academic dons of his generation.

Professor Beckett, despite being an other-wordly old bachelor, was another civilising influence. He would sometimes entertain our small class to dinner in his home, and the conversation was such that if you were talking nonsense, you knew about it very quickly because Beckett or the others would put forward arguments better and more subtle than your own. My Queen's history experience in that extended tutorial system was probably the next best thing to an Oxford or Cambridge education.

Away from my studies, Queen's had many other stimulations. One of my associates was a young English student, Michael Emmerson, who is credited with starting the Queen's Festival in 1953. Michael was also a colourful figure around the campus and, in summer, he would stroll about wearing a big straw hat and sandals. This was very different from the rest of us, who dressed conservatively in flannels, sports jackets, shirts and ties, and Hush Puppy shoes, if we could afford them. Michael was small in stature but he quickly became an influential figure who exuded great charm. He also had a tremendous entrepreneurial spirit, and he was able to persuade the university authorities, and others, to fund many of his ideas. He went on to manage Sir James Galway, the phenomenal Belfast flautist, and he became a senior executive with an international recording company.

Emmerson, like Coulter, and some of the others I have mentioned here, personified the air of creativity and exciting buzz around the campus in those days. My close friend Geoff Martin became the Student President, and he and others – like Ian Rainey, who later became a successful international banker and management head hunter – persuaded me to dip my toe into student politics.

I became a member of the Students' Representative Council, and in my final year, they asked me to write an article for the Students'

Handbook. Naturally I chose student sport as the topic and I clearly remember writing the article when I was spending a weekend at home in Bessbrook. The copy flowed quickly and easily on a subject which I knew inside out, and it was at that moment that I decided to make my career in journalism. It was a 'Road to Damascus' experience, but I had no background in journalism, and I had no idea about how to break in to newspapers.

In the last part of my final year I was heavily involved in working for my exams, but I also had to look for a job. In those days, a graduate could in theory pick and choose employment, but I was having little success. So I had to sit down and work out why I was not impressing prospective employers. Then I was granted an interview by the Chief Executive of the Regent Oil company in London. He talked to me in his office and told me how good his company was. When he asked if I had any questions, I said. "What can you offer me, compared to your competitors?" He looked at me narrowly, but we went on talking, and eventually he offered me a job on the spot. I told him I would think about it, but when I left his office and walked across Hyde Park, I was elated. I didn't want to be an oil executive, but I was learning how to sell myself to top executives.

I desperately wanted to be a journalist, so I wrote to the Thomson Organisation which owned the *Belfast Telegraph*. I was eventually interviewed by a senior figure from London, and a letter from the *Telegraph* arrived a week later. I excitedly opened the envelope, but my joy diminished when I discovered that they were offering me a job as an advertising representative. Not having any experience of newspapers, I did not know what to do. I thought that if I accepted the sales job I might move across to journalism, but my sixth sense told me that I would be going down the wrong road in doing that. It seemed a step too far moving from advertising into journalism. So, with much misgiving – and a good deal of courage – I decided to turn down the *Telegraph* job, with the excuse that I was going on a world tour. In fact, I was going nowhere!

Meanwhile, I was sitting my finals which proved to be as difficult as I had expected. Before they started, I bumped into Professor Beckett in the Queen's cloisters and he advised me to take the weekend off and read Jane Austen. I thought he had taken leave of his senses. I needed every second for my desperate swotting. In the course of one week, we were examined on a huge corpus of three years' work, and I have rarely experienced such pressure in my life. In fact one of my recurring nightmares since then has been that of wakening up in a cold sweat and supposedly in the midst of my history finals. This always tells me that I am working too hard, but the relief each time I wake up is always wonderful.

Eventually I staggered out of my finals and was later awarded a respectable second-class honours degree. I remember celebrating with Austin Currie and walking around the Queen's quadrangle at 3 am on an early summer morning in June 1963, just to make sure that our names were indeed on the notice board, with our degrees safely on the list for display.

My graduation day was a mixture of relief and apprehension. I was glad that it was all over, but I had no money and no clue about what I would do next. I was glad that my mother Lena and my grandfather Thomas were in the audience in the Whitla Hall, and I was especially glad that his financial support for me had proved so worthwhile. However, as I sat despondently among the rows of gowned graduates, I thought that my 'brave new world' of Queen's had slowly turned sour. I seemed to be going nowhere fast. However just then, a remark from the Vice-Chancellor, Dr Michael Grant, caught my attention.

Grant was not the best Vice-Chancellor that Queen's ever had, but he was a leading historian who was shrewd enough to write bestsellers on ancient history, including a life of St Paul. During his address to the new graduates he said, "Most of you here today will do very nicely in life." I could not understand exactly what he meant by that, but his remark gave me hope. I was determined I had not come this far to fail, and that I would do my best to make a successful career for myself. I had not done badly up to that point, I reasoned. But as I picked up my treasured BA (Hons), there was apprehension beneath my smile. I was twenty-three and unemployed, and I did not have a clue about what to do next.

My Honours degree in Modern History did not guarantee me a job, but in retrospect my experience at Queen's gave me far much more than I had realised. It had given me confidence, an ability to read widely and to summarise complex subjects clearly, an education from some of the academics who were world class historians in their special field, a knack for making contacts, and also a number of lifelong friends. In short, I had developed some of the main qualities needed for a successful career in journalism.

The big challenge now was to catch the eye of an editor and to talk my way in, but that would be much harder than I realised. I needed more experience than my one article about sport for the Queen's Students' Handbook. It was time to get moving.

CHAPTER SEVEN

Make or Break

Nowadays many university graduates take a 'gap' year after their studies to travel around the world and forget about academic life for a period. However my 'gap' year was spent back at Queen's University in working for a post-graduate diploma, and also trying to break into journalism.

The decision to do so was not quite as well-planned as it seems. In the weeks immediately after graduating in July 1963, my mind was in a whirl. The first challenge was to get a temporary job, so I returned to Eastbourne in Sussex where I had been working as a bus conductor during previous summers. Eastbourne was in a different class to Great Yarmouth, and I enjoyed being there.

The buses were better, so was the weather, and the town had an air of sophistication which Great Yarmouth lacked. It had a splendid concert hall where I first heard Ponchielli's 'Dance of the Hours' played by the British Concert Orchestra under the baton of the entertainer Vic Oliver, who was Sir Winston Churchill's son-in-law and also a serious musician. It was my first experience of a full orchestra playing 'live', and the experience hooked me onto the classics for the rest of my life. Eastbourne was also near London, and the town itself was a good place for partying. There were several ladies' colleges, and no shortage of fun. One night a law student called John Haire and I turned up at a dance, and we discovered that there were scores of girls standing on the other side of the room without partners. I don't know who was the more bemused – the crowd of girls or the two students from Northern Ireland.

Despite such distractions, reality beckoned and as the summer wore on I still had no permanent job. My friend Geoff Martin visited Eastbourne to see Chris Harte, a mutual friend, and one morning he and I had breakfast.

With typical directness he said, "It's time you got yourself organised." We had a long talk and I decided to return to Queen's to study for a Diploma in Education and also to seek a toe-hold in the student newspaper *Gown*.

It was difficult to obtain a Dip Ed scholarship because I, and a few others, had applied for a grant after the closing date. This obstacle was overcome in high places, though only after questions had been asked in the Stormont Parliament, but in the end all the late-comers were accepted.

The course was much less challenging than the intellectual demands of the Honours History degree, but one of the main problems was Professor Knox, the head of the education department.

He was an overbearing man, and I noticed how the other education students bore the verbal slings and arrows from Knox without dissent. I was not keen to enter a profession which seemed so subservient from the outset, but I still needed my Diploma in case I failed to get into journalism.

Nevertheless there were some encouraging developments. My first essay for my education tutor was marked "Good, but tends to journalese", and I thought "Whoopee!" I also enjoyed teaching practice, particularly at the Royal Belfast Academical Institution, which was a law unto itself and where at least one teacher smoked in the classroom. I learned from 'Inst' the importance of grabbing the attention of a class at the start of the lesson, and holding it throughout. This helped me to realise later on that the same principles apply to a good article or a memorable speech.

My domestic arrangements had changed, and I was fortunate enough to find good accommodation in the Cliftonville Road area, which I shared with Morris Brown, my pal from Bessbrook, and also Charlie Wilson, who became a lifelong friend. Both were medical students approaching their final year, so there was much less partying than previously. Sadly, however, one party to celebrate Charlie's birthday on 22 November 1963 finished before it began when we heard that President John F Kennedy had been assassinated in Dallas. It remains true that everyone knows exactly where they were and what they were doing on the night that Jack Kennedy died.

My landlord in Easton Crescent was Jack Feely, a charming Southerner who had a ladies' hairdressing business in Castle Street. His wife Eileen mothered 'her' three students, as well as two children of her own, and she even gave advice – sometimes unrequested – about our girlfriends.

The Queen's hops were still in full swing, and I remember walking home from the university area and across to West Belfast, with only the occasional interruption from a harmless drunk or a passer-by looking for a light for his cigarette. Sadly, however, the same streets were to be overwhelmed by violence and danger only a few years later as the Troubles erupted in total ferocity. Meanwhile my attempts at breaking into student journalism were more successful than my education studies. Because of my background in hockey, I became sports editor of *Gown* fairly quickly.

Then disaster struck. The newspaper was sued for libel, the printer would not carry on without a financial indemnity against future legal action, and the entire staff of *Gown* resigned – apart from me. I did not see the point of doing so because the paper had made big mistakes, and if everyone had resigned there would be no-one left to start a rescue mission.

So within weeks of returning to Queen's I had become editor of *Gown*, which had seemed impossible back in my first year. However there were major obstacles – I had no staff and no money, but I had good backers.

Two members of the Gown Trust – John Willoughby Wilson and Brian Garrett – were lawyers and they helped me to plan a way ahead, with the assistance of the Queen's Librarian Peter Havard-Williams. The idea was to launch a financial appeal among the students to provide an indemnity for the printer.

I was recruiting my own supporters, including Jimmy Riddell, a man with his ear to the ground, who eventually became a Professor at Queen's. The *Gown* appeal caught the attention of the media, and I was interviewed by Denis Tuohy, who later on was one the first two anchor-presenters of BBC Two television network. My interview was awful. I told Riddell that I was 'rubbish'. He replied helpfully "Well, at least you were sincere."

The appeal went well, and we raised enough money to reassure the printer to take on *Gown* again. Some of the biggest donations came from the snooker and billiards players in the old Students' Union, which was regarded by some people as a den of iniquity. It was ruled with a rod of iron by a retired army officer Samuel Billington, known to everyone as 'The Major'. He barked loudly at everyone with commendable egalitarian derision, but he did so with a twinkle in his eye, and we liked him.

The old Students' Union was a convivial place and the building itself, though small, was much more attractive than the replacement Students' Union on University Road. This was built on the site of the much-mourned Queen's Elms student residences which were torn down to make way for the new Union. It is still one of the most depressing buildings in Belfast, both inside and outside.

Happily for me, *Gown* was back in business and I was recruiting staff. Jimmy Riddell, a noted oarsman, took over sport, Gerry Loughran who later became a senior civil servant was economics editor, Eamonn McCann who developed into an ever-controversial newspaper columnist, wrote an occasional article for me (on the back of a big brown envelope) and an Englishman called Tony provided a satirical column.

Soon after we re-started *Gown* it won an award as 'Best Irish Student Publication of the Year'. I modestly confess that this was not due to me, but to the work of one of my predecessors, but I was more than happy to travel to Dublin to collect the award from Terence de Vere White, the then Literary Editor of the *Irish Times*.

Back in Belfast we splashed the picture of me receiving the award on the front page of *Gown*. It had been a remarkable turn around in my fortunes within a short period, and not for the first or last time, I had snatched success from the jaws of failure.

Unfortunately my educational studies were not going well. Because I was so busy with *Gown*, I was not attending lectures. However, I had also been applying for teaching jobs, just in case, and I accepted a post in Kenya, subject to gaining my Education Diploma.

However my Professor Harry Knox had other ideas. One morning I opened a letter which demanded that I explain to him why he should not stop my scholarship allowance because I was not attending lectures.

This was an invitation to a verbal roasting, and I decided that submission to Knox was the best way of survival. His rollicking lasted forever, it seemed, and as he invented ever new ways of castigating me, I kept my mouth shut. When he eventually ran out of invective and breath, which I knew he would, he glared at me silently.

I then admitted that I was wrong, arrogant, careless, unappreciative, gormless, rude, silly and all the other things he had called me. I told him that I had secured a job teaching in Kenya, that I needed a Dip Ed, and that I would work hard to catch up. He knew that I was not afraid of him, and also that I really had a job in Kenya. So his anger subsided somewhat. He told me to work hard and wished me well. I had learned at first hand that "a soft answer turneth away wrath", and it was one lesson I never forgot.

In the event I buckled down, read Harry Knox's textbook on education, and rehashed his lectures in the final examination. Just before it began, he gave me a broad wink, as if to say "You'll do!", and I duly had my Diploma in Education.

Kenya was now beckoning, and I still had no job in journalism. However I had written to the Editor of the *Belfast Telegraph* John E Sayers, who – to my surprise – asked me to come for an interview. Before doing so I asked a law student Ted Jones to see if his cousin Cal McCrystal, a well-known *Belfast Telegraph* journalist who later became a star reporter with the *Sunday Times*, if he would give me a few tips.

Cal asked me to meet him in McGlade's, a famed journalists' bar behind the *Telegraph* which was run by the gentlemanly proprietor Frank McGlade who always had a flower or a sprig of heather in his buttonhole. I arrived on time but there was only one customer in the lounge bar, and he was far too well-dressed to be a journalist. I was looking for a Humphrey Bogart figure in a dirty raincoat and trilby hat with a 'Press' ticket in the headband,

I waited in vain for the 'Bogart' figure to appear. Eventually I nervously asked old Jack the barman "Have you seen Cal McCrystal in here today?" He replied "That's Cal at the end of the bar!" So the figure who was dressed like a top business man was in fact the journalist I was looking for. I was impressed.

Cal did not have much time to spend with me, but he was helpful, and I still remember his final piece of advice: "You will probably not become rich financially through journalism, but if you stick with it and are successful, you will have a very rich career." How right he was.

About a week later, I went for my interview with Jack Sayers, the Editor of the *Telegraph* which in those days was selling over 200,000 copies daily and was the most influential media outlet in the land. I had no idea that Sayers was one of the best editors in the long history of the *Telegraph*, or that he had a distinguished naval record, or that he had worked in Churchill's Map Room during the Second World War.

Nor did I know, unfortunately, that Jack was a snob. He asked me "Are you related to Colonel McCreary from Campbell College?" I replied "No, sir, I went to Newry Grammar School." Silence. Then Sayers said "Did you play rugger?" I replied "No sir, I played hockey." Another silence. I knew that the interview was not going well, and my heart was sinking.

Then Sayers said "I see you went to Queen's. Tell me about your time there." So I plucked up courage and told him how I had helped to save *Gown*, and how much I wanted to be a journalist.

There was another silence, and then – miraculously – Jack began to smile. I had made a breakthrough. He said "McCreary, that's a remarkable story. I am going to take a chance on you and offer you a job as a trainee. I will pay you £900 a year, and you will start on 1 September. That's the date when the paper started and when I began in the *Telegraph* too. I will make you a damn good journalist. Good day young man, and I will see you in two month's time."

I left Sayers' office in a daze. On the way to the lift I was passed by the *Telegraph* sports editor Malcolm Brodie who even in 1964 was a legendary journalist. I thought "Brodie doesn't know me from Adam, but my God, I am going to be working with people like him. I can't believe it".

I made my way downstairs and out into Royal Avenue where I waited for a bus back to our apartment on the Cliftonville Road. I don't know how I got there, because I was so excited that my feet did not seem to touch the ground. I was going to be a professional journalist, and I was going to work with the top people in the *Belfast Telegraph*.

On 1 September 1964 I reported for duty at the *Telegraph* and I was taken up to the big editorial room where I sat near the duty news editor Cecil Deeney, a friendly man who welcomed me warmly. I was wearing my good suit, in fact the only suit I had, and my Queen's graduate tie.

I was fascinated by the loud buzz of a busy newsroom, with reporters furiously typing their copy and yelling "Copy" – whereupon a young boy or girl would grab the typed sheets and carry them quickly down the large room to give them to the sub-editors. It was obvious that time was important, that deadlines were looming, and that the newsroom was not a place for indecision.

Suddenly a grizzled old cigar-chomping reporter called Billy Morrow yelled out to me "Copy, boy", and thrust his script into my hand. I did not know what to do, but Deeney came to the rescue. He said "Billy, catch yourself on. This is Alf McCreary, and he is not a copy boy. He's our new trainee graduate from Queen's University."

Billy Morrow, who was the paper's Agricultural Correspondent took back his copy, flashed me a lopsided grin through his nicotine-stained teeth, and went on hammering on his ancient typewriter. It was clear that these journalists were not impressed by having a new Queen's graduate in their midst.

My second day in the *Telegraph* was not encouraging. Cecil Deeney asked me if I had any stories up my sleeve. I told him that there was a big shortage of student accommodation at Queen's. This was a story I had covered in *Gown*, and I knew that it wasn't 'hard news' any more.

Nevertheless, Deeney called over Robin Harris, a skilled young reporter, and asked him to help me. I said to Robin "This is not a big enough story for the *Telegraph*." He replied "Don't worry. Tell me what you know, and I will type it out for you."

I was now working on a story which I knew would not stand up, but no-one was listening to me. My copy was passed on to the acting chief sub-editor John Brown, an ex-pupil of Newry Grammar School, and he was making it a page one 'splash' – in other words the biggest story on page one, and therefore the most important in that day's paper.

I could not stop this literary juggernaut from crashing, but meanwhile I saw the Editor-in-Chief John E Sayers striding down the room and waving a galley-proof of my story. "Who wrote this?" he demanded. I replied nervously "I did." He glared at me and snorted "Good God man, that's not a page one lead!", and he promptly threw my morning's work into the waste bin.

My erstwhile supporters melted away, without a word of commiseration, and there was nothing at all from Jack Sayers who walked back silently to his office. I stood alone in the centre of the big room, mentally licking my wounds. I went back to my accommodation that evening and I was convinced that I would be fired the next day. I was on probation, and I thought that Sayers was bound to realise his mistake in hiring me.

After a sleepless night, I turned up for work the next morning. No-one said a word about the previous day, as they busied themselves with producing a new paper. I realised that these things happen under pressure, and that people were not blaming me.

After several weeks on the *Telegraph*. I was seconded for three months to the London Polytechnic in Regent Street to join the first United Kingdom graduates' journalism training scheme. We were taught by experts in newspaper law, shorthand, sub-editing and other important aspects of journalism.

I don't know how many of us took it all in. The class was a raffish bunch. They included Simon Scott-Plummer from *The Times*, Ray Steading from the *Daily Mirror* group, and an amiable northerner called Ray Connolly who eventually became a top show business reporter, and an expert on The Beatles.

The course was useful, but hardly riveting. However it was good to be back in London for three months. I stayed in the Earls Court with all the other Aussies, and made regular visits down to Eastbourne where I still had good friends from my days as a student bus-conductor. In London I also had a great opportunity to watch Chelsea football team playing regularly at Stamford Bridge, and also to visit the theatre as often as my meagre income would allow. One of my most vivid memories is of skipping a training session at the London Poly and 'mitching' off to the National Theatre to watch Sir Laurence Olivier playing Othello in a matinee performance, with Billie Whitelaw as Desdemona.

When my course finished I had to leave the delights of London and settle down to my new career in Northern Ireland. In news terms it was a backwater, but I was not to know then that Northern Ireland would not remain a media backwater for long.

The first months of 1964 were taken up with basic training 'on the job'. My first day in the Belfast Petty Sessions Court was spent with a hard-nosed reporter called Robin Walsh, who much later became

Editor of BBC Television's 9 pm main news in London and eventually the Controller of BBC Northern Ireland.

Walsh said "You take Number One Court and I'll cover Number Two. We'll meet in the Press Room later." So off I went, with little knowledge of the law or the court system, but Walsh (and other court experts like Ivan McMichael) were helpful, and I soon picked up the basics.

I discovered that the courts were generally a grim repository of human misery, enlivened by the odd flash of humour. One Saturday morning I was covering the Belfast Petty Sessions, during which an elderly vagrant faced a charge of wilful damage because he had hurled an iron grating through the plate-glass window of a department store.

The Resident Magistrate John Long was familiar with the old character who had appeared before him previously, and he knew that the 'wilful damage' was a desperate ploy by the man to spend some time in the warmth of a prison cell, where he would receive regular meals each day.

The magistrate peered at the defendant and asked rhetorically "What am I to do with you? If I impose a fine you won't be able to pay it. All right then, I sentence you to seven days in Crumlin Road prison."

The old vagrant cleared his throat, looked straight at the magistrate and said "Thank you, John. You're not a bad ould bastard." As the prisoner shuffled out of the dock, all of us in the court had a quiet chuckle. We had just witnessed a wise magistrate handing down a sentence in which justice and mercy were combined.

Other forms of court justice were not so clear to a young reporter like me. One day I was writing up a case in the Press Room of the Crumlin Road courthouse when a bewigged barrister burst in without warning, with a rough looking character in tow. The barrister whipped off his wig, and yelled "Look here son, you're up for larceny. Everyone bloody well knows you did it and if you plead not guilty you'll take up everybody's time, and people want to go for lunch. So you will frigging well plead guilty and you'll do less time in Crumlin Road prison. OK?" The rough young man and his barrister then left the Press Room, without even a glance in my direction, and went back into court. I was learning how the law worked at the sharp end of the legal system.

On another occasion I reported on a case where a hardened criminal was found guilty of yet another burglary. I listened carefully while his defence lawyer pleaded eloquently for leniency. When he had finished the judge kept on scribbling on his notepad, with his head down. Without looking up he said "Eight years. Take him away." There was a gasp around the courtroom. It may have been justice, but there was no humanity in the court that morning.

This was all part of the routine training of a young reporter. The other journalists in the *Telegraph* had learned their trade as juniors in weekly newspapers, so I had a great deal to learn, and very quickly.

I soon realised that a degree in history, or any other subject, did not equip me for a career as a reporter. My knowledge of the Carolingian Empire or the rise and fall of the Hapsburgs was of little use when I was sent down to Holywood to tell a woman that her under-age daughter had eloped the previous day and had been married at Gretna Green. Her mother started crying, and I was sorry for her. I knew however that my job was to get good quotes and to file my story as quickly as I could.

The news editor John Rooks was a tough individual who bawled out his reporters regularly. Rooks seemed to yell at people equally, and this developed a rough camaraderie among us. One day the criticism was so bad that a reporter hurled a huge typewriter at Rooks' head. If he had not ducked, it would have killed him. Nevertheless John Rooks was a sound newspaperman. One morning he yelled at me for my alleged failure to write a story properly, so I plucked up courage and said "John I'm a beginner, you are supposed to be training me, so you show me how to do it." He grabbed his typewriter, harrumphed a great deal, started to write the story himself, but became diverted and never finished it. I walked away without a word, and John rarely troubled me again.

I also learned how to work with the police, but it was not as simple as it seemed. One night I shared a lift to a jazz festival at Crom Castle in Fermanagh with Ian Hill a former *Gown* editor and also a colleague of mine, who then worked in a now-defunct paper called *Ulster Week*. I quite enjoyed Hill's company, despite his tall tales and pretensions. Sadly, he was not particularly reliable, as I found out later that night.

I had arranged with Hill to meet him on a certain spot because I needed a lift home, but he did not turn up. So I was stuck. Then I had a brainwave. I went over to a police inspector, told him that I was a journalist, and asked if anyone could give me a lift home. He was less than helpful and simply walked off. Then a constable came over and said "Son, you did the wrong thing there. If you had asked me to help you, I would have sorted you out." Eventually I got a lift back in a mobile fish and chip van as far as Portadown, and then I caught the early train to Belfast. I learned not to approach a senior policeman in quite the same way again.

The first nine months of my training were challenging, and I was learning a lot. I was aware, however, that my life outside journalism was about to change. My flatmates Charlie and Morris were sitting their medical finals, and they would soon become housemen in local hospitals. This meant that our cosy arrangement of living together on the Cliftonville Road would change, and I would need to find a place for myself.

On a soft summer evening in June 1965 I finished as the late reporter in the *Telegraph*, and walked up to Queen's, resplendent in my three-piece John Collier suit, complete with lapels on my waistcoat. I knew that the medical final results were being announced there by the Dean of Medicine, the formidable Professor John Henry Biggart. My friend Charlie passed, much to our delight, and he and I went on a long liquid celebration, which started at the old Oak pub on the Grosvenor Road.

At some point in the evening we made our unsteady way across to Bostock House, the Royal Victoria Hospital's residence for nurses where a dance was taking place. The place was too noisy and crowded for me, and I said to myself "Let's get out of here, this is all too much."

So we left Bostock, and by some mysterious process which I have never quite fathomed, I was driven in Charlie's car to another milestone in my own destiny. Somehow we arrived at another dance in a large hut at the City Hospital. Charlie started talking to an attractive girl called Rosemary, whom he knew from previous meetings in their school days. He was not to know that night that he and Rosemary would became an 'item' and that they would marry a couple of years afterwards.

I was minding my own business when suddenly I spotted across the room a tall, beautiful-looking girl with dark hair. She was wearing a pink gingham dress in the style of the times, and I thought to myself "Wow!" She was chatting to another man who had shared digs with me, and this was an excuse for me to go over and speak to this most attractive young stranger. I was fuelled by the arrogance of youth as well as curiosity, and also by the spirit of the evening, so I introduced myself to her.

She was called Hilary Fitzsimons, and within a short time we were dancing together. When the dance ended I walked her home to her flat in Dunluce Avenue, and on parting I said that I would be in touch.

On my way home I told myself "That's a really lovely girl. She's far too good for a rolling stone like you." Nevertheless, I did ask her out, and we went to a dance in the Belfast Boat Club. Within a short time we were 'going steady' and things were beginning to change in my life.

The situation had improved dramatically since I had finished my history finals two years earlier with no prospect of employment. I now had a staff job in the top Northern Ireland newspaper, I had a steady girlfriend and I was about to find accommodation where for the first time I would be living on my own.

It was a little daunting, but also exciting, and I knew that my 'brave new world' was even better than I had expected. It was like my first year at Queen's all over again, but I felt that I was also a bit wiser. The next few years would show me whether this was true or not.

CHAPTER EIGHT

The Calm Before the Storm

IN THE EARLY Sixties Northern Ireland was relatively peaceful, and becoming more prosperous. The border war waged by the IRA in the Fifties had petered out, and the Unionist leader Captain Terence O'Neill, who succeeded the hardline Lord Brookeborough, was extending the hand of friendship to the Roman Catholic and nationalist community.

O'Neill had the enthusiastic backing of the *Belfast Telegraph* under Jack Sayers, and the political bridge-building was matched by an encouraging growth of inward investment. This was pioneered by the dynamic Minister of Commerce Brian Faulkner who despite his industrial and commercial vision, was an uncompromising unionist, and he was certainly not in the O'Neill camp.

As a young reporter I was aware of what was happening politically, but it was on a level far above my pay station. I was too inexperienced to become part of the paper's skilled political team, and my role was to learn basic reporting the hard way.

This meant the continued routine of the courts, collecting mind-numbing data from the Records Office and elsewhere, and acting as an editorial dogsbody. This included reporting on planning appeals about the siting of advertising hoardings, which were lucrative for the legal fraternity, but boring for me.

However on one dramatic day my lowly position as a trainee reporter was elevated to a role of temporary importance. On 14 January 1965 Terence O'Neill surprised everyone by hosting a secret meeting at Stormont with the Taioseach Sean Lemass, the first time that an Irish Premier had visited Stormont.

It was an imaginative move by O'Neill, but he had not told his backbenchers, and he was to pay dearly for it later on when he lost the confidence of his party, and eventually had to resign. In all truth if he had told his MPs about the meeting in advance, there would have been an uproar, so the hapless O'Neill was in a no-win situation from the start.

Unfortunately for him, his arch political enemy, the die-hard Unionist Ian Paisley and his supporters had been tipped off when the meeting was breaking up. They arrived en masse at Stormont but were unable to do much about it, and they vented their fury by throwing snowballs at the Irish Premier's car as it left the Stormont estate.

I was blissfully unaware of the unfolding drama as I sat in on a dreary planning appeal in the Stormont building. However in an urgent call, the *Telegraph* news desk hauled me out of the planning appeal and told me to leave immediately and pick up what I could on the Paisley story. By the time I arrived at the scene the protest was nearly over, but I filed a few sentences to keep the newsdesk in touch while a more experienced reporter made his way to Stormont.

This incident made me realise that a reporter at every level was required to be instantly available to cover any breaking story. The Paisley snowball protest was comical, but it had a serious intent, and I was to hear much more about the Reverend Dr Ian Paisley and his followers in the years to come.

For the most part, however, my early years at the *Telegraph* were the same mixture of stories that most young journalists encounter when learning the business. Occasionally there were exciting 'markings' – a term used by the news editor who would 'mark' your name in his big dairy prior to the morning editorial conference.

One morning John Rooks said to me, with a chuckle "Go up to Queen's and ask that famous fiddler to play you a tune." In translation this meant "Get up to the University fast and try to get an interview with the world famous violinist Yehudi Menuhin, who is receiving an honorary degree today."

I assumed that the *Telegraph* had already phoned ahead for permission to speak to Menuhin, and my experience of Queen's made me realise that I needed to get to their star graduand before the ceremony began. When I arrived at the Lodge at Lennoxvale, and nervously rang the bell, the door was opened by the Vice-Chancellor's elegant Swedish wife Sophie Grant, When I asked if I could interview Mr Menuhin, she said "You will have to wait for a while, because he's practising." I did not know whether that meant he was practising the violin or practising yoga, of which he was a noted devotee. So I kept my mouth shut and waited to meet the great man, all the while wondering what I would ask him.

He duly appeared, a slight and charming figure, and we had a short interview, the details of which I cannot remember. However I had my brief brush with greatness, and I filed my story. Not long afterwards I talked to another star celebrity in the shapely form of Anne Sidney from Poole, Dorset who was the then current Miss World. I shared a taxi with her on the way to her hotel. Again I cannot remember what we talked about, but her leggy glamour left a lasting impression on me.

On another slow August news day I was suddenly despatched to Nutts Corner airport to meet another VIP, Lord Mountbatten, who had flown in from London and he was on his way to his Classiebawn Castle in Co Sligo where he spent part of the summer each year.

On the way up to the airport. I wondered what I was going to ask him at such short notice. I did not have time to do my homework and to prepare questions about his exceptional international career. I reckoned that if he agreed to meet me, our encounter would be swift, and that he would exchange some pleasantries about stopping off briefly in Northern Ireland.

I was correct in my assumptions, and I was learning yet again one of the important differences between journalism and the world of academe. In university publications, an academic will not say something even as harmless as "It's a good day", without a string of learned quotations from other academics to back up that statement. In journalism there is also a need for expert sources, but usually little time or space to tell a complex story concisely to a mass audience. I was learning in the *Belfast Telegraph* to develop an entirely new mindset and discipline from that of an honours graduate in history.

What now impresses me about that day I met Mountbatten, was the relative lack of security surrounding him, compared to that given to Royal figures and leading personalities today. He had only one plain-clothes bodyguard as he walked from the aeroplane. Mountbatten gave me a short, friendly interview as we both stood on the tarmac.

His style was like that of Prince Philip, a bit sharp, teasing, funny, but memorable.

This sophisticated man of the world made me feel like a professional, and not like a young regional reporter learning the job. Then with a cheery wave he set off to Classiebawn by motor car. On that August summer day we had no idea that some fourteen years later Lord Mountbatten would emerge from his Classiebawn Castle for one last time, and set off innocently in a small boat in which the Provisional IRA blew him up as he fished off shore with his family and friends.

Sometimes, by contrast, there were humorous encounters with well known people. One day I was sent to the airport to interview the Roman Catholic Primate Cardinal William Conway. My photographer colleague, an Englishman with no knowledge of the Irish Catholic Church, waited until I had finished talking to Conway, who then asked him conversationally "How's your wife and family." The photographer replied "They're fine sir. What about yours?" Conway looked at him as if he had two heads.

Despite the lighter moments, there were long periods of drudgery in trying to write stories in a province where there was little news. It took a long time to get my first by-line in print (ie a reporter's name on a story) but that only lasted a couple of hours. I had written about the Captain of the Belfast–Liverpool ferry, the *Ulster Prince*, and the subs had given me a by-line. However an eagle-eyed colleague told the news editor that the story had already appeared in the *Sunday Express*. So my name was taken off the report, through no fault of my own, and I only noticed what had happened afterwards, when I looked up a later edition on the paper. Nobody took me aside to explain why.

In such conditions a young reporter can lose heart, and a word of praise from a senior colleague can go a long way. One day I wrote an article about the graffiti on Belfast Technical College, which shows how hard it was to fill a paper in those days. I thought my story wasn't bad, but again there was no by-line. However, our assistant chief sub-editor Tommy Edgar said to me quietly "That was a great piece you wrote about the Tech." His kind words made my day, and I still try to praise the work of young colleagues who might benefit from an appreciative comment in a competitive world.

I was only the fifth graduate to join the *Telegraph*, and in the early

Top left: Standing up for myself at the age of five.
Top right: Later with my mother Lena McCreary.
Bottom: Later still with my grandparents Thomas
and Mary Anne (Minnie) McCreary.

Top left: With my Aunt Jean. *Top right:* Life as a freckled youth. *Bottom:* The Boys Class at Bessbrook PE School shortly after the end of the Second World War.

Football family. *Top:* Bessbrook Strollers, winners of the Irish Junior Cup in 1945, with my uncle Bill McCreary in the back row, fourth from the right. *Bottom:* The Evergreen football team won the Summer League Cup in 1957. The author is back row fourth left, with lifetime friends Morris Brown, front row extreme left, and Graham McAleer, front row third from the left.

Evergreen FC Cup & League Winners of Newry under Eighteen Summer League 1957
Top row   B.Aulds J.Gregory A.Mc Cleary J.Doran S.Aulds S. Mc Givern Manager
Bottom Row MBrown G.Mc Givern G.McALEER F. Rush Capt. H. Williamson B.Burns

Top: Newry Grammar School First XI around 1958, with the author, front row second from the left, Geoff Martin, front row third from the left, and his brother Robin, also in the front row on the extreme right.

Bottom: Geoff Martin with the Reverend Sydney Carser, a much-loved minister of Bessbrook Presbyterian Church, at a family christening.

Queen's University days.

Top: Working on the buses in Eastbourne with colleague Ken Houston.

Bottom left: My finals in Modern History, with the dreaded exam papers.

Bottom right: My Hons BA graduation photograph, in July 1963.

Gown
an independent newspaper

GOWN TOO SUCCESSFUL ?

Friday, 6th December, 1963. Vol. 10. No. 3. 5d.

During the past few weeks, the future of Gown has been the subject of considerable speculation at all levels within the university and elsewhere. At the time of going to press it seems likely that this will be the last Gown — as we know it.

The main cause of Gown's present position is lack of finance, but we must make the position clear on this point. Gown is NOT on the verge of bankruptcy. In fact, Gown is and always has been, solvent; though the revenue from advertising and sales was usually just sufficient to cover our production costs. The newspaper first came into existence in 1953, and under a series of editors, including Shirley Anderson, Ian J. Hill, John Trew and Cy Jameson, it has carefully built up a first rate reputation in student journalism within the British Isles. During this period, its circulation also has soared from three hundred to over two thousand copies.

Guarantee Fund

Newspapers today are a business concern, and even though Gown is a student newspaper, it has grown to such an extent that it must be placed on a sound business footing. In other words Gown needs a Guarantee Fund not merely to cover production costs, but also to assure our printer that we, like any other newspaper, will be able to meet any commitments or liabilities which may arise in the future. The printers' demand for a guarantee has not arisen overnight; on the contrary, they have shown a great deal of patience in the past. But printing is a business proposition and they quite understandably will print a newspaper only on condition that it also is organised as a business proposition. This applies to all other printers as well.

Money

Where will this money come from? The university is legally unable to give financial backing to an independent body such as Gown. Even if this were possible, we would be unwilling to surrender our independence. We depend for assistance, therefore, on those people who are sufficiently public spirited to en-

sure that, in this day and age, Queen's University, Belfast—like any other university in the United Kingdom—will still have a student newspaper. In particular we turn to YOU, the students, because as students we all should make a tremendous effort to ensure that OUR newspaper stays alive. It would be stretching optimism to the point of impertinence to expect the help of outside interest if we ourselves failed to give a tangible indication of our determination to guarantee Gown's existence.

Future

A student news[...] tions. First, it sh[...] to and from all se[...] versity and this i[...] portant at Queen's[...] is the only real[...] Secondly, it should[...]

The Editor receives, on behalf of Gown, the top award for the best university newspaper in Ireland, at the Irish Universities Editors' Conference in Dublin. The award, which was won under the Editorship of Cy Jameson, was handed over by the Editor of The Irish Times.

sent to the Front and to the public at large, the opinion of the student body on issues vital to the interests of all three. Gown's overall record, despite the justified criticism of, few [...]

HOW YOU CAN HELP

This is how the money and the names will be collected:

Seven appeal points will be set up throughout university premises. They are:

1. THE McMORDIE HALL, from 10.30 — 5.
2. THE GREAT HALL (Steward's door) from 10.30 — 5.
3. THE SOUTH [...]

At each point there will be a copy of the petition. Donors will sign their names on this, and at the same time will be issued with a receipt for the amount they have given. We think that 2/6 is not too large a sum to give to guarantee Gown's existence. Morning coffee for a week, a drink [...]

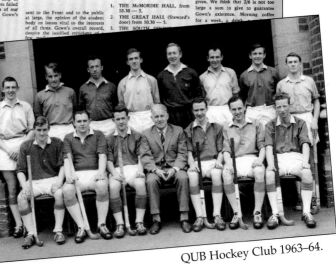

This page, top:
Collecting an award for the University newspaper *Gown*. This was part of a successful campaign to save the paper from bankruptcy. It also led to my career in journalism. *Bottom:* My last year in the Queen's Hockey First XI.

QUB Hockey Club 1963–64.

Opposite page, top: Last days in the shipyard.
Bottom left: A letter following my book on 'Old Bushmills'. *Bottom right:* In troubled Derry/Londonderry.

THE YARD

'Nothing is impossible' in this town of 9,600 where men challenge the elements and themselves—and economics

THE long trek over the Bridge and down into the shipyard is not so much a walk as a pilgrimage. This is the hard world of the cloth-cap Belfast man; the territory of the tall gantries and the giant cranes that dominate the city; the cauldron of din and steel where gnarled men in soiled work-clothes fashion lengths of raw metal and wood and glass into objects of power and grace.

In the shipyard, men challenge the elements and themselves in their search for daily bread. The 'Yard is rooted in industry and surrounded by steel, but it is as close to nature as the sea itself. It is also relatively unknown to the thousands of outsiders who pass daily its huge yellow cranes with the black writing emblazoned on the crosspiece.

This is the tight little world of the turners, the iron sorters, caulkers, platers and welders, the bull runty and countless others. This is the stage where the actors have exotic nicknames like Skiboo, Heavy Dog, Mountain Goat, Too Much Soup, Obado, Flannel Feet, Give Us A Match, Light-Duty Brown, of Cheyenne and Hookie and Rodeo. The shipyard has a life and a language of its own.

Its size alone is impressive. It is a small town, covering 270 acres and employing 9,600 men. They are building two tankers and two bulk carriers at a total deadweight of 800,000 tons. Last year they launched 656,000 tons. They do things in a big way at the 'Yard.

Yet, like so many Ulstermen, they do not talk big. Ulstermen are wary of eloquent statements of pride or love or creation. A nod or half-smile from an Ulsterman can convey more sometimes than a thousand words.

Billy Thompson, a senior foreman welder, has been in the shipyard 41 years, since he was 17. His father, his father's father, and his great-grandfather were all shipyardmen. He is a cousin of the late Sam Thompson, whose pen underlined the artistry of some shipyardmen as he fought for a better society. Billy Thompson himself has a finely-shaped pair of hands that are a witness to craftsmanship without betraying undue strength.

"Things have improved since the old days," he said. "There is more humanity now, there are more facilities.

Alf McCreary, centre, talks to steelworkers during a visit to the shipyard. From left are: Bertie Waring, senior foreman; Walter Jones and Tommy Webster. "Things have changed since the old days. There is more humanity now."

concrete floors in those days."

Even today welding is a hard job. The inside of a tanker is like a huge operating theatre with tubes and lengths of piping leading to and from the patient. The innards of a tanker are corridors of catwalks with grizzled men in d a n k e r i n h o l e s a n d

At the end of a year of crisis for Harland and Wolff,

ALF McCREARY

has been talking

who make the shi

to go to work in Bally-murphy at the present time, and you don't really expect them to come here," said one man with a hard realism that shows no illusions about the facts of l life in Northern Ireland. Ship-

Down at the finishing yard the Essi Camilla, a Norwegian bulk carrier, was being prepared for her final trials. It is in the finishing yard that order emerges from chaos. It is here that the huge vessel which once was an idea now has shape and style and a future. It is difficult to stand on the bridge of such a vessel and not feel some pride at this glimpse of a more constructive face of Belfast. It is also difficult to ignore the shipyard humour. "Don't touch that rudder, mister, or you'll have this thing streamin' d o w n High Street."

Pride and craftsmanship is one thing, but a balance-sheet is another. And in a world where foreign governments subsidise their shipyards, sometimes heavily, the Belfast shipyard will find life, if there is life at all, extremely difficult.

Sir Brian Morton, the new chairman since October, is optimistic, understandably. No man will take on such a job if he thinks that a shipyard will become a graveyard. In his own dapper and charming way, he has dealt with a p p a r e n t l y hopeless situations before. In Londonderry, he tried to w e l d together two quite different traditions and helped to create something new. But the Belfast shipyard is not the Londonderry Development Commission. The message in Belfast is clear. The Government will cover the expected losses on the present order book, but the new orders will have to make money. There will be no more hand-outs.

"The market is not dead," said Sir Brian, with calculated caginess. "The problem is that people have been mesmerised by the situation in the tanker market. There are other types of ship.

"Nothing is impossible. If we can continue to project that attitude to the men, and given a climb out of the world recession, we can compete with any unsubsidised shipyard. Personally I give Harland and Wolff more than a fighting chance."

It is too early to say whether this is an accurate assessment or merely brave words. Down on the shop floor, and among the gangways and the gantries, the men are trying hard to help themselves. Doubtless, there are still expert skivers but the possible

ALFIE. McCREARY.
WHISKEY (BOOK.
COLUMN.
BELFAST TELEGRAPH.
ROYAL AVENUE.
BELFAST.

> ' At the moment the abiding reality, apart from the feeling of death, is the total lack of communication across the divide. The story of Derry is a tale of two cities. It is symptomatic of Northern Ireland and of Ireland and its people. Its messages 'we shall overcome' and 'not an inch' are mutually contradictory. '

Derry: a tale of two cities

TUESDAY: ALF McCREARY, Provincial Journalist of the Year, reports from Bogside.

LONDONDERRY is a city caught in the cold hand of death. A piercing wind sweeps across Loch Foyle. The weak sun fades in a wintry sky that promises snow. The bitter weather matches the mood of the city.

Derry is like a prolonged wake. The main streets are empty. The shops are closed. Soldiers with rifles at the ready, shelter wearily in shop doorways surveying the bleak scene.

Policemen in twos huddle from the cold, trying to look as inconspicuous as their conspicuous black uniforms allow. Buses are scarce.

Food is hard to find if you are a visitor. Hotels serve only residents — mostly reporters and television crews, a multi-lingual babble of observers here to record the latest agonies. It is a place where people fend for themselves.

The deaths of 13 people hang over everything like a cold dark cloud. The sense of mourning either spontaneous, calculated or enforced, is inescapable. Derry is making sure that everyone knows what has happened.

Re-inforced

It is one thing to read about Derry or to watch the TV bulletins from the warmth of an armchair.

But when you come through this icy city, tired and hungry and watch the faces of the Derry people, the atmosphere of death, desolation and degradation eats into your bones.

If anyone believes that the events of Sunday have shocked people into a common humanity they can forget it. The communal slaughter has reinforced prejudices on both sides and left those in the middle with a greater burden of reconciliation.

Down in the Bogside where the bar arcades rust and crumble the blood of a dead man still mingles with the rain water in the gutter. Here they talk bitterly of what they call the brutality of British Paratroopers.

Sunday, they say, was "the last straw." But few can think of anything beyond a vague allusion to a united Ireland.

united as never before. The Bogsider thinks and reacts already as if he was part of a United Ireland.

The immediate signs are ominous. "You can bet your sweet life that there will be trouble after the funerals," said one man.

The attitude in the Protestant quarter is as predictable as the writing on an Orange wall. There is a sense of shock but it is tempered with a feeling of inevitability that something like this had to happen.

The sympathy is genuine in humanitarian terms but it is like a sympathy for people on another planet.

I talked to Protestants who felt that the trouble had been caused by the actions over the years of the Civil Rights leaders.

There was no questioning of the Army's action. One woman said she felt terribly sorry for the soldiers and for the taunts and insults that they had to take.

One minister there was indeed sympathetic for the victims and their families but there was perhaps more shock than sympathy.

"It is as if a man had been playing with something for long enough and eventually it got him," he said.

It was almost as if a terrible judgment had taken place.

He said: "There was a time when Christ took a whip. At times this is the only way to deal with these things."

He said it was terrible the way people argued over death. His job was not to hold a brief for either side.

"Blessed are the peacemakers," he reminded me. "But not peace at any price."

One man who had been associated with the Loyalist cause said that some good might come out of the suffering, if it showed that Stormont and Westminster were prepared to exercise the rule of law and stand behind their obligations.

Reaction

Again there was sympathy for the bereaved but there was the implication that at some time the security forces had to stand up and do a job expected of them.

There were degrees of Protestant reaction. One young man said he felt ashamed that authority and the people had not been big enough to work out a solution "before it came to this."

He said: "I have a feeling of empty-

Two of the toughest assignments of my career. *This page:* Bloody Sunday, in January 1972. *Opposite page:* The Kingsmills massacre, in January 1976.

A sombre scene, all too common in South Armagh, as one of the 10 Protestants assassinated on Monday night was laid to rest yesterday.

'THESE MEN WERE MY FRIENDS'

JAMES McWHIRTER, Walter Chapman, Reginald Chapman, Robert Chambers . . . suddenly a writer's nightmare comes true. The dead men in a mass killing are the people from my home village. The names become flesh and blood — now cold, frozen, mutilated.

I knew the men from Bessbrook because I grew up with them, played football with them, shared with them the bundle of life in that picturesque little village. James McWhirter, a solid family man, used to drive the old mill lorry. His wife, now his widow, always had a cheerful word with me when I returned home. Mrs. McWhirter, today surrounded by friends and family, is shocked and desolate.

Reginald Chapman and Robert Chambers were boys when I left Bessbrook. The memories of quick-eyed, darting youngsters flood back, memories of the village with stirring victories on the football field and communal thoughts so rich and warm that you would hold some of them close to your heart for the rest of your life in any corner of the world.

Walter Chapman was an old school pal. We sat in the same classroom in the dingy old public elementary school. We shared the same teachers, the same fights, the same privations, the same football field.

MUTILATED

A personal reaction by Belfast Telegraph staff writer Alf McCreary to the deaths of 10 men from his home village of Bessbrook.

The men were shot on Monday. They were buried yesterday.

A search for culprits, like blind men tilting at windmills. But there was no talk of revenge, only of suffering.

One relative said, "I cried before I went into the morgue. I expected the worst, and it was the worst. They pulled down the sheets and there they

ALFRED McCREARY, who received the Journalist of the Year award from James Prior.

Top left: At the Savoy Hotel London with *Belfast Telegraph* editor Eugene Wason for the UK National Press Awards where I was named as Provincial Journalist of the Year. *Bottom:* Other award-winners included George Melly, Keith Waterhouse and John Pilger. *Top right:* With Northern Ireland Secretary James Prior at the Northern Ireland Press Awards, later on in my career.

JUDGES

Tom Hopkinson, C.B.E., Chairman
Michael Foot, M.P., Peter Harland, Charles Jervis, O.B.E., Charles W̶...
Sydney Jacobson, Editorial Director, I.P.C. Newspapers Ltd., Non-voting Organiser

AWARDS

 JOURNALIST OF THE YEAR
ALASTAIR HETHERINGTON,
THE GUARDIAN

 INTERNATIONAL REPORTER
OF THE YEAR
JOHN PILGER, DAILY MIRROR

*Runner-up: Jeremy Campbell,
Evening Standard*

 YOUNG JOURNALIST OF THE YEAR
(25 OR UNDER)
JANICE CAVE, SOUTHEND EVENING ECHO

*Runners-up: Henry Macrory, Kent Messenger
Julian Norridge, Evening Standard*

 PROVINCIAL JOURNALIST
OF THE YEAR
ALF McCREARY, BELFAST TELEGRAPH

*Runner-up: Peter Blacklock,
Southend Evening Echo*

 NEWS REPORTER OF THE YEAR
MONTY METH, DAILY MAIL

Runner-up: Anthony Shrimsley, The Sun

 CRITIC OF THE YEAR
GEORGE MELLY, THE OBSERVER

*Runner-up: Philip Hope-Wallace,
The Guardian*

 DESCRIPTIVE WRITER
OF THE YEAR (TWO AWARDS)

VINCENT MULCHRONE, DAILY MAIL

KEITH WATERHOUSE, DAILY MIRROR

 SPORTS WRITER
OF THE YEAR
FRANK BUTLER, NEWS OF THE WORLD

Runner-up: Neil Allen, The Times

 WOMAN'S PAGE
JOURNALIST OF THE YEAR
ELIZABETH PROSSER, THE SUN

Runner-up: Moira Keenan, The Times

 CAMPAIGNING JOURNALIST
OF THE YEAR
COLIN BRANNIGAN, THE STAR, SHEFFIELD

 SPECIAL AWARD
KEN GARDNER, THE PEOPLE

Above: Bridge-building, with a Roman Catholic priest Fr Denis Faul, left, and a Presbyterian Minister, the Reverend Donald Gillies, on the right. This picture summarises clearly the *Belfast Telegraph*'s policy of bridge-building between the two communities during the decades of the Troubles. *(Belfast Telegraph)*

Belfast Cathedral

A SERVICE OF THANKSGIVING

FOR THE LIFE AND WORK OF

ADMIRAL OF THE FLEET

EARL MOUNTBATTEN OF BURMA

25 JUNE 1900 — 27 AUGUST 1979

SUNDAY, 9 September, 1979 at 3.30 p.m.

Top: Pictured during my early career, circa 1965, with Lord Mountbatten at the old Belfast airport, on his way to his summer home at Classiebawn Castle in Sligo. *Bottom:* Some fourteen years later he was murdered near there by the Provisional IRA. These two pictures summarise the huge deterioration in the security situation within a relatively short time.

Top: With my mentor and spiritual hero the Reverend Dr Ray Davey, the Founder of the Corrymeela Community, some years before his death. *Centre:* The cover of my first Corrymeela book, designed by my artist friend and colleague, the late Rowel Friers.

A selection of the excellent drawings by Rowel Friers which summarised memorable moments in my career. *Top left:* At the end of several years as a television critic for the *Ireland's Saturday Night*. *Bottom left:* After my unhappy assignment to Blackpool where I interviewed Frank Carson, but later 'missed' Hurricane Higgins.
Above: My departure from Queen's later on to take up full-time writing.

Pictured at a presentation to Alf from his Editorial colleagues of a Rowel Friers cartoon and a wrist watch by BT Editor Roy Lilley are (from right) Sam McMurray, chief sub editor; Barry White, leader writer; Eddie Sterling, picture editor; Michael Drake, agricultural correspondent; Derek Black, leader writer; Martin Lindsay, deputy news editor; Tom Carson, features editor; and Desmond McMullan, assistant editor.

Alf McCreary is off to tell the Queen's story to the world

BT CHIEF features writer, leader writer and columnist Alf McCreary has taken over an appointment as the new information director at Queen's University.

He is heading a department aimed at bringing the work of the university to a wider audience.

The Vice-Chancellor, Dr. Peter Froggatt, said the appointment followed a report compiled by a working party which defined a policy of information, publicity and public relations.

Dr. Froggatt admitted that in the past the University had neglected to some extent, to tell the public what was going on there in its various departments.

"The appointment of Mr. McCreary is the first step we are taking to try to remedy this deficiency in our information and communication," he added.

Alf, who took up the post on January 1, said: "The university has an important story to tell of its excellence and its contribution to the community. I believe it is at the heart of the Northern Ireland community and my role is to present this story of Queen's to a wider audience, not only at home but throughout the UK and indeed, the rest of the world because we have Queen's graduates throughout the world in key positions.

"Queen's is a very modest place which doesn't like to boast but I think it is important to tell people what a good job it does," he added.

Alf (44), a graduate of Queen's is married and has three children. He has won several major prizes including two British National Press awards and in 1983 the Rothman's Journalist of the Year Award in Northern Ireland.

ONE of Alf's last assignments for the BT was to cover a strike of binmen in Craigavad. He is here seen tasting a binman's life, showing that it can be just a step from a bin lorry to Queen's University.

Top: My last days as a staff member of the *Belfast Telegraph*. *Bottom:* my final assignment as a 'binman'. The caption notes "It can be just a short step from a bin lorry to Queen's University."

days I had to work hard to prove that I was not just another academic dropping in from Queen's. The greatest compliment my colleagues paid to me was to accept me as one of them. One day I came into the office proudly wearing a brand new short coat, which was styled then as a 'car coat'. Eddie McIlwaine, who went on from the *Telegraph* to be a reporter with the *Daily Mirror*, had a sharp wit, and he said to me "I like your car coat. All you need now is a car to go with it!" Everybody fell about laughing at my expense, but I knew that I was one of the team.

Norman Jenkinson, our feisty news editor, said to me years later "It's good to get graduate trainees." I replied "Jenks, you are a hypocrite – do you remember the hard time some of you guys gave me when I started?" He said "Don't worry, you made it. Graduates have little knowledge of journalism, but we can train them. What they have, more than many other people, is a wide general knowledge. They know, for example, that Mozart was a composer, and not a racehorse. That's important in journalism."

As the Sixties wore on, I was aware that storm clouds were beginning to cast shadows over the future of Northern Ireland. In 1964 rioting broke out on the Falls Road, Belfast when the police forcibly removed an Irish tricolour flag from the window of the Irish Republican headquarters.

Two years later several leading Loyalists, including the infamous Gusty Spence, were given long prison sentences for their part in the murder of a young Catholic barman at a pub in the Shankill Road area. Despite the best efforts of the Prime Minister Terence O'Neill and his colleagues, the shadow of the gunman was once again threatening us all.

At the time, however, I had little idea of how bad the situation would become in a very short time. I had read Irish history at Queen's, I was reporting on 'Community Weeks' in Newry and other places where former IRA men were taking part in 'pram races' with leading Unionists. It seemed on the surface as if the worst of Irish history was in the past; but we were wrong.

§

In the meantime I was enjoying myself in the 'Swinging Sixties' and building up my career. Jack Sayers was most supportive, and appointed me as the *Telegraph's* 'Army Correspondent'. One of my first major assignments was to travel to West Berlin to join the Royal Inniskilling Fusiliers on their tour of duty there in late 1965. It was an exciting prospect for a young journalist to travel to the heart of Berlin at the height of the Cold War.

Just before I left, Sayers called me in to his office. I expected a detailed military briefing from my editor who had had such a good war record. However, I was disappointed. He looked me straight in the eye and said "Remember, young man, on this trip the Army pays for everything!" That was my total briefing. I was learning about the hard realities of newspaper finances.

The Berlin visit was the most memorable experience I had had in journalism up to that stage. I flew into a snow-bound city in mid-winter and stayed in the officer's mess, where I was treated with great politeness and hospitality. One of the Inniskillings' duties was to help guard Spandau Prison, where Hitler's former colleague Rudolf Hess was incarcerated, and I was taken on tour with different platoons.

One very special visit was a journey into the Russian sector in East Berlin, because the British and the Americans had legal international rights to do so. The Inniskillings dressed me in an officer's uniform and I joined my colleagues in a jeep as we drove past grim young Russian soldiers standing ram-rod straight on the very Iron Curtain border itself. I was probably one of the first 'embedded' journalists from the West to travel with Allied forces there since the end of the Second World War. I was only twenty-five years old, and I really felt that I was touching history.

On the first day of that trip to Berlin I wanted to show the *Telegraph* that I was not wasting my time, so I filed a story about the regimental swineherd who hailed from Bellaghy, or some other rural part of faraway Ulster. This resulted in a furious phone call from John Rooks on the news desk. He bawled: "We haven't sent you to Berlin to write about pigshit. Go out a get a proper story." Rooks was rough, but he was right.

The Inniskillings' Colonel was Terry Troy. He was a martinet and wherever he went all heels, except mine, clicked to attention. I had been told to bring my dinner jacket to Berlin, where Colonel Troy and his wife had invited me to dine with them. There was the usual verbal jousting as the Colonel tried to place me in the Northern Ireland pecking order.

Had I gone to Campbell College? No. I had gone to Newry Grammar School. Silence. Then I said casually "I read Modern History at Queen's, before I entered journalism." I was back 'in' again, and we got on famously.

Troy was a hard man, but his wife brought out the soft side in him. I realised that he loved his regiment, and he was aware that the Inniskillings faced huge cuts, if not extinction, in the next Defence Review. I wrote a major feature for the *Belfast Telegraph* which was titled "The Royal Inniskillings' Greatest Fight Is Off the Battlefield". Colonel Troy wrote me a generous letter afterwards, and I was sorry that his campaign to save the Inniskillings later failed.

I also covered quite a few Army stories back in Northern Ireland, including the erection of a Bailey Bridge over the Sixmilewater River in Antrim, which was the only news which the troops generated in those days. It was a calm prelude to the horrendous task which the Army faced a few years later in keeping people from both sides in Northern Ireland at bay, to prevent many of them killing one another.

The social life associated with Army stories in the peaceful days of the mid-Sixties was great, but I was to soldiering what Boot was to journalism in Evelyn Waugh's satirical novel *Scoop*. One of my experiences included a journey from Garlochhead in Scotland to Glasgow and then on to the ferry travelling to Belfast, with the regimental band. Once on the boat they disappeared en masse into the bar, and I realised that in civilian life many of the same group doubled as members of a local Temperance Silver Band.

Sometimes I covered particularly fascinating stories, including one morning in Otterburn in England when I joined soldiers hiding in the thick undergrowth of the moors while they guided Phantom bombers from a base near London to attack practice targets 'behind enemy lines'. The technology from ground to aircraft was amazingly precise, and frightening in its killing power.

The turning point in my brief Army coverage came after reporting on an exercise with an Irish regiment on Luneburg Heath in Germany. One evening after dinner I watched a training film which showed clearly how I could defend myself by killing an attacker with a few well-planned blows. I decided that there were better ways to use my time as a journalist, and I talked my way out of covering such assignments, due to other reporting pressures.

My first big writing break came when I was asked to write a television column by the paper's Deputy Editor Freddie Gamble, whom we all respected and liked. He said to me "Have you got a wee television set?" I replied "Yes". Then he said "Good I want you to deputise for two weeks for our regular television critic Hastings Maguinness".

The column ran in the quaintly named *Ireland's Saturday Night* sports paper, which had a big circulation because of the great demand for the local football, rugby, hockey and other results. This was my first opportunity to write a column, at a time when few journalists were invited to do so because editors felt that hard news sold more papers than comment.

After my two-week stint was over, Freddie said "I like your style. You 'knock' very adroitly. So I'll keep you on." I was sorry for poor old Hastings who had lost his column, but that was the way it worked. I was now the television critic with a regular column which was well-read because people always liked to compare their own views with those of the columnist. Television programmes were fewer in those days, and often worse than today.

Local television was full of lively young things, and the UTV station had opened only a few years earlier, in 1959. There was an air of excitement in UTV, and even the reality of merely appearing on television helped to make people a star. UTV produced household names such as Ivor Mills, Brian Durkan, Anne Gregg, Tommy James, Jimmy Green and others, and I made many good friends among the other staff including Anne and Alan Hailes. The overlord was Brumwell 'Brum' Henderson who presided over what he called his 'fun factory'.

Brum was immensely charming, and larger than life, but you had to watch him. He could be professionally tricky, and I always had to be aware of the possibility of his symbolic knife slicing silently into my ribs. To his credit, however, he ran as good a television station as he could, and people liked working in his 'fun factory'.

However, UTV was not above criticism, and one week I wrote a fierce column claiming that "This new station has too many chiefs and not enough Indians." Fred Gamble said "I think this is alright but we had better ask Jack Sayers to look at it." So he handed the Editor my galley proof as we walked along a corridor into the newsroom. Sayers ignored me completely, took out his red pen, turned to Gamble said "Good God Fred, we can't say this!", and promptly crossed out half my column, right on our deadline. I am not sure how we managed after that, but with the help of expert compositors downstairs like Billy Kerr and Ronnie McCausland, we somehow filled the sudden gap that had appeared in the television page.

The BBC was a much more staid station than its brash young competitor UTV. I said this one night after working hours to Waldo Maguire, the Ulsterman who was Northern Ireland Controller. Waldo poured himself another stiff 'Black Bush' and said "You are right, but most of my staff are family people, and I don't have the heart to start a bloodbath." These were different days indeed in the world of television.

One BBC presenter I admired was Larry McCoubrey who held the place together even in the midst of frequent technical chaos. Nevertheless he had been hurt by one of my critiques, and this came to a head when we shared a drink one afternoon in Tangiers, as part of a Press junket organised by British Airways. I explained to him my view, and we agreed to differ. Then he said "Praise me if you can, knock me if you feel it's justified, but above all don't ignore me!" That is still the plaintive cry of all those who earn their living in the exposed and sometimes surreal world of broadcasting and writing.

I continued to write my television column for many years, and even today it is remembered by those old enough to recall the early days of television in Northern Ireland. I enjoyed it immensely, because it gave me a high profile, and the rare opportunity to hone my skills as a columnist.

For some years I also covered hockey matches at weekends. Many of the players were my team-mates or opponents from my early days playing for Queen's, and I would have loved to have continued with them. I was asked to join YMCA to take over eventually from their British Olympic goalie Harry Cahill, but to show willing I had to start in the lower ranks. My first match with YMCA III team went well and afterwards my newly-acquainted right back said to me "Keep it up goalie, you're not bad." I did not tell him that only a year earlier I had played in goal for the British Universities team against the Germans in Munich. However I knew that I could not play and report at the same time, and my hockey career ground to a halt. Journalism had to come first.

I now look back with wonder at why I put so much effort into reporting these games for such little financial reward, but it kept me in touch with my roots. I am still amazed at the low level of technology which we used. Our first rule was to make sure that we were near a phone that was actually working. The former hockey editor of the *Telegraph* Carl Anderson and I often reminisced about covering games on the Lisnagarvey complex near Lisburn which is now the site of the large Sprucefield shopping centre. To file our half-time reports we had to race down a lane, cross a busy road, enter a small petrol/diesel filling-station, and use the phone in the back store surrounded by bags of potatoes and other assorted clutter. In terms of technology, compared to today, we were not that far ahead of carrier pigeons.

However I had more serious topics to cover, and Jack Sayers appointed me as the paper's New City Correspondent. This was an important post because the Stormont government was planning a new city in the Portadown–Lurgan area and this was a good opportunity for our paper to keep abreast of the latest news.

In my new role I was given access to the top civil servants, and also to the Minister of Development William Craig, a leading Unionist who later became the notorious bete noir of the civil rights campaigners in Northern Ireland.

I met Craig in his Stormont Office and he showed me his plans for the development of forest parks and other tourist attractions. His enthusiasm was infectious and I could see that he really believed that there was a bright future for Northern Ireland. He had no inkling, nor had I, that his plans for that bright future would shortly be in ruins in a political meltdown that was partly of his own making.

The 'new city' never reached the potential envisaged by the early planners, because of complex factors including politics and resignations. Sadly even its name was divisive. The *Telegraph* invited its readers to submit suggestions, and Jack Sayers toyed with the idea of 'Ulidia', an ancient name for Ulster.

However, the Stormont government with typical mule-headed stupidity chose the name Craigavon, as a tribute to the first Unionist Prime Minister Lord Craigavon. By doing so, they squandered the opportunity to create a new project which would have the support of everyone, including unionists and nationalists.

I was appalled by the government's lack of foresight, but it was typical of the major blunders which the Unionists made around that time. Instead of establishing a second Northern Ireland university in Derry/Londonderry, with its largely nationalist population, they chose the safe unionist territory of Coleraine. The Unionist councillors in Belfast with an unsurprising lack of imagination also tried to name a new bridge over the River Lagan the 'Carson Bridge', in honour of Lord Carson, one of the fierce opponents of Home Rule who was a Unionist hero.

However the then Governor of Northern Ireland Lord Erskine of Rerrick courageously intervened, and it was named the 'Queen Elizabeth Bridge'. This still had 'unionist' connotations, and was therefore divisive to non-unionists.

The intervention of Lord Erskine further fuelled the noisy campaign by Paisley and other anti-O'Neillites. I was aware that despite everything which the *Belfast Telegraph* was doing to support O'Neill and to prevent Northern Ireland from sliding back into a sectarian bloodbath, the storm clouds were gathering.

There was little I could do personally to prevent this. I was at an age when the challenges and distractions of my daily life were more important to me than the long-term future of Northern Ireland.

Unfortunately, however, major changes were on the way, and I had no idea how far-reaching they would prove to be, both personally and professionally.

CHAPTER NINE

The Storm Breaks

"THE SIXTIES... were young men's years. Our world was richer, smaller, but was it better? We were better turned out, better turned on, but were we happier? Life was a hard day's night, and the Beatles were king. If you lived in Alabama, or Pinkville, or Saigon, or India, most of Africa, or most of Asia, it was a different story. But if you were a white Anglo-Saxon with a pound in your pocket, a girl on your arm and food in your belly, the Sixties was a great time to be alive."

These words were part of an article which I wrote for the *Belfast Telegraph* to summarise the broad view of the 'Swinging Sixties', and they mirrored the thoughts about my career and private life.

The *Belfast Telegraph* did not pay well, but the newsroom was lively and we had the camaraderie of knowing that we worked for a top newspaper which was widely read and was playing a significant role in the political and cultural life of Northern Ireland.

There were many rich characters in the newsroom including the Snooker Correspondent Ronnie Harper whose wisecracking imagination prompted him to tell me that he had played out of golf bunkers so big that he swore he saw a camel train passing through several of them.

Jack Magowan, our talkative and likeable boxing correspondent was famous for his fractured prose, including his observation that "This fighter's 'glass jaw' is his Achilles heel!" Harry Duff, the Racing Greyhound correspondent, was small and round, like a ripe tomato, very friendly, and at times virtually unintelligible. His stock reply to every question was "Wye nat?", and I continue to drive my family mad by repeating Harry's reply when they ask my advice about doing something.

As a young journalist I was receiving a first class training under the steady eye of Jack Sayers and his senior staff. I was taught about the importance of speed, integrity, balanced reporting and, above all, accuracy.

One Saturday morning I received the dreaded note from Sayers "Please see me – JES." This was usually the prelude to a difficult encounter with the Editor-in-Chief. When I entered Jack's office he was incandescent with rage. He yelled at me "I promised to make you a good journalist, but why are you reporting rubbish like this?" I had committed the grave mistake, in his eyes, of reading the wrong line about shipping in my visit to the then austere Belfast Harbour Office, and recording a million tons less than it should have been.

It was hardly a hanging offence, but the real story was that Jack Sayers, the former naval officer who was fixated by shipping, had been teased about this inaccurate report by his pals over lunch in the Ulster Reform Club. Jack's justified tirade ruined my weekend, but he taught me the importance of accuracy, and I still hate making mistakes.

Despite my excellent training in the *Telegraph* I was getting restless. I was still a rolling stone and I was looking for outlets in London and much further afield, without knowing, of course, that if I stayed on in Belfast I would soon be covering one of the most important stories of my career.

My private life was moving along happily until one morning my girlfriend Hilary told me that she was leaving to take up a post as a physiotherapist in Calgary General Hospital in Canada.

I did not think that this was a great idea, but there was nothing I could do about it. However I had already planned to visit New York and to travel across to the West Coast that autumn, to celebrate my 27th birthday, and as Hilary was setting off for Canada around the same time, we agreed to meet in Montreal to visit Expo '67.

After a wonderful few days in New York with my Uncle Bill and his wife Eileen, during which I memorably saw Lisa Minnelli and Joel Grey in the original Broadway production of the hit musical *Cabaret*, I travelled overnight by bus to Montreal airport, where Hilary and I had planned to meet after she arrived on a flight from Shannon Airport.

However it was so big and busy that we could not find each other. As I was about the leave for the last time on an downwards elevator I heard an agonised yell from Hilary on the floor above. She was changing money at a bank till and she had spotted me at the last minute. She ran to meet me, but it was a narrow shave. We had not chosen an alternative venue in which to meet, and in those days there were no mobile phones.

No doubt we would have worked out some other way of meeting up, but I don't know what we would have done if we had missed each other entirely in Montreal. Happily, however, we did meet, if only just, and we enjoyed Expo '67 together.

A few days later, before leaving to travel separately to San Francisco and Calgary, we stayed in Syracuse in New York state where I had an appointment with the Dean of the highly-regarded university School of Journalism. The meeting was worthwhile, because it convinced me that my career lay working in journalism and not in teaching it.

However my peace of mind was disturbed at the prospect of leaving Hilary. We sadly said our heartfelt "good-byes" at Syracuse bus station, and set off on our very separate ways. We had no firm commitment to meet again, despite our very strong bond, but we promised to stay closely in touch. Looking back, we were taking a big gamble on our future, but we were young, and we were still looking for adventure.

My sadness at leaving Hilary was partly compensated by my long journey on a Greyhound bus to Chicago and then through the mid-west and on to San Francisco itself. This was a special offer of "99 Days for 99 Dollars", and around each corner there was a new vista. It was exactly what my 'rolling stone' instincts enjoyed most. This feeling of adventure was summarised much later by one of my friends who said "You are at your happiest when you are boarding a bus or train or plane on the way to a new story, with a notebook in your hand."

San Francisco, at the height of the Flower Power in 1967, was a marvellous mixture of colour, music, hippies and other assorted odd-balls, and also the breathtaking scenery, architecture and culture of one of the world's greatest cities.

I stayed with Andy Duffin, an old Queen's pal who had the distinction of being the first Ulster-born Roman Catholic president of the Students' Representative Council. One Sunday afternoon he drove me in his red

Ford Mustang to a Romanesque amphitheatre in the Californian hills where a jazz concert was due to take place.

I was so impressed by the hot sunshine and the orange groves that I paid little attention to the musicians in powder-blue suits who were assembling on the stage. Then at 4 pm a handsome man in a white suit stepped onto the stage from the shadows, clicked his fingers and the band swung into its signature tune 'Take the A-Train'. I thought "Oh, my God this is Duke Ellington and his Band!" As my jaw dropped, Andy Duffin chuckled and said "I bet you didn't expect this."

After that memorable moment with one of the world's top jazz bands among the orange groves of California, it was all down hill. I returned to Belfast, by way of a short visit to the Grand Canyon, and my wanderlust was curbed by the confines of the sub-editors' room in the *Belfast Telegraph*.

I disliked sub-editing, partly because no-one offered me proper training. The genial Chief Sub-Editor Hastings Maguinness, who always called me 'Ralph McCleary' said to me one day "Lay out this page, son" and walked off. He might as well have told me "Take this Maserati and drive it."

I had little interest in design and lay-out, and I disliked being cooped up in a room with affable but mostly middle-aged men, some of whom were a little too smart-assed for my liking.

I had chosen to become a journalist to see the world, but I had to persevere with my sub-editor's training in Belfast. To compound my misery, my treasured white Mini was stolen on Christmas Eve while I was drinking with my friends in McGlade's Bar. So I had to spend the night in my empty flat in Belfast, and travel to Newry on Christmas morning in a rickety old UTA bus to have lunch with my family in Bessbrook.

The New Year was no better. I went to a party hosted by my friend Gloria Hunniford and her then husband the late Don Keating, and got a lift back to my dark and empty flat in Belfast. I still had no car, so the next morning I had to travel by bus to Downpatrick Court where I covered a case about a farmer allegedly polluting a stream, and also about another man allegedly urinating on a neighbour's lawn. It was not riveting copy.

That evening I travelled back to Belfast again by bus, bought some liver and bacon in a butcher's shop and cooked a solitary meal in my draughty apartment. There I was, without my formerly steady girlfriend who was living in Canada, also without a car, and apparently without any prospects of improving my position as a journalist.

If anyone had wished me a "Happy New Year" I would not have been impressed. However, I was about to learn another important lesson. Life can change totally within an amazingly short period, and that's what happened to me.

Sadly, however, on 10 January 1968 Hilary's father the Reverend James Fitzsimons died suddenly from a heart attack. He and his wife Dr Winifred Fitzsimons were very special people. I was extremely fond of both of them, and I had visited them regularly when Hilary was in Canada.

I went to the funeral at Second Dunboe Presbyterian Church near Coleraine to pay my respects to the family and also to represent Hilary, who had then decided to end her job in Calgary and come home. However she was prevented from getting back in time for the funeral because of a snowstorm in Toronto.

A couple of days later she returned to Belfast and on the way to the airport by bus I glanced at my horoscope in a newspaper. I have never believed in horoscopes since the time I had to write them for a couple of days because we had lost the agency copy. However my horoscope in that morning's paper stated "From today everything will get better", and it did.

When Hilary and I met again, the smouldering flames of romance grew even stronger, and within a short time we were married. The rolling stone had stopped rolling, and Belfast was now home.

In the early summer my career in the *Belfast Telegraph* also took a dramatic twist for the better. My colleague Godfrey Fitzsimons (no relation to Hilary) had accepted a post with the *Irish Times*, and the *Telegraph* was looking for a replacement feature writer and leader-writer.

Much to my amazement Jack Sayers appointed me to the job on a six months trial, and there was no turning back. It was a huge promotion for me, and something akin to being plucked from the relative obscurity of the backbenches at Westminster to become a junior member of the Cabinet.

The leader-writers team of two in those days were the heavyweight political commentators Martin Wallace, who was Deputy Editor, and Barry White. I marvelled that they could write incisive leaders at speed on almost any subject, and always to a tight deadline.

My first experience of leader-writing was alarming. Jack Sayers tended to give short, sharp briefings, and often on the hoof. One morning he said to Barry "Let's give Terence O'Neill a boost, he needs it." Then he said to me "Alf, write three pars in support of the New University", and off he went. I struggled long and hard to write a helpful editorial for the NUU and took it in to Jack Sayers. He scanned it quickly and said tersely "This will not do. Try again." I left his office in a state of quiet desperation, because the deadline was approaching and I did not know what to do. I showed Barry White my leader, and asked for his advice. Barry read through my work, continued typing his own leader at the same time, and said "Put the first paragraph last, and tweak the middle paragraph a bit, and you should be OK."

I did exactly that and took it in to Sayers again. He read it, beamed at me and said "You are a quick learner!" My mini-crisis was over, and I remained ever-grateful to the imperturbable Barry White for his advice. After many years of writing leaders on every subject imaginable, my colleagues nicknamed me 'A man for all seasons'. I continue to enjoy writing leaders for the *Belfast Telegraph*, after all these years, and I still remember Jack Sayer's advice that "Writing leaders is a rare skill but it is essentially an endless variation on obvious themes."

Another important aspect of my new job was writing features, which gave me an opportunity to range much more widely than a reporter was normally allowed to do. This was the era when facts were more important than opinions, and few reporters apart from the specialists were given by-lines.

I relished my new freedom as the paper's sole 'feature-writer', and at a time when the *Telegraph* was embracing fully the concept of large feature articles.

I really had the best of both worlds. In the mornings I was writing in-depth leaders and political commentary, and in the afternoon I was living the life of a widely-ranging feature writer. Part of the paper's admirable policy was to bring variety to its readers, and not to dwell solely on the bad news which was all too plentiful.

Accordingly I wrote about everything from an afternoon's greyhound coursing in Ballymena, to a descriptive 'colour piece' on concert featuring the comedian James Young in Rathfriland and also a substantial article on the former Irish President Eamonn De Valera. At the same time I was still writing my weekly television column. No young journalist could have asked for more variety or more opportunities to develop his or her skills.

In the meantime, the political situation was deteriorating alarmingly. The Unionist government was unwilling or unable to move quickly enough to meet the demands of the well-organised civil rights campaign led by John Hume and others, and which was partly modelled on the USA campaign led by Martin Luther King.

However I always wondered why it had taken the Roman Catholic and Nationalist community so long to assert themselves and to demand their rights in Northern Ireland. The earlier Nationalist leaders seemed to me to have been remarkably supine and ineffective, until the emergence of a whole new generation of educated young people who knew how to play hard-ball politics.

One of these people, as I have noted earlier, was my old class-mate at Queen's Austin Currie who did more than most to start the civil rights momentum. He was then a Stormont MP and on 20 June 1968 he squatted in a house in Caledon which had been allocated to an unmarried Protestant tenant, even though many Catholic families could not get a house. In doing so he was drawing attention to the disgracefully inequitable system of housing allocation operated by local councils in Northern Ireland.

After a long Province-wide campaign, matters came to a head on 5 October 1968 when the RUC batoned a civil rights march in Londonderry, during which the ebullient SDLP leader Gerry Fitt was hit on the head in full view of the television cameras, and he subsequently never allowed anyone to forget it.

This made headlines in all the national media, and the Unionist government led by Terence O'Neill was on the back foot. Towards Christmas, however, the situation cooled slightly and Jack Sayers instructed me to write an important series on "The 50 Day Revolution." Jack assumed that the worst was over, but he was misjudging the situation, and he was not the only one to do so.

Jack asked his new personal assistant Roy Lilley to help me. Roy had returned from a promising career in London, and later went on to become one of the best editors in the history of the *Belfast Telegraph*. He also became one of my closest lifelong friends.

Roy Lilley gave me advice on how to handle the assignment, but left the groundwork reporting to me. With my new found freedom I was able to report on the grassroots views in Derry and elsewhere in Northern Ireland. I really felt that I was coming of age as a journalist and reporting one of the biggest running stories in the history of the *Belfast Telegraph* and of Northern Ireland.

I was also delighted that Jack Sayers confirmed my new appointment with a charming handwritten letter, which I have kept and which I still treasure, and I was also given a modest salary increase several weeks later.

The future looked bright personally and professionally, but as 1969 swept in there were more big changes on the way. Northern Ireland was descending into violent upheaval, and sadly my mentor Jack Sayers fell into ill health and had to retire in 1969. He died shortly afterwards.

Jack had a vision of a peaceful, integrated Northern Ireland, but he was far ahead of his time. If the Unionists had shared his vision and had moved much earlier to embrace the Irish Nationalist and Roman Catholic minority in meaningful power-sharing, the tragedy of the next four decades of death and destruction might have been avoided.

Jack had guided the *Telegraph* to a pre-eminent position in Northern Ireland journalism, and it had the biggest circulation in its history, with a forty percent readership among all the adults in Northern Ireland. Sadly, however, this campaigning newspaper was a courageous lone voice in a political wilderness.

Sayers must have been heartbroken as he watched helplessly while Northern Ireland steadily moved towards disaster. He may have felt that he had failed, but his vision of power-sharing between the main political blocks was fulfilled eventually. The pity is that it took several decades to do so, but even today Sayers's words in a leading article in the *Belfast Telegraph* of 5 November 1968 send out the same challenge and warning: "The threat to Northern Ireland's future is not… the IRA or even Nationalism. It comes from Protestant Ulstermen who will not allow themselves to be liberated from the delusion that every Roman Catholic is their enemy."

The new editor of the *Belfast Telegraph* was Eugene Wason, an avuncular Scotsman with a wide experience of editing newspapers, including the *Sunday Chronicle*, the *Sunday Mail* in Scotland, the *Africa Daily Post* in Rhodesia and the *Evening Post* in Hemel Hempstead.

He was the first non-Ulsterman to edit the *Belfast Telegraph*, and his style was different to that of his predecessors. Not surprisingly, Eugene knew little about the complex situation in Ulster, but he soon made it clear that he was prepared to consult wisely with those who did.

His main role was to keep the *Telegraph* on track with its courageous policy of backing power-sharing and relating to its readers of all political backgrounds. His management role was also to groom his successor as editor, and he soon realised that the obvious choice was Roy Lilley, who had been an ace political correspondent in Belfast and London and had one of the best analytical brains available to any editor.

Under Wason the leader-writers' morning conference played a vital role in charting a clear path for the paper through the maze of political deadlock and violence that was leading the Province to a deadend.

The conferences lasted sometimes up to an hour, and the debate was frank and free. As a relative newcomer to this august gathering I was treated with the same respect as all the others in arguing my case. There was generally a broad consensus on the best way forward and after the morning briefing it fell to Barry White and me to write the day's leaders. Later on we were joined by Edmund Curran, who became a close writing colleague, and who succeeded Roy Lilley much later as editor.

Eugene Wason presided over the leader-writers' conference with a shrewd paternalism. He said little, but listened a lot. He would speak out on certain topics but, given the complexities of the war raging all around him, he was sometimes out of his depth.

On such occasions we would say politely "With respect Mr Wason…" One day he retorted with his customary humour "Gentlemen, when you say to me 'With respect', does that mean you think I am talking bollocks?" We all said "Yes", amid laughter. Eugene was a good editor, and he recognised his own limitations.

He also had a fresh approach to journalism, and he set about changing the somewhat dated style of the *Telegraph*. Early on he stunned everyone by suggesting that the paper should run a story on "The happiest dog in Belfast." He was far ahead of his time regarding tabloid journalism in Northern Ireland, and it took years for his colleagues to accept his suggestion for a story about "The happiest dog in Belfast."

He also wrote only one leading article for the paper, even though he was the editor. It was titled "The Strange Case of Papwa Segolum", and it was about a golfer who had won the Rhodesian Open but who was presented with his prize on the lawn outside the golf club because he was black. Eugene had been a courageous opponent of Ian Smith, and his newspaper had been banned in 1964 after only eight months in business because of its opposition to the ruling regime.

Eugene Wason was also a good diplomat. One day I went into his office to ask him for a rise. Our lovely baby daughter Emma Jane had arrived, and money was tight. When I asked Eugene for a £100 rise, he put his thumbs through his red braces, leaned back in his chair, adjusted his ample belly for maximum comfort, and said to me "My dear boy, you are one of my best writers. On your day you write like an angel. I would love to give you a rise of £200, because you deserve it. But I have no money available to give to you." Nevertheless I thanked him for listening to me, and walked out of his office with a lilt in my step. He had not given me a penny, but he had made me feel good about my work. People who did not know Eugene dismissed him as a 'lightweight'. In reality he was a clever and brave man, and he often demonstrated the wisdom of Solomon.

Under his editorship the *Telegraph* maintained its political authority and gravitas, but it was also open to new ideas and to new methods of reporting. I was given great opportunities as a feature writer, and this included many in-depth profiles and interviews with major figures, and all the time breaking new ground in journalism.

One of my early interviewees was the Army chief Lieutenant-General Sir Ian Freeland whom I profiled in a 2,000 word article on 9 February 1970 under the simple title "The General". At that time he had one of the most thankless jobs in Northern Ireland, which was tearing itself apart. Freeland was polite, but a little stiff during our long interview. However, I was also able to speak to his wife privately. She was pretty, bubbly and without inhibitions, unlike her husband, who was constrained from speaking freely because of his high office.

Lady Freeland told me about another side to the man. She said that they had met at the races in India, had fallen in love and had married two years later, in 1940, though they had only seen each other regularly for about a month. She was twenty, and he was twenty-seven. She said "It was a bit mad, wasn't it, but it has worked out fine." She also told me "If he has a fault, it is that he is maddeningly tidy. He is certainly not infallible. If the car breaks down he gets into a fearful flap. He pretends that he knows how to fix it, but he is not really very mechanical." I thought "What a lucky man to have such a lovely wife."

Before we published the article there were discreet 'feelers' from Army headquarters in Lisburn to see if they could read it in advance, which is anathema to all journalists. It transpired later that the General was not so much worried about what he had told me but about what his wife might have told me about him. We published the article unchanged, and the only thing missing was the General's nickname, which I had been unable to find out. I later discovered that, behind his back, they called him "Smiling Death".

This was no surprise to me, because during my research for the article one of the General's aides had told me "If you get on the wrong side of him, you will not last long. Professionally, he can be ruthless." Yet behind the image of the hard professional, was the reality of the man who told me "I have felt rather despairing lately. There are enough troublemakers out there, and simple people to follow them. One realises the difficulty, but I cannot solve it. My job is to keep the peace while the politicians try to solve it."

Such a long and revealing interview with a top general might be more commonplace in the media nowadays but in the Northern Ireland of the early Troubles this was part of the *Belfast Telegraph's* ground-breaking journalism.

Throughout that period the Troubles steadily worsened, and culminated in a vicious and prolonged pitched battle in Londonderry between the RUC and civil rights protestors in August 1969. The Irish Premier Jack Lynch sent 'field hospitals' to Irish border areas, and eventually troops were called in to help the exhausted police. In October there were serious clashes between Loyalists and the Army in the Shankill Road area of Belfast where three people were killed, including the first policeman to die, Constable Victor Arbuckle. The situation in Northern Ireland was spiralling out of control.

During that period our office in the *Belfast Telegraph* became a Mecca for major figures in national and international journalism who needed an in-depth briefing on Northern Ireland. I remember the award-winning *Guardian* reporter Harry Jackson returning from covering the rioting in Derry. He shook his head ruefully and said to us "Those people are not looking for a solution. Both sides are still looking for a victory." His words have always stayed in my mind as a incisive and accurate summary of most of Northern Ireland throughout the Troubles. Sadly, in some areas this still applies today.

As the years progressed the situation became worse. The Unionists were dominated by hardliners and were continually unable to out-manoeuvre their political opponents. The political deadlock helped to create a vacuum which was filled by the militant, vicious and well-organised Provisional IRA. This in turn led to the rise of equally vicious Loyalist paramilitary groups. Another dark milestone was reached on 6 February 1971 when Gunner Robert Curtis was the first British soldier to die in the Troubles. A few weeks later three Scottish soldiers were murdered by the Provisional IRA, and their bodies were dumped at Ligoniel on the outskirts of Belfast.

The atrocities on all sides were deeply traumatising, especially to those who believed that after the improvements of the early Sixties, the 'Irish question' which had poisoned Anglo-Irish relations for so long had been confined to the dustbin of history.

Despite the desperate efforts of London and Stormont politicians to quell the gathering storm, Northern Ireland became a basket-case Province, which was wracked by fear, bigotry, violence, bloody-mindedness, pain, political deadlock and extreme danger.

Unlike my cross-channel and international colleagues, who could fly off after a tour of duty, I had to make the best of Northern Ireland because it was my home. I too shared the apprehension, fear and uncertainty of many other people. As a political commentator I was continually appalled by the stupidity of those on all sides who refused to see reason, but I knew that there was no easy way out of the deep and dangerous swamp into which we had driven ourselves.

Yet as a journalist, I also felt – a little guiltily perhaps – the exhilaration of covering one of the most important stories of my lifetime, and working with some of the national and international big names in journalism.

For long periods I was a part-time correspondent, or 'stringer', for such highly-regarded titles as *The Guardian*, *Time* magazine and the *Christian Science Monitor* in Boston, and other publications.

The late Sixties had been bad, but as the early Seventies grew steadily worse, there were two important personal milestones. In 1970 I had entered a portfolio of my articles for the British National Press Awards. To my great surprise I was chosen as the British Provincial Journalist of the Year, the first time (to my knowledge) that this award had come to Northern Ireland. The judges' citation read "A great deal of distinguished reporting is going on in the Provincial Press. For his moving and illuminating commentary on the much-reported situation in Northern Ireland, the award goes to Alf McCreary."

One of my featured articles was "A Letter to the first baby of 1971", in which I stated "If you want to change things you will have to be prepared to do it yourself. If you want an end to bigotry, double standards and stubborn stupidity you will have to speak out and make a stand in the club and in the pub, in the boardroom and on the shop floor. It will be a tough job and you can leave your kid gloves at home…"

I travelled to London with my editor Eugene Wason to pick up my prize at a splendid lunch in the Savoy Hotel London, where I rubbed shoulders with such legendary figures in national journalism as Hugh Cudlipp and Keith Waterhouse of the *Daily Mirror*, Vincent Mulchrone of the *Daily Mail*, and Charles Wintour, the editor of the *Evening Standard* who was one of the judges of the Awards competition. To my delight he later commissioned me to write articles for his authoritative London evening paper at a time when Mary Kenny was his Features Editor. My prize for the Award was a golden pen, which was later stolen from our home by burglars, but I never forgot the joy of that day in London at the British National Press Awards.

All of this boosted my confidence greatly, while also awakening my journalist's wanderlust again. I was also grateful for the many messages of support back home, including a card from my mother which read "Congratulations, I am very proud of you." One of the letters I most liked was from Godfrey Fitzsimons whose job I had taken over in the *Telegraph*. He wrote, with typically wry humour: "Of course it's the seat you're sitting on that done it. The genius rubbed off my ass onto your ass!"

However the most important event in my life in the very tough year of 1971 had nothing to do directly with journalism. My wife Hilary was pregnant and we decided that she would have the baby in Carrickfergus Hospital rather than the Royal Victoria Hospital in Belfast. It proved to be one of the most fortuitous decisions of our lives.

So early in the morning of 9 August 1971, we had to drive quickly to Carrickfergus because the birth of our child was imminent. I left Hilary in the hospital and went back home to snatch a few hours sleep.

I was unaware that in the meantime all hell had broken out in West Belfast. Early that morning the Army had forcibly lifted 300 people in a dawn raids in Republican areas and they were being interned without trial. This was one of the biggest ever mistakes by the government in Northern Ireland, and also one of the most powerful catalysts for IRA recruitment during the entire Troubles.

Following the internment raids there was sustained violence in Belfast, Derry and other places. However I also had other things in my mind. I had to drive our daughter Emma, aged nearly three, across Belfast on my own to leave her with my wife's Auntie Winnie and Granny Fitzsimons who had agreed to look after her while Hilary was in hospital.

As I drove across the city from North Belfast, I saw to my horror that the timber yards at the docks had been set on fire, and that the Corporation buses were being taken off duty. People were scurrying to safety throughout the city, and there was desperation and danger everywhere.

After leaving off Emma I made my way to the *Belfast Telegraph* where my colleagues were working under immense pressure. In mid-morning my phone rang, and a voice said "This is a nurse from Carrickfergus Hospital. Your wife has just had a baby boy. Congratulations!"

I walked into the large newsroom in a semi-daze, with a big smile on my face. I passed the editor Eugene Wason who was hurrying away from the newsdesk with a worried frown. He said to me "What are you smiling at on a day like this?" I replied "My wife's just had a baby boy." Eugene's frown broke into a beaming smile. He said "Congratulations – take the afternoon off." Which I did.

I drove through the fear-filled Belfast streets to Carrickfergus hospital where Hilary and I held our first-born son, Mark James McCreary. It was so poignant that every word of my "Letter to the first baby of 1971" which was published in the *Telegraph* just over eight months earlier could equally have applied to our little boy Mark.

As I nursed him again later that night I also thought about a news story that was breaking just as I was leaving the *Telegraph* that afternoon. Several people had been shot dead in fierce gun-battles raging across West Belfast.

I thought of the joy of our family that day and also of the despair of the other families whose loved ones had died. Here was life and death, joy and sorrow, good news and bad news, and all so intertwined in my personal and professional life.

My world was now bright and promising, and more so than I could ever have expected, but there was no escaping from the dark shadows all around us. The storm was now threatening to overwhelm us all.

CHAPTER TEN

The Eye of the Storm

THE GRIM MOOD of the early Seventies was so bad that I was tempted at times to move away from Northern Ireland with my family and to leave it to itself.

In an article published in July 1970, I wrote about returning to Belfast from a holiday in Connemara where Hilary and I had spent part of our honeymoon two years earlier in the beautiful Renvyle House Hotel. This time it was different from those previous days of relative peace. I wrote glumly "I pointed my car towards Belfast and drove more in hope than conviction. As I swept round a corner near Balmoral a billowing cloud of black smoke spiralled into the sky... Coming from the heart of the Falls–Shankill area it could mean only one thing.

"Soon enough I was piecing together, with the help of press and radio reports, the events that had led to more deaths, more destruction and more homeless people. It is not pleasant for an Ulsterman to come back to a city where misery and death stalk the streets. For one wild moment there is a temptation to drive round it, past it, away from it, to leave it to its troubles."

The article was published by the *Belfast Telegraph* and also by the *Irish Times*, after the editor Douglas Gageby spotted it in the Northern paper. Douglas was an outstanding editor, and a charismatic person for whom I had great regard.

After the internment crisis of 1971, the violence increased dramatically, and 1972 began in the worst way possible. On 30 January – a day which came to be known as Bloody Sunday – thirteen civilians were shot dead and another was fatally wounded by British paratroopers during a banned civil rights march in Londonderry.

This was one of the major turning points of the Troubles. It massively increased Provisional IRA recruitment, polarised opinion even further, and cast a dark shadow over the whole island. The Irish government recalled its ambassador from London, and a mob burned down the British Embassy in Dublin.

I watched with dismay the television news on the Sunday evening of the killings, and the next day the *Belfast Telegraph* sent me to Derry to report on the aftermath of the shootings. It was a sombre assignment in a place which was in such deep mourning. I stayed in a hotel on the outskirts of the city with other journalists as we all tried to piece together the bloody pieces of a horrible jigsaw.

On the Tuesday morning I managed to persuade a doctor's wife to drive me down into the Bogside to interview some of the residents there, and I asked her to take with us a reporter from the *Glasgow Herald*. She said to the young journalist "When I take you into the Bogside, keep your mouth shut because of your accent. Some of the paratroopers were Scottish."

In my report, which was published by the *Belfast Telegraph* and *The Journal* in Newcastle-upon-Tyne, I wrote: "Londonderry is a city caught in the cold hand of death. A piercing wind sweeps across Lough Foyle. The weak sun fades in a wintry sky that promises snow. The bitter weather marches the mood of the city.

"Derry is like a prolonged wake. The main streets are empty. The shops are closed. Soldiers with rifles at the ready shelter wearily in shop doorways, surveying the bleak scene. It is a place where people fend for themselves.

"At the moment the abiding reality, apart from the feelings of death, is the total lack of communication across the divide. The story of Derry is a tale of two cities. It is symptomatic of Northern Ireland and of Ireland and its people. Its messages 'We shall overcome' and 'Not an inch' are mutually contradictory. Its continuing tragedy is that there seems to be nothing as yet to fill the emptiness. There is too much faith, not enough hope, and too little charity."

The next day I reported from a local Roman Catholic Church on the funeral service for the victims. Before it started, I walked up to the front of the church and slowly read all the name plates on the coffins. I was all too aware that each wooden box held the remains of a human being who had been alive and vibrant only a few days previously.

It was a dreadful situation, personally and professionally. There was no escaping the mood of death, destruction and mourning, and yet I had to remain detached enough to get my story and to meet a tight deadline for the final edition of that day's *Telegraph*. I remember leaving the church, and running along empty streets, all the time praying that I would find a public telephone that actually worked. Life without mobile phones was more difficult for a reporter in those days.

To my relief, I made my deadline and almost immediately the presses in Belfast started rolling with our page one lead. In my report I stated "They buried their dead under a leaden sky as the rain poured down. The coffins were borne out of the black church on a windswept hill. The relatives, some weeping, some restrained and pale, followed the coffins from the church. So too did Cardinal Conway, a striking figure in his scarlet robes."

Earlier, in the church, the atmosphere was highly emotional. A sobbing woman was half-carried up the aisle moaning "My wee Paddy". In the congregation another woman began screaming hysterically as relatives tried to comfort her.

Then up in the gallery a girl's sweet clear voice sang 'Through All The Changing Scenes of Life' to the tune of Winchester. As a Protestant I said to myself "That's one of our hymn tunes too," and I thought of the grotesque sectarian divisions in our society which had been created falsely in the name of the bad religion which had allowed itself to become too mixed up with politics.

As I travelled silently back to Belfast I thought of the terrible scenes I had witnessed in those three days. It was too early to apportion blame, and I had been trained as a reporter not to jump to conclusions. It took many years of expensive legal inquiries to get to the truth, and for the British Prime Minister to apologise on behalf of the British to the families of the victims, and rightly so. David Cameron, addressing the House of Commons after the publication of the Saville Report on 15 June 2010, described the paratroopers actions as "both unjustified and unjustifiable".

However on the day I left Derry after the funerals, the killings were almost too much to take in. All I could remember was the overpowering feeling of having reported on an immense human tragedy.

Almost inevitably the violence escalated. On Saturday 4 March two people were killed and over seventy were injured, some horribly so, when a bomb went off without warning in the crowded Abercorn Restaurant in the Cornmarket area of Belfast.

I was in a Queen's University sports pavilion at Upper Malone, several miles away, when I heard the dull sickening thud of the large explosion. I had no idea where it had taken place, but it sounded bad. It was one of the first of many such thuds of terror which intruded upon our lives with such horrendous consequences, for many years to come.

The deaths and casualties in the Abercorn explosion were fewer than in many later atrocities, but because the Abercorn was one of the first, the shock was immense.

The *Belfast Telegraph* ran a page one picture of an injured woman being helped by rescue workers, and the paper caught the public mood by stating "This newspaper, like others, can no longer find headlines adequate enough to convey the misery. Nothing that is said, nothing that is written, seems shocking enough. And the words of condemnation have all been heard before."

The situation in Northern Ireland was virtually out of control, and it was no surprise that less than three weeks after the Abercorn explosion, the British government suspended the Stormont administration and introduced direct rule from London.

This was another major turning point in the downward spiral of violence and political deadlock. At the request of Charles Wintour, the editor of the *London Evening Standard*, I quickly wrote a major feature for his newspaper which was headlined "Requiem to Ulster". I stated "The passing of Stormont, temporarily or otherwise, marks the failure of a system and a way of life… in the meantime we face dark, dangerous and difficult days." Sadly this was to prove all too true.

Ironically on the same evening that direct rule came into force I was interviewing at length William Craig, the former Minister of Home Affairs, who was a fierce opponent of the civil rights movement and whose steadfast opposition to Captain Terence O'Neill had helped to bring him down. Before I went to Craig's home I recalled a comment which an English MP had made to me about him. He said "Years ago, he was a young, rather progressive figure. Now he seems to have shrunk within himself. The man is a long way behind his eyes. It's like talking to a mask."

As I talked to Craig in his elegantly furnished home in south Belfast his telephone in the hall kept ringing. This was distracting, and I wondered why on earth he did not answer it. Eventually he left the room, lifted the phone and stayed on the line for a long time.

I thought that this was bad manners but I was in no position to rebuke such a powerful political figure, particularly as I was depending on him for my extended interview. Eventually he returned to the room, apologised for the delay and said "I've just been speaking to a man who rings me up every night and threatens to kill me. Now where were we in our interview...?"

This struck me as odd behaviour, but then Bill Craig, though charming and polite, was an odd man – or perhaps no more or less odd than many of the political figures during that period in the history of Northern Ireland. We finished our interview after midnight, and I ended my extensive profile for the paper with these words "I remembered the unionist who had described Bill Craig to me as 'the strong man of Ulster.' I thought about Samson as I drove home. He was a strong man too."

Craig never regained his pre-eminence in Northern Ireland politics, and he died in 2011 after a long and debilitating illness. The *Belfast Telegraph's* obituary, summed him up fairly: "Despite his charm, his lack of diplomacy at key moments in Northern Ireland's history helped to stoke up political extremism."

Another strong politician from those days was Brian Faulkner, who eventually became leader of the Unionist Party and Prime Minister of Northern Ireland. I only met him once, by arrangement, at his home in County Down. The trouble was that he had forgotten about our appointment.

When I arrived at his large house he was clearly preparing to leave for another meeting, but as we talked I could see his brain whirring. He was deciding whether to pack me off politely, or to take the opportunity of giving an extended interview which would be prominently displayed in the *Belfast Telegraph*.

He decided quickly on the latter course of action. Although I did not approve of his hard-line unionism, I found him to be charismatic and persuasive. He said "I came in the hard way, standing on street corners, on top of lorries, putting my case, and that of the Unionist Party." The tragedy about Faulkner was that the Unionist Party stupidly left it too late to offer him the leadership of the Unionist Party, and preferred instead the much less able figures from the 'big house' – Terence O'Neill and James Chichester-Clark.

If Faulkner had succeeded to the leadership several years earlier he might just have turned the Unionist Party around far enough to create an effective power-sharing government with politicians from the Roman Catholic minority, and this which might have helped to mitigate some of the worst of the Troubles.

O'Neill had undoubtedly shown courage in trying to build bridges with his political opponents several years earlier, but his diffident manner won him little support. He talked like someone from a different political planet, and referred to Londonderry/Derry as "London-dree." This was a sure sign that he was out of touch with the grass roots on both sides. He was an amateur compared to his brash and highly-focused political rival Ian Paisley, and even in his own ranks he lacked the common touch. I only interviewed him once, in his home at Ahoghill. It was an autumn evening and when I walked across the white carpet of his living room, he carefully bent down and picked up the stray leaves that had fallen off my shoes. It was a harmless gesture on his part, but somehow he immediately made me feel at ill at ease.

Nevertheless, Terence O'Neill deserves credit for his vision in trying to head off the storm. If more people had heeded him sooner, there would have been less bloodshed and misery in Northern Ireland.

One particularly exotic Ulster-based politician in that broad period of Northern Ireland's history was Enoch Powell, who was the Unionist MP at Westminster for South Down. Powell was too clever by far to be part of the unionist establishment, but he needed a Westminster seat after parting company with the Conservative Party, and South Down came to his rescue.

Some years earlier he had been sacked from the Shadow Cabinet by Edward Heath after his controversial "Rivers of Blood" speech on immigration. He had been a big beast in the Westminster jungle, and even though he worked hard to counter the accusation that he was a 'carpetbagger' in South Down, I was aware that politically he had seen better days.

I interviewed him one morning in a small room in the House of Commons at Westminster. As he approached me he had a hammer in one hand, and his shoe in the other. He said "Don't worry I am not going to hammer you because you are a journalist. I am going to hammer down a nail in my shoe."

Powell was not an easy man to interview, as I soon found out. I asked him "Is it true that whenever Edward Heath lost the General Election, you sang a 'Te Deum' while you were shaving?" (A 'Te Deum' was an early Christian hymn of praise.)

Powell paused, his eyes narrowed like a cat that was stalking a mouse and then replied "What an interesting way you put your question. When you said 'whenever' did you mean 'every time Heath lost the election?' or was that merely an Ulster use of the word 'when'?" I thought to myself "Powell is trying to intimidate me already".

However, I persevered, and I ended up with a good interview with this difficult yet courteous man. I still recall his final reply when I asked him about his guiding principle in life. He said "My guiding principle is to get through each day, but also 'so to pass through things temporal, that finally we lose not the thing eternal.' That's religious terminology, and I mean it in a religious sense."

Enoch Powell was an intellectual giant among political pygmies in Northern Ireland, but like so many clever men he also ended up by out-smarting himself and having to settle for a political career that was less distinguished than it might have been.

Most of the Unionist politicians were helpful and friendly enough, but they were slightly buttoned-up compared to the nationalists who were more approachable. Gerry Fitt of the SDLP was a clever and funny grass-roots politician, who had served on Atlantic convoys to Russia in merchant ships during the Second World War. He had educated himself about law and politics, and later he had an important political career at Stormont and Westminster, as he attempted with others to bring order out of the political chaos in Northern Ireland.

However I remember him most fondly for his great sense of humour, and I recall him telling hilarious stories about his adventures abroad, as he sat in his terraced house on the Antrim Road in Belfast.

Sadly he had to leave his Belfast home and live in London after he was forced out by republican thugs. Gerry was not a superstitious man, nor was he religious in the ordinary way, but he said to me once "I don't go to church but when I enter a plane I say a wee prayer. Its like backing a horse both ways!"

When he was appointed as Deputy Chief Executive of the 1974 power-sharing Northern Ireland Executive, he strode up the long terrace of steps to the Stormont building, which was the seat of government. He was carrying a bright new leather case, the first time that anyone in the media had seen him do so. When he finally succumbed to reporters' question to look inside, they found only a tin of Andrews' Liver Salts!

Gerry had a notoriously bad stomach, and on one occasion when he collapsed in the Stormont chamber he was immediately rushed to hospital. Gerry later told with relish how one of the ambulance men recognised him and said "Gerry, you are my MP and I have a wee case I want you to fight for me." Gerry said "I was bleeding to death and I was in no condition to fight my own case, never mind his!"

Another remarkable nationalist politician was Paddy Devlin, who for a brief period was Minister of Health and Social Services in the short-lived Northern Ireland Executive. Paddy had been a member of the old IRA in his youth and a champion boxer, but his politics had moved to the centre-left and he was a keen supporter of power-sharing.

I knew Paddy well, but when I went up to his home in West Belfast for his first major interview I said "Good morning Minister". He looked at me in astonishment and said "For f—ck's sake call me Paddy!"

His two police minders roared with laughter. When they were driving us past the old unemployment benefits office in Belfast, which was known colloquially as 'the Buroo' I tried to give Paddy a cue for a good quote by saying "Many a time you fought people's cases in there, as a councillor, but now you're the Minister."

I was hoping that he would say something like "Indeed, times are changing for the better." However his reply was direct, and unprintable. He said "You are too f—king right!" More laughter all round.

When we arrived at his Stormont office, he beckoned me over to his big Ministerial desk. He reached down slowly, opened a drawer, and solemnly pulled out a large pistol. He said "That's my protection." Then he took a brown envelope from his desk and polished his big brown boots, before – as a good Labour man – striding in to the canteen to join the queue of other workers in his department.

On another occasion I met Paddy in Donegal, where I was playing in a very low-key golf tournament with several friends from the North. Paddy was on holiday in Donegal, and suddenly he emerged from behind a bunker, with his two Irish police minders in blue raincoats.

He joined me on the fairway, and as we went around the course, he kept saying to me "Great shot". Eventually I said "Paddy, I'm playing rubbish!" I did not know until then that he had sight problems, which were even worse than mine on the golf course.

However there was a bonus for me. As we walked, Paddy kept giving me all the latest inside information about developments at Stormont. I was by no means the best golfer that day, but I was one of the best informed journalists in Ireland, north or south.

I was fond of Paddy. He cultivated a rough, tough exterior, but he was a kind and sensitive man who really had the best interests of all the people at heart.

John Hume in his heyday was a towering political figure, and ever-friendly and helpful wherever I met him – in his native Derry or Belfast or somewhere in Europe. One evening I was returning to Belfast and I met him in the luggage queue at Aldergrove airport.

We had a fascinating chat, and as we walked together from the baggage carousel, he was struggling with a brown paper parcel. It was wrapped with string, which was cutting his fingers. He said "I'm bringing back some wine from Brussels but this string is killing me!" He left me with a cheery wave as he went to this car, with his raincoat over one arm.

I said to myself "There's one of the most important politicians in Europe and he's lugging home a case of wine whereas some of his European colleagues are travelling back in limousines." John was always a man of the people, and he carried his fame much more lightly than his wine.

Oliver Napier, another leading Catholic politician, was a founder member and a long-time leader of the cross-community Alliance Party. He was also a good friend, and as a solicitor he helped me with one or two legal problems. We always stayed close, and in his later years of ill-health we met together regularly for lunch in Belfast.

I saw him in hospital during his last illness, and luckily we had the whole of visiting time together. Though he was frail, his mind was sharp, and he entertained me with a long discourse on the inside story of working with Edward Heath and other politicians in drawing up the Sunningdale Agreement. It was like being involved in a political master class. Sadly, Oliver died only a few days later, and I still miss his company.

The politics of Northern Ireland could be tough and brutal, and they took a toll on many of the leading figures who were continually embroiled in controversy.

Not surprisingly, this controversy was part of the daily life of journalists who covered politics during the Troubles. The *Belfast Telegraph* continued with its policy of bridge-building despite strong opposition from hard-line unionists, and even from some quarters within the *Telegraph* building itself in Royal Avenue.

The media was accused by many people of stirring up the violence, and there were those who thought that "Ulster is a lovely wee Province and there is no need to report all this bad news." People said to me frequently "You journalists never report the truth." My stock reply was "You tell me your truth, and I will tell you mine."

The terrible events of 1972 continued, and on 21 July nine people died and 130 others were injured – some very badly – in a series of more than twenty bombs which were detonated all over Belfast by the Provisional IRA. The Provisionals claimed that they had given warnings but these were totally inadequate to prevent widespread carnage, panic and destruction. As the dull thuds of terror reverberated across the city, I left the *Belfast Telegraph* early and drove home with my colleague John Wallace, the paper's Political Correspondent.

We watched the news reports on television, which showed rescue workers shovelling bits of bodies in plastic bags. My wife was in tears when she saw the pictures, but I was in a professional mode and was busy soaking up all the details of the death and destruction.

It was only afterwards that the utter horror of what happened sank in to my consciousness. Nine innocent people had died, and many others had been injured in a savage attack by the Provisional IRA which had shown no regard for human life. It was one of the worst atrocities of the Troubles, and proved that Republicans could be every bit as brutal – if not more so – than all the others involved in the unending conflict.

The year 1972 proved to the worst of the Troubles, and of the 470 people who died there were 322 civilians. In the same year there were 4876 injuries, including 3813 to civilians.[1]

It was bad enough to have to report such awful statistics but even worse to live in a society where your fellow citizens could do such dreadful things to one another. Throughout the Troubles I experienced a deep internal struggle between my professional duties as a journalist and my personal feelings as a human being living full-time in the community.

As the violence continued, the politicians were unable to reach agreement on a stable power-sharing administration. After a cross-party conference with the Prime Minister Edward Heath at Sunningdale late in 1973, a new power-sharing Northern Ireland Executive was formed early in 1974.

Tragically this was to be short lived because Unionists could not accept the proposal for a Council of Ireland, which would involve limited input from the Dublin Government. The Unionists would discover bitterly that they would have to accept much greater Dublin involvement in their affairs later on.

The Northern Ireland Executive was brought down by a prolonged power strike in May 1974, which was organised by the Ulster Workers Council, backed by Loyalist paramilitary groups. Professionally this was another big story to cover, but personally it was deeply unsettling. The province was without power for long periods, but in our own home we were more fortunate than others because we had a small Aga cooker, on which we could heat food and water, and help to supply the needs of some of our neighbours.

My real worry, however, was about the future of Northern Ireland. It was frightening enough to have to run the gauntlet of car bombs and 'no warning' explosions in and around Belfast as part of my daily job, but the UWC strike was threatening the rule of law in a way which meant that no-one was safe. The future for me and my family, and for thousands of others, seemed bleak because there was the continued prospect of violent upheaval, but without any political settlement on the horizon.

---

[1] Sydney Elliott and WD Flackes, *Northern Ireland: A Political Directory 1968–1999*, Blackstaff Press, 1999, pp681–84

Towards the end of the strike I had planned a holiday break in Donegal with my family. On the way to the border beyond Derry we passed garages where petrol was being rationed, and it was a relief to be getting away from it all – even for a short period. As ever, the situation was not without its black humour. On a BBC Radio interview the President of the Ulster Farmer's Union was asked if the agricultural industry was facing great difficulties because of the power cuts. He replied "It's not just facing difficulties, hi. It's lying on the flat o it's beck!" You could always trust an Ulster farmer to get to the point.

After my short break in Donegal, which gave me much food for thought, I began to fear more and more for the future of our two children growing up in such a troubled province. One Saturday morning Roy Lilley and I talked over the situation after our weekly game of golf at the beautiful course at Massereene, near Antrim.

We knew many of the inside stories about the political and security situation at the time. After a long, objective, and detailed analysis, we regretfully concluded that there was a strong likelihood that Northern Ireland would slide into total civil war, or something very near to it.

It seemed to me that I should do something about this soon, for the sake of my family. I therefore decided to use my summer holidays to go to Canada and try to find a job as a journalist, though for obvious reasons I could not tell my editor about this. Canada seemed attractive as a country of opportunity for a young family, and I always had a hankering to live there for a while – possibly because I might have done so anyway if Hilary had not come back to Northern Ireland after the sudden death of her father in 1968.

So in July 1974 I travelled to Calgary, Edmonton and Victoria in Vancouver Island to look for a job. It was a lonely journey because I knew that I would be giving up a great deal professionally if I left Northern Ireland, and it would take me quite some time to pick up the nuances of Canadian politics. It would also take me even longer to make a name for myself in a foreign environment where nobody had ever heard of me.

I met senior journalists on the main papers of all three centres, but with respect to them, I soon realised how provincial Canadian journalism was, compared to the red-hot story that was the daily staple of journalism in Northern Ireland. That was probably one of the main reasons why I eventually decided not to settle in Canada, apart from the fact that I would have to give up my job in Belfast, which I liked, and go over there on six months' probation.

I also realised that journalism did not have quite the same standing in the provinces of Canada. In Calgary I had a beer with several journalists from *The Herald*. One of them said excitedly "I've managed to get an interview with a brain surgeon." This was regarded as a major scoop, but I said to myself "Several of my friends in Northern Ireland *are* brain surgeons!"

In Edmonton I met my old school friend John Brown who was then Chief Sub-editor of *The Journal* and he told me how devastatingly cold it could be there all winter, with the ice cracking the trees as he made his way to work each morning at 6 am. I did not fancy that.

I also went to Victoria Island which was a favourite place of retirement for older Canadians escaping from the freezing winters of the mid-West. The island was much bigger than I had anticipated, and the capital Victoria had its pseudo-English attractions, but on a wet day it reminded me of Donaghadee and the County Down coast during a miserable Ulster summer.

Though my mind was in turmoil about whether to stay in Canada or not, the traveller in me took over and I enjoyed seeing all these new places. In Calgary I visited the famous Stampede with my friend Lesley Trueman and her husband Keith who had settled there.

I described the Calgary Stampede later as "a kind of cowboy and Indian Twelfth of July, without the politics. They even had a World Chicken-Dance championship. This is an Indian version of the World Pipe Band Championship – if few enough people in the world do it, you can always claim universal status."

During my visit to Canada I depended on the warm hospitality of friends and relations from back home. In Vancouver, I stayed with Leonora, the sister of my Bessbrook friend Morris Brown, and her family. In Victoria Island I stayed with June and Steve Wynne, whom I knew from their Belfast days, and I also met Peter McMullen, the former Rugby Correspondent of the *Belfast Telegraph* who had emigrated to Canada.

In Victoria I had lunch with Hugh Love, the brother of the BBC's well-known broadcaster Walter Love in Belfast. Hugh was a leader-writer in a newspaper in Victoria, and as he talked about the subjects he covered, I realised that my work in Belfast – and that of my colleagues as well – was in a different league of journalism as we covered a virtual civil war.

However I was grateful for all the help which my friends had given me, and I was not short of advice. As I boarded the plane from Vancouver to Belfast, I was looking forward to meeting my family and friends, but I was apprehensive about leaving a prosperous and settled country like Canada, and returning to the danger and uncertainty of a Northern Ireland that was tearing itself apart.

However, after much heart-searching, for all kinds of personal and professional reasons, and after talking it over with my wife Hilary, we decided to stay in Northern Ireland. When I entered the leader-writers' room on my first day back at the *Belfast Telegraph*, the atmosphere in the city was grim. There had been more explosions in Belfast during my absence, and the windows of several buildings nearby in Royal Avenue had been blown out. Belfast seemed even more wounded and broken than when I had left it, compared to the places I had seen in Canada where they were building up their cities and there were tall construction cranes everywhere.

In the *Belfast Telegraph* my colleague Barry White – who always seemed to type while he talked – said to me laconically "Oh, I see you you're back. Don't you realise that Northern Ireland is going down the drain?" I nodded in dumb agreement, but Barry then said "The good news, of course, is that this place is more interesting for a journalist than Canada." He was right.

Belfast was indeed grim, dangerous and depressing but for me it was the only story in town. I knew that, as a journalist, I had made the correct decision to come back home.

CHAPTER ELEVEN

Sunshine and Shadows

FOLLOWING MY RETURN from Canada in the summer of 1974, I settled down once again to the ordinary and yet extraordinary pattern of life in Northern Ireland during the ongoing Troubles.

Life was ordinary in the sense that children had to be taken to and collected from school, bills had to be paid, people went to and from their place of work, and tried to get on with life as normally as possible.

However the Province was extraordinary because there were armed soldiers and police everywhere, security barriers, peace walls, road blocks and the blood-drip of killings and maimings caused by one or other of the protagonists in the dispute.

Northern Ireland was truly a place apart, which few outsiders understood and which regularly perpelexed even the most hardened of insiders. The isolation of the Province from the rest of the United Kingdom was underlined by the extraordinary announcement in November from the British Ministry of Defence that the names of soldiers killed in the conflict in Northern Ireland would not be added to war memorials because Northern Ireland was not regarded as a war zone.

The Provisonal IRA had no illusions about this, and it carried the war closer to the heartland of Britain by exploding two bombs in the centre of Birmingham on 21 November 1974. They killed twenty-one people and injured more than 160 others in one of the worst acts of carnage in the Troubles.

The British public had been accustomed to the daily litany of deaths and injuries in Northern Ireland, and there had been deadly Irish terrorist attacks in the United Kingdom, including the deaths of seven people after an Official IRA car bomb attack on Aldershot military barracks on

22 February 1972. However, the Birmingham bombs brought a different dimension to terrorist attacks in the United Kingdom.

The first that I heard of the Birmingham bombs was on the morning afterwards when Edmund Curran, my senior colleague in the *Belfast Telegraph*, rang me early in my hotel in London where I had been working on another assignment. It was obvious that I needed to get to Birmingham to report on the aftermath of the Birmingham bombs for the next day's paper.

I reached there early on the Friday afternoon. Birmingham was a city I did not know, and I had no contacts there. So I had to start from scratch and file a report for an early deadline.

The obvious first move, as in any strange city, was to find a friendly taxi-man who would take me to the area where the bombs had exploded in two pubs called The Mulberry Bush and The Tavern in the Town.

When he heard my accent, he gave me exactly the same advice that the doctor's wife in Derry had given to the young Glasgow reporter during the days after the Bloody Sunday killings. The Birmingham taxi driver who was called Gregory Caulwell told me "With your accent, I would not go out alone in Birmingham tonight." A helpful reporter from the *Birmingham Post* said to me "This is not the best place in the world to be Irish at the moment."

Because I was working on my own, with a tight deadline to meet, I had to make the best of the time at my disposal. I was also aware that, for the first time, I was reporting to a Northern Ireland readership about a major terrorist atrocity in England. Just under two years previously I had reported on the funerals of thirteen civilians shot dead by paratroopers in Derry, which seemed at the time to be unsurpassable in scale. Now I was conscious of reporting on an even bigger tragedy where twenty-one civilians had been murdered in Birmingham as a result of terrorist bombs.

Despite my tight deadline in Birmingham I managed to talk to a wide cross section of people. A hospital official told me "The IRA in their vicious way have tried to achieve their ends in Ulster. We in Britain reacted academically... but it was so remote."

Such violence was no longer 'academic' in the heart of Birmingham. I wrote in my report as an Ulsterman in Birmingham that night "You have heard it all before, you have smelt the sulphur in the air, you have felt the lurch down, down in the pit of your stomach, you may even have shed the tears, but you cannot tell the people of Birmingham tonight that you understand. They do not want the Ulsterman's understanding or sympathy.

"The reality of Birmingham tonight is that of two silent, shattered pubs in the centre of a grim and deserted site, and they hold unthinking hatred. Few Irish eyes will smile tonight, or for many nights to come."

I was anxious to research my story accurately and to send it to my editor as quickly as possible. It was only after my report had been filed and the adrenalin had stopped flowing that I thought about the horror of it all in human terms. More people dead, more injured, this time on the other side of the Irish Sea, and for what purpose?

The next morning I had breakfast in a leading Birmingham hotel, and the two tables next to me were filled with numerous reporters and photographers from the *Daily Mirror* and the *Daily Mail* who were making their presence felt. As I dined alone I wondered how my article for the *Belfast Telegraph* would compare to the vast output of these two national newspapers with much more resources and staff than we had to cover the story.

It took several months for me to find out, but I was surprised and pleased to discover that I was named runner-up as Reporter of the Year in the 1974 British National Press Awards, partly for my coverage from Birmingham. It was a great pity, however, that the subject matter had been so sombre and shocking.

The Birmingham bombings also created great controversy when six men jailed for the crimes had their sentences quashed, after a long campaign to prove their innocence. The campaigners included the men's families as well as politicians, clergy, lawyers and journalists on both sides of the Irish Sea. The 'Birmingham Six' were freed at the Old Bailey in March 1991, nearly seventeen years after the bombings, and the quashing of their convictions raised fundamental and very serious questions about the way in which the local police force and the British legal system had dealt with the whole issue.

All of this was played out for years after the bombings, but on that night in Birmingham I was conscious – as I had been when covering the funeral of the thirteen people shot dead on Bloody Sunday – that I was reporting on a major human tragedy,

Back home, the violence and political deadlock continued, the litany of misery seemed unending, and yet there was the continuing paradox that life in Northern Ireland was continuing as normal, or as near normal as possible in an overall abnormal situation.

Accordingly I continued to report on many non-violence and non-political stories inside and outside Northern Ireland. The *Belfast Telegraph*, which was strict on expenses, rarely paid for overseas trips, but this did not preventing me from writing during my visits abroad which were financed by other organisations, or from my own pocket.

One of my most memorable assignments was in New York where I reported on the real 'Kojak' and not the Telly Savalas portrayal of a fictional policeman in an popular television series with the same name.

I met the real Kojak in the city's notorious 9th precinct which was full of violence, drug-dealing and prostitution. The policeman in charge was Inspector Robert Houlihan, a nattily dressed and urbane senior officer who told me "Sure, we get on with the Kojak team filming here, but television police shows tend to be sensational."

Nevertheless the statistics of crime in Inspector Houlihan's 'patch' was impressive. In 1974 there were 2019 robberies, 770 knifings, shootings and other assaults, 138 reported rapes and forty-one murders – and all in an area less than a mile square.

I thanked Houlihan for his courtesy to me and accepted his offer of a ride in a police car with two of his officers. We were quickly called to the scene of a suspected break-in, and I later reported the incident in these words: "Officer Tellone went in first, easing his gun from his holster. Leidy was second, his gun now at the ready. McCreary was third, armed with a notebook and pencil." The call-out turned out to be a false alarm, but I felt that I was taking risks that I could well do without, particularly as there were many similar risks back home.

It was time to go. On the way to the underground station, the two New York cops showed me the Bowery bums and the street-walkers. A beautifully shaped woman with red hair walked near the car. "That's quite a girl", I said conversationally to one of my companions. "Yeah" he replied "She's gorgeous, but she's a fella. She has had special treatment to create her big 'boobs'. This is police work, New York style!"

§

In those days there were much fewer 'celebrity' stories than today, when people actively court publicity, often with little to commend them. However I discovered back in the Seventies that 'real' celebrities were often willing to talk if you had a thick enough skin to ring them, or their agents, directly, and to ask for an interview.

One morning I read in the *Daily Mail* that the author Frederick Forsyth was staying with his family in a Dublin hotel. Having just written his thriller called *The Day of the Jackal* he was at the height of his fame, and I decided to ring him. His wife was from Northern Ireland, and I reckon that he might have heard of the *Belfast Telegraph*.

My request for an interview was granted and I travelled down to Dublin to interview Forsyth at length. He was charming and full of anecdotes about his writing, and it made a great interview which was a scoop for the *Belfast Telegraph* at the height of the Troubles.

Around the same period I discovered that the actress Sylvia Kristel was filming in the Isle of Man. She was a beautiful young woman who had been making her name in the Emmanuelle movies, which were the sensational 'skin-flicks' of their time.

Her Isle of Man filming was on a more serious artistic subject, which is probably why she was willing to attract some different publicity about her career. I interviewed her in her hotel in Douglas at the end of a long day of filming at an outside location. She was tired, and when she came into her apartment bedroom she looked decidedly unglamourous in her thick black tights and a plain grey sheath dress.

After our interview she invited me to dine with her and her companion Ian McShane, the actor, and the two of us went downstairs to the dining room while she changed for dinner. We chatted mainly about football while we waited for Sylvia to make her entrance.

Eventually she wafted in to the dining room, with a swish of great beauty. She was wearing a gorgeous dress and a large white hat. She turned every head in the room. This was star quality, and I basked in the reflected glory as she sat down at our table. It seemed somehow sad that such a stunning young woman was famous only for her semi-pornographic 'skin-flicks'.

She had a turbulent personal life and had been a heavy smoker, and also used cocaine. She died in 2012 at the age of sixty.

Another young woman whose life was ruined by literally too much exposure was Maria Schneider who starred with Marlon Brando in 'Last Tango in Paris'. This sexually explicit movie was banned in parts of Britain, though the Corporation allowed it to be shown in Belfast.

I wrote a full page review for the *Belfast Telegraph* in the lyrical language of a young 'avant-garde film critic', or so I thought! However my down-to-earth editor Roy Lilley made it plain that he thought that my copy was chiefly artistic 'guff'.

I wrote "This is a beautiful, haunting, tragic film about loneliness, lack of communication and emptiness… in the end the loneliness of Brando becomes the loneliness of every man who faces death. In musical terms it reminded me strikingly of Tchaikovsky's Sixth Symphony, with its passages of light, brilliance and gaity, but its inevitable tragic end."

Later on Maria Schneider said that she had felt "violated and exploited" by the film, from which her career never really recovered. She died from cancer in 2011, aged fifty-eight.

Despite the high-flown prose of my film review, my editor thought that 'Last Tango' was nothing but pornographic rubbish but, to his credit, he did not change a word of my report. However it is worth noting now, with the passage of time, that I was able to range so widely with my writing for the *Telegraph*, yet all the while grounded in the reality of the violence that was waxing and waning like a deadly tide all across Northern Ireland and well beyond it.

In 1975 my career in the *Belfast Telegraph* took another upward turn when the editor gave me a new Wednesday slot in which I could write whatever I liked, within the laws of libel. This was after ten years of writing a weekly column about television. Though I knew that I would miss my television column, which had built a wide readership on a subject about which everyone was an 'expert', I relished the opportunity for a new challenge.

I was also aware that throughout that period the *Telegraph* did not pay for my television rental or licence which were expensive for a relatively impecunious journalist in those days. This was because one of the Managing Directors had made the odd decision that if he had to provide the television critic with a set, he would also have to provide a car for his motoring correspondent!

In my final television column on 12 June 1975 I wrote "The end of an affair is often sad and sentimental. The end of my affair with a mistress as lively, infuriating and unpredictable as television is sentimental. You outgrow the subject of your affections, but the withdrawal symptoms remain.

"Television criticism is a lonely occupation. Everyone is a television critic, to a degree, but the writer who is paid professionally to give an opinion, is obliged to deliver what is on his mind. But the critic who has no strong opinions either way on most programmes is failing to give the reader a firm marker by which he can judge his or her own opinion. It is better to be read than dead."

I ended my final column by answering the most frequent question I had been asked by readers "How much television do you watch? Always I say 'As much as I can.' To turn that into 500 television columns is a trade secret that I will pass on to my successor. Meantime, thanks for all the letters. I really have enjoyed my ten-year affair with television."

The column was taken over by my colleague Keith Baker who had often deputised for me on my holidays, and who later went on to become a senior executive with the BBC in Northern Ireland.

I set the tone of my new Wednesday column in June 1975 by writing "I like chic ladies with long legs, people who keep to their principles, poetry, the Antrim Coast on a clear day, the Ulsterman's wicked but superb sense of humour... the west of Ireland, optimists, the west of Canada, people who care, good writing, cosy firesides, an evening with Tchaikovsky, a well-delivered speech, a smile on a wet Monday, sinking a long putt, children and hot summer days with the family among the roses."

My Wednesday column continued for another nine years, and it gave me great satisfaction and made me many friends. It is one of the great privileges of journalism to be given a weekly column to air your views, and I have been fortunate to write columns of different kinds for nearly fifty years. William Rees-Mogg, a former editor of *The Times* once claimed that it is the duty of a columnist to be entertaining but not necessarily to be accurate all the time. I disagree with his claim about accuracy, but the first duty of any columnist writing about any subject is to be eminently readable – a quality that is often lacking nowadays.

Writing about everyday events with a light and often serious touch, and interviewing celebrities or reviewing topical movies, was always a therapy for me in those troubled times, but there was no escape from the constant violence.

Early in 1976 I had to report on one of the worst atrocities of the Troubles which took place near my home village of Bessbrook. This engulfed me in personal sorrow and a sadness and nostalgia for the peaceful days of my boyhood. It was hard for me to believe that such savagery could take place in a South Armagh setting which I had known so well.

On 5 January 1976, twelve mill workers were ambushed at Kingsmills in their van when they were returning home from Glenanne. They were ordered to line up by their unknown assailants who asked which men were Catholics. When one said that he was Catholic, the attackers told him to run for safety, and then cold-bloodedly shot the rest, all Protestants. Ten died almost instantly, and one man, Alan Black, was left for dead. Fortunately he survived and was able to provide details of the horror which he and his former workmates had encountered.

The attack took place on the night after two young Catholic men John Martin Reavey and his brother Brian had been shot dead in their home at Whitecross, not far from Kingsmills. A third brother, Anthony, was also shot, and he died from his injuries nearly a month later. Three members of the O'Dowd family also died in an attack some fifteen miles away.

The Kingsmills massacre had the hallmarks of a ghastly retaliation for the murder of the Reaveys and the O'Dowds, and it caused widespread shock throughout Ireland. In an editorial the next day the *Irish Times* stated "The headless coachman is driving Northern Ireland full tilt down the road to hell."

The Unionist MP Harold McCusker said "I am extremely scared that my country is facing anarchy", and the Roman Catholic Primate Cardinal William Conway said that those who took a life for a life "were spitting in the face of Christ."

The Kingsmills massacre had taken place around 6 pm on a dank winter evening, and shortly afterwards I had a phone call from Roy Lilley who told me what had happened. He said "I want you to go down to Bessbrook tomorrow to file a report for the paper. I know that it will be hard for you to do this, but you are the best person on my staff to cover this story."

When I arrived in Bessbrook early the next morning, the first thing I noticed was the drooping Christmas tree in the village square in front of the house in Wakefield Terrace where I had grown up as a boy. I noted later in my newspaper report that "A communal death in a tiny village stuns everyone. The pervading feeling of death in Bessbrook is as real as the grey clouds scudding across the sky, as dank as the cold rain pattering down. Even the forlorn Christmas tree lurches to one side, as if recoiling from the community horror that surrounds it."

I had known personally some of the men who had died. They included my school mate Walter Chapman. He had shared the primitive resources of my boys' primary school, as well as the rigours of studying under the martinet head teacher Jemmy Darragh so long ago, and he had also worked with me as a temporary Christmas postman in and around Bessbrook.

I also had known another victim, Jimmy McWhirter. He was a quiet, obliging man who had driven the Bessbrook mill lorry for many years, and had ferried our troop of Boy Scouts to and from Belfast Harbour when they had gone for their annual camp to the Isle of Man.

My Aunt Jean was a near neighbour of the widowed Mrs McWhirter, and she said that I should attend the wake to show my respect for the family. I did so, and met Mrs McWhirter who remembered me clearly from my boyhood days. She was deeply shocked, and yet remarkably dignified in her sudden sorrow.

Later I wrote in my newspaper report "Every wake is the same. People try to make conversation, afraid of saying the wrong thing, or of not saying the right thing, or they try to avoid those awful gaps which we all know where the silence of eternity hangs heavy in the air.

"And the bereaved repeating their story again and again; the rest of us thinking about the empty chair, when the funeral is over, and the friends have gone. There was horror, too, mostly unspoken. What ran through those men's minds as they were lined up to be shot. 'Thank God, they weren't tortured', said one man. Small consolation."

Later on I talked to Danny Chapman, whom I had known in my boyhood partly because he exercised his greyhounds which passed our house in The Gardens, to which we had moved from Wakefield Terrace.

Danny was a man of few words but he told me graphically about having to identify his nephews Walter and Reggie Chapman.

He said "I cried before I went into the morgue. I expected the worst, and it was the worst. They pulled down the sheets, and there they were, lying, dead like dogs with their teeth showing. It was as awful as that. I saw mine lying dead like dogs, you can print that."

I later reported that "I leave Bessbrook, my home village, with a heavy heart but with a deeply questioning mind. Maybe after this massacre, or a thousand 'Bessbrooks', enough people will get the point. Meanwhile as these words on this page in time crumble to dust, and the body of my schoolmate Walter Chapman rots in his grave, the principle will still apply, namely that we will either learn to learn to live together or we will die together. Thus far, we're learning a lot about dying together."

Later that evening, after I had filed my copy I rang my editor Roy Lilley at home. I said "The Bessbrook funerals are taking place tomorrow. I want to be there, but I don't think that I would be able to write about them." He replied "I understand. By all means go to Bessbrook, but there's no need to write about it."

The funerals were as sad as I expected, and perhaps even more so, for an unusual reason. They were essentially private funerals for the bereaved families and friends, and for the people of Bessbrook and the surrounding areas because they had lost some of their own.

However it was also an intensely public occasion when leading politicians like the Reverend Dr Ian Paisley and people from other parties, as well as senior clergy, turned up to pay their respects, and there were television cameras everywhere.

In such a large crowd it was difficult to find a quiet space for private mediation, but in the midst of the melee outside Bessbrook Presbyterian Church, which I had known so well as a boy, I was joined by my mother Lena. She knew that I would be at the funerals, and she came to meet me outside the church.

"Isn't this awful?" she whispered "All those dead people, and poor Walter Chapman your chum from school." Then she told me something that shook me rigid, even on that terrible day. She said "Your father Norman is inside the church. He waited outside and pretended that he was an aide of Ian Paisley. When Paisley arrived he showed him to a seat at the front of the church, and then sat near him. That's typical of your father Norman."

It was typical indeed of Norman's outrageous opportunism, and his sheer brass neck. I listened to my mother in silence, but her eyes told me everything. On that day of all days I promised myself once and for all I would do all I could meet this absent man who had been so much part of my life. I resolved to do so, whatever the effort involved in meeting him, and whatever the emotional cost of doing so.

However, that would be a task for the future. In the meantime my career was pointing me in directions far beyond those I had anticipated as a newspaper journalist. I had already written and had published my first book. And on 16 March 1976 I spoke in Belfast Cathedral for the first time. This was during a Lenten service, with the theme "What sort of a society are we looking for?"

Prior to the service I had received a written death threat, possibly because of my well-known and forcefully expressed support for ecumenism. I showed the letter to a senior policeman who said "Don't worry about this. It's fan mail! If people really want to kill you, they won't tell you in advance."

Suitably relieved I entered the pulpit in Belfast Cathedral and spoke to an audience of people from all backgrounds – which, for a beginner like me, was a nerve-wracking experience.

I addressed the main theme "What sort of a society are we looking for?" and I said: "That question was asked by Terence O'Neill seven years ago, and what is our answer today? The answer is still all around us, in the 1,500 crosses, in our broken, battered buildings, in the cries of the bereaved, in the silence of suffering, in the faces of our children.

"On this day, the day of St Patrick when all the world thinks of Ireland, this community is known all over the world for its hatred, its passions, its coldness, its lack of mercy, its abiding death.

"We have a short fuse, and a long memory, we look forward, not back, to 1690 and 1916. We lack vision, we lack compassion, we lack statesmen, we lack politicians. We even lack ideas."

I went on to say "I look forward to a society where I can walk without fear in Royal Avenue, or East Belfast or the Bogside. I want a society where we will have politics and not a sectarian pantomime, where tomorrow is more important than today.

"I look forward to the day when we in Ulster will use our brains (and we have them) and not our brawn; where power will come from the pen and not the sword; from the ballot box and not the barrel of a gun. I look forward to the day when I can look into the eyes of my children and know that this is a fit place for a child to live."

However I ended my address with a warning; "The way ahead is full of danger. I see much more blood and tears. There is no simple way out. There are many false Messiahs, in clerical garb or otherwise, who offer their vision of Heaven, but forget to mention the Hell. Both sides want to win, but who in God's name is looking for a solution?

"Perhaps the main task of the people of goodwill is to survive, and to wait for the smoke to clear. If we get a new chance, and we may not, we must learn to communicate with one another, or perish."

The speech drained me, and later that night, in a mood of tiredness and near despair at the continuing violence I said to my wife Hilary "I wonder if my address today was worth the effort, was anyone really paying attention, will it do any good?"

She replied firmly "You must never think that. Your job is to write the words and deliver them. You may never know the effect they will have on other people."

She was right. Later on, the law of unexpected consequences reminded me that my words had not been wasted. Nine months later I was invited to the launch of a Corrymeela peace group in a very tough area outside Belfast. I said to one of the organisers "I must congratulate you in starting this group. Where did you get the idea from?"

She replied "I heard you speaking in Belfast Cathedral on St Patrick's Day, this year, and I also heard the Corrymeela leader the Reverend Ray Davey speaking later that day in Down Cathedral. You both inspired me to start up this new peace group."

Her words made me realise that I had been a man of little faith. Life often provides an inspiring and humbling experience, even when we cannot see a way forward. In the midst of all the violence in Northern Ireland in those days, there were always the seeds of hope for a better future, and I had met and worked with some remarkable peace-makers whom I will describe in the next chapter.

CHAPTER TWELVE

The Peace-Makers

THROUGHOUT THE EARLY years of the Troubles, there were seemingly endless reports on the violence and political deadlock. While the politicians could claim to have been doing their best to stop the mayhem, the efforts of ordinary people on the ground to make peace were usually lost in the small print of daily reporting.

I was particularly aware of some of the bridge-building efforts between people from both the main communities because I knew of the existence of the Corrymeela Community. Significantly, this had been established in the years before the Troubles started, and Corrymeela was the visionary outreach of the Reverend Ray Davey, and his supporters from a broad range of religious backgrounds.

Ray Davey was one of the most remarkable men I ever encountered. I first met him in 1959 at Queen's University, where he was the first Presbyterian chaplain, and we remained close friends until his death in 2012.

Ray Davey and his wife Kathleen were two people who exemplified the best of Christianity. They were generous of spirit, helpful, and convivial company, and although they were self-effacing and gentle, they had a great inner strength and conviction that helped them to overcome the challenges and obstacles which they faced, and also to inspire people of all faiths and of none.

Ray, the son of a Presbyterian minister in Dunmurry, was born in 1915 and educated at the Royal Belfast Academical Institution. He looked set to follow his father's footsteps and become a minister. After further education at Queen's University, Assembly's College and New

College Edinburgh, he came Assistant Minister at Bangor Presbyterian Church.

He was an excellent rugby player and was a member of the Ulster team which was unbeaten by the famous All Blacks team in their 1935 tour. Ray, then only twenty, was the Ulster full-back and he later told me that if he had managed to score points with his drop-kick to win the game near the end, he would have felt even then that his life's ambition had been already achieved.

However he was destined for greater things. Instead of becoming another conventional Presbyterian minister with his own church somewhere in Northern Ireland, he became a YMCA volunteer in 1940 and served in North Africa during the Second World War.

It was planned that his ordination as a minister would take place in Jerusalem, but he was captured in Tobruk, and he often recalled that grim experience with typical humour by repeating the words of the German officer who ended his freedom – "For you, my friend, ze war is over."

Ray was incarcerated in prison camps in Italy and Germany, where he learned the need for peaceful co-existence among large groups of his fellow prisoners where morale was low and boredom was often high.

Towards the end of the War he was in a prison near Dresden, which suffered disastrously from Allied bombing, and the experience affected him deeply.

Between 13–15 February 1945 British and US bomber aircraft dropped around 3,900 tons of high explosives on the city, and some 25,000 people, including civilian men, women and children, perished.

Ray Davey wrote graphically later on about his experiences in a powerful book titled *The War Diaries* which he had secretly compiled during his time in the prison camps. Even today it remains a fine example of reporting, worthy of any professional war correspondent.

The prison camp in which he was held was only 20km outside Dresden and he later wrote of his visit to the shattered city. "The atmosphere in Dresden brings one back to the reality and grimness of war. I felt strangely uncomfortable walking around the sorrows of this once-beautiful city.

"In some of the streets it was like climbing on the Giant's Causeway. Places that had been the hub of human activity and action are now still, and few people pass by. I don't think that one could find a habitable building in 10 square miles in the central area.

"I climbed round to the remains of the Domkirche, a month ago probably the most beautiful church in the city. Now it is but a mass of ugly masonry, with the statue of Martin Luther, legless, lying face down in the street, blown 10–15 yards from its pedestal."[1]

Even today when I read Ray's words I am taken aback by the picture of the destruction in Dresden in 1945, and I understand even more how his war experiences affected this gentle and sensitive man.

A few days after the war finished, Ray ended his book with the following words: "War in Europe is finished, all the horrors. Next step is reconstruction and planning, so that people will be able to live happier lives, free from want, fear, hate, suffering, destruction.

"Government plans, social security, housing, education. Will all this be enough? What is the answer? Change people's hearts. Things that make wars and unhappiness are not just Hitlers and Mussolinis, but are things in our own lives – greed, pride, dishonesty, lack of consideration. If we are to overcome these things, we must become different ourselves."[2]

Those words were written on 17 May 1945, but if Ray had only known it then, they could also be applied to his native province for the next half-century and more.

He told me later on that he had two choices. "I could have allowed my war experience to grind me down completely, or I could decide to make the best of it. I chose the latter course. After the war, the challenge of trying to do something about conflict stayed with me, especially in my own society which was so polarised."

This was the calibre of the man I met who was the Presbyterian chaplain at Queen's when I was only 19, and for as long as I knew Ray I was continually impressed by the depth of his faith, his practicality and his vision.

In my early days at Queen's, I sometimes visited the Presbyterian Chaplaincy where Ray and Kathleen held Sunday night meetings. I went to the meetings not because of my religion, but because there was

---

[1] Ray Davey, *The War Diaries: From Prisoner-of-War to Peacemaker*, Brehon Press, 2005, pp208–09
[2] Op cit, p22

little else to do in Belfast on a Sunday night in 1959. Besides, at that stage I fancied myself as a 'lapsed Presbyterian', but I suspect that the faith of my rural Presbyterian upbringing was still steeply embedded in me.

One Sunday night at the Queen's Presbyterian Chaplaincy I listened to the minister of Fisherwick, the Reverend Jack Withers, who was one of the best speakers of his generation. I was impressed by what he said and how he said it, but I noticed that after he had finished his address, he took out a packet of Gallagher's Green cigarettes and lit up. I was utterly shocked. I could not believe that a Presbyterian minister, of all people, could be so 'un-Christian' as to smoke in public, or in private. I now realise, with amusement, how conservative I was in those days.

During my time at Queen's I saw Ray Davey from time to time but I did not play an active role in the Presbyterian Chaplaincy, nor in the hard work of establishing Corrymeela.

On 30 October 1965 – some three years before the Troubles began – the Corrymeela Centre was opened in a refurbished former holiday fellowship building at Ballycastle. It was set high on a cliff, with magnificent views over Rathlin Island.

The aim was to make Corrymeela a Christian centre and an open village for "all people of goodwill who are willing to meet each other and to work together for the good of all; open to all sorts of new ventures and experiments in fellowship, study and worship; open to all sorts of people. This is part of our vision. We know that we are only at the beginning, and there is much to be done."

This visionary mandate was intended to be wide enough for people from all backgrounds in a divided province and beyond it, but it is difficult for the modern generation to comprehend fully just how revolutionary it was then. In 1965, Ulster's religious and political life maintained a cultural and social apartheid which was about to explode into decades of bitter conflict. The lack of determination and effort in previous years to build bridges between the two main communities would come back to haunt everyone.

Although I never became a member of the Corrymeela Community, I approved of its objectives, and I wrote about its work quite often because it was doing good things and I wanted people to know about it.

One of my first visits was to report for the *Belfast Telegraph* on a cross-community seminar where one of the guest speakers was the new Nationalist MP for Tyrone – none other than my former Queen's colleague Austin Currie. I was impressed that Austin had risen to prominence so quickly after graduating, but I was perhaps even more impressed by his new VW Beetle which I thought then was the height of earthly success!

Some ten years later I started writing my first book about Corrymeela. The idea came to me when I was driving to troubled Derry/Londonderry one morning on a reporting assignment. I had seen so much distress in that lovely city, and I had reported frequently on its many sorrows.

I was already writing a book about the victims of violence, but that project had stalled for reasons beyond my control – which I shall explain in the next chapter.

In the meantime, I felt it was right to devote my energies to a book about the work of people who were working for peace, although they were gaining little recognition or publicity for doing so.

I contacted Ray Davey and he immediately backed my idea. The first step was to get a publisher, and Ray contacted a Methodist minister the Reverend Wilbur Forker. He ran – among many other things – a small publishing company called Christian Journals Ltd, with post-box registrations in Belfast, Dublin and Ottawa.

Forker was no ordinary minister. He was an exotic character who had worked with the World Council of Churches in Geneva and, when I met him, he was an adviser to the American investment guru and millionaire Sir John Templeton.

Each year Sir John funded a richly-endowed Templeton Prize for the most significant advances in religion in the previous twelve months, and Forker was the administrator who helped to run it. The Templeton Prize was presented to the winner in London by the Duke of Edinburgh, so it was obvious that my new publisher had some highly impressive contacts.

Forker lived in a large house at the top of the Malone Road in Belfast, and he often boasted to me that his stamp collection was worth even more than his house. I had never met a man quite like him. He was different in every way from a typical Methodist minister, but I was grateful for his support.

The book was relatively short, though closely argued and tightly written, and I completed it inside a year. Ray and Kathleen Davey were most helpful in setting up interviews, and I recall some moving, and amusing, stories about the work of Corrymeela and its people.

I told the story of Johnny, from a hardline Protestant area, who went to Corrymeela for a week and became friendly with an American lady – but he did not know that she was a nun.

At the end of the visit his friend said "Johnny, you were very friendly with that wee nun." "You're wrong" said Johnny "She's not a nun. She's wearing the uniform of a district nurse." He could not accept that he had been talking to a nun, but the experience undoubtedly broadened his outlook. Another pensioner outlined the barrenness of the lost years when he said "If we had had places like Corrymeela fifty years ago, we would not have any of these troubles today."

There were also flashes of humour, like that of a young boy from a troubled area who had misbehaved at Corrymeela and had set fire to a hayfield. Ray Davey gave him a stern lecture and asked "How did you manage to do it?" The boy replied "I used matches, but it took nine of them to get the damn thing lit." Ray could scarcely hide a smile.

The main thrust of the book, titled *Corrymeela, the Search for Peace*, was to show that reconciliation was possible across the religious, social and community divides, and that small acorns might some day grow into tall oaks. The book also showed that reconciliation in the blood, sweat and guts of the Ulster conflict required well-intentioned people to have their feet firmly on the ground.

The book did well, and went into several editions. It was launched in Belfast in 1975 and shortly afterwards Wilbur Forker decided on an English launch. He chose St Bride's Church in Fleet Street, which was at that time near the centre of the British national newspaper industry.

As we met at Belfast airport en route to London for the press conference I asked Forker "Where are the books?" He was stingy about giving away books, and he had only a couple in his briefcase. Undaunted, however, he held the press conference with aplomb in St Bride's Church, and this led – among other things – to a glowing review of the book in *The Times* by their Religion Correspondent Clifford Longley. Only Forker would have had the nerve to hold a London press conference, with just a couple of books available.

Later that year Ray Davey and I went to New York for an American launch, which also went well. I recall Gloria Hunniford, who was then working for BBC Radio Ulster, ringing me early in New York for a 'live' interview on her radio programme in Belfast. Those were heady days indeed.

Ray and I did various radio programmes and presentations in and around New York. However the only time I saw him angry was when one of our contacts let us down by making a hash of one meeting at which Ray was due to speak. I discovered then the reality of righteous anger. Beneath Ray's gentle exterior there was a core of steel that had been fashioned by the rigours of war, and which others, who had not experienced such conflict, could not have understood.

The breakthrough in our New York visit came when Wilbur Forker sold the rights of the Corrymeela book to an American publisher. The negotiations took place when Forker and I lunched together with an editor from Hawthorn Books, in the exclusive Yale Club in New York. Forker was able to use the Club because of his close connection with John Templeton, a Yale graduate. It was an impressive setting in which to do business, and I was delighted to have a New York publisher.

The American edition of the book also did well, and it was reviewed favourably by a succession of newspapers across the States. One day I received a package from a newspaper in the mid-West, which included an impressively decorated parchment. The editor of the paper informed me that I had been made an Honorary Member of the 'Mark Twain Society'. I was not sure what that meant exactly, but I was honoured nevertheless.

Before we left America, Ray and I went to a celebratory dinner with my Uncle Bill, who took us to one of the best restaurants in New York, called Maxwell's Plum. Before the meal I ordered a 'Rusty Nail'. Ray asked me "Why on earth do you need a rusty nail?" However he soon realised that this was the name of a powerful cocktail, and not a small metal object, and he smiled at me knowingly, with a conspiratorial wink. Bill McCreary took it all in, and laughed across the table.

For the rest of Ray's life, every time we met together in company, he would look at me with that little smile hovering on his lips and he would say "Watch the rusty nails!" No-one else ever knew what we were talking about. It was always our little secret. I not only admired and respected Ray. I also loved him as a mentor and a friend, and I shall never forget him.

The work of the Corrymeela Community has continued to the present day, and it has made – and still makes – a significant contribution to the work of reconciliation across the divides. Although it has attracted several fine leaders and volunteers from different backgrounds, its formative thrust came from Ray Davey and his experience of the need for community togetherness in the midst of conflict. Without Ray there might not have been a Corrymeela.

In the last pages of his *War Diaries* he wrote, on May Day 1945, "I feel now that I need some touchstone to bind all my life into one again; some flame to ignite the whole fire of my life. I think that it will take a big job to do this. Much I would like to say if only I could articulate it and put it into an ordered whole, a philosophy of life, a credo."

Ray eventually found his credo, his philosophy and his 'big job' in Corrymeela, and in doing so he blessed and inspired many other people.

Though Ray Davey and his colleagues were pioneers in bridge-building, there were others who were also taking courageous steps to try to bring peace. I remember the Church leaders who secretly met leaders of the Provisional IRA at an hotel in Feakle, County Clare in December 1974.

The peace bid ultimately ended in failure, and there was an element of the 'Keystone Cops' involvement when the IRA men hurriedly left the hotel just before Irish Special Branch officers had entered it, apparently after a tip-off.

Afterwards, the Unionists severely criticised the churchmen, and not surprisingly the churches stressed that the clergy were acting on their own initiative. They were hung out to dry because church committees and assemblies are nervous about offending people, and too cumbersome for swift, decisive and brave initiatives.

I knew several of the senior clergy who had gone to Feakle, and I had worked with some of them in writing stories about bridge-building. They included the Church of Ireland Bishop Dr Arthur Butler, an independently minded man who had also raised the ire of the Unionist establishment by preaching a sermon in Belfast Cathedral at the Memorial Service to the late Lord Brookeborough, and suggesting that he had been less than perfect.

Canon Bill Arlow, another member of the Feakle delegation, suffered from heart trouble, but he had tremendous moral strength and courage in trying to build bridges. The Reverend Dr Eric Gallagher, whom I also knew well, was an erudite and clear-minded former Methodist President, and behind his sometimes formal exterior he was a kind and humorous man.

The Reverend Dr Jack Weir, who was also at Feakle, was the Clerk of the Presbyterian General Assembly and a former Moderator of the Church. He was intelligent and streetwise, which was a formidable combination. He also had a short fuse, but no-one underestimated his initiative and courage, and his broad, international outlook.

I once worked with Jack when I was the English-speaking rapporteur at a meeting in Crete of the European Council of Churches. This was held before the Berlin Wall came down, and many of the East European clerics at the Conference were aware that Big Brother from Moscow had his eye on them.

During a coffee break Jack Weir and I looked at several groups of Orthodox Archbishops and Bishops speaking to each other in huddles. Jack said to me "Those guys could teach even Ian Paisley a thing or two about politics."

The senior clerics who went to Feakle told few people about what they intended to do – partly for secrecy reasons and partly because they knew that official sanctions from their ruling bodies would be long-winded, doubtful and in the end too late.

By taking the initiative at Feakle, they showed that peace-making was not easy, but they also blazed a trail for later clergy who made significant contributions at different times to making and keeping the peace. They included Robin Eames, John Dunlop, Harold Good, Gerry Reynolds, Alex Reid and many, many others.

During the Seventies and Eighties I seemed destined to work with many bridge-builders, including those who had been complete strangers to me. One summer our family went for a holiday to the Burren in County Clare.

Our children were playing outside our holiday house, and they befriended a black Labrador puppy which was romping beside its owner. We exchanged polite greetings, and the dog's owner turned out to be Dr Brendan O'Regan, a visionary Irishman who helped to establish a cross-border and cross-community organisation called Co-Operation North, which later became known as Co-Operation Ireland.

Brendan, whom I came to like very much, was a leading entrepreneur, who as the former Chairman of the Shannon Free Airport Development Company, virtually invented the concept of an international duty-free airport.

He was also a former Chairman of the Irish Tourist Board, and he used his considerable range of contacts to establish his new peace organisation which became a force for good in Northern Ireland and the Irish Republic.

Later on he told me about the essence of his philosophy, when he talked to me for a book I was writing about the bridge-builders.[3]

He said "Peace-making is a very difficult task, and it requires the best possible abilities and organisation, and long term professional commitment. It is at least as difficult a job in a country as promoting industry or tourism, and in Ireland it is more important than either." I agreed with him wholeheartedly.

Brendan also had a hand in producing the first ever Irish coffee. He told me that one day he spotted a tray of duck that was being carried into the Shannon restaurant. He said to the chef Joseph Sheridan "This lacks eye appeal". The chef grabbed a handful of red currants which were being prepared for another dish, sprinkled them over the roast duck and said "Now its got eye appeal!"

A couple of days later, Sheridan set before Brendan what appeared to be the first Irish Coffee and asked him triumphantly "How's that for eye appeal?"

O'Regan told me later "People may say that others had mixed the same ingredients before, but I believe that Joseph Sheridan was the man who first gave it 'eye appeal,' with its distinctive white collar."

Brendan and I remained friends for many years until his death, and I did what I could to help to promote Co-Operation North. We did not meet often, because he lived in the south west of Ireland, but when we did he always reminded me of the article I had written after we first met in the Burren, which I described as a place "Where the silence is a bandage for healing the wounds of the world."

Another influential businessman who did much to build-bridges was Sir Anthony O'Reilly, who in the mid-Seventies was the President and Chief Executive of the Heinz Corporation. He was also a co-founder

[3] Alf McCreary, *Profiles of Hope*, Christian Journals Ltd, 1981

and Chairman of The Ireland Fund, which was set up in 1976 for the creation of the shamrock of "Peace, culture and charity in Ireland, North and South." Since then it has raised some US $350 millions to fund peace and reconciliation initiatives as well as cultural, educational and community development in many parts of Ireland.

O'Reilly's co-founder in 1976 was Dan Rooney, the prominent businessman who owned the Pittsburgh Steelers football team, and later became the US Ambassador to Ireland.

In his earlier life O'Reilly had made an international reputation as an outstanding rugby player who won his first cap for Ireland at 18, and went on to win twenty-eight more. He also had a distinguished record with the British Lions and the Barbarians.

However there was much more to the man than his sporting achievements. The first time I met him was when I interviewed him for an in-depth profile in the *Belfast Telegraph*. This was probably the first article of its kind on the man who was eventually to take over the paper.

I found O'Reilly to be a man of great charisma, and also a razor-sharp brain. He had a broad social vision even beyond his entrepreneurial interests, and he was deeply committed in helping to heal the wounds in his native land. He was also one of the most articulate and wittiest people I had ever met.

We developed a good working relationship, and later on I also profiled him for a weekly radio series which I was presenting for BBC Northern Ireland. I was deeply interested in his peace work, and he agreed to be interviewed for a book I was writing about the bridge-builders, some years after my Corrymeela book had been published.

One of the problems was in trying to pin down a time and place where I could interview this busy man. Then one day, at short notice, he invited me down to have dinner with him at his large house in County Kildare.

When he rang I had just finished recording a BBC programme, and I headed off straight for Kildare in my best Marks and Spencer brown denims. There was no time to change, so I hoped that I would not be too badly dressed for dinner.

I need not have worried, because I felt that I was anonymous among a large number of Heinz executives from the UK who had also been

155

invited to dinner. I noticed that the lady on my left was wearing a diamond bracelet, the real thing.

After dinner we all went into a larger room, and I wondered when I would get to interview O'Reilly. He kept disappearing with various executives, presumably for business huddles in another part of the building.

Around midnight someone put on a tape recording of the revealing interview I had done with him for the BBC, and the room went quiet as everyone listened intently. It was one way of letting all these people discover more about the inner man.

Around 12.30 am, when I had almost given up hope of interviewing O'Reilly, he invited me into an ante-room, with two glasses of fine white wine. I turned on my tape recorder and Tony O'Reilly talked for nearly an hour about helping to make peace in Ireland.

It was a riveting dissertation, and I remember it especially because O'Reilly was one of the only two people I have interviewed whose words translated almost exactly onto the page.

Let me explain. Most people unwittingly use two forms of language – one for speaking and another for writing, and they are not quite the same. In this respect Tony O'Reilly was exceptional. My interview with him was repeated almost verbatim in my book, which was later published by Marshall Pickering under the title *Tried By Fire*, with a foreword by the then Archbishop of Canterbury Dr Robert Runcie, a fine, courageous Christian whom I knew personally.

There was also an introduction by his Middle East envoy Terry Waite who later suffered a long and tortuous imprisonment in the Lebanon, where he was kept for long periods in solitary confinement. Ironically, Terry Waite, whom I also interviewed in depth, was the only other person I met who shared Tony O'Reilly's ability to talk in prose that was inherently literature.

Many people in those days thought privately that the peace-makers were well meaning but naïve, though they would not always say that to their faces. I put the point to Tony O'Reilly, and his reply was instructive.

He said "Cynicism is a cul-de-sac in which too many Irish people reside. To me you need the innocence of enthusiasm, you need the naïvete of knowing that it works elsewhere, and therefore it should be applied by people who have concern that they should bring a restful innocence to bear on the Irish question, because assuredly in Ireland the Irish have failed to solve it. Therefore it is legitimate for us to claim some authority, be it the authority of innocence and naïvete, to try to make a contribution towards a solution."

Tony O'Reilly and I stayed in touch for a number of years after we met during which time he, unexpectedly, invited me to the Gala Centenary Dinner of Ballymena Rugby Club, where he was one of the main speakers. When I arrived in 'black-tie' attire I could not find my name on the guest list, and I thought that there had been some mistake.

I spoke to Syd Millar, a famed Ballymena clubman and international Irish rugby player and British Lion who eventually became chairman of the International Rugby Board, from 2003–07. He said "Of course you are on the guest list – you are at the top table!" To my surprise, O'Reilly had placed me as a member of a row of British Lions players, including Willie John McBride, Cliff Morgan, and himself.

As a mere hockey player who had only managed to achieve interprovincial caps as a schoolboy and teenager, and British and Irish Universities caps later on, I kept my head down in such illustrious rugby company.

When the speeches were over there was a rush to the top table by the other guests who wanted the autographs of these outstanding rugby internationals. While they were busy signing, one guest put an empty page in front of me and asked for my autograph. I said to him "I'm not an international rugby star, I'm a writer with the *Belfast Telegraph*." He paused, and then said "Just sign the page anyway, sure you'll do to start me off." There's no place like Ulster to cut a man down to size.

In later years, sadly, I lost touch with Tony O'Reilly but I always admired him for the skill, time and effort he put in to helping the situation in Northern Ireland, and I was delighted when he received his well-deserved Honorary Knighthood for his work.

Among the wide range of bridge-builders in that period one woman deserves special mention. Saidie Patterson who lived at Woodvale in Belfast was a doughty trade union campaigner and a committed Methodist with a courageous big heart. On occasions she would write to me after I had written an article attacking the hardliners, while other people remained silent.

Sometimes I was worried about what I had written because, unlike visiting journalists, I lived in Belfast and not all that far from some of the worst areas of violence. However one particular letter from Saidie was most encouraging. In her broad blue script she wrote "That was a courageous column this week. Don't worry. Just you keep on keepin' on." She never could have known how much she had strengthened me.

Over many years, peace came dropping slow in Northern Ireland and there is still some way to go. It would be wrong to suggest that the people I have mentioned in this chapter were the only important peacemakers, but they were among the pioneers in the darkest of days.

It is also difficult to assess just exactly what effect they had, but it is my deep conviction that if these people had not been there, the situation would have been much, much worse.

I still look on Ray Davey as the first trailblazer on the difficult path to peace, and I always remember – and try to apply – the Corrymeela motto "It is better to light a candle than to curse the darkness."

During the worst of the Troubles the small candles of light here and there grew into larger flames, even though Northern Ireland as a whole was still moving steadily into the heart of darkness. Sadly, I was to witness all too much of the pain and suffering of that darkness as I met and wrote about some of the victims of violence and their families and friends. I shall take you into that heart of darkness in the next chapter.

CHAPTER THIRTEEN

The Heart of Darkness

MY IDEA FOR a book about the victims of violence arose partly from a series of articles which I wrote for the *Belfast Telegraph* about the Royal Victoria Hospital.

I was given permission by the hospital administrators to write about the work of medical and nursing and support staff in dealing with the casualties of the conflict, and I formed a good relationship with a leading general surgeon called Willoughby Wilson.

He allowed me to watch him operate on a wounded policeman, as I stood at the edge of the theatre, fully gowned and masked, and with a pencil and notebook in my hand. One of the other masked and gowned doctors in the theatre was Aires Barros D'Sa, a friend of mine from my Queen's days. His eyes were asking "What the hell are you doing here", and I replied in kind "I'll tell you later."

Suddenly Willoughby called me over to the table to explain what he was doing. The anaesthetist Maurice Brown said dryly "If you are going to faint, pleased don't faint over the patient." However I had no intention of fainting, and I listened to Willoughby intently as he explained the technical details of the operation.

I did not understand clearly what he was saying, so I told him "I am writing for a mass audience out there, and I'd be grateful if you could talk in the plain language which people outside the hospital can understand." Willoughby then spoke in simpler terms, as most clever people can do when explaining their specialty. It is usually the second-raters and the poseurs who hide behind jargon.

Afterwards we had coffee together. I said "Willoughby, you told me that you often hear the best jokes during an operation. Why did things go suddenly quiet?" He replied "There were complications, and we almost lost the patient."

Willoughby looked exhausted, and angry. He said "I was on duty last night, and I was called in around 4 am because of an emergency. There were two hoodlums who had been shot in a gunfight, and an elderly lady who was suffering from peritonitis. However I had to take first the patient who was the most ill, and that was one of the gunmen. That kind of thing really gets to me."

I liked Willoughby, who was a charming man with a good sense of humour; but he too was a victim of the violence because he had had to deal with so much tragedy. I saw him break down in tears at a conference one evening when he was talking about his work, and he did the same during a BBC radio recording with me on another occasion.

I realised from speaking to Willoughby and others that there was a huge range of inspiring human stories associated with a big hospital during the Troubles, and I decided to try to write a book about the Royal.

I also had a deeper motive in trying to show that this famous hospital, which was in the middle of an urban paramilitary battleground used by all the main protagonists, could also be a haven of peace and healing. In the Royal there was no 'Protestant' or 'Catholic', or 'Loyalist' or 'Republican' blood, but only the pain and suffering of people from all sides.

I had no experience up to then of writing books, and this one turned out to be a remarkable test of my stamina and initiative, as well as emotionally demanding. (My Corrymeela book came later.)

The first task was to find a publisher, and after much effort to persuade people that this was a good idea, it was accepted by The Blackstaff Press, which in those days was under an entirely different management from its modern counterparts.

I needed to carry out intensive research on some of the personal stories of victims of violence, and also among the Royal staff. I sought the official backing from the hospital, but to my dismay, I was turned down. The senior medical staff discussed my request at a special meeting, but they were worried about giving a writer a free hand to write about their hospital.

Even though the chairman of the medical staff committee Professor

Harold Rodgers later on backed what I was trying to do, he was unable to have the original decision reversed.

I was therefore dependent on the help from senior figures like Willoughby Wilson, and also the head of the accident and emergency department William Rutherford, a tall, saintly and slow-talking man whose sentences never seemed quite to end.

Others who helped me included Professor Frank Pantridge, who led the team which invented the miniature heart defibrillator which could be carried in a Mobile Coronary Care Unit, including a suitably equipped ambulance or other mobile vehicle. In effect this was the same as bringing the 'hospital' to the patient, rather than the other way round. Pantridge had discovered that the first sixteen minutes or so were crucial to the survival of a heart attack patient, and the invention of the Mobile Coronary Care Unit has saved millions of lives all over the world.

Pantridge, like many brilliant men, was also an eccentric, and I had difficulty in arranging a meeting with him. When we eventually got together, I was wearing my Queen's graduate's tie, which was the kind of thing I knew he would notice. As we talked, he barked at me from his big, black leather chair which he had swivelled round so much that all I could see was his back .

I tired of this calculated ploy to impress me, and I asked boldly "Professor Pantridge, do you usually talk to people through the back of your head?" He whirled his chair round in astonishment, and realised that I was not in the least intimidated by him. After that we got on very well.

Frank Pantridge was most helpful, and behind the bombastic image I think he was a rather lonely man. He was a great doctor who helped to save the lives of millions of people, but his endless war with bureaucracy made him many enemies, and he never received the knighthood he deserved – which was an absolute disgrace.

My research with the victims of violence was immensely enriched by those men and women who had suffered greatly, and who were willing to talk to me about their experiences.

I was aware that even the cliché 'victims of violence' had become a neat mental box which removed them some distance from the rest of us. In reality, most of them had been in the wrong place at the wrong time, and these 'victims of violence' were ordinary people, flesh and blood, just like you and me.

One of the first people I interviewed was a pretty young woman called Jennifer McNern who had lost both her legs as a result of the Abercorn bomb blast of 4 March 1972. Her sister Rosaleen was also badly injured in the bomb, and lost two arms and a leg. Other people lost limbs and eyes in the blast. As part of my research, I obtained pictures taken in the operating theatre of the hospital but they were too gruesome to publish.

Another victim was Jimmy Stewart who had lost both legs in the blast. A neighbour of mine, Tom McFarlane, was also injured and the dramatic picture of his blood-spattered face was splashed all over the newspapers. Fortunately Tom was not as badly injured as he looked, and he made a good recovery. However his injury underlined the fact that almost everyone in Northern Ireland knows someone, or someone who belonged to someone, who was killed or injured in the Troubles.

On the day of the Abercorn bombing, the centre of Belfast was crowded with shoppers. In the afternoon the popular Abercorn Restaurant in Cornmarket was packed with people.

At 4.29 pm a bomb exploded in the restaurant without warning, killing two young girls and injuring many other people, some horrifically so.

Though no organisation claimed responsibility for the bomb at the time, it was later thought to be the work of the Provisional IRA, though they had initially blamed Loyalist paramilitaries for the atrocity – which the latter denied.

Whoever was responsible, they callously caused immense suffering and pain for ordinary, innocent people. From my detailed researches carried out much later on with the help of experts, I discovered that the bomb, which was in a large handbag, had been left under a table near the back of the Abercorn, and the force of the explosion created a crater three feet across and eight inches deep. It was electronically detonated, with the help of a small clock – possibly a travelling alarm clock.

At a pre-selected time, the alarm rang, the winder-key rotated and completed an electrical contact through a battery linked to a detonator in the charge.

Technical experts told me that a bomb of that type caused an initial shock wave travelling at around 13,000 miles per hour. This pulverised the floor and caused the ground to shudder. However the main damage was caused by a blast wave which travelled at 600 miles per hour and had a tearing, heaving, wrecking motion.

In the confined space of the Abercorn restaurant, the bomb caused incredible damage and injury among the 150 casualties. Personal belongings, including shopping bags, toys, scraps of paper and beads were hurled everywhere amid the choking dust, and beside cups and saucers, plates and scraps of food. Knives and forks were embedded in civilian bodies, and the leg of a table protruded through one victim's thigh.

Dr 'Minty' Bereen, a senior consultant anaesthetist, who worked feverishly later that night with his medical colleagues to help the victims, had previous experience of conflict as a member of the Royal Army Medical Corps in the desert campaign during the Second World War.

He told me later on "My first reaction, on seeing the casualties of the Abercorn bomb was 'My God, this is El Alamein all over again.'"

In a tragic twist of circumstances, Dr Bereen was working on the victims of the Abercorn bomb without knowing that his daughter Janet had died in the blast, along with another girl Anne Francis Owens, who only eight months earlier, had been injured in another explosion in Belfast.

Janet and her parents had lived in Hampton Park, Belfast 7, and the police had found a torn document among her belongings with the lettering 'een,pton,ast,7'. They eventually traced Dr Bereen later on and asked him to go to the 'Laganbank'. To a doctor that could mean only one thing – it was a code word for the city mortuary. His daughter Janet was dead.

Nearly forty years later, as I re-read my notes of that terrible event, I recall the sadness, shock and terror of those years, which were repeated so many times throughout the next three decades and more of violence.

I also recall my apprehension about interviewing some of the victims of the Abercorn. I had never met anyone badly injured in a bomb. How could I ask them about their injuries, without appearing intrusive, and – perhaps even worse – sounding like a professional writer whose main aim was just to get his story?

The first person I interviewed, a couple of years after the Abercorn, was Jennifer McNern who together with her sister Rosaleen, had agreed to talk to me at their home near London.

Jennifer and I made an arrangement to meet outside an underground station. As I waited, a car stopped beside me and a groomed young woman asked me to step inside. It was Jennifer, and she was driving the car only with her arms, in the specially-equipped vehicle.

After a few minutes she parked outside a small supermarket, handed me some money and said "Could you please go in and buy me a pint of milk and a loaf of bread. It's easier for you to do it, because I have no legs." She said it so matter-of-factly that I lost my apprehension about the interview, and later I listened carefully as she and her sister told me their remarkable story.

They had been shopping in Belfast for clothes in advance of Rosaleen's wedding later that year to Brendan Murrin, a young Donegal man. They went in to the Abercorn for a coffee, and as they were about to pay the bill, the bomb went off without warning.

During our long interview in London they told me about their months of painful recovery. Jennifer summed up their tremendous courage and strength of mind by telling me " There were bad moments but I felt that I just had to 'catch myself on.'

"I knew that I would have to 'do without'. It is so disheartening for doctors if you reject help. You could not afford to think of yourself all the time, or keep saying 'me, me, me' and become hysterical. The whole family was involved, apart from Rosaleen and myself, and you had to think of them as well."

Their courage was exemplified on the day that Rosaleen and Brendan were married, as planned, in August 1972, and Jennifer was one of the bridesmaids. The story of 'the McNern sisters' has stayed with me ever since, and has often reminded me of the deeply human dimension to the suffering of the Troubles.

I also talked at length to Jimmy Stewart, who had also been badly injured in the Abercorn. He had called in for a snack, and when he had finished he set out for the cash desk to pay his bill. He never made it. The last thing he saw from the corner of his eye was a bright, green glow as the bomb went off.

Like Jennifer and Rosaleen he, too, went through many months of difficult and painful recuperation as he tried to adjust to the grim reality of losing both legs. He was a deeply committed Christian and he and his fiancé Florrie were married in 1974 in the Welcome Evangelical Church at Cambrai Street in Belfast.

When I was researching my story about Jimmy I recall going to his house one afternoon. He had taken off his artificial legs and he was sitting on his stumps. He asked me how I was, and I replied by telling him about some of my worries and grouses on that day.

After I had finished I asked Jimmy "How are you?" He replied "Oh, I can't complain." I realised all too well that I had been doing all the complaining, and his words still challenge me.

I have dwelt at some length about the Abercorn bomb because it was one of the first big atrocities of the Troubles, and its human aftermath affected me deeply because I had come to know some of the victims so well. Though there were to be many more victims of the Troubles, the story of the Abercorn underlined the dreadful human cost of the violence that hung like a dark, evil cloud over all the people of Northern Ireland for so long.

§

Another remarkable story of the Troubles was that of Alan Black, one of the two survivors of the Kingsmills massacre in 1976. Some time later I interviewed Alan in his home in Bessbrook, where he told me some of the details of the attack and his survival, which he had not previously mentioned to any journalist.

On that terrible night, several gunmen ordered the millworkers out of their van and, as I have noted earlier, they asked Catholics to identify themselves. Richard Hughes, the only Catholic, spoke up, despite whispers to him from the others, all Protestants, to stay quiet. They all thought that he was going to be killed. Instead the gunmen told him to run for it, and they turned their guns on the rest of the men standing in a line.

Between 150 and 200 rounds of ammunition were fired. Thermos flasks were scattered across the road, and the lid of a lunch box lay on the top half of a pair of dentures, which were soaked with blood and rain.

A Christian tract, which had belonged to one of the men, had a poignant headline – "Herald of Hope – a message of salvation, healing, comfort, good cheer and encouragement to the needy, the unsaved."

For the men who had lined up fearfully in the darkness, there was no healing, comfort, good cheer or encouragement that night. They were all mown down in the hail of bullets. They included Alan Black who lay still and was left for dead, while the gunmen melted away.

As Alan lay helplessly on the road, one driver came on the scene, but he or she drove on. Fortunately another motorist and his wife were passing by, and they stopped. They raised the alarm, and help was quickly on its way.

An ambulance from Daisy Hill Hospital in Newry sped to the scene. The ambulance crew – Sean Murphy and Michael Mallon – checked for survivors, and found Alan Black lying on the ground, semi-conscious. They decided quickly to take him to the hospital, and this almost certainly helped to save his life.

As Alan Black told this story to me in the peace and tranquillity of his home in Bessbrook many months later, I could hardly take in what he was saying. It sounded more like a scene from a television drama than the reality of life and death at Kingsmills, near the church where my mother had been married. In fact she was an aunt through marriage of Alan Black. It all seemed so direct and personal.

Alan told me that as he lay in the back of the ambulance, one of the attendants looked after him, but he was conscious enough to notice that the driver eventually made radio contact with the hospital. He said "Ten black, one white." Alan thought "That does not make sense. I am the only Black in here." He did not realise that the driver had been talking in code to the hospital authorities who were quickly summoning senior staff and making ready an operating theatre for the badly-injured man in the ambulance.

By the time Alan arrived in Daisy Hill Hospital a senior team was waiting for him. The life-saving measures started immediately in the casualty department even before he went to the theatre. His leather jacket and overalls were hacked off to save time.

Alan told me later that the first chaplain to arrive at the hospital came over to him at once. He was a local priest called Father Devlin, who asked Alan if he was a Catholic in order to administer the Last Rites. Alan said "No, Father, but I could do with a prayer anyway." One of Alan's hands was badly smashed, but the priest took his other good hand, and prayed with him.

It was a poignant symbol of human solidarity. Even in the bitterness of Northern Ireland, a Catholic priest and a young Protestant man could share the comfort of a prayer in the shadow of death.

The surgeons and other staff worked hard to save Alan's life, despite the eighteen bullet holes in his body. He told me later about his long road to recovery, and about the turning point in his recuperation.

He said "On the Sunday after the shooting, I lay in hospital very depressed. I felt myself going down and letting myself go. The nurses seemed to know this too. They came and they talked to me, and somehow it seemed to pass.

"Somehow, and I don't know how, they took me out of that depression, and I began to fight back. That Sunday was a turning point. I began to live again in a positive way. I began to think of my wife and family. From that day, I really became a survivor."

When Alan had finished telling me his story, there was a silence between us. I had never heard anything like it, and his story of life and death, and of courage and kindness, was unforgettable.

I then asked Alan if he had been back to the scene of the shooting. He said "No" but after some thought he agreed to drive there with me. It was only a few miles away.

When we got out of the car, Alan noticed that someone had put a wreath on the brow of a small hill where they reckoned that the shooting had taken place. Alan said to me "I'm not sure that it's in the right place. One of the things I remember most about the shooting was the fact that I was lying face down in the hollow, and the rainwater trickling down the road helped to cool my face."

As he talked I realised to my horror that I was standing on the spot known only to Alan and to the killers, who had claimed membership of the so-called Republican Action Force. The killings were thought to be a retaliation for the murder of members of two Catholic families in the area in previous days.

Such obscene tit-for-tat killings defied all reason in those days of madness. More than anything else, my experience of talking to Alan Black about the Kingsmills massacre brought home to me the reality and brutality of the violence of those days, when even a remote country ditch could become a killing-field.

Even today, as I write these words, I recoil at the sadness of it all, and I am all too conscious of the sheer depth of violence and suffering which followed in the decades after the Kingsmills massacre – which should in itself have been a big enough warning to the people of Northern Ireland that "enough is enough".

Tragically the violence went on and on, and the policy-makers were sucked into the trap of "the politics of the latest atrocity" – just as the horror of one incident began to fade, it was replaced by another – sometimes worse – incident.

The MP Gerry Fitt coined the term "Whataboutery" – people would say "Your side killed and injured these people". The reply would come "What about those who were killed and injured by your side the last time?" In such a perverse situation, the suffering of ordinary people was too often reduced to a footnote in the ongoing political wrangling and deadlock.

However, in the midst of all this there was some dark humour. An ambulance-man called Robin Shields told me of the time when his crew was called to help a shipyard man who had been injured at his home in Sandy Row, Belfast.

Apparently when he awoke early one morning to prepare for his work, he went downstairs to prepare a cooked breakfast for himself.

He lit the gas cooker and put on the pan to fry some eggs. Suddenly the lightbulb in the kitchen went out. So he stood on a chair, and reached up to replace the bulb. However he received a sharp electric shock which made him lose his balance. On his way down his hand hit the handle of the frying pan which ejected two half-fried eggs onto his face, and also put out the cooker, but the gas was still flowing freely.

Meanwhile his wife upstairs had heard the commotion. She raced down, saw the kitchen in darkness and lit a match. Boom! This caused an explosion and blew out part of the kitchen.

The noise alerted the neighbours. The ambulance arrived quickly, and when Robin Shields and his colleagues were carrying the injured man out of his house on a stretcher, one little lady bystander said plaintively "It's not his day!"

Sadly, however, there was an even darker element to that story. Some years after Robin talked to me, he too became a victim of violence. He was a former police reservist as well as an ambulance supervisor and he was shot dead on 30 September 1980 by the Provisional IRA as he sat at his desk in the ambulance depot at the Royal Victoria Hospital.

For many months I steadily continued my research into the life-saving and healing work of the hospitals, but my manuscript itself almost became a victim of literary annihilation. The then management of The Blackstaff Press had accepted the book, but halfway through my research they changed their minds.

They decided for no clear reason, as far as I could see, that they did not want to proceed with the publication. It was a cruel way to treat a young writer, and I did not have enough experience about the legalities of the publishing business to challenge them.

I was devastated. It felt as if something inside me had been aborted, and I placed the unpublished manuscript in a cupboard in my study. I was unable to read it or even look at it. I knew that it had the potential to be an important book, but my confidence was shattered.

As usual, I put a brave face on things, and I turned to something else, which eventually became a book on the peace-makers. However, I was beginning to believe that my book on the victims of violence would never be published, but again the law of unexpected consequences kicked in. Hilary and I were at a dinner party in the home of a BBC staffer in Belfast, and one of the guests was a senior producer from London.

He mentioned that he was thinking of filming a major television documentary on the Royal. Hilary said loyally "My husband has written a book on the Royal." I quickly interjected "It's not yet finished…"

However, I was paying full attention to the London-based BBC producer, because he was confirming what I already knew – namely that I was on the right track, if only I could find a publisher.

So I took fresh heart, and turned back to my unfinished manuscript. I tightened up a couple of the early chapters, and sent them to a London publisher, with an explanatory background synopsis.

However these were returned, with a polite letter from the publishers explaining that it would make a good book, but that it would not be right for their market. I sent off my manuscript to thirteen other publishers, and I could have papered my study with polite rejection letters.

Just as I was beginning to lose heart, I met a man called Alan Anderson, who was then the managing director of the *Belfast News Letter*. The company also had a publishing section, and Alan agreed to read my manuscript. I was delighted when he decided to publish it under the imprint of Century Books.

I worked busily to complete my research and writing. By this time word had spread in the medical world about my project, and instead of approaching hospital staff to talk to me, they were asking me to talk to them – all unofficially of course.

There was a point, however, when I could take no more of it. The suffering and heartbreak on all sides was so great that I, too, was in danger of becoming a victim – like my surgeon friend Willoughby Wilson.

I clearly remember the day when I decided that I had had enough. I was interviewing a boy called Tony Meli who was badly injured when a transistor radio exploded in his hand. It had been handed in to his father's café the day before, and Tony Meli senior placed it on a shelf, thinking that someone would return the next day to claim it.

That morning young Tony innocently reached for the radio and turned it on. In the resultant explosion he lost a forearm and an eye. Tony told me his story in the front room of my home in Belfast, where he and his father had come to meet me.

My wife brought in some tea, and orange juice for young Tony. As he talked to me, I noticed that he was trying – with limited success – to lift the glass of orange juice with the metal callipers which the doctors had attached to what was left of his forearm. As I watched him, I thought of my own children, and of the discomfort and handicap of this innocent young boy.

For me this was an interview too far. I just could not take any more, and after Tony and his father had left, I decided that I would stop my research. I had already seen and heard too much.

Eventually my book, titled simply *Survivors*, was published in October 1976, and we had a memorable launch in the Dunadry Inn, which was attended by many of the people featured in the book.

Survivors became a local bestseller, and went into a second edition. In that sense it was a success, but its shocking stories of the suffering of innocent people did not prevent the violence continuing, and even getting worse.

However, I was immensely glad that a number of the victims of violence in the earlier years of the Troubles had been given probably their first opportunity by a book author to talk in depth about what had happened to them.

It was this which made all my hard work and struggles in producing the book so worthwhile. At least these people were getting their voices heard.

Sadly, however, there were hundreds of other deaths and thousands of injuries to come, and so many other stories to be told. By the end of 1976, there were 1866 deaths, and by the end of 1999 the total had risen to 3636.[1]

Nearly forty years after writing and publishing my book *Survivors*, I still find it difficult to watch or listen to, or to read about, many of those people who chose to use violence for political ends, and who strut around as if the murder and suffering they caused had nothing to do with them. In too many quarters there is still an all-too-convenient amnesia about the Troubles, where the victims are forgotten about as human beings.

This makes me more convinced than ever that all the victims of violence should be encouraged to tell their stories, and that they should be given a proper environment in which to do so.

This will be an infinitely difficult task for the government and its agencies to achieve, but a solution must be found. From my experience of writing in depth about some of the victims of violence, I am certain that until the voices of all these people are heard telling their own stories, there will not be proper healing or peace in this part of our island which has experienced so much of the heart of darkness. This, in many ways, is the greatest unfinished business of all.

The suffering in Northern Ireland was bad enough but I was about to embark on a journey where I encountered human suffering and deprivation on a world scale.

On the day after my *Survivors* book was launched, I took a plane to Geneva, then to Amsterdam and eventually to Africa, Asia, the Far East and Central America to report on the poor, ill and starving people of the developing world.

That, however, was a dimension of human suffering on a huge scale that shook me to my core, and helped to put the Northern Ireland Troubles into a very different perspective.

---

[1] *Lost-Lives*, Mainstream Publishing, 1999, pp1473–74

CHAPTER FOURTEEN

Third Degree

THROUGHOUT THE TROUBLES, I was aware that Northern Ireland was not the only place in turmoil, and that there was deprivation and suffering in other parts of the world on an even greater scale.

However the sheer degree of this was brought home to me when I carried out extensive research in Africa, Asia and Central America between 1976–77 to write a book for the British churches' development agency Christian Aid.

This opportunity to travel and to report on an international scale arose from a phone call a couple of years earlier from the Reverend Ian McDowell, who was then head of Christian Aid in Ireland.

On the eve of Christian Aid week he asked me if I would consider writing a story about famine in India. When he rang I was deep in an article about violence in Northern Ireland, and I had no time – or indeed inclination to drop everything to accede to his request.

However, a few days later on Christian Aid Sunday my local minister the Reverend Fergie Marshall, who was an outstanding orator, issued a challenge from the pulpit in Whitehouse Presbyterian Church. He said "Sometimes the easiest way to help Christian Aid is simply to give them a donation, but have you ever considered giving them some of your time and your skills as well?"

His challenge stirred something deep inside me, and the next day I contacted Ian McDowell to find out if he was still interested in a story about India.

He most certainly was, and he filled in some details for me. I spoke to my editor Roy Lilley, and that week the *Belfast Telegraph* ran my story about how a small donation could help to save the life of a child in India.

I wrote it in a very direct, personal way, and suggested that even a small sum from each reader could work wonders. We also ran a picture of a wide-eyed and appealing Indian child, and the combined effect was amazing.

Hundreds of *Telegraph* readers donated money and we raised more than £600 for Christian Aid which was a considerable sum in the mid-Seventies. This was an impressive response from people in Northern Ireland who were also trying to survive during the worst of the Troubles.

Even more surprising was the reaction from my hard-headed journalistic colleagues in the *Telegraph*. They said "That was a moving piece you wrote. If somebody makes a collection around the newsroom each week, we'll donate something."

I said "Great!", and then looked round for someone to volunteer as a collector, but there was only me. I took up the challenge gladly, and in the weekly collection I learned a great deal about my fellow journalists. Some of those whom I expected to be obvious donors never seemed to have the right change, and many others from whom I had not expected much, turned out to be the most generous and most regular givers of all.

As this weekly collection continued, I was also wondering privately if I could help Christian Aid in an even more direct way. After much thought I wrote to the London headquarters, though my letter must have seemed naïve to those who read it. I offered to help their work, but underlined that I could not contemplate moving to London, for family and professional reasons.

Much to my surprise I received a letter back from the Christian Aid publicity chief Hugh Samson asking me to meet him, and offering to come to Belfast to do so. I knew that something important was in the offing, because nobody visited Belfast in those days unless they had to.

We agreed to meet in the Dunadry Inn, near the international airport, because it was too much to ask a stranger from London to risk going into the centre of Belfast. Hugh Samson was an engaging and positive man who was looking for a journalist to travel to various parts of the developing world, and write about Christian Aid.

He said to me "This would require you to travel extensively to places like Africa, Asia and Latin-America. Would it be possible for you to do that?" I breathed in deeply, and tried not to appear too much like an eager country bumpkin. Would I travel around the world and report on my journeys? Would I heck! It had always been my ambition to let my pen take me around the world. The big challenge was how to make it happen.

Hugh Samson wanted me to spend several months travelling, but that seemed impossible for a staff journalist working in Belfast in the midst of the Troubles, especially as an extended leave of absence or a 'sabbatical' was then unheard of.

There was also the important question about my home life and responsibilities – was it fair to ask my wife Hilary to cope on her own with two small children for a long period while I was away?

I told Hilary about the offer, which was obviously in aid of a good cause, and she was immediately and totally supportive. I then had a long talk with Roy Lilley and he generously gave me a leave of absence for several months, because he knew how important the offer was to me.

This was partly because he also supported world development, and partly because regular files in the paper about problems like hunger and disease on a world scale might help some of the *Belfast Telegraph's* readers to look at the Northern Ireland Troubles from a different perspective.

I was deeply appreciative of the support from Hilary and Roy because without their help, the trip would not have been possible. It was decided that I would travel from October 1976, until the end of April 1977, with a break back home at Christmas.

Before I left the *Telegraph*, my colleagues organised a small farewell party, during which one of my colleagues, christened me 'Father Teresa'. As several of us stood around chatting, one of our sharp-witted sports writers Colin McMullan asked me "How are you going to travel to these places?" I replied innocently "I'm going by air". Colin replied "Oh, I thought that you were going to walk on the water!", and when he said that everyone else doubled up with laughter, at my expense.

That's what I liked about the *Belfast Telegraph* in those days. We were not well paid, we worked in often dangerous circumstances, but we were almost like an extended family. Whatever I did and wherever I went, I was one of them, and that collective loyalty and respect for one another was important to me.

So on the day after my *Survivors* book was published I flew to Geneva to talk to officials from the World Council of Churches who gave me background information on some of the problems in the developing world.

Two days later I went to Amsterdam to meet the Reverend Aat Van Rhijn, with whom I had worked as a Northern Ireland member of a Dutch-Irish group which was organising conferences in Holland to try to build bridges with different groups involved in the Troubles in Ulster.

Aat introduced me to several people in Holland who had extensive practical experience of working in the developing world, but my real education started when my KLM jumbo jet touched down in Nairobi, and I began to learn about the harsh realities of life in Kenya, and later on in Tanzania, the Sudan and Tunisia, and many other places.

I met several Kenyan officials working for the local churches council and their associated development agencies and staff. One of my first visits was to a place called Mathare Valley, a sprawling slum where around 80,000 poor people crowded in to a patchwork of dirt some four kilometres square.

I later wrote about it in these words: "There is a stench about Mathare Valley, with its human excretia at random and with the goats rummaging in the refuse tips beside the ramshackle buildings. Mathare Valley is off the tourist track, yet it is only a short distance from Nairobi's glittering showpiece centre. In one of the leading international hotels there, a single cocktail with the suggestive name 'The Persuader' costs as much as it would take to buy fifteen meals in the slums of Mathare Valley."

I decided early on in my journey that one of the best ways to underline world poverty to a wide readership in the UK and the USA was to write for the *Belfast Telegraph* and for the *Christian Science Monitor* in Boston about the plight of ordinary human beings, and not to be daunted by the overwhelming statistics of hunger and disease.

In a book titled *Up With People* which was later published by Collins of London, I set the scene for so much of which I experienced in my travels.

"The face of the Third World is the meat of statistic on the bone of hunger, the gnawing reality of suffering and death. It is an emergent skeleton, increasingly meaningless in the inevitability of its magnitude.

"The face of the Third World is clouded by economic arguments, obscured by policy statements, distorted by ignorance, prejudice and propaganda.

"Yet the constant mirror is the face of humanity itself, blood of blood and flesh of flesh: North and South, rich and poor, a man and a woman, earthland and city slum. The face of the Third World is the face of... Margaret Mumbua."

I met Margaret who was living in a hut with a cardboard roof in Mathare Valley. She lived there with her husband and four children, and another two had died in childbirth. Her husband found odd jobs as a labourer and she was a temporary cook.

They scraped along until disaster struck. Her husband was killed in a car accident, and she and her children went to live with her father. Life was a little better, but when he died Margaret and her children had to leave the family's patch of land.

As the eldest child, Margaret should have inherited it, but she was prevented from doing so by her male relatives. So she and her children were reduced to begging.

She told me "Some people were kind, they gave me money and we managed to stay alive somehow. But no-one would take us in. I suppose that if they had done so they were afraid that they could not get us out again. So we had to sleep rough, out in the open, in alleyways, wherever we could find a place."

One day she met a friend of her late father, who gave her money and put her in touch with a doctor. Eventually she was directed to a nutrition centre established to help the poor of Mathare Valley.

She said "My baby son Christopher was so hungry that at first he used to stuff the food into his eyes and ears and nose as well as his mouth. He thought that each meal might be his last. Then he used to hide his food in his high chair, for the same reason. Gradually he was nursed back to normal, and we all got a bit better."

Margaret was given a job as a weaver, and earned a small sum each month through piece-work. She spent the money on food, charcoal and water. Food was still scarce, with only the basics to live on. Margaret was still vulnerable because she suffered from ulcers, and if she took any time off work, she was not paid.

She told me "I struggle on. I get very depressed when I think of my husband and the dead children. You live from day to day and you wait to see what the next day brings. I am twenty-five, but sometimes I feel that it is too late for me to marry again. Who would want to marry me, with all my problems? I often feel lonely, especially at night when I can't sleep."

Margaret's plight touched me deeply. She was the first person I interviewed in depth in the Third World, and her suffering was different to what I had experienced among many of the people I had interviewed back home in Northern Ireland.

However her plight was real, and no less deadly. I had witnessed some terrible situations in Northern Ireland, but this was different. Back home the vast majority of the people had food, shelter and medicine, but Margaret Mumbua was typical of many millions of people throughout the Third World, both then and now. She had nothing at all, except four hungry children, a cardboard roof over her hut which was worth a total of just £70, and only the clothes she stood in. She did not even have hope, but she had courage and dignity in the midst of her travails.

However my journey with Christian Aid was not totally without hope, and I visited several projects where people were engaged in productive self-help schemes. I came to understand one of the great slogans of development workers and agencies "If you give a man a fish, you feed him for a day. If you teach him how to fish, you feed him for life."

The next stage of my journey, to the depths of Southern Sudan, taught me many lessons. I discovered the kindness of so many of the African people, and I discovered something about myself, and how much I took for granted in my comfort zone in the developed world.

In Sudan I reported on an ingenious Christian Aid project where a French engineer built concrete boats for navigation on the River Nile. This helped to create employments for people from the local area.

At first I could not work out how 'concrete' boats would not sink. But coming from the city of Belfast where Harland and Wolff had built hundreds of iron vessels, I should have known better.

However I learned about something more than shipbuilding in Southern Sudan. I learned about hunger, deprivation and survival. One day I had lunch with the French engineer at a roadside 'restaurant', which was little more than a mud hut.

I ordered 'roast lamb', which seemed to be the only dish on the menu.

When it was eventually served, it was covered with flies. Instinctively, I wanted to send it back, but my companion said "This is all they have got. Just remove the flies, which are dead anyhow, and then eat the meat. Otherwise you will go hungry." I did exactly what he suggested, but I learned a lesson about taking even the most basic things for granted.

I learned many other things in Southern Sudan. One day set off on a long journey with several companions towards a place called Wau. We travelled in the back of a lorry, and my only sustenance was a carton of fruit juice.

Somewhere on our journey we had a tyre 'blow-out'. There were no garages anywhere so the driver and his helpers had to change the heavy tyre themselves. As we huddled round the vehicle I noticed that several tall Dinka warriors had emerged from the forest, and they were watching us intently.

They were naked, apart from loincloths, and their slim muscular bodies and their faces were daubed with white paint. They carried large spears, and I became apprehensive about what they might do.

However I need not have worried. They were simply curious, and after a while they had seen enough and they melted back into the forest.

We changed the tyre and completed our journey to a small village in a clearing. I was given a grass hut in which to sleep, and as there was no food, I was resigned to going to bed hungry. However before I turned in, I went for a walk in the moonlight, and I could hear the sounds of African drumbeats and dancing. I was told later on that I had been walking in an area full of poisonous snakes, and if I had been bitten there was no antidote. Clearly someone had been looking after me.

The next day I lay in my grass hut, and the lack of food as well as the intense heat was making me weak. However, every two hours a black lady from the next hut brought me a cup of hot tea, which kept me going. I have always remembered that spontaneous act of kindness from a woman, who by our material standards in the West, had very little. It seemed to me obvious that I should do everything I could to help people like her by publicising their plight and trying to raise funds to help them.

I spent a couple of days living on black tea until an American missionary whom I had met told me that he was going out to forage for food. Eventually someone gave him a tin of macaroni, and we ate macaroni stew beside a campfire, while we listened on a longwave radio to a 'live' football match between Liverpool and Manchester United. It was one of the most memorable meals of my lifetime, because my hunger was so intense.

The same missionary introduced me to an American doctor in the local hospital where many of the patients were Africans who had suffered from lion bites or spear wounds. One evening in late November we went to the doctor's home where people were rehearsing Christmas carols. The physician was a strange character who refused to talk to me because I was a journalist.

I did not mind this at all, but every time I hear that beautiful and ancient carol 'O Come O Come Emmanuel', I think of that steamy night in Southern Sudan with a group of Americans and Europeans rehearsing Christmas carols.

Being so far away from home, it was almost impossible to keep in touch with my wife and friends. There were no cell phones, and not even faxes. However I was often reminded of home in other ways. One day I visited a remote village in Southern Sudan, and suddenly – among all the local Dinka people – a white woman said to me "You're a long way from home!" She turned out to be a Belfast girl called Carol who had trained in the Royal Victoria Hospital as a nurse and was working with the people of Southern Sudan. I was delighted to meet her, and to hear the Belfast accent again. I have often wondered about whatever happened to her. There are not many people in the world who can say "I last met you in a Dinka village near Wau."

I eventually left Southern Sudan and spent a few fascinating days in Khartoum, before travelling on to Nigeria – or so I thought. However there was a sudden change of plan, and I was being switched to Tunisia, many hundreds of miles away.

I arrived at the airport in Khartoum and realised that the only money I had with me was a US $100 travellers' cheque. However when I tried to change it, the bank teller went beserk. Apparently my official bank papers were not the right colour, and he refused to give me anything.

I was absolutely stuck. I then appealed for help to an Englishman, who was the only person in the queue behind me, but he said "Sorry old chap, have to rush for my plane, you'll have to sort it out yourself."

It was easier said than done. I was in Khartoum airport, without cash and where no English was spoken. Thoroughly confused and dispirited at this stage, I mistakenly joined a queue of Muslims and very nearly boarded a flight to Riyadh instead of one to Cairo, where I was heading en route to Tunis.

I eventually boarded the right plane, and I arrived in Cairo at 2 am with no money and no hotel, and I had to join the passport queue with a melee of pilgrims coming back from Mecca. I soon discovered that my elbows were more effective than good manners.

After some delay I cleared passport control and hailed a taxi, and the driver took me to a hotel near the docks. When we arrived, I raced upstairs, made sure that they would cash my cheque and then went back down to pay the driver, all the while hoping that he had not driven off with my luggage.

I then went to my room, sat on the side of the bed and took off one of my shoes, which broke in half. It had been one of those days. However my problem the next morning was to get to the airport in time, and also to let Hilary know where I was. The former was easier than the latter. The hotel had no telex, and the phones were dodgy, so I realised that I would have to contact Hilary if and when I could, and to tell her was I was going to Tunisia and not Nigeria, as she had expected. However, I was unable to do so.

I arrived at the airport in good time, and soon realised how wise I had been. My flight to Tunis was leaving early! I went to the ticket desk and tried to find out what was happening. The lady spoke no English, so I tried to talk to her in my broken French.

Then a voice behind me said "Don't worry, buddy, I'll handle this." He was a Canadian called Frank McGuinness who spoke fluent French and he quickly sorted things out. We sat together on the flight, and as we travelled across the Libyan desert I told him about my unsuccessful attempt to contact my wife.

He said "It's simple. When I get to my hotel in Tunis I'll phone my wife at our apartment in London, and she can phone your wife in Belfast." That seemed to me to be an amazingly practical solution, after my previous weeks in remote areas where phones were almost non-existent.

As we approached Tunis, I told Frank about my work with Christian Aid, and asked him for a lift into the city centre where I could find somewhere to stay for the night.

He agreed, and we set off in a taxi. We drove through the city late at night, and on the far side the taxi stopped at his hotel, the Tunis Hilton. He leapt out, leaving me in the back seat, and then he returned after a brief interval. He said "I've organised you a room for the night!" I replied "Frank, I can't afford the Hilton! I'm working for a charity."

He said "The room is on me. It's all part of the good cause you are supporting." I thanked him sincerely and made my way to a beautiful bedroom. After spending nearly two months in mud huts, this was luxury indeed.

I will never forget the kindness of Frank McGuinness who showed me more than almost anyone else I have known the depth of the story of the Good Samaritan. I was completely and utterly the victim of circumstances beyond my control, but Frank McGuinness chose not to walk on by. The experience also taught me that a spontaneous act of kindness is never wasted nor does it go un-noticed. Our every act of kindness will be repaid, but often in ways which we will never know about, or need to know.

After a week working in Tunis, I met up with Hilary in London, looking as lovely as ever, and then I spent the rest of that Christmas at home in Belfast. On the way back from Tunis, however, I had travelled into London from Gatwick Airport I had noticed that the people on the train had looked cold and pinched, and that the London Christmas lights were secular and half-hearted looking, without either warmth or cheer.

When I returned to Belfast, I went to the City Hall and stood for a long time looking at the resplendent Christmas tree and lights, and at the shoppers hurrying about. This was during the second worst year of the Troubles, but there was still a great Christmas atmosphere everywhere. I said to myself "What a magnificent and unbelievable city this is, despite the Troubles. If Belfast did not exist, we would have to invent it."

During the Christmas festivities, I went to a dinner party where an acquaintance said to me "I've had a really big problem this Christmas." I asked, with concern, "What was that?" He replied "I just managed to buy my new Rover before the price increase." I looked at him in disbelief. After all I had seen in Africa, where most people's "really big problem" was trying to stay alive, I could not comprehend this man's selfishness and warped value system. I did not know whether to be angry with him, or to pity him.

After that Christmas of 1976, I went back to the developing world and travelled to India and many other places. It was in Sri Lanka that I was taught one of the greatest lessons of all.

One day I was visiting a tea plantation with a Jesuit priest from Naples. We entered a hut where a young woman was lying along a straw pallet on the mud floor. She looked emaciated, and the priest told me that she was suffering from TB.

I said, without thinking, "That's not too bad. You can buy the drugs to help her." He said "Yes, but it's not as easy as that. I can buy her the drugs, but there is no guarantee that her family will have enough food to help her maintain her recovery. The drugs are expensive, and I have to balance her needs against those of dozens of local children whose sight can be saved quite inexpensively by buying the right drugs to help them."

Then he stared hard at me and asked me a question which I will never forget. He said "Do you think I like having to play God?" I stared back at him silently, for there was nothing I could say to help him in his terrible dilemma.

I stepped out of the gloom of that hut, with the dying girl on the pallet of straw, and I emerged into the strong sunlight and looked at the enormous natural beauty of the tea plantations all around me, and I thought to myself "Oh my God, I used to worry about my golf handicap…"

I finished my first major Third World trip three months later, and this was only the beginning of some three decades of such visits with the help of Christian Aid and Tearfund, during which time I wrote and broadcast extensively about the needs of the developing world.

During this time I also visited Tanzania, India, Rwanda, Guatemala, Paraguay, Chile, Vietnam, Cambodia and many other places where I encountered most of the same problems which I had seen on my first trip to Africa. I also discovered that many of these places had at least one thing in common with Northern Ireland – they were all troubled areas, but they also looked very beautiful.

Back home I also gave many talks and I helped to raise money for these causes, and in this work I realised how tremendously generous the people of Northern Ireland are to those in need.

The readers of the *Belfast Telegraph* continued to support me, and I regularly received a sizeable cheque from a man in Derry/Londonderry who asked me simply to "Pass this on to help those in need."

One afternoon I returned to the *Telegraph* after lunch, and the doorman handed me a white stuffed envelope. It looked to be the usual kind of envelope full of religious tracts or abuse from a reader who thought that I had lost my way in life.

To my surprise, the envelope contained £200 in banknotes, and there was a scrawled letter which stated "Dear Alf, I have been following your travels with interest, please use this where it is most needed." The letter was unsigned, and there was no request for a receipt. The money was given to me in total trust.

I sent the money to a contact in post-war Vietnam, and I was told later that it helped to buy meals for hundreds of children in a local orphanage. This was all reward I needed, just to know that the money had been so well spent.

My initial journey to Africa, Asia and Latin America was the start of a much longer, lifetime journey in reporting from the developing world. When I left Belfast in 1976 I thought that I knew something about suffering. However, when I returned to the *Telegraph* as a full-time journalist in the spring of 1977, I was a changed person.

I often said to myself "If all our people from both main communities in Northern Ireland were forced to spend a year in any of the countries I have just visited, and they had to experience the hunger and sickness of those I have met in the developing world, they would be only too glad to return to the beauty and the plenty of Northern Ireland, and they would agree to share it in a dozen different ways."

That's what my heart told me. However my head told me that the search for peace in Northern Ireland would continue to be long, bloody, messy, bad-tempered and extremely difficult. And so it proved.

CHAPTER FIFTEEN

Back to Basics

WHEN I RETURNED to Northern Ireland in May 1977 after six months of travelling around the world, the reality of the Troubles closed in quickly again.

It was not quite like Sir Winston Churchill's description of Ireland after the cataclysm of the First World War when he wrote about "the dreary steeples" of Fermanagh and Tyrone emerging from the mists, but it was confining and soul-destroying nevertheless.

I had been to places like Kenya, Tanzania, the Sudan, India, Sri Lanka and Guatemala where the majority of people were trying to survive from day to day, but back in Northern Ireland we were fighting a war about identity – Orange versus Green, Protestant and Roman Catholic, Unionist, Nationalist, Republican, British or Irish. It all seemed so obscene against the background of a wider world where vast numbers of people were starving, and dying of hunger and disease.

In a *Belfast Telegraph* article capturing a "Sense of the Seventies", I wrote the following words "In Northern Ireland it was the decade of disappointment as the bitter integrity of the Unionist–Nationalist quarrel outlasted all other considerations, even life, peace and prosperity. It was a decade of blood, and of guts spattered over streets again and again, as attitudes hardened and the cries of pain fell on deaf ears.

"The Ulster people, Protestants and Catholics, are in the main a very kind, a very open and a much misunderstood people. However it remains to me a mystery why as a community they seem to lose their sanity when they go to the polls. A community divided against itself permanently, however caring and however good in human terms, ultimately cannot stand."

In the midst of this mayhem it was a privilege to be a member of the *Belfast Telegraph's* leader-writing team during one of the best periods in the long history of the paper's printed edition. This was decades before the internet, mobile phones and other hi-tech developments provided a potentially vast readership on a worldwide scale.

The *Telegraph's* daily editorial conference, chaired by Roy Lilley or the Deputy Editor Edmund Curran, could last up to an hour, and sometimes even longer. After a debate in which each individual was listened to carefully, the newspaper's editorial line on that day would emerge.

Then it was up to my colleagues Barry White, Derek Black and me to write the leader as succinctly as possible and always to a tight deadline. There was so little time available that the Editor or his Deputy usually had no time for an extensive re-write.

Not surprisingly, the leader-writing team was well informed about the current events of the day, and also about the political nuances involved.

Our managing director Bob Crane was a shrewd chief executive, and several times a year he hosted superb lunches in the *Belfast Telegraph* boardroom where the editorial team had the opportunity to talk informally with some of the leading public figures of the day.

They included political, church and business leaders, and the *Telegraph* lunches were highly regarded by the policy makers as an means of briefing the opinion formers, including the political correspondents and columnists.

In those days the Northern Ireland Secretary of State had overall political responsibility for the Province in association with the current Prime Minister, and the majority of these people, from both main parties in Westminster, were heavyweight politicians.

One such was the jovial James Prior who was Secretary of State at a time of particularly high tensions. He was also one of the liveliest guests at our *Telegraph* luncheon club, and I still remember his reply to one question from a colleague who asked him if he had really wanted to come to Northern Ireland. He took a sip of wine and then said with a chortle "I wanted to be Foreign Secretary, but Margaret would have none of it." The 'Margaret' of course, was none other than the Prime Minister Margaret Thatcher, and she regarded Prior as one of the Cabinet 'Wets'.

I then asked Prior what he really thought of the people of Northern Ireland. With another chortle he said "I have never been in a place with so many really lovely people, and so many absolute sh–ts!". Given the sort of people Jim Prior had to deal with, that was probably a fair comment.

Another Northern Ireland Secretary who did become Foreign Secretary later on was Douglas Hurd. During one of our *Telegraph* lunches, when we journalists were keen to grill him about the latest details from No 10 Downing Street, he suddenly asked Bob Crane about the new computerised production process in the *Belfast Telegraph*.

Bob had many fine qualities, but he could be a bore about computers, so twenty minutes later he was still explaining our production process to Hurd.

I murmured to one of Hurd's several bright young Oxbridge aides "I think that your boss is being very clever by using up our valuable interrogation time in talking about computers."

"Not at all" replied the aide in a plummy public school accent. "I think that the Secretary of State is being most generous with his time in talking to you people."

Whereupon, I turned to my left and whispered to the Stormont chief press officer David Gilliland, who was well known for his wit and cynicism. I asked him "David, is the Secretary of State's aide a clever person, or not clever at all?"

Gilliland's eyes glinted behind his glasses as he replied "The person to whom you are referring is not as clever as he thinks." Not for the first time, I was aware that many of these 'bright' young people drafted in from the Westminster 'village' were not that politically bright at all.

Incidentally it was Gilliland who was credited with one of the best political 'one-liners' of the Troubles. One day there was a loud noise outside Stormont Castle as a helicopter, carrying a not particularly popular junior minister, descended to the helipad. Gilliland went to the window of his office. He watched the helicopter slowly touch down, and then announced to his waiting colleagues "The ego has landed!" The laughter nearly drowned out the noise of the helicopter.

The *Belfast Telegraph* lunches were also attended by leading Irish politicians, including Dr Garret Fitzgerald who as Taioseach and Opposition leader in the Irish Parliament played a significant role in Anglo-Irish politics.

Garret was a likeable man, without the pomposity of some other politicians at his level. He arrived at the back door of the *Telegraph*, slightly late, and those of us who attended the lunch were not quite sure how he got there. We had a hunch that someone had dropped him off by car near the building, and that he had made his own way to our office.

Given the tensions of those times, and the fact that Fitzgerald was a high profile Irish politician, there was a risk in going 'walkabout' in downtown Belfast, but that was Garret. Once inside our boardroom, he started talking in torrents of sentences, and he rarely paused for breath during the next two hours. He was fascinating, and he was obviously a decent human being. Garrett not only represented the best of Irish politics, but he could talk for Ireland as well.

Another memorable guest at one of our *Telegraph* lunches was the Roman Catholic Primate Cardinal Tomás Ó Fiaich. He was disliked by the majority of the unionist population, partly because of his direct manner of speech and his sturdy advocacy of Irish Republicanism.

However, his private persona was different. Ó Fiaich was an unapologetic, old-fashioned and adamantly non-violent Irish Republican from Crossmaglen, and he was also outgoing, and warm-hearted. His parties at his Episcopal house in Armagh city embraced people from all backgrounds, and I recall the amusement of a former Irish Presbyterian Moderator who told me that the Cardinal's party-piece was to sing 'The Ould Orange Flute', an anti-Catholic song, in Irish!

When the Cardinal came to our *Belfast Telegraph* luncheon, he immediately took off his jacket, reached for a glass of whiskey and lit up a cigarette. He seemed like an unassuming parish priest who was looking forward to a good lunch, and a bit of 'craic'.

Ó Fiaich was a great guest – open, witty and not afraid to speak his mind. He visited us at a time when the local Bishop was a Dr Philbin, originally from the west of Ireland. Philbin was ultra-conservative, and given the turmoil of Northern Ireland in those days, he was undoubtedly the wrong man in the wrong place at the wrong time.

This was alluded to by the editor Roy Lilley, who in an infinitely layered and polite question asked the Cardinal, as the head of the Catholic Church in Ireland "What are you going to do about Bishop Philbin?"

Ó Fiaich, with a glass in his hand and a twinkle in his eye, looked at Lilley and replied with a question of his own "Roy, what would YOU do with Bishop Philbin?"

The Cardinal was no fan of Philbin, but we realised that even a Catholic Primate could do nothing about an individual Bishop, whose ultimate line manager was the Pope himself.

Looking back on those lunches at the *Belfast Telegraph*, it was great to discover more about the real human beings behind the public image. The lunches also helped us to keep well-informed about the latest developments in the political and cultural landscape.

The *Belfast Telegraph's* constant editorial line was to back political power-sharing between the two main communities in Northern Ireland, and also to affirm the link with the rest of the United Kingdom. The power-sharing policy infuriated hardline unionists, but the paper's pro-union policy was anathema to many nationalists and republicans. Nevertheless it was a source of pride among the *Telegraph* journalists that their paper was widely read by people from all sides of the political, religious and cultural divides.

It was also a tribute to the skills and the collegiality of the editorial team that the leaders were written concisely under such pressure, and they were rarely changed. Sometimes the line of the main leader was so clear on a major topic that it was relatively straightforward for the writer to complete it.

However the smaller second leader could be quite tricky to craft. This was sometimes because no obvious subject presented itself, and the writer had to develop a skill in word play around an obvious theme like spring, summer, autumn and winter. With such long experience, I became so adept at this that my colleagues christened me "A man for all seasons."

However this formula could become seriously unstuck, and dramatically so on one occasion. On Monday, 27 August 1979, it was a slow news menu in the early morning, and I had to write a three sentence leader on the delights of a Bank Holiday.

This was not as easy as its sounds, because you have to possess certain skills to write about nothing much, but yet to make it interesting. The same applies to other creative skills. It was well known, for example, that the comedian and entertainer Les Dawson was able to play the piano deliberately badly, as part of his act, simply because he was an accomplished pianist.

Having completed my 'Bank Holiday' leader near lunchtime I went to the canteen, where my wife phoned me urgently. I was then the Ireland Correspondent of the prestigious *Christian Science Monitor* newspaper in Boston, and Hilary told me that they were trying to contact me urgently.

"Why?" I asked her innocently. She said "Lord Mountbatten has just been murdered by the IRA in Sligo. Have you not heard?" No I hadn't heard, because in the ensuing frantic rescheduling of the *Belfast Telegraph* to catch up with the sensational events of that day, our news desk team had forgotten to tell me what had happened. Sometimes the least informed people are those who work inside newspapers.

One of my immediate tasks was to contact David Anable, the overseas news editor of the *Christian Science Monitor* in Boston, to find out what kind of report he wanted from me. Then I had to phone *Time* magazine and *Newsweek* in London and New York, as I was filling in for their regular correspondents in Belfast who were on holiday.

The *Time* correspondent in London asked me to find him a room somewhere near Mullaghmore in Sligo where Lord Mountbatten had been murdered. He said "It may be hard to find a bed for me, but I'm happy to share with old Al from *Newsweek*. We worked together in Vietnam."

Despite the bad news of the day, it was fascinating to be working with these international correspondents, but sadly, as the day wore on, the news became even worse.

Near Warrenpoint eighteen British paratroopers were killed in a Provisional IRA bomb after they were lured into a trap at Narrow Water Castle. It is thought that the bomb was detonated across the nearby estuary on Irish Republic territory. It was the single biggest list of death and serious injuries at that point of the Troubles.

The events of those years now read like details of a war long forgotten, but horrifying and intensely disturbing at the time. Almost every day there were murders, bombs, roadblocks, and all kinds of confrontations, against a background of political deadlock.

In February 1978 twelve civilians died and over twenty were badly injured in a Provisional IRA firebomb attack at La Mon House Hotel near Belfast. Almost exactly a year later eleven men, known as the Shankill butchers, were found guilty of the gruesome torture and murder of nineteen innocent Catholics, and jailed for life.

Over a month later Airey Neave, the Tory spokesman on Northern Ireland and a close friend of Margaret Thatcher, died in a booby-trap bomb planted at the heart of Westminster by Irish INLA Republican terrorists.

Then only two weeks later, four policemen died in a 1,000 lb bomb detonated near Bessbrook, my native village. And so it went on and on. It was clear on all sides that there was not going to be the slightest prospect of peace in Northern Ireland any time soon.

The grim statistics told their own tale. By the end of the Seventies over 2,000 people had died since the Troubles began, and there were obviously many more deaths and injuries to come. The statistics themselves were bad enough but the real heartbreak and horror were contained in the deeply moving human stories of people who had lost loved ones, or who had to deal with relatives who were traumatised by severe injuries.

One mother whose son had been shot dead by the Provisional IRA 'by mistake' wrote me a heart-rending letter of appreciation because I had expressed my deep sympathy for her and her family in one of my weekly columns. It still disturbs me to think that an innocent young man could be murdered 'by mistake' and that his mother's grief would be intensified beyond measure by such callous and random savagery.

I replied to her privately and expressed my own despair at the killings which went on and on, and no-one seemed able to stop them.

Yet even in those terrible times, there was the paradox that people tried to live their lives as normally as possible, despite the extraordinary dangers and stresses of daily life.

For example, the most important event in my life in 1977 had nothing to do with journalism or the Troubles. It was the birth of our third child Matthew, on 16 September of that year. I saw Hilary in the maternity unit before the birth, and those were the days when the majority of men definitely did not attend the arrival of the child. Perhaps we were the poorer for this, but it never occurred to most of us that we ought to be present to support our wives and to welcome our new-born child into the world.

I left Hilary in labour – that sounds awful now – and went back home to await the arrival of our baby. Once the child was delivered I rushed back to the hospital. Hilary was still groggy, but there was our healthy boy lying beside her in a hospital incubator.

We decided later to call him Matthew, partly because this means 'gift of God' and partly because I felt that 'Matthew McCreary' would make a good name for a writer. Little did I realise then that he would eventually become a fine journalist and that, of course, his wife Orla and all his friends would call him 'Matt'.

Back in my professional mode I continued to write articles about more 'normal' situations, as well as commenting on the hard news of the continuing violence and political in-fighting.

I wrote my leaders in the mornings, and this left me free on most afternoons and evenings to report on other non-political stories. It was an opportunity to write about the good news, as well as the bad, and I was fortunate enough to have an editor who backed me practising in this dual role.

Thus my writing portfolio included some exotic stories, given the background of Northern Ireland. During one routine assignment in Crossmaglen, which was at the heart of the border 'bandit country' I talked to the proprietor of a guest house who offered to take me to dinner.

The fact that anyone would open a guest house in Crossmaglen at that time of upheaval was a news story in itself, and the proprietor's invitation to dinner was an offer I did not want to refuse.

He asked me "Would you like to go to a Vietnamese restaurant near here?" As he spoke, the house was shaken by the roar of a British Army helicopter overhead on its mission to carry food and other supplies to the beleaguered troops who were stationed in Crossmaglen.

I thought that I had misheard him and I asked "Are you serious, there can't be a Vietnamese restaurant near Crossmaglen? He said "I'm not joking. One of the Vietnamese boat people who were rescued and allowed to settle in the United Kingdom came to live in Portadown, and he has opened a restaurant in Crossmaglen which serves Vietnamese food."

I reported this in the *Belfast Telegraph*, and it was picked up by most of the national newspapers, and also by the BBC Radio 4 network. My story about this Crossmaglen 'exotica' had struck a chord with a wide audience.

Another off-beat story arose from the night when I reported on a female wrestling match between 'Cherokee Princess' and 'Klondyke Kate' at an hotel in Cushendun, on the Antrim coast. Those were the days when male wrestling was immensely popular on television, chiefly through the antics of people like the feared Mick McManus.

It took the public a long time to realise that wrestling was largely a theatrical extravaganza which had little to do with reality. This was underlined by the obituary much later of Mick McManus who was described thus in *The Independent* newspaper: "For all his tough-guy image, he was actually a quiet, polite and gentle man. In later life he collected antiques, developing a particular expertise in porcelain."

Probably the Cherokee Princess and Klondyke Kate were also gentle and courteous in private, but they were professionally enough at wrestling to entertain a large audience that night in Cushendun.

Afterwards I talked to the Cherokee Princess, who was billed as "The World's Most Beautiful Lady Wrestler." She was called Gloria Young and she looked most attractive in her red jacket and black tights.

She told me that she was twenty-four, and unmarried, and that she lived in Wales. She had not long returned from cabaret in the Far East where she doubled as a 'fire-eater'. She also said that she was a pianist, with three grades from the Royal College of Music. She liked wrestling, though she feared a permanent injury. However she appreciated the money, and she was saving to buy a business.

Her opponent that night – Klondyke Kate – was billed as "a big lady, mean and nasty" was a young lady from Stoke-on-Trent who liked working in Northern Ireland because of the friendliness of the people.

I noticed, however, that the two ladies did not fraternise after their wrestling bout, and I wrote later that "There are areas where only the foolish intrude to reason why."

There were also male wrestlers on the bill, including a man who had the stage name of "Dirty Darki – The Referee's Nightmare". Afterwards, he outlined for me some of the classic wrestling holds, and when he put his thumb on my wind-pipe and started to press it, I knew instantly that wrestling was not for me.

During this part of my career I was still able to travel overseas quite frequently, and where possible I sent or brought back reports for the *Belfast Telegraph*.

These included a story from Miami where I was due to meet an elderly entrepreneur called Kaplan, who had been one of the first distributors of Old Bushmills whiskey in the USA.

This was part of my extensive research for a book on the history of Old Bushmills, which had been commissioned by the then managing director Bill McCourt, who also became a good friend.

Unfortunately Mr Kaplan was living in an old people's home in Miami and was too ill to see me, but his wife was a generous host. She paid for my stay in a nearby apartment block. One evening as I watched people dancing after dinner, I noticed that a good looking young man was escorting different old ladies on to the dance floor.

I initially thought that he was being very kind to possibly his grandmother and some of her friends. However I was disabused of this kindly, if naïve notion, when an nearby diner told me that the old ladies were paying the young man to dance with them. It was the only time that I ever saw a gigolo in action.

During that trip to Miami I also went for a massage, which I rarely do. I was partly curious to find out what happened in a resort full of rich, elderly and mostly overweight businessmen. When it came to my turn, the male proprietor of the heath spa said to me "Who do you want to massage you – the black girl, or the girl from the islands?" I was by this stage a long way from my Bessbrook boyhood, and I replied hesitantly "I don't know, maybe the girl from the islands, I don't really care." He replied "It's your bad luck buddy, you're getting me."

All the other sweaty figures in the sauna roared with laughter at this 'Irish' guy who had fallen for one of the oldest jokes imaginable.

When my book on Old Bushmills was finished we called it *Spirit of the Age*, and it was publicised on television in New York, during a snowstorm, and launched in San Diego, during a heat wave. This was exotica indeed, and I well remember the reception on St Patrick's Day in an upmarket San Diego restaurant.

It was launched by the Irish Republic's Education Minister George

Birmingham. He was one of the Dublin government's ministers who were in the USA on a Paddy's Day charm offensive. I felt it a great irony that an 'Orange' labelled whiskey was being launched in the USA by a Dublin minister on St Patrick's Day.

However the venue was not inappropriate because many thousands of Ulster emigrants had made the long trek to California in previous decades and had brought with them the folk memory, and sometimes the products, of the Old Bushmills distillery.

In fact when I landed in San Diego airport from New York, I noticed large advertisements urging people to try an 'Ambush' – a mixture of Old Bushmills and a beverage called Amarillo. The irony of that was not lost on me either, because the word 'ambush' had a very different meaning where I lived.

After the launch in San Diego, the restaurant staff rearranged the tables and it was quickly full of people celebrating St Patrick's Day. I noticed a barman wearing a priest's collar, but that apparently was his usual party piece on special days. I also noticed that the resident pianist was playing superbly, and when I went over to pay my compliments to him, I realised that he was reading the *New York Times* while he played.

Before I left America on that visit I spent a day and night in San Francisco. I did not have an 'Irish' tie, so I bought one in a local drapery store. It was made in Belfast, which made me feel at home! The next day I had my final television appearance in that hectic nationwide book promotional tour.

It was a live broadcast from the sunny grounds of a women's prison outside San Francisco. This was a unique experience for me as I watched the female inmates pass by in brown prison uniform. I also received some professional tips from another author on the programme who was doing a coast-to-coast tour to promote her own best-selling book *Vietnam Nurse*.

That night I boarded a British Airways jet in San Francisco and flew along the North Pole route to London, and from thence back to Belfast and its grim reality.

Every time I completed a foreign assignment and came back to Belfast in those days, there was a cultural shock, no matter how many times I had experienced this previously. In this case it was hard to readjust from the wonderful experiences in New York, San Diego and

San Francisco, and to try to get used again to the bombs, the barbed wire, and the barbed politics at home.

However there was no way of avoiding all this, short of leaving Northern Ireland, which my wife and I had decided not to do, for family and other reasons. There was also the constant lure of my professional life – Northern Ireland was still THE big story, I was committed to bridge-building, and I wanted to see it through to the end.

Against this continued backdrop, the year 1981 was a watershed for me both personally and professionally. In August of that year my beloved mother-in-law Dr Winifred Fitzsimons died at the age of sixty-two after an illness. She was a true Christian, and she lived with quiet and impressive saintliness. She had been widowed some twenty-three years previously by the untimely death of her husband, the Reverend James Fitzsimons who had died at fifty-six from a heart attack.

My mother-in-law had graduated from Queen's University with a degree in medicine, but apart from her early post-graduate days, she had not practised while rearing her four children. After her husband's death, she took fresh medical training and spent the rest of her career as a family practitioner in Coleraine, where her kindness and medical skills were appreciated by many people.

She and I became close friends, and her early death deeply affected my wife Hilary, and the wider family. I paid tribute to my mother-in-law at her funeral in First Coleraine Presbyterian Church. She was buried in the graveyard of Second Dunboe Presbyterian Church. After the interment, two craggy old bachelor farmers, who had been my mother-in-law's patients, came up to me at the graveside and one of them said to me shyly "That was a quare good tribute you paid to Dr Fitzsimons in the church. There was'ne a word you couldn't stand over." That was a great tribute indeed to my much loved mother-in-law and close friend, now so sadly departed.

A few days before her death, however, I had experienced quite different emotions when I was involved in one of the most interesting assignments of my career. I was sent to London to report on the wedding of Prince Charles and Lady Diana Spencer in St Paul's Cathedral.

I was the only reporter there from Northern Ireland, and I sat in the same row as Maeve Binchy, the novelist who was then the London editor of the *Irish Times*. Though the media were crammed into a corner of the

Cathedral near the front, we had a better view than the American First Lady Nancy Reagan, who was seated well down the Church. However the best view of all was reserved for the willowy and beautiful Princess Grace of Monaco, who was seated near the High Altar.

It was an historic and glittering occasion, and for me the service was particularly memorable because of the fine music, and also the mellifluous tones of George Thomas, who was at that time the Speaker of the House of Commons. He read beautifully from St Paul's masterpiece on "Faith, Hope and Charity" from the New Testament, in the unsurpassable poetry of the King James Version. (My mother-in-law used to say that "St Paul did not make this up, he simply wrote it down!")

Prince Charles' first Royal Wedding was also memorable for me in another way because the media area was so crowded that the world-famous New Zealand soprano Dame Kiri Te Kanawa trod heavily on my foot by accident, as she made her way to the television gantry to sing live a Mozart aria for a worldwide audience of many millions.

I reported in the *Belfast Telegraph* that "it was indubitably the day for the big occasion with the pageantry of Church and State layered upon pomp and circumstance. Yet through it all the little human touches were a reminder there was more to this day than the first wedding of a Prince of Wales in St Paul's since 1501..." I concluded my report in this way: "It was something which people who were lucky enough to be there will never forget. Prince Charles himself had said 'I want everyone to come out of the Cathedral having had a marvellous musical and emotional experience'. And that's exactly what it had been. Happy and glorious."

That was then. The subsequent failure of the marriage and the untimely death of Diana was a great tragedy, but perhaps – with hindsight – the breakdown between these two young people with so much emotional and psychological baggage was inevitable.

I returned from the Royal Wedding to yet another stark contrast. Northern Ireland was in the throes of dealing with the Provisional IRA hunger-strikes which was one of the most controversial and polarising developments of the entire Troubles, and which I will mention later on.

However, away from the sinister and disturbing daily news about the hunger-strikes, I found that my career was moving in yet another direction as the presenter of a BBC series of radio profiles on well-known people in Northern Ireland and from much further afield. This gave me a fascinating insight into the lives of many figures who were already national celebrities before that term became so badly abused. Life behind the headlines is often quite different to what members of the public might suppose, and that's why I wanted to talk to the people who were making the headlines, and to try to find out what they were really like.

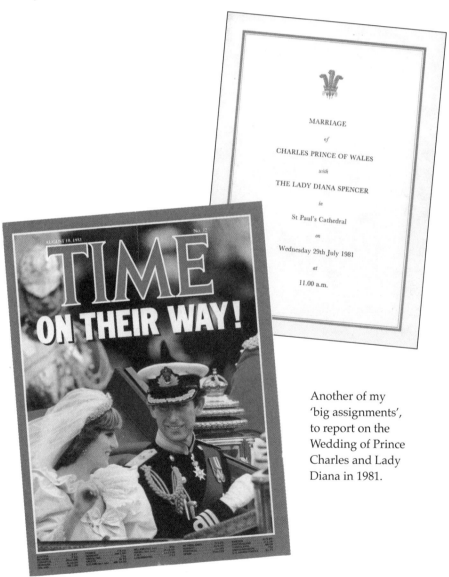

Another of my 'big assignments', to report on the Wedding of Prince Charles and Lady Diana in 1981.

CHAPTER SIXTEEN

Behind the Headlines

ONE OF THE advantages of being a writer is that you can come to know people behind their public image.

This is an advantage because most people do not get close to many well-known public figures. The disadvantage is that when you do so, you sometimes see them, warts and all.

One of my more memorable in-depth interviews was with the late Frank Carson, who was a brilliant comedian but also a man who had a hard edge behind his image of a folksy and funny storyteller.

I first met Frank in the mid-Sixties when I was a television critic with the *Belfast Telegraph*, or to be more precise, with the *Ireland's Saturday Night*. I was invited to join a panel to choose applications from a long list of hopefuls for a BBC Northern Ireland television talent contest.

There were numerous acts, and some of dubious quality, including a man who played the tin whistle – down his nose. He did not make the final list.

Frank Carson was in a different league. He was then relatively unknown, and he was earning his living as a plasterer. Immediately he entered the studio, I spotted him as an obvious finalist for the competition. Frank was not only funny during his act, but all the time.

Some comedians have a dark side and they are not all funny off stage, but Carson never stopped telling jokes. I am not sure if he won the BBC Northern Ireland finals that year, but later on he became a national hit when he won a television network talent competition. He never needed to go back to plastering again.

Frank was at the height of his fame when I travelled to Blackpool to meet him. He was topping the bill in a local theatre with the pop star Lulu, but beforehand we had lunch at his home in Blackpool.

He never stopped talking, and I hardly stopped laughing throughout the lunch. He told me a story about his experiences as a British serviceman in the Second World War, and particularly about one mission in the Middle East.

He said "My commanding officer and I were invited to afternoon tea by a village chieftain. When the tea was served, we were surprised when he slowly poured milk into a saucer. Not to be outdone by this, or to appear to be impolite, my Commanding Officer and I looked at each other and then solemnly did the same thing.

"Then the chieftain kneeled down slowly and set down the saucer with milk for his pet cat, which promptly lapped it up. We were left hold a saucer of milk each, and we did not know what to do with it. So we also knelt down and gave our milk to the cat as well. That was its lucky day!"

Our lunch was served in Frank's Blackpool home by a charming lady, and half way through the meal he introduced us. He said "This is the wife, and we've been married for thirty years. It seems just like yesterday." I replied innocently "How nice!", and he ended with his punch-line "...and you know what a lousy day yesterday was!"

Laugh, laugh, laugh – it never stopped. Even at the theatre the impromptu jokes went on. The man was nerveless. During the interval Frank told a series of jokes to Lulu, who was so doubled up with laughter that she almost missed her cue for her entrance on stage for the second half.

At the end of the show Frank bade me goodbye and I went away with memories of a top comedian whose talent matched his massive ego. I also recalled that when we arrived outside the theatre, Frank had said to me "Watch this."

He parked his large vehicle on double yellow lines outside the theatre, and just across the street from a parked police patrol car. When one of the policemen came across to investigate what was happening, with a parking ticket no doubt at the ready, Frank rolled down his driver's window and said to the police officer "It's only me, it's the way I tell them!"

The policeman said "Frank. It's you!", and he visibly relaxed as he laughed his way back to the patrol car. Then Frank said to me, with a wink "Now that they know it's me, I can park on this double yellow line all day." Frank Carson had developed a tough skin in a tough business, and he was nobody's fool.

After I left Frank at the theatre, I made my way back to my overnight guesthouse. Blackpool, despite its worldly downmarket charms, did not impress me. I was glad to be on my way out of it the next morning, except that my destination was Accrington. It was there that I had arranged to meet Alex 'Hurricane' Higgins, who was then the current Snooker World Champion, and also an Ulster folk hero with feet of clay.

I trudged through Accrington in the rain to a local pub where I expected Higgins to turn up and to honour our pre-arranged appointment. I waited, and waited, and waited. I knew that Higgins could be unreliable, but I thought that he would be keen to be featured in the biggest paper in Northern Ireland, and that he would at least turn up.

After forty-five minutes I became tired of waiting, and I asked the barman if he had seen Higgins recently. He gave me a look of pity and said "Alex was in here earlier, but he has cleared off to Blackpool for the weekend."

No Higgins, no interview, no major profile for the *Belfast Telegraph*. I asked myself "How could you have been so naïve? Did you really expect Hurricane Higgins to keep his word?"

I went back into the pouring rain, carrying my suitcase, and headed towards the railway station. On the way there a lady, who looked like part of the cast of Coronation Street, was standing in her doorway. She said cheerily "Are you going on your holidays luv?" I smiled at her weakly through clenched teeth, but I thought it better not to answer her, in the circumstances.

I was thinking to myself "No I am not going on holiday. I am returning to Belfast in the rain, and without my 'exclusive' interview with Hurricane Higgins. And I am never, ever, going back to Accrington again."

However, given the law of unexpected consequences, I was to meet the 'Hurricane', or what was left of him, many years later. This time he could not escape from me. He was dead.

Despite his outstanding skills as a snooker player, Higgins had a troubled life. His marriage failed, he lost his position as the world's top snooker player, he drank too much, he fell out with too many people, and his life became one big mess.

On top of all that he developed throat cancer, and died after a long illness. The self-styled 'People's Champion' was no more, but his friends and the plain people of Belfast gave him a good send-off, and much better, perhaps, than he deserved.

I invited myself to his funeral service in St Anne's Cathedral by offering to write a 'colour piece' for the *Belfast Telegraph*. Although the service was due to begin at 11.30 am, I arrived early to watch the build-up.

The funeral was a surreal affair, with the coffin in an ornate hearse drawn by black horses while members of the public lined part of the processional route to pay their last respects.

When I arrived at the Cathedral, I was prevented from going through the front door by two bulky young men in dark glasses, who asked for my name. I told them that I was reporting the funeral for the *Belfast Telegraph*, but they were unimpressed. "No meeja" they said "Just friends of Alex, and other invited guests."

So, I needed the assistance of the then Dean of Belfast Dr Houston McKelvey who told the two heavies on the main door to let me in.

Once inside I asked the Dean "The funeral cortege has arrived an hour early. What are you going to do now?" He replied "Once they come in we'll keep them here. If we let them leave they might not come back again!"

In the event, it was an impressive service which was attended by Higgins' friends and by most of the world's best-known snooker players, and other sporting figures.

The Dean preached a generous sermon along the lines of "Who are we to cast the first stone?", and Higgins' daughter read a moving poetic tribute to her dad.

At the end, the mourners filed out of the Cathedral, including ordinary members of the public who had filled the empty media seats along the side of the church.

As I prepared to leave, one wee Belfast woman said to me "Are you the meeja?" I replied "Yes, I'm writing a report for the *Telegraph*. Do you want to give me a quote about Alex?"

She replied "I was not a great snooker fan, but I always enjoyed watching him on television." I wrote down her words dutifully, and asked for her name because a journalist is always glad of a quote for a 'colour piece'.

As I walked away, she came after me and said "There was another thing I want to say about Alex – he didn't give a sh–t about anybody!" She was absolutely right, but her comment was not for publication.

During those years I interviewed so many people that I could write a book about them. However it is sobering to realise that most people are 'famous' for a short period, and then the public forgets about them quite quickly, in a world where the daily news and the lust for new 'celebrities' are insatiable.

I also discovered the big difference between interviewing people for a long article in a newspaper, and talking to them in depth for a radio programme. In newspapers the emphasis is on the quality of the writing, but in broadcasting the clarity of voice and a good sense of timing are important also. However the supreme requirement in all interviews is an ability to listen intently, and to know when a good story is developing.

In the early Eighties the BBC asked me to present a series of radio profiles on well-known personalities, as I mentioned earlier. I accepted the invitation enthusiastically as another development in my career, even though I had little or no training for radio. I am amazed that I had the courage to take on the challenge, and that the BBC had given me the opportunity to do so.

I was prepared to learn 'on the job', which was the way in which the BBC operated in those days. It was a nerve-wracking experience, but I made up for my lack of experience by building up a top-class list of interviewees for my weekly programme, which was recorded. It was called "People in Profile" and it was a local version of Desert Island Discs, during which each interviewee talked about his or her career, and chose some favourite music.

My first guest was the Secretary of State for Northern Ireland Humphrey Atkins, and this was a scoop. The trouble was that I did not have enough experience to tell the bosses that the Secretary of State was coming into the BBC building, where the interview was to take place.

When the top 'suits' found out, about an hour before the recording began, they went into a flap, but it was too late to repair my breach of protocol in not telling them in advance. I found this all rather amusing.

The interview went well. I respected Atkins, who was regarded as a political lightweight compared to the first Tory Secretary of State Willie Whitelaw, who was a heavyweight in every respect.

However Humphrey Atkins was smart enough to end up as Deputy Foreign Minister when he left the Northern Ireland job, which he must have found frustrating and unrewarding.

I recall one evening when he invited my wife Hilary and I to dinner at Hillsborough Castle, together with around a dozen people from other walks of life in Northern Ireland.

The dinner passed pleasantly enough, but after the coffee stage the ladies were asked to move into a separate room, and the men stayed with the Secretary of State as the port was passed round. Even now it is hard to believe that such a 'sexist' arrangement still prevailed at Hillsborough Castle at that time.

As we passed the port around the dining table, each person gave his views about the current situation in Northern Ireland. Unfortunately, our lack of agreement on the major issues underlined exactly why Northern Ireland was in such a sectarian and political deadlock, with the resultant violence that was swirling all around us.

Atkins listened to each speaker carefully, and at the end he could not conceal his exasperation. He said "I have listened to everyone here, and there is one big difference between you and me. I fought against the Germans during the Second World War and I have learned to move on. It is clear to me that you people still cannot forgive or forget the past."

Atkins knew exactly what the trouble was in Northern Ireland, and he had summarised our lengthy round-table discussion in a nutshell.

§

One of my most memorable radio interviews took place by chance after I attended a music recital at the home of the Marquess of Dufferin and Ava at Clandeboye. I had been invited by a financier called Harry McIlroy who was the head of a bank in Belfast, and whom I had profiled earlier in the *Belfast Telegraph*.

The recital was a black tie affair, and it was the first time that my young son Matthew had seen me in evening dress. With his child-like enthusiasm and his early gift for observation and language he said "Dad, you look like a real gentleman!"

During the recital I noticed that one member of the audience looked remarkably like the actor and film star Peter O'Toole who had achieved worldwide fame in the David Lean's film 'Lawrence of Arabia'.

I kept glancing at this man discreetly to make sure that I was right, and eventually I said to my self "He IS Peter O'Toole." As soon as the interval began I made a beeline for him, before anyone else had the chance to talk to him.

I said "Mr O'Toole I run a BBC radio programme and one of my recent guests was the Ulster-born actor Harry Towb. He mentioned that he had worked with you on a series of short stories by Sean O'Faolain."

O'Toole replied "Yes, dear boy, I remember Harry well, but we worked on stories by Frank O'Connor, not O'Faolain". I then said "I would be delighted if you would consider appearing on my radio programme. I could interview you here perhaps tomorrow, if you were free." He replied "I'll think about it, dear boy. Ring me in the morning."

I could not believe that I might actually get O'Toole to agree, and the next day, near noon, I rang him. I happened to be in Holywood, County Down where I was working on a feature for the *Belfast Telegraph*.

When I rang Clandeboye House, a very precise butler answered. When I asked to speak to "Mr O'Toole", he asked "From where are you phoning?"

I replied "Holywood", and he went off to tell O'Toole who came to the phone immediately. It was only afterwards that I realised that O'Toole must have thought that the call was from "Hollywood, California" and not "Holywood, County Down."

I asked O'Toole if he would like to be interviewed, and to my amazement he agreed. He said "Come down to Clandeboye and we will have afternoon tea. We can talk afterwards."

I could not believe my luck, but the big problem was to get a producer from the BBC to come with me, at such short notice, and to bring an old-fashioned and very heavy recording machine.

Fortunately my producer Charlie Warmington was free, and we set off for Clandeboye. Charlie was one of the most helpful people with whom I worked at the BBC, and he was the only one who helped me with voice-training for broadcasting.

On the way to Clandeboye I said to Charlie "What do we do if O'Toole asks us for a fee? Our top rate is only fifty quid a programme." Charlie replied "I know it's only peanuts, but you'll have to tell him beforehand."

O'Toole received us graciously, but I had the tricky job of finally hooking my big fish. So I said "Mr O'Toole I am grateful that you have agreed to be interviewed, but we have a fixed fee and we can only pay you £50." There was a short silence, and then he waved his hand and said "Dear boy, give the money to charity!"

Much relieved, I began my interview while Charlie looked after the technicalities of the interview. It went well. O'Toole was a natural broadcaster with a gift for language, and he had a huge fund of stories.

He talked about serving in the Royal Navy during the Second World War. He said "Our vessel put in to Londonderry and a few of us wanted to go somewhere for a drink. We were told that there was great Guinness in Donegal, but Royal Navy people were not allowed to go there because it was a foreign country and Eire was neutral during the war.

"However we solved the problem. We heard that people turned a blind eye to the rules, and that if we left our naval hats at the customs hut on the border, nobody would say a word. So we did exactly that, and we had a blinder of a night in Donegal. The Guinness, dear boy, was wonderful!"

For many months afterwards I smiled at the thought of 'Lawrence of Arabia' removing his Royal Navy headgear and leaving it in a customs post on the Irish border, while he enjoying the forbidden delights of Guinness in Donegal.

The challenge of following up the Peter O'Toole interview was to maintain the same standard, and a surprising number of high-profile people visited Northern Ireland even at the height of the Troubles. They included the American singer-songwriter Harry Chapin who gave me one of the best interviews of the series.

He talked with insight and humour, and yet he was serious about the important things in life, like love, creativity and fulfilment. I remember well one of his statements – "If you ain't busy living, you're busy dying."

Tragically, Chapin himself died soon after our interview, when he was involved in a horrific motor accident in upstate New York. The untimely death of this talented young man who had so much to offer was difficult to accept or understand, then and now.

There were also some outstanding local characters who appeared in my "People in Profile" series. One morning my producer and I went to the Europa Hotel to meet George Best who had agreed to talk to us.

Not surprisingly Best did not appear, although I caught up with him later on, and in a very different context. On that morning in the Europa, however, we were stuck for a subject for the next week's programme so I suggested to my producer that we should try Rinty Monaghan, a former world champion flyweight boxer who, in his day, was probably even better known locally than a more recent Ulster world champion Barry McGuigan.

We contacted Rinty, who was delighted to be invited, and we did the interview in the studio. I had known about Rinty in my boyhood, when he was a sporting folk hero, and I even remembered that he had narrowly beaten the Glaswegian Jackie Paterson for the world title in 1948. He had a remarkable story to tell about his early difficulties as a Roman Catholic in the Harland and Wolff shipyard, and his stirring boxing victories, as well as his later career as a Belfast taxi driver.

One of his trademarks was to sing 'When Irish Eyes Are Smiling' at each successful bout on his way to the world championship. So my producer and I thought it would be fitting to allow him to sing it at the end of the recording.

That meant that he had to remain quiet until we gave him his cue to sing. However he was nervous, and every ten seconds he would look me in the eye and ask "Do I do it nae?" Each time I shook my head, but eventually we got the timing right. I looked across at Rinty, nodded my head, and instantly he burst into song. His performance was a fitting finale to an historic programme, and also a tribute to his outstanding career as a professional boxer.

Despite the sense of creativity in talking to such fascinating people, and making radio programmes about them, I was never totally happy working for the BBC. There were many good people in the Corporation, some of whom have been friends of mine over a long period, but there were too many others who were arrogant, insecure and with limited talent.

My experience at the BBC was not unique, but it contrasted with my time in the *Belfast Telegraph* where I had been working for so long. Of course there were rows and rivalries within the *Telegraph* staff, but there was also an atmosphere of mutual respect and camaraderie, which I rarely found at the BBC. I have never understood how so many creative people could sustain such dedication and stamina to make a lifelong career in an atmosphere which could descend at times into such a bear-pit of insecurity, envy and hubris.

Nevertheless I still remained grateful to the BBC for the opportunity to have branched into regular broadcasting, and I met some remarkable people. I was glad to have made the programmes, but I was also glad to move on.

Some of my most challenging writing assignments were associated with major events like Royal visits, and particularly those of Queen Elizabeth II, who came to Northern Ireland with commendable regularity even during the worst of the Troubles.

In August 1977 she came to Belfast as part of her Silver Jubilee celebrations, and I was sent to Hillsborough Castle to report on her arrival there. It was a particularly challenging visit for Her Majesty because she was required to travel by helicopter for the first time.

She and the Duke of Edinburgh were based on the Royal Yacht *Britannia* which was moored in Belfast Harbour, and it was felt that the Royal couple should travel as little as possible by road, because of the security situation.

When the Queen and Prince Philip landed at Hillsborough by helicopter I was part of a small group of reporters who were positioned not far away. The Queen was wearing an outfit which the *Irish Times* later reported was a "Kelly green" colour. As she passed closely by there was no clear hint of how she felt about the helicopter journey, though some experienced 'Royal watchers' thought that she looked rather tense.

Later that morning she held an investiture in Hillsborough Castle and I remember standing outside the building beside Prince Philip who was his usual unpredictable self but on that day, sadly for us, there were none of politically incorrect quips which so endeared him to the British public.

When I finished my report from Hillsborough I went to the Lower Falls in Belfast where the Army was dealing with violent protesters.

Later in the afternoon I was in time for my son Mark's birthday party in our back garden, which was roughly equidistant from where the rioting had taken place in Belfast, and the site where the Queen's yacht was moored in Belfast Harbour. It was always difficult to adjust to the two worlds of work and family in a city like Belfast where peace and war lived cheek by jowl.

Later in my career I met the Queen on two separate occasions – once in Westminster Abbey after a service to honour the civilian victims of war and their families. They included Joan Wilson and her daughter Julie-Anne who had invited me to join them in the famous Jerusalem Chamber. I had no idea that the Queen was present, until a senior cleric from the Abbey murmured to us "Her Majesty will be with you in a moment." Suddenly there was the Queen, right in front of us. I was impressed by her professionalism and authority. The Queen is relatively small in stature, but her presence fills every room she enters.

The next time I met the Queen was in Buckingham Palace when I was invited to an Investiture Ceremony to receive an MBE for my services to journalism and charity in Northern Ireland.

I had been told by others who had been to the Palace to arrive there early in order to get a good seat for my family, so my wife Hilary, daughter Emma and son Matthew and I were some of the first to arrive outside the gates. My son Mark and his wife Angela and their baby daughter Molly were living in Australia at that time, and they were unable to attend the Investiture Ceremony.

As I was standing outside the gates of Buckingham Palace and waiting to get in, a man joining the queue said to me, to my great surprise, "Aren't you the boy from Bessbrook?" He was the minister from a South Armagh church, and the father of Ruth McCartney, the talented music director of the choirs of Methodist College Belfast which had won many national awards. Ruth was also being honoured at the Palace, and deservedly so.

The Queen filled the large Palace ballroom with her presence, and for my family and me it was one of the days of a lifetime, and I am sure that it was the same for all the others who received awards. When I hear of people I know who have been given a decoration I am delighted for them, because it really is a special occasion. I respect those who decline such an honour, but I disapprove of others who do so, and then leak it to the media. That is the height of bad manners.

§

One of my most memorable reporting assignments was in June 1984 when President Ronald Reagan and the First Lady Nancy visited the Irish Republic.

This was the first visit by a US President to Ireland since John F Kennedy in the Sixties, and there was a air of anticipation in all parts of the island, including the North.

The visit was partly a pre-election campaign by Reagan who had recently discovered his Irish roots, and the Irish-American vote was valuable for any campaigning US President.

I was sent to cover his visit to the small village of Ballyporeen in Tipperary, where an enterprising publican had opened new premises which he named 'The Ronald Reagan Lounge'. It seemed too good an electoral opportunity for Reagan to miss, especially as the new mobile television cameras could broadcast his visit 'live' to every part of the USA.

I arrived in Ballyporeen on the day before his visit, to discover that the American Secret Service staff had combed every cranny for security threats, even the sewers. However they were not so secret themselves because, incongruously, they all wore light-coloured raincoats, which were instantly conspicuous.

I also noticed one huge wall-advertisement for Irish whiskey which read "Black Bush – The President's Choice." By the next morning, however, it had been altered by the Secret Service to read "Black Bush – the Residents' Choice". I thought naively that this was because the President did not like whiskey, but I was told that the term 'Black Bush' has a different connotation in the USA.

When President Reagan eventually reached Ballyporeen there was the usual flurry of the excitement and sense of drama that accompanies all visits by such famous people. As the President and his large entourage slowly walked down the main street, they were accompanied by a tall US Naval officer who was carrying a large holdall, known as 'The Football'.

This was said to contain the codes to help the President counter a sudden nuclear attack from Russia, at a time when the Cold War was still dangerously chilly. It occurred to me that the naval officer with the large bag could be a decoy, and that the road-sweeper standing nearby was the man with the real secrets.

In the afternoon the President visited the pub which was named after him, and I was one of the several Irish journalists who were roped off in a corner of the 'Ronald Reagan' bar, together with the hardened White House corps who were travelling with him.

As soon as the President entered, followed by his wife Nancy whose eyes never left his face, someone thrust a pint of Smithwick's beer into his hand. It had been tested by the Secret Service, and it was an obvious photo opportunity. This led to a *Daily Mail* newspaper story the next day about the "Guinn-less President."

Back in the 'Ronald Reagan' bar, a grizzled US reporter whispered to me "Look out for the baby, buddy." The wife of the pub owner had recently given birth to a daughter whom they had christened Nancy, for obvious reasons.

Sure enough, the Secret Service men removed the pint from Reagan's outstretched hand, even before he could take a sip, and suddenly the President was left holding the baby.

Then an American reporter asked him, for the benefit of the huge US audience watching the live broadcast "Mr President they named the pub after you, but they christened the baby after the First Lady – what do you think of that?"

There was a silence. All I could hear was the whirring of a helicopter hovering over the pub. Nancy gazed intently at her husband. Still no comment. Was the most powerful man in the world lost for words? Had he even understood the question? Eventually he said "Well, you guys, let's say this is 'fortunes of war!'" Everyone laughed with relief. The US President was still clearly able to function.

Then Ronald Reagan was hurried by his bodyguards to another part of the building, and in doing so he passed about two feet way from me. To my astonishment he was being told off by a burly female security chief who was bristling with radio and microphone antennae. She snapped "Mr President you are already twenty minutes late, and your staff cannot tolerate this." I suddenly felt sorry for Reagan. He was by no means young, and he was clearly under pressure, despite being the most powerful man in the world.

When the US President was ushered into a side room, I was hustled out of the building, with the other reporters. As I was hurried by Presidential aides along the street outside, and past the cheering crowds, I noticed several things.

Outside the pub a large van was filled with heavily-armed security men. In front of them was the President's black limousine which was empty, apart from a lone submachine gun on the back seat; and a solitary ambulance was parked in the back yard of the pub.

All of this brought home to me the vulnerability of so many major public figures, and perhaps most of all the President of the United States.

In later years I made an in-depth study of Reagan who was one of the great post-war US Presidents, and also a remarkable man. He was much more than the mere B-movie actor which, his many critics suggested, was his only real claim to fame.

It had been a privilege to report at first hand on the visit of President Ronald Reagan to Ireland. However I did not know at the time that this would be my last major assignment as a full-time staff member of the *Belfast Telegraph*. My career was to take yet another unexpected turning, and away from daily journalism and newspaper work. But more about that later...

CHAPTER SEVENTEEN

On the Move

M Y DECISION TO leave the *Belfast Telegraph* was not taken lightly or suddenly. It was the result of a long period of self-analysis, when I tried to answer two questions – "Do I want to spend the rest of my working life in the *Belfast Telegraph* and secondly, do I want to try a career outside daily journalism?"

Neither question was easy to answer. The *Telegraph* was giving me a fulfilling career, and I had experienced in the newspaper more freedom, writing opportunities, challenges, variation and international travel than most of my peers, apart from the high-profile sports editor Malcolm Brodie. He was a fine, supportive colleague with a generous spirit and a fund of fascinating and funny stories about the many ramifications of sport in general and of soccer in particular.

By the early Eighties I had been in the *Telegraph* for nearly twenty years, and for most of them I had been reporting in detail about the Troubles. I had interviewed a large number of the protagonists and the victims, I had written countless editorials, analyses, columns and major features about the continuing deadlock in Northern Ireland, and I was running out of words.

For example, each leader-writer was required to put his own brief headline on the editorial he had just written. One of those which I often used about the latest atrocity was "Murder Most Foul". Sadly, even these words became hackneyed, and there seemed to be almost nothing new to say about the horror of the Troubles, and the suffering of the people on all sides.

The situation was made infinitely worse by the Republican hunger-strikes in 1981 when ten Provisional IRA men starved themselves to death between 1 March and 3 October in an attempt to win significant political concessions from the British government.

Much has been written elsewhere about this tragic episode in Anglo-Irish relations, but in essence it was a fight to the death – literally – between the formidable British Prime Minister Margaret Thatcher and the militant Republicans.

To put it bluntly, Mrs Thatcher won, and I cannot think of any other British post-war Prime Minister who would have had the steel to face down the Republicans in this way. The action of the hunger-strikers totally polarised the community. Their fellow Republicans naturally regarded them as heroes but the Loyalists viewed them with hostility and derision – which was symbolised by their graffiti about Bobby Sands, the most high-profile hunger-striker of all. A large wall slogan stated, with supreme disdain, "We will never forget you, Jimmy Sands."

The hunger-strike was a well known political weapon used by Republicans in Irish history, and however ghoulish or suicidal the 1981 deaths appeared to be among non-Republicans, there must be some recognition of the commitment of young men to starve themselves to death, however misplaced or unattainable their objectives were.

Although the news of the hunger-strikes filled many broadcast bulletins and newspapers, I had little involvement in reporting them directly, though I wrote a large number editorials and analyses about them for the *Telegraph* and the *Christian Science Monitor* in Boston. By that time I was fully occupied as a commentator, and leader and feature writer, and the daily reporting was being carried out by a new generation of news journalists.

Some of my vivid personal recollections of those terrible days are about Bobby Sands. One evening at a gathering of former hockey players I met a man who had been his teacher when he lived in Rathcoole, which had been a mixed housing estate before the Troubles. He told me that Sands had been "a nice wee lad" before someone had thrown a missile through the window of his home in Rathcoole.

This gave me an entirely different dimension to the young man who was starving himself to death in prison, and I wrote about this in a profile I was preparing for *Time* magazine in New York. I received a named 'by-line' on my article from that internationally-acclaimed magazine which normally reserved by-lines only for their senior correspondents and staffers.

My other memory of Sands centres around my reporting for the *Christian Science Monitor* in Boston. During that period the London editor was David Willis, a top-flight journalist who had previously been the bureau chief in Moscow.

During a weekend in early May 1981 when Bobby Sands was lingering near death, I mentioned to Willis, who had travelled to Belfast just like hundreds of other international journalists to cover the hunger-strikes, that I was going to Waringstown to report on a cricket match for our weekend evening sports paper, the *Ireland's Saturday Night*.

The village of Waringstown, which is some two miles south east of Lurgan in County Armagh, has a long tradition of producing champion cricket teams. They play in picturesque and leafy surroundings which are worthy of anywhere in England itself, the home of cricket.

I did not know that Willis was a cricket fanatic, who had formed a team during his time in Moscow, and he could not believe that I was reporting on cricket during the weekend of such international media coverage of the death of Bobby Sands.

Willis enthusiastically accompanied me to Waringstown and the next week the *Christian Science Monitor* carried an account of a cricket match in Northern Ireland during that sombre weekend previously, as well as an incisive report by Willis on the life and death of Bobby Sands. It was another striking example of peace and war existing side by side within the complex society of Northern Ireland, a dimension which is largely unknown and unintelligible to outsiders.

My other memory of that traumatic period was of a visit by Mother Teresa to the Corrymeela centre in Ballycastle. At a press conference one reporter asked her what she thought of the hunger-strikes and she replied that she found it difficult to understand why people in Ireland were starving themselves to death while people in her own country were dying because of the lack of food.

This was interpreted wrongly by some of the media as an attack by Mother Teresa on the hunger-strikers, but it was nothing of the sort. It was, however, an attempt by her to put the disturbing and sad episode of the Irish hunger-strikes into an entirely different context.

Nevertheless, they were of pivotal significance at that time and they still play an important role in sustaining the ethos of militant Republicanism in Ireland.

The hunger-strikes ended late in 1981, but they left deep wounds in the socio-political life of the Northern Ireland communities which will still take a long time to heal, if ever.

It was clear to me after the hunger-strikes ended that the political deadlock and violence which had trapped Northern Ireland in the past would continue for decades, and so it proved.

In theory I had the choice of staying with the *Belfast Telegraph* and reporting and commenting on much the same kind of stories about violence, political deadlock and human suffering, or looking for a different challenge.

The problem was that my work outside the *Belfast Telegraph* was generated largely by my reputation with the paper, and I was taking on commitments which brought me far away from Northern Ireland.

In 1981 I was invited to the 'Salzburg Seminar', which was run by Harvard University in association with the US government, to take part in a major international conference on the role of the media in society. It was a delight for me to travel from Munich to Salzburg on the 'Mozart Express', and later to meet so many people from different countries in Europe and the Middle East and to find out how they were dealing with their problems.

However the participants (not all of whom were journalists) expressed dissatisfaction with how the seminar was being run and, probably because they knew I was a newspaper reporter and therefore used to questioning authority, they asked me to talk to the organisers. I did so, and the Seminar Director invited me to produce and to present a verbal report to the plenary session within two days.

With difficulty, but also enjoyment, I interviewed everyone involved, and I was able to present a plenary report which seemed to please everybody, including the management. Afterwards a lecturer called Jon White from the then Cranfield Institute of Technology said to me "You're a one-man band. I don't think that you will be staying in your present job much longer." I laughed off his kind remarks, but I remembered what he had said.

On another occasion, I accepted an invitation to address an international conference in Washington on the effects of sustained violence within a local community, and I told the stories of some of the victims I had interviewed in Northern Ireland.

It was a formidable challenge for me, particularly as one of the speakers was the then First Lady Rosalynn Carter, the wife of the US President Jimmy Carter. However I was given an attentive hearing by a large audience which wanted to know more about the effects of the violence in Northern Ireland.

However there was only one discordant note, for me, which was struck by a questioner who had roots in the South Armagh area where I had also been brought up. His question was based on views which he had formed while growing up there some fifty years previously, and I was disappointed that he had learned nothing and had forgotten nothing about his native province since then. Sadly, he had never moved on from the sectarianism with which he had experienced in South Armagh.

The Washington trip was a good opportunity to visit that great city for the first time, but on my return to Belfast it was difficult to settle down to the daily treadmill of events in Northern Ireland with its daily stories of its suffering, its violence, and its long snakes of mourners filing out of Protestant or Roman Catholic churches to pay their last respects to murdered family or friends.

During that same period I also had the opportunity to visit another part of the world which had experienced immense suffering, and which was much greater than anything I had known in Northern Ireland.

Under the sponsorship of Christian Aid, the development agency of the British Council of Churches, I was invited with two other Europeans and an American to visit Vietnam and Cambodia to report on some of the post-conflict developments in both countries.

We spent several days in Ho Chi Minh city which was known formerly as Saigon. It was fascinating to note the developments there since the end of the war, but it was also sad to discover the many orphans in the streets, and particularly a little daughter of a former and long-departed American GI who took my hand and asked me if I could be her 'daddy'.

The children in Vietnam had seen few Europeans, and they assumed that we were Russians, because of the many people from that country who were working as 'advisers' to the Vietnamese government.

The main purpose of our visit was to concentrate on Cambodia which was just beginning to recover from the genocide of the Pol Pot regime, during which the Khmer Rouge and its supporters were responsible for the deaths of an estimated two million people from 1975–79.

People were forced to leave the cities and to work up to twelve hours a day, without a break. Children were separated from their parents, and given a leadership role in torture and executions. The Khmer Rouge tried to transform Cambodia into a classless rural society. They abolished money, schools, churches and other institutions.

It was an insanely murderous period when the main targets for forced labour, brutality and slaughter were the so-called 'intellectuals'. This label was so widely misinterpreted by members of the Pol Pot regime that the victims included intellectuals whose only 'crime' was to wear glasses.

My companions and I met one charming young girl whose fiancé had managed to leave on a commercial plane for Paris just before the Pol Pot clamp-down, and she was supposed to follow him two days later. Sadly she was too late, and she was forced to stay on in Cambodia, with little possibility of seeing her fiancé ever again.

On our way up country in Cambodia to visit an area where dissidents from the Pol Pot regime were still active, we were told that several Russians had been murdered recently on the road along which we intended to travel. This was ominous, because in a crisis we most certainly could have been mistaken for Russians. I was naturally worried about this, but after much heart-searching I told myself "You've been working for many years during some of the worst Troubles in Northern Ireland, so what are you worried about over here?"

As it turned out, the main danger to me was not from the Pol Pot rebels, but from my own foolishness. On our way north to the area of the world famous Ankor Wat Temples, we stopped at a roadside 'café' for refreshments. This was little more than a shack, but it provided a place to rest and to shelter from the searing heat.

My companions wisely chose bottled drinks but I asked for iced tea. To this day I cannot figure out why I was so stupid, because the 'iced' tea was not made with bottled water, but with the water from the local river. As a result I developed chronic stomach problems and had to survive for the rest of the trip on scrambled eggs and hot, black tea, which was the only food I could keep down.

I also had to spend a lot of my time on toilets, and this was rather difficult – to put it politely – in areas where there was no running water. It was a situation which tested even the greatest charity among companions travelling in rough places.

One of my worst moments came during a midnight visit to the toilet in a half-empty hotel, where I watched by torchlight the multi-coloured insects crawling over my feet as I listened to the clanking of the chains of a monkey which had broken from its pen and was roaming around in the darkness of the building. At that point I said to myself "What in God's name am I doing here? I want to go home!"

However the visit was memorable for many other reasons. It was inspiring to visit people in places where they were re-building their lives with the help of Christian Aid in association with the local churches. Most of those people had been left with nothing, and they were showing immense determination and courage in starting all over again.

I also had the opportunity to visit the beautiful Ankor Wat complex of 12th century Buddhist temples, and also to bathe in a river nearby while the local militia with ancient rifles guarded us from any Pol Pot insurgents who might be lingering in the area.

Eventually the militia men became fed up with their guard duty, and joined the rest of us who were swimming in the river, while multi-coloured parrots and jungle-fowl flew over our heads. However, my swim in the filthy river, despite the beautiful surroundings, may not have been helpful for my stomach condition!

That night we met for a meal with a contingent from the Cambodian Army and, to my amazement, I ended up dancing with several female officers in an Asiatic version of an Irish reel. You do strange things when you are in strange places!

On a more serious note, the visit to Vietnam and Cambodia reminded me that the human suffering on a vast scale in those countries had put our own suffering in Northern Ireland into a much sharper perspective. I shall never forget the horror of the genocide museum in Phnom Penh with hundreds of human skulls displayed in long grim rows, and other evidence of the prolonged torture and death of innocent people.

When I returned home after that short but unforgettable visit to Vietnam and Cambodia, it was once again hard to readjust to my work in Belfast, and it became more and more difficult to see a peaceful way forward for Northern Ireland.

There were still many major news stories which made grim headlines – including in that broad period, the escape of thirty-eight Provisional IRA men from the Maze Prison on 25 September 1983, which was one of the biggest escapes from a British prison in history. During that serious incident a prison officer was stabbed, and he later died. Only nineteen escapees were recaptured, within a few days, and the others remained on the run.

Then on 21 November of that year three elders died in a savage Republican attack on Darkley Pentecostal Church in South Armagh, and seven other people were injured. The shooting was claimed by the so-called 'Catholic Reaction Force', but some time later the notorious Dominic McGlinchy, one of the leaders of the ruthless Irish National Liberation Army, claimed that members of his organisation had been involved, though he denied personal responsibility.

There was no shortage of incidents, but after writing so many editorials and other articles which attempted to make some sense of Northern Ireland and its tortured politics, and seemingly unending violence, I began to see myself doing this for the rest of my professional career. Maybe it really was time to try to move on, before it became too late to do so. I was then in my early forties, and it was getting late for a major career change.

Ironically it was during this period that I won most of my awards as a journalist. In 1980 I received a Certificate of Merit in a Media Peace Prize competition organised by the United Nations Association.

The awards were presented at a London ceremony by Dr Conor Cruise O'Brien, formerly a leading politician in Dublin who later became Editor-in-Chief of *The Observer* newspaper. He paid tribute to my work and, more importantly, to my newspaper.

He said "I would like to say a special word of commendation to Mr McCreary of the *Belfast Telegraph* for his work for peace in grindingly difficult circumstances over many years.

"The *Belfast Telegraph* is historically one of the only artefacts which reaches some part of both communities, and not only one, in Northern

Ireland. In the precarious and even dangerous work of spanning the gap, the *Telegraph* and Mr McCreary deserve our praise."

These words were particularly welcome from a man who knew, more than most others at that London reception, about the reality of life in Northern Ireland, and the difficulties which all journalists faced in working in the Province at that time.

Not long afterwards, in the first Rothman's Press Awards for Northern Ireland, I was chosen as Feature Writer of the Year. Ironically the prize was presented to me by Kirkland Blair, a senior London-based executive with Rothman's, who had been my Scout Master in Bessbrook many years earlier.

Then I was given the same award in 1982, and a year later I was named as runner-up Columnist of the Year, Feature Writer of the Year, and finally as the Northern Ireland Journalist of the Year.

I was particularly surprised because having won a big award the previous year, I was not expecting anything more. Just before the awards dinner began in the Culloden Hotel, the Chairman of the Judges Robin Walsh said to me "You've no chance this year, sunshine. Just enjoy yourself with a good dinner and the refreshments." I believed him, and I was in a mellow mood when the results were announced.

I had no idea that I would have to leave my seat to go up to the front not just once, but three times, until it became almost embarrassing to do so. Nevertheless I was pleased that my work was being recognised in this way. The awards were handed over by the Secretary of State James Prior who remained unflappable, and chortled merrily as he watched the journalists letting their hair down at a function where there was a free bar.

In one sense these awards meant that there was little left for me to achieve professionally, especially as I was happy to remain as a writer rather than to pursue a career within the editorial management team. The awards also meant that it was harder to leave the paper because my reputation was secure and I was fortunate in being able to cover the kind of stories which were best suited to my temperament and to my style of writing.

However the desire for new challenges persisted, but I knew that if I wanted to change my job, I would need to stay in Northern Ireland.

This was partly for family reasons at a time when our children were in good schools locally.

Apart from ensuring that the children's education was not interrupted, I was particularly keen to stay in Northern Ireland where many of my long-term friends and wider family were living, and Belfast had become very much my 'home' city.

§

In the summer of 1984 I applied for a newly-created job in Queen's University which was looking for its first Director of Information. I had retained an affection for Queen's since I went up there as an undergraduate in 1959, and I felt that it would be the right challenge for me to help the University to promote itself through the media.

However the struggle in my head was whether or not I wanted to leave the freedom and creativity of daily newspaper journalism, and to face the demands of working within the possibly stultifying administration and the challenging academic atmosphere of a big university. I knew that such a step might be difficult, and I wondered if I was prepared to make that leap. The only way was to find out.

I spent a long period thinking carefully about all the possible issues involved, and the decision was not easy. I decided, however, that I would have no sense of failure if I did not get the job. The real failure would be in not applying.

I remember a family holiday in the Cotswolds at that time, and my thoughts were continually about my possible career switch. I felt that if I had to stop writing as a journalist, I would no longer be the same 'Alf McCreary'.

I eventually applied for the University job, and after a long delay I was interviewed by a large panel of senior figures at the University, including the Vice-Chancellor Professor Sir Peter Froggatt. I told the panel that I would need a written assurance that I could continue to write as a freelance if they appointed me.

I was not being presumptuous, but eminently practical. There was no point in accepting a job where I would be restricted to a totally administrative role. Peter Froggatt, who knew his Old Testament backwards, understood my point immediately, and said "Mr McCreary you would be very wise to have this in writing, because there may arise a King who knows not Joseph!" He was saying, in other words, that future Vice-Chancellors and other senior university figures might not look so favourably on me, and that I would be better to have this agreement included in my job contract. It was good advice.

When I returned home my wife Hilary said "How did you do?" I replied, slightly amazed, "I think I may have talked myself into it!" Later that evening Professor Colin Campbell the Pro-Vice Chancellor in charge of the new appointment, phoned to offer me the job. Once that happened my mind was clear, and I accepted the post, subject to salary and other important matters to be agreed. However I spent the next few days in a daze, wondering what I had done.

The news about the appointment was later published on page one of the *Belfast Telegraph* – it was a slow news day! The morning after the story appeared, I was standing at a bus stop with two ladies, complete strangers, who were talking about me. One said "I know yer big man there. He used to work in the Telly." Her companion said "How do you know?" She said "I read it in the paper. He used to be Alf McCreary."

That's what I felt like inside. I used to be 'Alf McCreary' but I was embarking on a totally new journey with an unknown destination. My *Telegraph* colleagues gave me a warm send-off, and presented me with an inscribed watch, and a wonderful drawing by our then resident cartoonist Rowel Friers, who was a highly-skilled and well-known artist in his own right.

The caption read "McCreary swops Smarties for Quality Street." This was a reference to my time as the journalists' 'Father of Chapel', in effect the union 'shop-steward'. I repeatedly warned my colleagues during wage negotiations that "Whatever rise they give you, it's still only the equivalent of chocolate Smarties."

The implication was that by accepting a key management job at Queen's I was going on to greater things. Certainly the salary would be much better, and the challenge was exciting at that point in my career.

However a part of me was also sad at leaving the *Telegraph*. It had been hard work, but the paper had been good to me, and I was leaving behind many trusted and talented colleagues with whom I had shared so many frightening, depressing and also inspiring stories about one of the worst periods in the history of Northern Ireland.

I knew that I would miss particularly the camaraderie of the leader-writing team, and above all the advice, professional expertise and friendship of my editor Roy Lilley.

However it was time to move on. I knew instinctively that my new career at Queen's would provide major challenges but I had no idea of how great those challenges would be. All too soon I would find out...

CHAPTER EIGHTEEN

Queen's Re-Visited

O N AN ICY morning in early January 1985, I reported for work on my first day as Information Director and Head of Information at the Queen's University of Belfast.

With such a grand title for a job in such a respected institution, some people might have supposed that the Vice-Chancellor himself would have been at the front entrance to welcome me.

I am joking, of course. Almost as soon as I arrived, however, the Vice-Chancellor Sir Peter Froggatt wrote me a charming note of welcome and soon afterwards we had a long, helpful talk in his office.

However on the frosty morning when I arrived in the ugly, box-like administration building overlooking the beautiful Victorian quadrangle at Queen's, I discovered that no-one had provided me with a desk in my empty office – even though the University had known several weeks previously about the date of my arrival.

I was not perturbed, but I formed an instant opinion that the University's administration was somewhat antiquated, and subsequent events proved that I was not far wrong.

Soon I also discovered that some people in the administration building stopped for morning coffee and afternoon tea at specific times, and it was best not to try to do business, even by phone, within these fixed parameters. The administration building was also closed at lunchtime each day, at precisely the time that it was most needed by students and staff who were otherwise occupied with lectures or tutorials during normal business hours.

However I realised later on that the Queen's administration was as efficient, if not more so, as most other national institutions of its kind, within a widespread university ambience rooted in past centuries but which needed to be brought up to speed for the rapidly-changing modern world.

The majority of my administration colleagues at Queen's were friendly, agreeable and helpful, although there some who seemed to go out of their way to irritate me, and I could have cheerfully strangled them! Again I am joking, and I am sure that on many occasions the feelings were mutual.

One of the bigger problems, however, was in decision making. During my early years at Queen's there was a prevalent culture among some managers and academics that the best way to do business was not to make a decision, if it was possible to fudge the issue. This was difficult to accept because I had come from a newspaper background where decisions had to be taken quickly.

In a newspaper, the editor's decision is final, right or wrong. Otherwise chaos ensues. In university life, a decision is made, often with effort, and it is liable to be changed within a few days. I discovered that the purpose was not necessarily to make the right decision, but, at all costs, not to get anything wrong, even if this meant no decision. This was often the 'wrong' decision anyway.

This ethos fitted in perfectly with the prevailing committee system where much the same people met together regularly, when they wore a particular hat, and then many of them met again at another committee, but wearing a different hat. Sometimes it seemed like a complex game of musical hats and chairs.

Another striking feature of life on the Queen's campus was the frequency of 'crisis' meetings. I soon realised that we seemed to have a 'crisis' at least once a fortnight. In reality a committee meeting was sometimes a good excuse, in many cases, for another round of talking, and often no more than that.

Of course there were many important issues to consider and not a few real crises, but too many meetings were a waste of time.

The administrators at Queen's took some getting used to, but the academics were in a league by themselves. I had been warned by a senior figure that "Academics are trained to come to a conclusion but not necessarily to make a decision. There are those also who think they are so smart that they outsmart themselves. Remember this – no matter how long you stay at Queen's and or what you achieve, they will never understand or appreciate what you are trying to do." It was prophetic advice, and I needed to hear it.

I was also given humorous advice by one of our senior porters who said to me "I can always spot the professors who come here for a big conference. If you watch them at the refreshment breaks, them's the boys who don't know how to work the coffee machines".

I gradually realised that some academics felt that they knew everything about everything. Their arrogance was as breathtaking as it was limitless. However I took comfort from knowing that many academics did indeed outsmart themselves, and I appreciated the comment from Sir Eric (later Lord) Ashby, one of the finest Vice-Chancellors in the history of Queen's. He once said that an academic was not necessarily better than a bin-man in conducting his or her personal life.

At Queen's the academics fitted into several broad categories. There were the high-flyers and international experts who did not need help in gaining them publicity. Some of the top people were also the nicer human beings, though I once received a waspish letter from a distinguished scientist whom I had interviewed for our university magazine.

I was taken aback by this, but I realised later that I had asked him mostly personal questions and little about his specialised subject, which I knew nothing about. This painful episode reminded me of a quote from Carl Jung: "You can debate anything with an academic but don't ask him personal questions because he will be unlikely to know how to handle his emotions, and he will never forgive you for doing that."

The second broad group of academics at Queen's were those on their way up, and could be pushy, but they were smart enough to know that my colleagues and I in the Information Office were doing our best to increase their profile, and that of Queen's.

A third, much larger group, consisted of people who were just happy to go on teaching and carrying out research, and they appreciated my help in gaining them some media recognition, just as much as I appreciated their expertise and realism.

There was also a small group of troublemakers who knew how to apply the University's regulations to their own advantage, and finally there were some individuals who, sadly, were totally and irredeemably idiotic.

There is, of course, an element of caricature in my remarks about my university colleagues, some of whom no doubt found me as puzzling at times, as I did them.

Since then I have mellowed, and I realise that many academics were not aware of the extreme pressures of time and the editorial space and deadlines with which my colleagues and I had to grapple. Nor did I always understand fully the challenges which they were facing during a period of demanding government-driven assessments, at a time when university budgets were being cut. It was against this complex background that I embarked on my role to "tell the world about Queen's" and to help "to tell Queen's about itself."

I was helped greatly by the Vice-Chancellor Sir Peter Froggatt, who knew what I was trying to do. Early on at one cocktail party – always a dangerous place because people could often wield a verbal knife even at a social occasion – a senior official complained to him "McCreary is always thinking of the worst headlines." Froggatt replied "Indeed so. That's his job." He understood that a publicist always thinks of the best and the worst possible headlines.

It was also a culture shock to be on the other side of the table from my former fellow professionals in the media. I never tried to mislead them, and I told them as much as I could.

For example, if reporters discovered that we were keeping a lion on the campus, it was my job to react to this dangerous situation. However if they had not found out that there was also a tiger roaming around Queen's, it was not my role to do their reporting for them.

This is not as mythical as it seems. Long before my time a well-known member of staff, Dr Dickie Hunter, staged 'Hunter's Circus' in Belfast every Christmas. He was a colourful figure who strode around the campus in a black coat, red scarf and large hat. Dickie was a former Anatomy lecturer, and he held the senior post of University Secretary from 1937–48.

During his summer holidays he toured Europe to look for suitable jugglers and tightrope walkers for his annual Circus, where he served as Ringmaster, complete with a pink coat, top hat and a whip.

Sometimes I felt that in my role as Head of Information at Queen's I was the ringmaster as well as the spokesman for the University's three-ring circus.

In essence a person in my job needed to be a maverick whom the media assumed was on the University's side, and whom the University believed to be on the side of the media. The only way to do the job properly was to be prepared to lose it every other day by standing up to often arrogant and self-serving academics about the error of their ways. However, there were compensations in helping others who really wanted to work with me and my staff in raising their profile and who had the best interests of the University at heart.

My first few years at Queen's went well. I recruited new staff and we produced a first generation of glossy publications which were part of the University's drive to recruit students. These publications were similar to those in other United Kingdom universities, and we measured up well in comparison to the others.

One of the more difficult tasks, however, was to change the image of Queen's, which had grown greatly in size since I had been an undergraduate there over twenty-five years previously.

The University was almost seven times bigger, and it had been through a difficult period during the worst of the Troubles. Several staff and students had been murdered or wounded by paramilitaries, and the Students' Union was perceived by many Unionists as a bastion of Republicanism and a 'cold house' for Protestants.

Queen's also had the problem of appearing stuffy and elitist. This had arisen partly from its history when it had been regarded as the university for the children of the Ulster middle classes, and most of them Protestants.

However this had changed drastically with the influx of large numbers of Catholic students from the end of the Fifties and who brought to the university a much more cross-community atmosphere.

Queen's as an institution made a major mistake in its response to the Lockwood Committee which set out in the Sixties to provide a blueprint for Higher Education in Northern Ireland. The Queen's response was self-serving and dismissive, and it failed to grasp the opportunity for the expansion of higher education in the Province. As one expert observer has pointed out "Queen's played its hand badly in the early 1960s and had to live with the consequence for the rest of the century."[1]

The Stormont government accepted the Lockwood Committee's recommendations, but they made the political mistake of establishing the New University of Ulster (NUU) in unionist Coleraine, and not in nationalist Derry.

Nevertheless, Queen's had to look over its shoulder nervously at a new third-level competitor in Northern Ireland. This became even more acute with the establishment in 1984 of the University of Ulster under its dynamic first Vice-Chancellor Sir Derek Birley. He had been the Director of the original Ulster College, recommended by Lockwood. This became the Northern Ireland Polytechnic and it was amalgamated with the NUU to become the University of Ulster.

It was part of my task to help the hitherto slightly aloof Queen's establishment begin to win back friends and to influence the right people. This was a formidable challenge, but I was part of a senior team in the University who knew that Queen's could not afford to rest on its laurels.

Unlike some of my more competitive Queen's colleagues, I had a regard for the University of Ulster, where the staff were keen to turn what had been the progressive Polytechnic into as good an institution as the University of Ulster could be.

I also had a regard for Professor Sir Derek Birley, whom I had interviewed in depth for the *Belfast Telegraph* several years previously. When I came to his office at Jordanstown, he complimented me on my articles, and I suspected that this was an attempt to butter me up.

I soon realised that Birley really had read my articles carefully, and that his comments deserved to be taken seriously. Our interview lasted a couple of hours until lunchtime, and then Derek asked me to share a glass or two of Old Bushmills with him. I declined because I had a deadline to meet, but I could have talked to him all afternoon.

Before I left, Birley gave me a signed copy of a book he had written on cricket called *The Willow Wand*. I only discovered years later that this was a classic of cricket literature. It was described by John Arlott, the influential cricket commentator as "A quite remarkable cricket book; it is also witty, scholarly, readable and thought-provoking." Years later I

---

[1] Prof Leslie A Clarkson, *A University in Troubled Times*, Four Courts Press, 2004, p37

met Birley at a university dinner, and he was still complimentary about my writing, even when he had no need to be. He was a tough character, but he was a first-class educationalist who made a major contribution to higher education in Northern Ireland.

My task in helping to raise the profile of Queen's was assisted greatly by the nomination of the University to host the prestigious 1987 British Association for the Advancement of Science, for the first time since 1952.

This was a major event during which scientists gathered together each year to present the latest discoveries in the world of science.

My role was to provide the national and international media with the best resources possible, and with my Information Office and other colleagues we did just this. I went to great lengths to get all the details right, including even the seating and position of the tea and coffee dispensers in the Press room.

I was also assisted by a specially-recruited team of students, and I appointed as the leader a young man called Lembit Opik, who had roots in Northern Ireland. He later became, for a period, a high-profile Liberal Democrat MP. Lembit was resourceful, highly intelligent and a good leader, and I was not surprised when he achieved such a profile later on.

The British Association meeting went so well that Queen's was awarded a British Airways Trophy at the Northern Ireland Tourist Board Awards in 1987. In a subsequent edition of the Queen's Newsletter we ran a picture of Sir Gordon Beveridge, the Vice-Chancellor holding the coveted Award, which was a bird-like statue, with Denis Wilson a senior administrative colleague beside both of us.

I worked closely with Denis who usually knew much of what was happening at Queen's. He often used the word 'consorbient' to describe something that was virtually indescribable, but I never had the nerve to slip it into one of the Vice-Chancellor's speeches, or to use in print – until now.

The British Airways Award was one measure of the success of the British Association meeting at Queen's. Another was the comment from a former *Belfast Telegraph* colleague Joe Gorrod, later of the *Daily Mirror*, who expressed to me his amazement at the range of topics covered by the British Association. I reckoned that when a hard-bitten *Mirror* man like Joe was enthused by science in this way, we really had got the message across. Joe, who sadly died recently, was one of the great 'characters' of Northern Ireland journalism.

The British Association meeting was marked also by the publication of a book titled *Province, City and People*, which was edited by my academic colleagues Professor Ronnie Buchanan, one of my former teachers, and Professor Brian Walker, with whom I was to write a history of Queen's later on. It was titled *Degrees of Excellence*.

The 1987 BA book was a series of essays which gave a good overview of life in Northern Ireland, and the introduction was provided by the relatively new Vice-Chancellor Sir Gordon Beveridge. Having re-read this recently, I am almost certain that I wrote most of it myself, which was part of my job.

Gordon Beveridge, a chemical engineer by training, had a different style to that of his predecessor Sir Peter Froggatt, with a background in medicine.

I liked working with Peter, and I was sorry that he left office within eighteen months of my arrival. He had courageously faced enormous challenges in keeping Queen's functioning as efficiently as possible in the tides of violence which swirled around the University and sometimes inside the campus itself. That was no mean achievement.

Gordon Beveridge was very much an engineer and he did not have the same natural fluency of Peter Froggatt. Shortly after his arrival Gordon asked me to draft him a speech for an annual dinner he was due to address.

I had not written any speeches before, except my own, so I went into the nearby Botanic Gardens and sat in the late summer sun while I drafted an address for my new boss. Gordon was delighted. He said "You write the way I speak!"

From that moment I was tasked with writing every speech which he delivered during his long tenure as Vice-Chancellor. This was demanding at times, but it was also an honour to be part of the public voice of the University at that level. It also gave me almost instant access to the Vice-Chancellor, and that was important in the academic jungle where there lurked many powerful big beasts who often crossed my path.

I have many vivid personal recollections of my years at Queen's. I was fortunate enough to interview the former Vice-Chancellor and later Chancellor Lord Ashby at his home in Cambridge, where he had gone after his time at Queen's. He was a man of immense charm, and even in his mid-eighties he had a sharp intellect and a clear recollection of his days at Queen's for which he had retained a special affection.

Following our interview for my profile of Ashby in our Queen's letter magazine, I offered to send him a draft copy. His reply was typical. He said "Don't bother. I would only be tempted to change it" I often wished that other Queen's figures had been the same!

My role at Queen's also enabled me to learn much more about universities in the British Isles and further afield. After a few years my colleagues in the Information Offices of the UK elected me Chairman of their association, and later I also became Chairman of the European Universities information and public relations officers group EUPRIO.

The latter appointment was a surprise. I was a UK representative on the group, and at a meeting in Paris, preceded by lunch, I was feeling mellow at our board meeting in the Ecole Des Mines. The outgoing chairman was Ray Footman of the University of Edinburgh and the intention was to invite a Danish representative to take the chair.

To our surprise, however, he announced that he was leaving university life to take up another career, and he proposed that I should become Chairman. The committee agreed and I spent several years as Chairman, where I appreciated the experience and advice of Ray Footman, and that of another good friend Dr Inge Knudsen from the University of Aarhus in Denmark who was a founding member and also a former chair of EUPRIO.

My experience with these groups gave me an invaluable insight into how the information offices in British, Irish and other European Universities carried out their work.

I have rich memories of organising a Public Relations seminar in Prague, and being questioned by a somewhat bewildered former Czech Army officer who had lived through the Cold War and who wanted to know what public relations in a democratic society was all about.

On the way home to Belfast, I was buying a coffee at Prague airport when a stranger with an Ulster accent came up to me and said "Aren't you Alf McCreary? I didn't like what you wrote about the Orangemen at Drumcree in your column!"

I looked at him for a moment and said "I don't think that you and

I are visiting Prague to talk about Drumcree." He replied "Perhaps you're right". This was all part of being in the public eye.

On another occasion I took time off from Queen's to attend a Remembrance Day service at the Thiepval Tower in France, with a group of people from the Shankill Road, where I served as a member of a cross-community committee in West Belfast. The group included Gusty Spence the leading UVF figure who had been jailed many years previously for his part in shooting a young Catholic barman in the city.

As we all lined up for the Remembrance Service at Thiepval, Gusty approached me carrying three wreaths. I was wearing a dark blazer and my Queen's graduate tie. He said "Ralph we have to lay 'thee' wreaths, and my mate Geordie and me have only two pair of hands. Would you lay a wreath for the Liverpool loyalists?"

I said nothing, but my mind was buzzing with the headlines that would appear if I helped Gusty – "Queen's Information Chief Lays Wreath For Liverpool Loyalists." After a few moments, Gusty looked at me and said "Maybe not", and off he went.

I realised that my European sorties sometimes took on a life of their own, and that I had to be careful not to create the wrong headlines. My real challenge, however, still lay at home as I worked with my staff and colleagues in trying to tell the world the good news about Queen's University, and also in trying to make the best of the bad news in the major upheavals that lay ahead. It promised to be no easy task.

CHAPTER NINETEEN

Best of Times, Worst of Times

O NE OF MY problems as Information Director at Queen's was trying to help my colleagues to understand the media's concept of 'news'. On one occasion I organised a press facility for the launch of an important new mainline computer by the then Secretary of State Sir Patrick Mayhew.

There was an impressive media attendance, and I knew why. The reporters were keen to 'doorstep' Mayhew about the latest killings, which overshadowed any news about a new computer, but my staff and I were still expected to get the Queen's computer story splashed all over the newspapers and television bulletins. However, the story was not quite as important to the outside world as some of my colleagues had thought.

However there was good news a-plenty about the University's celebrations in 1995 of its 150th anniversary, together with the Universities of Cork and Galway. These were the three Queen's Colleges which had been established in 1845 by Sir Robert Peel.

Details of the wide-ranging programme were outlined in the introduction to the 1994–95 Vice-Chancellor's Report, which I drafted, and which was beautifully produced by my Information Office colleagues.

The events fell into two broad categories – those which were organised jointly by the three universities, and those which they organised themselves.

The highlight of the joint celebrations was a splendid reception held in St James' Palace in London, which was attended by Her

Majesty Queen Elizabeth II and the Irish President Mary Robinson. This symbolised the long-standing connections between the three universities on the island of Ireland and also the warm relationship between the two Heads of State. This culminated in the Queen's historic visit to Ireland during the Presidency of Mary McAleese, who was herself a graduate and former Pro Vice-Chancellor of Queen's.

During the St James Palace reception I was in charge of publicity, together with other colleagues and a senior member of President Robinson's staff. On the night we had to work hard – with the aid of a pool photographer from the *Irish Independent* in London – to engineer a joint photograph of the Queen and President Robinson and their entourage.

It was particularly fitting that Mary Robinson was present, because only a few months earlier she had accepted an Honorary Law Degree from Queen's. Her visit to Belfast for the conferment in June 1995 also made history, because it symbolised the growing desire for normality between the two jurisdictions North and South. This was just three years before the signing of the Good Friday Agreement, but even in 1995, the political ice in the North was showing no signs of a thaw.

The Queen's University Sesquicentennial Celebrations also included a special concert by my old friend 'Dr' Phil Coulter who had been awarded an honorary degree by Queen's, and the broadcast from the campus of the BBC's radio flagships 'Mastermind', with Magnus Magnussen, and 'Any Questions' with Jonathan Dimbleby.

Queen's also ran a successful Community Week in which the public was invited into the main buildings. It was salutary to observe the gratitude of many people because they were 'allowed' inside some of the 'hallowed' precincts. It reminded me of how much we still had to do to connect Queen's with its local community.

There was also much about which Queen's could be proud during its special anniversary year. A Queen Elizabeth Anniversary Prize for excellence had been awarded to the Servicing the Legal System unit in the Law Faculty. This was one of only twenty-one prizes awarded nationally in a competition which had 200 entries.

There was more good news, with the award of six 'Excellent' categories in teaching, which brought the Queen's ratings to fifty percent, compared to the national average of twenty-five percent.

Queen's also had more good news in 1995 with the award of a Nobel Prize for Literature to the poet Seamus Heaney who was a graduate and a former member of staff. Later on that year, Queen's provided one of the venues for the visit of President Bill Clinton to Northern Ireland – the first US President to do so.

There was great anticipation in the Sir William Whitla Hall at Queen's as the invited audience waited eagerly for Clinton's arrival, following his memorable appearance at Belfast City Hall, where he switched on the Christmas lights.

During the build-up to Clinton's arrival at the Whitla Hall, where I was helping to look after the Press, I noticed that the Sinn Fein leaders Gerry Adams and Martin McGuinness – who at that stage were still in the publicity shadows – were engrossed in conversation with a gaggle of Church of Ireland Bishops. Over in a far corner a group of leading Unionists were in a huddle, talking mostly to themselves. It was not difficult to figure out which side was winning the propaganda battle.

Clinton at close range was most impressive as he 'worked the rope', and greeted scores of well-wishers, some of whom had travelled over from Washington. I was not surprised to notice also how his charisma impressed a large number of good-looking women.

What did surprise me, however, was his sheer ability to greet so many people with such warmth and individual attention in such a short space of time. One of our porters broke ranks and went to the top of the line to shake Clinton's hand. About forty-five minutes later when the President had almost finished his greetings, the same Queen's porter nipped to the end of the line and shook the President's hand a second time. Clinton said "Nice to see you again." That total recall on a very busy occasion was impressive.

Queen's could not have had a better 150th Anniversary, with positive headlines which would have been the envy of any other educational institution. Sadly, however, the University was still mired in controversies which arose from its pivotal position within the Northern Ireland community.

In the late-Eighties a report by the Fair Employment Agency found a significant imbalance in the University's employment of staff, and that Catholics were greatly under-represented in proportion to the denominational make up of the general population in Northern Ireland.

This caused embarrassment to the University, which was accused of being 'anti-Catholic', and Queen's took relatively swift action to deal with this problem. For those interested in the complex details of this chequered period in the history of Queen's, they are expertly analysed in a definitive book by a former Pro Vice-Chancellor Professor Leslie Clarkson. The publication is titled *A University in Troubled Times*, and it chronicles in depth the history of the University from 1945–2000. This was part of a trilogy of Queen's histories, including Moody and Beckett's monumental two-volume history of the University from 1845, and *Degrees of Excellence – The Story of Queen's 1845–1995*, which I wrote with Professor Brian Walker as mentioned earlier.

The fair employment issue at Queen's created much pain and resentment among many of the staff, including the alleged victims of discrimination and the alleged perpetrators. The poison and hurt of these allegations and counter-allegations, a number of which were duly upheld, swept through the system, and in publicity terms the University was constantly on the back foot.

There were endless leaks to the media, and my role was that of working constantly on damage limitation. The University's employment figures were indefensible in terms of fair employment, and the Senate had to take measures to ensure that such a sorry state of affairs would not occur again.

In the meantime, I had to deal daily with an intrusive and sometimes hostile media which was interested in only one story – the fair employment cases pending and how they were being handled.

The good headlines we generated in those difficult days were as rare as hen's teeth. The big story was always fair employment, and Queen's had been moved onto the political agenda in Northern Ireland where the pivotal issues continued to focus on the vexed relationship between the two main communities.

This period was one of the most difficult in my time at Queen's, but I tried to make the best of it. I felt sorry for the Vice-Chancellor Sir Gordon Beveridge who, as a Scotsman relatively newly arrived from Edinburgh and Glasgow, was out of his depth in the midst of this Northern Irish political, social, and denominational quagmire.

I recall one stressful Graduation Day ceremony where Sir Gordon had to deliver a complex speech about fair employment to the young graduands and their families who were entitled to something lighter on such a joyous occasion.

After the ceremony we held a packed Press conference in the Senate Room. Gordon managed well enough through a difficult period of questioning, but I winced at the reply to his final inquisitor. A reporter from the *Irish News* asked him if he would apologise for our shortcomings on fair employment. The Vice-Chancellor snapped back "No." Legally he may have been obliged to answer in this way, but it sounded too negative.

I could just see the bad headlines in the next day's newspapers. Afterwards Sir Gordon asked me "How did I do?" I replied "Not very well. You should have fudged the last question." Gordon, to his credit, was a high-principled man who was not prone to fudge or flattery.

Eventually the Senate announced measures to deal with the crisis, and to provide a clear path for the future. As Leslie Clarkson notes in his book "In spite of a number of cases before the Fair Employment Tribunal there was a growing appreciation that Queen's was tackling the discrimination issue effectively."[1]

Nevertheless it had been a difficult episode for everyone, and it was a nightmare for any Information Director to handle.

However, there was also a happier side to our graduations, and often the opportunity to meet with many well-known people. They included Brian Keenan, who had made headlines when he was imprisoned in Lebanon and who later wrote a superb book about it, titled *An Evil Cradling*. When Brian arrived at the Vice-Chancellor's Office, Gordon said "Mr Keenan this is Alf McCreary our Information Director!" Brian replied, "Yes, I know him. I used to read his Wednesday columns in the *Belfast Telegraph*!"

On another occasion Gordon, who had just arrived from the more formal social life of Edinburgh, introduced me to the then Lord Mayor of Belfast, Dixie Gilmore, who once ran a small grocery store where I shopped as a student. Gordon said "Lord Mayor, do you know our Information Director Alf McCreary?" Dixie replied "Gordon, do I know him? Sure I used to feed him!" The Vice-Chancellor looked slightly taken aback, but also amused, at the informality of the city in which he had come to live.

---

[1] Prof Leslie A Clarkson, *A University in Troubled Times*, Four Courts Press, 2004, p192

One of my most vivid memories of all was the day when Queen's conferred an honorary degree on the footballer George Best. At that time George was off the drink and he looked incredibly fit, and handsome. He was also immensely charming and signed copies of his new autobiography for my University colleagues and me.

He was due to receive his honorary degree at an afternoon ceremony, which often had a formal atmosphere but which was always handled with great style by Queen's. As the long snake of robed academics wound slowly into the building while a capacity audience stood to attention, the second last person in the line was George Best in his grey three-piece suit.

As George entered into the full view of that large audience, suddenly it seemed as if a thousand cameras were flashing while everyone took a picture of this superstar in their midst. It was the first time that I really understood what real stardom was all about. I felt privileged to have written the honorary degree citation for Best, in association with our Registrar James O'Kane, who then had the more difficult task of delivering it, which he did well.

During this period I was also able to travel widely on University business and also in my own time. I recall a particularly eventful trip with Christian Aid to report on development projects in Paraguay and Chile. On my first day in Santiago I was nearly mugged and I was also trapped by tear gas following a confrontation between security forces and protesters in the centre of the city. I remember thinking it distinctly odd that I had survived intact during more than two decades of the Troubles in Belfast but that I had been placed in such danger in Latin America.

During that visit I also brought a flag with me to commemorate "The Best of Belfast 1991". I was a member of a committee appointed by the then Junior Stormont Minister Richard Needham to highlight some of the attractions of Belfast, and to help with the planning of the visit of the Tall Ships to the Harbour.

The 1991 "Best of Belfast" Committee was one of the most fascinating and most argumentative groups I have ever encountered, but the campaign was a success and this was due in no small part to the visit of the Tall Ships which brought a welcome ray of light to a city that had been in darkness for far too long. So somewhere deep in Latin America there may still be a flag on display to commemorate my visit there, and also the "Best of Belfast 1991."

§

There were a number of situations in the Eighties when Queen's was dragged into the headlines by events which were beyond the University's control and which left it in a 'no-win' situation in terms of major publicity.

On 6 March 1988 a young Belfast woman called Mairead Farrell was one of three members of the Provisional IRA who were shot dead in Gibraltar by a unit from the British Army's SAS.

This created a huge controversy because the three were unarmed when they were killed, although they were alleged to have been preparing to attack British soldiers stationed in Gibraltar. After the shootings, the authorities in Spain discovered a car containing explosives and ammunition. It had been rented by Mairead Farrell under a false name. The authorities also found another car across the border from Gibraltar. It contained false passports and bomb-making equipment.

Queen's was pitched into the controversy because Mairead Farrell was one of its students, and Republican supporters demanded that the University should fly its flag on the main tower at half-mast, as it had done traditionally for a number of other deceased former students.

This demand left the University senior staff in a quandary. If the flag was flown at half-mast, this would further infuriate those in Northern Ireland who believed that Mairead Farrell had been on an IRA bombing mission and she and the others had received their just desserts. However, for some people this was not a clear-cut issue. They asked why the unarmed Provisional activists had been shot and not arrested.

The controversy raged on in Northern Ireland, while details of the mission of the IRA's active service unit in Gibraltar became clearer. In the end Queen's decided not to fly the flag at half-mast.

I remember standing with Gordon Beveridge on the back stairs of the main Lanyon Building while he and I put the finishing touches to a Press Release which my colleague Anne Langford and I had prepared for the media. Meanwhile a posse of reporters, including a man from

Queen's Information Director. *Top:* Good times, with distinguished Ulster journalist John Cole. *Bottom:* Bad times, yet another 'crisis' within the University's "three-ring circus."

Celebrating Queen's 150th birthday in 1995.

This page, top: My old friend Phil Coulter who gave a concert in the Whitla Hall.

Opposite page, top: Her Majesty Queen Elizabeth with Irish President Mary Robinson at a reception in St James' Palace, London for the three former 'Queen's Colleges'. *Centre:* President Bill Clinton. *Bottom:* presenting a copy of my Queen's history (co-author Professor Brian Walker) to President Robinson after she received an honorary degree from the University.

SESQUICENTENARY REUNION

1845 – 1995
QUEEN'S
150

DINNER

in the Great Hall of the University

Friday, 3 November 1995

1845 – 1995
QUEEN'S
150

Celebrating Queen's 150
Sesquicentenary Programme

Top: At Buckingham Palace in June 2004 to receive an MBE from the Queen.

Bottom: With my wife Hilary, daughter Emma and son Matthew.

Pictured with the Duke of Edinburgh *(top left)*, Senator George Mitchell *(top right)*, Archbishop Desmond Tutu *(centre left)*, Sir John Major *(centre right)*, and Lord Eames *(bottom)*.

Top: The Remembrance Day carnage at the Cenotaph in Enniskillen on 8 November 1987. (*Pacemaker*)

Bottom left: With Gordon Wilson at the launch of the book on his daughter Marie, who died in the Enniskillen explosion. *Bottom right:* My later biography of Gordon himself, which was published shortly after his death.

"Sorrow is a frost that settles on your heart"

As the 25th anniversary of the Enniskillen bombing approaches, Joan Wilson talks to **Alf McCreary** about the atrocity that killed her daughter Marie, injured her husband Gordon and changed her own life forever

Joan Wilson, whose daughter Marie died when a Provisional IRA bomb exploded without warning at the Enniskillen Cenotaph on November 8, 1987, is apprehensive about the 25th anniversary, which occurs next week.

Sitting in her Enniskillen home this week and surrounded by evocative family pictures, she tells me: "I would like to think that the anniversary would not trouble me so deeply, but it does. There are so many memories, and so many things I cannot get out of my mind.

"I remember vividly that morning when Marie left me to go to the service at the Cenotaph. I said to her 'Have you got your umbrella?' She said 'Yes, I have, mother. Don't fuss about me, I'll be alright.'

"Those were the last words we ever exchanged.

"The next time I saw her was on that afternoon in the Erne Hospital. She was lying in intensive care, wired up to a life-support machine. Her sister Julie Anne and I spoke to her and her eyelids flickered. I think she heard us, but she was too far gone to speak. She died shortly afterwards."

Marie, a student nurse, was one of 11 people who died in the blast that badly injured many others, including her father Gordon. He suffered a badly dislocated shoulder. They were trapped under tons of rubble, but despite the darkness inside, they finally managed to hold hands. Marie's last words to him were "Daddy, I love you very much".

That evening Gordon's words to a BBC reporter became one of the iconic messages of the Troubles. It received a massive local and international reaction, including a tribute from the Queen in her Christmas Day broadcast.

Gordon said: "I bear no ill-will. I bear no grudge. Dirty sort of talk is not going to bring her back to life. Don't ask me, please, for a purpose. I don't have an answer. But I know that there has to be a plan, and God is good. And we shall meet again."

Throughout the trauma of the very public funeral and the harrowing days, months and years afterwards, Joan Wilson was constantly at her husband's side, and she was a rock for the entire family.

Looking back on that devastating period now, she says: "I don't know how we got through it all, but the Lord has been my fortress and strength. Without His help I would not have survived. Every day I pray to Him, and I read my Bible. This gives me the strength to carry on."

Mrs Wilson will not be going to the ceremony at Enniskillen cenotaph on the 25th anniversary. "That would be too much for me, because it brings back so many memories," she says.

"I have never been able to go there, and I find it difficult to even pass near it. On the 25th anniversary I will go early to the local church with my family and friends, and compose myself prayerfully before the service begins."

Joan Wilson has had a quarter of a century to try to come to terms with what happened, but the raw wounds are still there.

TRAGEDY: Gordon Wilson and his daughter Marie

> I pray that they realise what they have done and repent. I have no bitterness for them, only pity

She reveals: "I still think of what might have been. Would Marie have followed her wish to be a full-time nurse, where would have her career taken her, would she have married and had children? Part of me knows that these thoughts are futile, but I cannot help thinking in this way."

Mrs Wilson still prays for the people who murdered Marie. She says: "I pray that they will realise what they have done and repent, and that they will seek forgiveness from God."

Like many of the families of other victims, she would want to ask the bombers why they killed innocent people.

She continues: "I have no bitterness for them, only pity. How can anyone lead a normal life knowing that they have killed and maimed other people? I also feel sorry for the parents of these people. If any of my children had done such a thing, it would be utterly dreadful."

Joan Wilson is also realistic about the doubtful possibility of the bombers being arrested and charged. "It has taken 25 long, hard years to get to where I am now, and no-one has been arrested," she says.

"However, I am now in a different place mentally. I don't really want to contemplate what would happen if they were arrested and charged. It would stir up the most awful memories for me.

"But I am certain of one thing. Whether or not they are brought to justice in this world, they will face justice in the world to come.

"On the great Day of Judgement, they will have to answer for their deeds. I am now content to leave all this in the hands of our Creator."

Joan has always been aware of others who died and were injured by the Enniskillen bomb, and of the sorrow of their families as well as the heartache of everyone who has been touched by the violence of the Troubles.

She explains: "This affects people from all backgrounds. I cannot bear to think of the suffering of those who were maimed, and it is impossible to describe the trauma of bereavement, unless you have experienced it yourself."

She has had to bear a series of particularly hard blows during her long life. As well as losing Marie in the Poppy Day massacre in 1987, her infant son Richard died in 1958 shortly after his birth and her other son, Peter, died in 1994 at the age of 38 in a car crash.

Then her husband Gordon died from a heart attack several months later.

She says: "We were married for 39 years and 10 months, and I still miss him terribly. He was my husband and my friend and companion.

"I miss his sense of fun, his conversation, just being with him and all the things that two people share in a long and happy marriage. I will miss him particularly during this anniversary period."

Joan has remained friendly with some well-known people like the former Irish Presidents Mary Robinson and Mary McAleese, but she has delib-

Top: The heartache of so many victims of the Troubles is summarised here by Joan Wilson in this *Belfast Telegraph* profile. *Bottom left:* With my daughter Emma and Joan and Gordon Wilson. *Bottom right:* Joan with our joint book on bereavement titled *All Shall Be Well.*

The Belfast Telegraph

MORNING EDITION

FRIDAY APRIL 8 2005   www.belfasttelegraph.co.uk   Price: 50p (€0.85)

The final amen

❛To stand in Rome on this special day is to be firmly rooted in the making of history❜

ALF McCREARY on the poignant last journey of Pope John Paul II, P4&5

Catholic Press and Information Office of Ireland

ACCREDITATION CARD

Pastoral Visit of John Paul II to Ireland 29th September–1st October 1979

B 1387

Name ALF MC CREARY

Nationality N. IRISH

Representing BELFAST TELEGRAPH

The funeral of Pope John Paul II in Rome was one of the biggest assignments of my career. I also kept my Press passes for the visit of the Pope to Knock in Co Mayo *(left)* and of US President Ronald Reagan to Ballyporeen in Co Tipperary *(opposite page, left)*, and also the Vatican Press Pass for the Pope's funeral *(opposite page, right)*.

Death of Pope John Paul II

Pilgrims' progress: And still they came — in their millions — to pay their final respects to the dead Pontiff lying in state in St Peter's historic basilica

An epic and moving farewell

Religious Affairs correspondent Alf McCreary reports from Rome

FINAL preparations were in place in Rome early today for the funeral of Pope John Paul II which has brought millions of pilgrims from all over the world to this historic city.

The Requiem Mass was due to begin at 9am local time as more than 200 presidents, prime ministers and statesmen and — significantly — the plain people of the world pay their last respects to one of history's most charismatic popes.

As the final tributes were being prepared and dignitaries were taking their places in St Peter's Square, all the many logistical pressures of this week were being forgotten in a modern take-over of this city which has been invaded so many times.

Today's hordes include possibly as many as two million Poles from the pope's homeland.

As final rehearsals were completed for the three-hour Mass to the strains of Gregorian chant, the Pope's simple coffin of plain Cyprus wood stood in the shadows of St Peter's — a continual reminder that we were all attending a funeral service.

Though millions had mourned this week, this had also been a celebration for a good life well lived.

Yet those of us sharing today's historic occasion were also aware that this marked the final human parting from a universally-known and loved figure.

This globe-trotting pope, who had circled the world a score of times, and had kissed the earth of many countries — including Ireland — would be making his last short journey to be buried beneath the Basilica, his face eventually to be covered with a white silk veil, his wooden casket hermetically sealed in a zinc coffin, and placed in yet another oak coffin and interred under a marble slab.

In the atmosphere of the ancient liturgy in Rome this morning, we were all aware that some day the world might talk about John Paul the Great.

But this was the last we would see of the earthly remains of the young Polish priest who had become such a majestic, often autocratic — but always a human — pope.

John Paul had retained his complex simplicity as a man of God.

The chief celebrant of the mass, Cardinal Joseph Ratzinger, theologically an ultra-conservative, is himself a contender to succeed John Paul II.

Yet even in the midst of today's ceremonies, there will also be thoughts of life and the future of the papacy, and that's how it should be.

The crowds were remaining remarkably patient, though there was a human temptation for everyone to try to spot celebrities including a trio of US presidents — George W Bush, Bill Clinton and George Bush Senior, as well as Prime Minister Tony Blair and, of course, Prince Charles.

Many other distinguished figures, known and unknown to the huge crowds, were taking their places. There was enough material for a month of celebrity magazines, despite the solemnity of the occasion, and the demands of the media age with reporters and cameramen busy in the midst of the crowd, but the sense of history overshadowed all.

Television is instant, but second-hand, but to stand in Rome on this special day was to be firmly rooted in the making of history.

As the final blessings were being prepared and the background music sounded across St Peter's Square, it was difficult not to think that Pope John Paul II, the supreme showman, would have approved of it all — a deeply religious ceremony yet with a riveting appeal for all of us here and those watching around the globe.

John Paul the Great was indeed being given a great farewell.

ULSTER FOLK & TRANSPORT MUSEUM

Exhibitions and Events 2005

Events

Blanket TV coverage of funeral

THE FUNERAL of Pope John Paul II will be broadcast live to viewers across Britain on ITV and BBC.

Both terrestrial channels will provide uninterrupted coverage of this morning's historic event from Rome.

On BBC 1, newsreader Huw Edwards will set the scene as mourners flock to St Peter's Square for the 9am funeral.

He will be joined in the studio by the Archbishop of Birmingham, the Most Rev Vincent Nichols, and church historian Professor Eamonn Duffy.

A BBC spokesman said the team would provide comment and analysis reflecting on "the spiritual significance of the ceremony", which is expected to last about two-and-a-half hours.

ITV1 will also air full coverage of the service from the Vatican, in addition to live coverage from Westminster Cathedral, Liverpool and Glasgow.

Alistair Stewart will anchor ITV's coverage in London from 8.50am. James Mates will be live at the Vatican during the service.

Studio guests will include leading Catholic writer and broadcaster Christina Odone.

An ITV spokesman said: "The programme will not only be providing full coverage of this historic religious service, but also an insight into the effect Pope John II's passing has had on the British public back home."

Sky News will provide live coverage from Rome, beginning from sunrise.

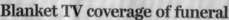

Festive spell in Manhattan makes for a simply magical experience

THERE is something in the New York air that makes sleep useless, wrote Simone De Bouvoir, and this is true. The city that never sleeps was pulsating and as exciting during our weekend visit recently, as it was some years ago when I first took a bite of 'The Big Apple'.

...... a score of visits I h........

...... through these stores was a priceless experience. Saks and Lord and Taylors were chic and elegant, but Macy's, though beautifully decorated, lacked that 'wow' factor ......of Manhattan.

hattan skyline.

No visit to New York, they say, is complete without a visit to a Broadway show. We went to see Chicago, a brilliant, brash, witty, cynical production, but an experience to be savoured — though we would ...... to pay for the

The familiar sights of New York, like the World Trade Center and the Empire State Building, remain breathtaking — even after several visits. This time the weather was right for both — great visibility, little wind, and the beauties of New York spread beneath us like a multi-faceted carpet. The World Trade Center was awesome by day, ... State Building was magical

---

Terrorists strike at the heart of modern man

A personal view by Alf McCreary, recently returned from New York

THE enormous sense of personal shock at the destruction of the twin towers of the World Trade Center in New York will be felt particularly by the many thousands of people, like me, who recently visited these once magnificent buildings.

Just over three weeks ago, I was there with my son Matthew at the height of the summer season. It was crowded, there were long queues, but the wait was worth it.

The World Trade Center offered stupendous views over New York harbour, the Statue of Liberty, Brooklyn, Manhattan and the Empire State building, which itself used to be the largest building in the city.

To visit the World Trade Centre was to pay homage to the vision of modern man. From the outside, it towered so far into the sky that it was almost impossible to photograph properly from the ground with an ordinary camera.

Once inside the building, you had a feeling that it was impregnable.

This, you believed, was the ultimate in construction – thousands of tons of steel, concrete and glass rising to the sky, as a witness to the creativity of 20th century technology.

Despite the sheer size of the twin towers, there was always a sense of order about the place, and I was there some 10 times in my career.

Once inside the building, you could whiz up the 110 storeys to the top in just over one minute – an incredible feat of engineering.

There was never any sense of being crowded the towers were so large that there was a place for everyone.

Built from 1966 to 1977, the vast complex consisted of five office buildings and a hotel and restaurant, connected by a vast underground concourse lined by shops, cafes and restaurants.

The World Trade Centre was the home

to 450 businesses and some 50,000 workers. And my heart goes out to the families of all those trapped and killed inside the buildings, and one shudders to think about the final toll of casualties in the midst of such carnage.

I took back not only on the magnificent views from the top of the World Trade Center, but also on the shops and restaurants at the bottom, including a cafe where I had a meal at the end of my visit.

I wonder today, with a sinking heart, about the young waitresses and all the office staff in that cafe.

Even after watching the re-run of the total collapse of the World Trade Center and the crumbling of the twin towers, it is almost impossible to take in what has happened.

This, and all the other attacks on the USA yesterday, will be a profound shock to the American people.

It is also a deep shock to the rest of the world whose people are faced with the enormous carnage perpetrated by such fanatical and evil people.

It is not just the Manhattan skyline that has changed for ever, but also the concept of international terrorism, as it plums a new depravity.

For the many Ulster people, like me, who visited the World Trade Center, this will be part of our own personal history.

Like the day President John F Kennedy was assassinated, we will remember the destruction of the World Trade Center, and the attacks on other American landmark buildings, and the horrific price in human suffering.

THE QUEEN expressed her growing disbelief and total shock" as devastation unfolded i the US.

In a message to US President George W Bush, she expressed heartfelt sympathy" and said her houghts and prayers were with mericans.

The Queen, who is at Balmoral in Scotland, was being pt closely in touch with developments, said Buckingham lace.

The full text of her message d: "It is with growing disbelief and total shock that I am

rorist attacks in the US. She described the attacks as "crimes

the very foundations of all our humanity

VISION OF DESTRUCTION: clouds of smoke billow into the Manhattan skyline following yesterday's attack on the World Trade Center

Queen, McAleese condemn 'crimes against humanity'

THE QUEEN

in the world, one of the greatest democracies of the world. It was

---

Above: One of the most dramatic stories I covered was the destruction of the Twin Towers at the World Trade Center, New York on 9/11. My column in the *News Letter* appeared the next day. Only months earlier I had visited the Twin Towers, and wrote about it for the *Belfast Telegraph*.

Alf McCreary

Religion Correspondent

'Showbiz priest' has his heart in the right place

religion

A nyone who watched the BBC television profile of Fr Brian D'Arcy this week, titled The Turbulent Priest, could not have escaped noticing the deep sadness at the heart of this sincere man of the cloth.

It was like watching a mid-life crisis up close, and in slow motion, but in the end Fr D'Arcy seems to have banished his major demons, for the medium-term at least.

This soul-searching was evident in his autobiography which I read some time ago, and he reached a major crossroads more recently when the Vatican tried to censure his outspoken column in the Sunday World newspaper.

This triggered off a deep inner debate about his role in life, whether he had been, and was ... this time and ...

Another dark chapter in our painful history

The murder of prison officer David Black this week is another dark day in our history, coming as it does just a week before the 25th anniversary of the Enniskillen bombing and our sad memories of so many other terrorist atrocities.

Words cannot fully convey the horror of such events, but in the widespread comments about the death of the prison officer, the Presbyterian Moderator Dr Roy Patton summed up the thoughts of all decent people.

He said: "Such evil violence contributes nothing to the new society that we are all helping to build, and is the complete opposite of the constructive part people like prison officers are taking in building a positive future."

Orange must get

Stand beside me

ONE of the most talked-about weddings of the year was that between the entertainer Daniel O'Donnell and Majella McLennan, which was given massive media coverage.

I, too, was at Kincasslagh in Donegal on behalf of this newspaper, and it was a day I won't forget.

Hundreds of Daniel fans braved the cold and damp weather outside St Mary's Church to wish the couple well. The bride, like others before her and since, was late, in this case by half-an-hour.

The church service seemed to take an eternity, with Daniel singing a solo, his concert partner Mary Duff singing two, and yet another one from his sister Margaret.

The bridal couple shook the hands of all 500 guests and then posed for photographs.

In the meantime the media photographers were worrying about the fast-fading light.

A BBC vehicle parked on Kincasslagh beach was in danger of being trapped by one of the highest tides of the year, and it could not be moved easily because the wedding limousines parked outside the church were blocking the way.

Understandably, there was relief all round when Daniel and Majella eventually posed at the door of the church, some three hours and ten minutes after the service had been due to start.

As they departed for the reception in Letterkenny I turned for home after a long, tiring day but I felt privileged to have been present at a quite extraordinary event.

It was extraordinary not least because the marriage took place in a Catholic church, even though the bride was a divorced mother with two children.

Many people have been wondering how this was possible, and some allege that this is easier if you are

Love and marriage ... Daniel and his bride, Majella

love, it must be an exclusive relationship, it must be permanent and both partners must be "open" to the possibility of having children. If any

as a bigamist falls foul of State laws.

However, the going gets tougher. Two paragraphs of Canon 1095 provide further clues. One refers to a

siderable immaturity, or a psychological condition or mental illness.

The non-consummation of a marriage is not enough in itself to lead to

This may explain why many people just give up on an annulment from the outset, though I am told that some 150 a year are granted in the

---

Above: One of the challenges of writing a weekly religion column is to keep in touch with current events, including the marriage of Daniel O'Donnell and Majella McLennan. This was the nearest thing to a 'Royal Wedding' in Donegal. The officiating priest was Fr Brian D'Arcy, pictured top.

Top: A family picture at the Linen Hall Library in Belfast where I was given honorary Life Membership. *Centre:* An invitation to the event. *Below:* With my daughter Emma.

Top: My *Titanic Port* book on the History of Belfast Harbour was launched at the Palace of Westminster, with the former Harland and Wolff Chairman Sir John Parker. *Centre:* With my wife Hilary at a Belfast Harbour Commissioners' reception in New York. *Bottom:* Presented to President Mary McAleese at her Official Residence in Phoenix Park in Dublin. On the left is the Harbour CEO Roy Adair, and on the right is the Chairman Dr Len O'Hagan.

For nearly forty years I reported from many parts of the Developing World for Tearfund and Christian Aid. *Top:* On an assignment at a water-project in Uganda in 2011. *Bottom:* Helping to clear the soil to build a new school in Rwanda in 2013. Both visits were with Tearfund.

Relative Values
Top: My elusive father Norman Leitch and his wife Doreen. *Centre:* With my Uncle Bill and my mother Lena at a family wedding in New York. *Below:* With my Aunt Jean, shortly before her ninetieth birthday.

Life's 'passing pleasures'

Top: With my only-ever 'big fish', caught in South Africa. *Centre:* getting close to 'Marilyn Monroe' at a 'Rat Pack' live concert in Las Vegas. *Bottom:* After my miraculous 'hole-in-one' at Massereene Golf Club, with my regular partner Roy Lilley.

the national ITN network, was waiting outside the building.

The Vice-Chancellor had just left a crucial meeting of a national university committee which had come to Queen's, and I wondered if his colleagues from other parts of the UK could really appreciate the gravity of the situation, and the pressure which Beveridge and the University were under.

Meanwhile a group of Republican students carrying black flags were circling around the Cenotaph outside Queen's, and a small number of Loyalist/Unionist students were goading them on from the sidelines. My heart sank even further because I knew from my experience as a journalist in reporting the Troubles that something big was about to blow, and that there would be huge trouble either on the campus, or somewhere else nearby.

Thankfully the Queen's term ended that weekend. Most of the students went home, and the immediate danger of physical violence within the University area diminished. However a week or so later, on 16 March 1988, the loyalist Michael Stone stormed into the Milltown cemetery in West Belfast during the paramilitary funerals of the three Provisional IRA activists shot dead in Gibraltar. Stone lobbed grenades and directed rifle fire at the mourners, killing three people and injuring nearly sixty others. He fled from the scene and was quickly arrested by police, who probably saved his life. My hunch about 'big trouble' brewing in Belfast had been correct.

The Gibraltar shootings and their aftermath had shown how impossible it was to carry out normal 'public relations' work at Queen's University. I don't believe that any of my Information Director colleagues in the British Isles or in Europe faced such major problems as I did. However even in the midst of the Mairead Farrell controversy I was also aware that this was not just a major issue for the University. It was also about the death of three more people in the Troubles, and about their bereaved families.

The next major public relations issue for Queen's arose a few years later when the University decided to drop the National Anthem from its graduation ceremonies. In any other part of the United Kingdom this would hardly have caused a ripple of comment, but in Northern Ireland it created major headlines because it cut to the heart of our troubles. Inevitably it raised once again the intractable problem of our identity – was the Province British or Irish, or neither, or a bit of both, or something different, such as 'Northern Irish', whatever that meant?

For decades the British National Anthem had been played at the beginning each graduation ceremony, but with the influx of greater numbers of Catholic students from the early Sixties onwards and the deepening political crises, this became a major controversy.

When the National Anthem was being played, some nationalist students sat rigidly in their seats while the unionist students stood up. This symbolised clearly the deep political division within Northern Ireland and within the student body.

As the complaints from the Irish nationalist lobby increased, so too did the media coverage of the graduation ceremonies which created more and more headlines. The 'anthem' controversy began to overshadow the good news of the graduations, and my colleagues and I were constantly on the alert for trouble. Prior to one summer graduation ceremony we were tipped off that a protest would take place on the platform of the Whitla Hall.

Accordingly we had two sturdy security men ready to assist our staff in dealing with any trouble. The ceremony passed smoothly until the moment when virtually the last of the graduates crossed the stage to shake the Vice-Chancellor's hand. Suddenly he grabbed the microphone and those of us in the wings who were expecting trouble immediately stiffened and looked to our security men to whisk the 'protestor' off the stage.

However, to our surprise and relief, he merely said "I would like to thank you all for giving me a great time at Queen's." Crisis over, we all relaxed; but the whole thing was ludicrous.

Nevertheless there were many people who believed firmly that Queen's was right to play the Anthem. After all, they argued, the University was funded largely by the British taxpayer and it was the 'Queen's' University, which had been named after Queen Victoria, as one of the then 'Queen's Colleges' in 1845.

Despite these persuasive and eminently legitimate considerations, the truth was that every year the celebration of graduation was overshadowed by political controversy.

The same applied to the Graduation parties on the splendid lawns of the quadrangle. Each year the music was provided by the band of the Royal Ulster Constabulary which ended the garden party with the National Anthem – and with the same result.

Some graduates and their families stood to attention, while others remained seated. On one occasion I watched an entire family perch itself precariously on a wooden bench in the quadrangle, in order to avoid standing for the Anthem.

Sadly, the National Anthem itself was being used as a political football, and it was being continually brought into disrepute. Clearly the University would have to do something about it, and also about the use of Irish language signs in the predominantly nationalist Students' Union which was also demonstrating its commitment to the Republican cause.

The trigger for the University to deal with these difficult issues at last was contained in the report of the consultants who had been employed to provide the University with a blueprint for creating a proper Fair Employment policy.

The recommendation stated: "The University, in the context of fulfilling its obligations to promote a neutral working environment, should consult widely and sensitively on the appropriateness of playing the National Anthem at graduation ceremonies, the RUC band playing at graduation ceremonies, and the use of Irish language in the Students' Union."

A Committee, of which I was a member, was set up to consider these issues, and its report was sent to the Senate, the governing body. As a result the Senate decided in December 1994 to drop the National Anthem from its Graduation ceremonies.

At the same meeting the Senate also agreed to offer an honorary degree to James Molyneaux, the Ulster Unionist leader. It was hard to credit the lack of joined-up thinking from such a body of intelligent and distinguished people as the Queen's University Senate. On the one hand they were honouring the Unionist leader, but on the other they were dropping the Anthem. If it was meant to be a 'quid pro quo', the Unionists were certainly not going to accept it.

I left the Senate meeting and resolved to have as quiet and as happy a Christmas as I could, for I knew that sooner rather than later the news would leak out and that there would be hell to pay. How right I was. To make matters worse, this promised to be a bad start for the celebrations of our 150th Anniversary which began early in 1995.

The uproar over Queen's decision to drop the Anthem soon made itself heard in the New Year. In a period when there were more 'leaks' from Queen's than in any broken-down housing estate in the country, the media reported that Jim Molyneaux had turned down the offer of an honorary degree because Queen's was dropping the Anthem.

The objections rained thick and fast onto the Queen's campus. As Professor Clarkson records in his book "By the time of the next meeting of Senate in February 1995, the University had received letters of objection from five borough or county councils, thirteen individual councillors and members of Parliament, eight organisations such as Orange lodges and 143 individuals".[2]

One elderly graduate returned his degree parchment to Queen's, after the media had been tipped off, and the story was carried in full in the local Press. There was also a meeting of graduates in the Whitla Hall later on, to protest about the dropping of the Anthem.

It was one of the largest graduate meetings of its kind in the history of Queen's. Those present included a wide range of professional people who rarely attended such meetings, but the importance of their presence was clear. They were protesting about what they perceived to be the dilution of their 'Britishness' because Queen's was dropping the Anthem. It was the middle-class equivalent of the working-class protest by furious Loyalists later on, when Belfast City Council voted in December 2012 to fly the Union Jack over the City Hall on designated days only, and not all the year round.

Unfortunately, the Vice-Chancellor Sir Gordon Beveridge completely misread the entire situation concerning the dropping of the Anthem. He had been advised, though certainly not by me, that the best way to deal publicly with the Anthem furore was to ignore it. This was fundamentally the wrong approach, and after several weeks during which Queen's continued to lose ground on this controversial and high-profile issue, a number of senior colleagues and I asked for a round-table meeting with Sir Gordon to express our grave reservations about the way in which the University was handling the situation.

Sadly, Gordon was almost a lone voice at the meeting, and the decision was taken eventually to go public with the University's response to the uproar. Significantly, the Vice-Chancellor chose not to lead the response,

---

[2] Prof Leslie A Clarkson, *A University in Troubled Times*, Four Courts Press, 2004, p190

and this was left to Professor Leslie Clarkson, who was then a Pro Vice-Chancellor.

I admired the way Leslie did this, with courage and eloquence. He was the one senior University figure on whom I could rely most often to take on a largely hostile Press during a period when Queen's had little good to say for itself. Later on he wrote me a personal letter in which he said, in effect, that we were left with few cards to play, but that we played them as best we could.

Rightly, Queen's stuck to its decision to drop the Anthem, and the world did not come to an end. The storm eventually subsided, as it did over the use of the RUC band and the Irish signs in the Students' Union. It had been a bruising period for the University and its public image, and I was not surprised when the top officials commissioned an outside firm of consultants to report, among other things, on the work of the Information Office.

It was the typical reaction of a demoralised management, some of whose decisions had made part of our work almost impossible. When the consultants' report was issued, it criticised some of the work of the Information Office, but the situation was interpreted in the local Press – and by people within Queen's – as a classic case of the critics 'blaming the messenger'.

Of course I had made mistakes, but I reckoned that anyone in the same position could not have done much better. I was particularly annoyed on behalf of my staff because they had worked extremely hard with me to create a professional approach to publicising the good news about Queen's, not least during the British Association meeting in 1987, the 150th Celebrations and through the many stories about the University's academic and other successes down the years. Sadly, however, people have short memories.

I was also disappointed that a number of powerful people within the University had not backed me as I hoped they should, and it was clear to me that my colleagues and I would face an uphill struggle to regain our place in the sun.

While I was pondering upon these issues, a friend rang me one day and said "Alfie what Queen's is doing to you is disgraceful. If I was you I would leave them to it, and go out and rebuild your writing career." This is what I did, but I waited for the right opportunity to present itself.

My decision to leave Queen's was similar to that which I had taken about leaving the *Belfast Telegraph* nearly twelve years previously. It was not taken on impulse and certainly not before I had weighed up all the arguments.

I had been at Queen's for a long time, and I had helped to mastermind a whole new output of promotional material, I had written all the Vice-Chancellor's speeches, I had helped to publicise hundreds of 'good news' stories about Queen's, and I been 'fire-fighting' the impact of the bad news for several years. It seemed unlikely that any of this would change in the foreseeable future.

I did not miss the daily hurly-burly of newspapers as such, but I wanted to extend my writing career beyond the promotional material for Queen's University. I was still attracted to the creative and raffish world of journalists, and it is no surprise that I made a point of attending two revealing sessions during one of the Queen's Festivals at which the BBC top-line reporters John Simpson and Fergal Keane talked about their careers.

They both said, in different ways, that they were essentially 'story tellers', and I thought "That's what I am as well." It was only a matter of time before I would seek to escape from the strait-jacket of university public relations and administration, and return to what I really wanted to do, which was to write full-time.

The opportunity came with yet another offer of a package for Queen's staff. My decision to apply was not only because of the latest developments. The previous few years had been stressful for everyone, including me, who had been at the heart of various crises. One Friday evening when I came home from work looking grey with fatigue my wife Hilary said to me "How was today?"

I replied "Not bad". I then outlined how I had managed to survive another stressful week in the office, but I was worried about the flashing knives re-appearing again during the coming week. Hilary looked at me for a moment and then she said coolly "You are beginning to talk just like another 'suit'. When I married you, I married a writer!"

I said nothing, but I knew she was right. At heart I knew that I was not a spin doctor or a career administrator. I was a writer, I had many stories to tell, and all of them were outside the daily life of a big university.

Eventually I signed up to leave Queen's, and as I thought about what I was about to do, I had some trepidation about re-establishing myself as a freelance writer at a time when most people of my age were thinking of early retirement. However, I was not to know then that I was about to embark upon one of the most productive, creative and fulfilling periods of my writing career.

CHAPTER TWENTY

New Horizons

ONE AFTERNOON IN mid-December 1996, I attended a meeting of business executives in the Canada Room in Queen's University.

I listened intently to the main speaker John Cole, a former *Belfast Telegraph* reporter who later became Deputy Editor of *The Guardian* newspaper and then the Political Editor of the BBC.

He was one of the best known journalists in the United Kingdom, and I had met him several times. He was a convivial Ulsterman who had not forgotten his roots and I was present some years earlier when Queen's had awarded him an honorary degree. In his acceptance speech he said that the two most intelligent people he had worked with during his career were the politician Reginald Maudling and the trade unionist George Woodcock.

As he addressed the business executives and Queen's staff members in the Canada Room all those years later I listened to Cole intently. Like most top journalists he had a fund of anecdotes about his career when he had worked with all kinds of distinguished people.

Afterwards, Sir Gordon Beveridge came over to me and said "I was watching your face when John Cole was speaking, and your expression told me where your heart really lies." It was a typically kind and perceptive comment from Gordon, whom I liked and respected.

However, I was not going to be working with Gordon much longer, because he took early retirement a few months afterwards. Even though I had signed up to leave Queen's, I was around long enough to witness some dramatic changes in the top management. Within a relatively short period three of the main people had gone.

Dr George Baird, the Secretary to the Academic Council died at an early age, after a short illness. He and I had joined the Queen's management team around the same time, and I knew how hard he had worked for the best interests of the University. I was particularly sad because his wife Honor had been a contemporary of mine in Bessbrook where her mother had been Principal of the Girls' PE School, next door to our classrooms where Jemmy Darragh had drummed English grammar and 'sums' into us.

Around the same period, another senior figure, the Pro Vice-Chancellor Mary McAleese, accepted the Fianna Fail nomination to campaign for the Presidency of Ireland, and she was ultimately successful.

I had worked quite closely with Mary whose many responsibilities at Queen's had included public relations. I was sorry that I was unable to get to know her better, but I was aware of her wide-ranging portfolio. One thing we had in common, however, was her regard for Queen's, and I shared her sentiments when she remarked, more than once "I love every stick and stone about this place."

I was pleased that she became such an outstanding President of Ireland, and that she was able to build on the groundwork of her predecessor President Mary Robinson to welcome the Queen on her historic visit to Ireland, which was such an important landmark in Anglo-Irish relations.

Even on formal occasions Mary McAleese had a charming informality. One afternoon when she was attending an anniversary function at Glencraig, Holywood for the Camphill Communities of Northern Ireland – of which our daughter Emma is a member – she spotted me in the audience of parents and friends of the Community. When she reached our table, she came over to me and with typical spontaneity she kissed me on the cheek and said "Hiya honey!" I said to my wife Hilary afterwards "There are not many wives who can say that their husband was kissed by a European Head of State who called him 'Honey!'"

I also had great regard for her husband Dr Martin McAleese who not only supported her selflessly, but also carried out important bridge-building work of his own in Northern Ireland.

Martin was a dentist by training and part of his practice had been in Bessbrook, where his surgery was in the very house at Wakefield Terrace where I had grown up as a boy.

The most important senior figure to leave Queen's around that time was the Vice-Chancellor Sir Gordon Beveridge who retired in 1997. This was no great surprise to some of us who were aware of the pressures he had constantly been under. No Vice-Chancellor since the end of the Second World War had quite so much to contend with.

Gordon Beveridge faced not only swingeing cuts in funding but also the problems caused by the political and cultural divisions in Northern Ireland which at times threatened to suck Queen's into a morass of misunderstanding and bitterness.

It was Gordon Beveridge's misfortune to come to Queen's during a period well-summarised by Leslie Clarkson in his book as a time of "austerity and anguish". Gordon helped to guide Queen's through a most difficult period, but he left the University a legacy of superbly refurbished buildings and a sound economic base for his successor, in the most stringent of circumstances.

Gordon Beveridge was a good and decent man, and history will be kinder to him than some of his contemporaries were. Tragically he died not long after his retirement, and I felt sad that he had not been given more time to share the more relaxed later years of his life with his wife Trudy and their family.

His successor was Professor Sir George Bain, a dynamic Canadian who had roots in Northern Ireland on his mother's side. He brought to Queen's a confidence, a clear direction to follow and a new impetus which helped to restore morale and to rebuild its considerable reputation. Queen's was fortunate to attract such a high-flyer who had been Head of the London Business School. His appointment by Queen's was a turning point, and it was one of the most crucial of any era within top management since the departure of Eric Ashby in 1959.

I was fortunate to work closely with George during my last months at Queen's. I liked his management style and his sense of humour. I watched him make one of his first speeches at Queen's, which was written for him by someone else.

As he ploughed on, his head dropped and I knew that he was bored. He asked me later "What did you think of it?" I replied "Not much. The point of your speech was not the technical importance of yet another dull computer but the fact that it was the result of a cross-border initiative. That was the real story." George replied "You are absolutely right."

From then on I wrote nearly all of his major speeches for the next few years. We worked well together and we often had great fun and satisfaction in doing so.

One of the main addresses we prepared was the citation when President Bill Clinton was awarded an honorary degree by Queen's. George Bain delivered it with aplomb, which he did with all his speeches. Only he and I, as well as his wife and key office staff, knew how much hard work and rehearsal had gone into it. George told me later that Clinton said that his speech was the best of the evening, and Clinton – no mean speaker himself – was right.

I was delighted to work with George over that period and also to meet again his wife Gwynneth. She had been a senior administrator at the University of Warwick and she had been a colleague of mine when we attended the annual meetings of the UK universities Information Officers group.

I left Queen's around the same time that the Good Friday Agreement was signed in the Spring of 1998, and I recall the agonising wait until it was finally ratified. I felt that this was a time for new beginnings – for Queen's under its new Vice-Chancellor Sir George Bain, for me as I embarked on a full time writing career, and most of all for the people of Northern Ireland in the new hopes that were being generated by the Good Friday Agreement after so many years of death, deadlock and darkness.

My staff in the University gave me some beautiful farewell gifts, including a handsome framed linen print of part of Seamus Heaney's poem 'The Cure at Troy', with the line which so aptly summarised the new Northern Ireland "where hope and history rhyme."

I was pleased to receive a signed copy of the poem because during my time as Information Director I had met Heaney, who had been only a couple of years ahead of me as a Queen's student. He had visited the University to open the Seamus Heaney Library and he later wrote me a private letter of thanks for the work of the Information Office in helping with the publicity for the event. It was typical of Heaney, who was another of those internationally-acclaimed Queen's contemporaries or near contemporaries of mine, including Phil Coulter, who remained impressively modest and true to their roots, despite their considerable worldly success.

When I left Queen's, the University organised a special lunch and a 'retirement' reception, which was customary for senior officers. They also presented me with a splendid cartoon by Rowel Friers with the caption "McCreary moves off in the 'Write' Direction."

It was most apt. I had no intention of retiring, and the very next day I went down to Larne to begin my first new assignment which was to begin a history of the Harbour. At lunchtime I drove to a park overlooking the Irish Sea, and as I ate my sandwiches in the warm Spring sunshine I realised that "with one leap, Jack was free."

It was partly a leap into the dark, because I had to rebuild my writing career, but I was glad that there were no more University committees, no more receptions, and no more phone calls from the media at all hours.

Nevertheless, I had enjoyed my career at Queen's. There were many good times, and I was privileged to have been able to give back something to my University which had given me so much. I remain intensely proud of Queen's, and I will always be a 'Queen's man'.

Even now when I walk through the Queen's quad, I sometimes pause and think of my teachers and fellow students of so long ago, and of the best of my administrative and academic colleagues later on. Queen's was a rich experience, and the University was extremely significant for me at important times in my life and career.

§

As a freelance my writing steadily gained momentum. During my years at Queen's I wrote occasionally for the *Belfast Telegraph*, and for the *News Letter*, which first appeared in 1737, and is the world's oldest continuous publication in English.

The editor Geoff Martin had remembered my poignant article about the former Stormont Prime Minister Captain Terence O'Neill putting his house up for auction at Ahoghill – a story which Geoff had also covered that day for a local Ballymena newspaper.

He asked me to write a column with the *News Letter*, which I did for several years, and later on this gave me the opportunity to comment upon one of the most important stories of my career. On 11 September 2001, popularly known as '9/11', almost 3000 people died in four co-ordinated al-Qaeda attacks on key targets in New York and Washington.

When two hijacked commercial jet liners were flown by Muslim fanatics into the World Trade Center in New York, the twin towers collapsed within two hours of the impact. In Washington the western side of the Pentagon was badly damaged by the impact of another plane which was flown into the building, and another plane which was targeted on Washington crashed at Shanksville, Pennsylvania after its passengers had tried heroically to overcome the hijackers.

Only a few weeks earlier I had been on the top of one of the towers in New York with my son Matthew, who had accompanied me on a summer break to the east coast of the USA. I remember the two of us attending a lunchtime concert featuring the Songs of the Auvergne, which was held in a beautiful seventeenth century church near the World Trade Center. Though the music was by Cantaloube, the atmosphere of that morning reminded me of Gershwin's 'Summertime, and the livin' is easy...'

After the concert, Matthew and I went to the tourist tower of World Trade Center complex. It was one of my favourite buildings which I had visited many times, and I always marvelled at the stunning views it afforded across New York city. The views were just as stunning this time, and I was delighted to share them with my younger son. When I was about to descend from the top on that hot August day, I patted the building and said "Au revoir, old friend, here's to the next time."

Sadly there was to be no "next time", because the Twin Towers crashed into rubble less than a month later. When the attacks took place I was back in Belfast, and like almost everyone else, I could not believe what was happening. That day was locked in my memory not only because of the terrorist attacks on the USA but also because my elder son Mark was leaving for Australia with his then girlfriend Angela, who later became his wife. In Australia he eventually became a senior journalist with the *Sydney Morning Herald*.

As we set out for Aldergrove airport, I asked my wife Hilary to drive the car because I was busily writing a column for the *News Letter*, and I had a deadline to meet. I tried to describe my feelings of shock and horror, which mirrored those of millions of people around the world.

I wrote "Even after watching the television re-run of the collapse of the World Trade Center, and the crumbling of the twin towers, it is almost impossible to take in what has happened.

"It is not just the Manhattan skyline that has changed forever, but also the concept of international terrorism as it plumbs a new depravity. For many people like me who visited the World Trade Center, this will become part of our personal history.

"Like the day President Kennedy was assassinated in Dallas, we will remember the destruction of the World Trade Center and the attacks on the other American landmark buildings, and the horrible price in human suffering."

Several weeks later I returned to New York when I was reporting on a previously-scheduled visit by the Ulster Orchestra which was giving a concert there. The city was still in shock, and I remember visiting fire stations where people had lost colleagues as they tried to save lives at the World Trade Center.

On the following Sunday I attended morning service in a large Anglican Church in downtown Manhattan where a packed congregation listened intently while the Duke of York read a Lesson.

That evening the Ulster Orchestra with its Principal Conductor Thierry Fischer performed superbly before a large audience at a concert in the city, and people were very much aware of the violence which had so disfigured both our countries, at different times. Before the concert began, a Stormont Minister Michael McGimpsey spoke to the audience movingly about our common suffering, and his words were appreciated by the New York people.

During my time in the city, I visited Ground Zero, which looked like Northern Ireland writ large. There was the same sense of shock, the rubble, the silent bystanders, the muted horror, and the inevitable question "Why?" Sadly I had seen so much of this before on a smaller scale, but you cannot measure the impact in numbers alone. When you stand on the ground where innocent people have been murdered, you are aware that irrespective of the numbers involved, these had been human beings with families and friends whose lives would never be the same again.

Near Ground Zero I met a US Army sergeant who told me that they had been sent to the area on the day after '9/11', and that now they were preparing to leave. I expressed my deep sympathies and explained that I came from Northern Ireland where my experience had helped me to understand, perhaps more than people from other countries, just how personal the '9/11' slaughter had been to the families involved and to the American people.

I felt like a war veteran who had witnessed and written about the aftermath of violence not only in my own country but also in Sri Lanka, Cambodia, Vietnam, and now the USA. I had written enough about war, and I wanted a new, more inspiring and hopeful subject to cover in depth. By that stage I was writing regularly again for the *Belfast Telegraph,* and the editor Edmund Curran invited me to become the Religion Correspondent of the paper.

The details were hammered out over lunch with the Features Editor John Caruth, and the News Editor Paul Connolly, and my career took another surprising turn. I had always been interested in religion in the widest sense, and many years earlier I had applied for the vacant post of Religion Correspondent of the *Irish Times,* when it was edited by Fergus Pyle. I was told later on by the news editor Donal Foley that I had missed the appointment "by the skin of your teeth."

Now I had the welcome and unexpected opportunity to work as the Religion Correspondent of the *Belfast Telegraph.* In my new role I was to encounter some of the best and the worst of human behaviour in settings both sacred and secular, and I was ready to begin another writing adventure as soon as possible.

CHAPTER TWENTY-ONE

God Has No Religion

MY INVOLVEMENT WITH religion began during my boyhood in Bessbrook when, like nearly all children of my generation, we had no choice in the matter.

I was sent to Sunday school and church every week, and I was aware that there was a God somewhere up there or out there, and that if I misbehaved He would put a black mark in his big book and punish me. This wrathful Old Testament figure was only part of the picture, and I also learned about the story of Jesus and also the redemption of the New Testament, though I was much too young to understand what it was all about.

From my early days, a person's religion did not bother me. Some of the other boys with whom I played were Catholics, which made no difference to me. One of my fellow soccer enthusiasts Graham McAleer, who was the centre-forward for our 'Evergreen' soccer team, remained a friend for a lifetime. My upbringing in a mixed environment like Bessbrook gave me a broad outlook on religion at an early stage, and it was only afterwards that I became aware of that privilege which many other people of my generation, and later generations, did not experience – with disastrous consequences for the small Province in which we all lived.

During my student days at Queen's University, I was impressed by the life and work of the Presbyterian Chaplain, the Reverend Ray Davey and, as I have noted earlier, it gave me an insight into practical Christianity at its best.

Several other people were pivotal to my spiritual awareness and they included my mother-in-law Dr Winifred Fitzsimons who showed how a Christian life, well-lived, could be a force for good.

During my career in the *Belfast Telegraph* it was impossible to escape the influence of religion during the Troubles. Almost every major story had a religious and political dimension, though I always believed that the Troubles were not about religion as such, in the strict theological sense of that term, but rather about the ostentatious display of complex cultural identities which often exploded into confrontations and violence.

The graffiti on the walls of Belfast and many other places was essentially a sectarian indicator as to which side was dominant in that area, and I suspected that it was easier to scrawl on a wall "To Hell with the Pope", rather than "To Hell with the Moderator of the General Assembly of the Presbyterian Church in Ireland." To write that latter slogan, you had to be able to spell properly, never mind understanding who or what a Moderator actually was, or did.

Activists from both main communities were not fighting about 'Transubstantiation' or the 'Thirty-Nine Articles' of the Reformation period of church history. Their set battles were about territory, and rigid boundaries along which people walked peacefully, but only with the permission of 'the other side'.

Sadly, however, religion was widely used as a tribal label and in many cases it was perverted into a political and cultural show of strength. Even in more recent times when Loyalist bands played sectarian tunes outside a Roman Catholic Church it was a shocking reminder that many of the young people were still trapped in the their cultural ghettoes where religion was disfigured, abused and mocked, or in real terms was virtually non-existent.

During my journeys in Africa, Asia, Latin America and other parts of the developing world I developed a wide experience of religious practice. In some countries like South Korea and the Islamist Sudan there was oppression of Christians, but in many other areas I found a refreshing co-operation between believers of all denominations in working together to help the poor, the sick, the hungry and the dispossessed.

It was not only in the developing world that I found new dimensions to religion. As an English-speaking rapporteur I attended a European

Conference of Churches meeting in Crete, which I mentioned earlier, and which gave me an insight into the Orthodox world of Christianity which I had known little about.

At the end of the conference those of us from many different countries who had been involved were invited to share in an Orthodox service in a small church in the hills of Crete. The men stood in the church on one side, and the women on the other.

A Russian Orthodox patriarch from Moscow presided, and he was assisted by Greek Orthodox priests from the local village. I noticed that while they did not speak the same language, they were at one as they followed the Orthodox Church liturgy.

For Protestants like me, and others from different backgrounds across Europe, it was difficult to follow what was happening but, ironically, the person who kept us all in line with the complex liturgy was a Jesuit priest from Rome. After the service, we all went back to the village hall where a 'fatted calf' had been roasted, and where they brought round the wine in plastic buckets.

It was all a long way from Bessbrook Presbyterian Church where I had first learned about religion, and I realised how much each version of Christianity spoke to different denominations in different ways. There was one God, but many varieties of worship, and I eventually came to the conclusion that what really mattered was how a person behaved, and not what he or she said they believed or thought they believed.

I often recalled a half-joking but also serious comment from Eddie Sterling, a former picture editor in the *Belfast Telegraph* who was a kind and helpful colleague. He used to say "When people tell me that they are 'Christians', I watch them like a hawk!"

This was his personal variation, no doubt, on the Biblical injunction "By their works shall ye know them." I was reminded of this vividly when I visited Vietnam to report on the development work of Christian Aid and its local partners. I spent some time there with a local woman doctor, who had suffered in the Vietnam War. During an American air raid on her village she had to seek refuge in the forest where she became ill and lost her unborn baby.

However she had not allowed that family tragedy to make her bitter, and I noticed how helpful she was to everyone. When I was leaving the village with a Vietnamese colleague I remarked "That doctor is a fine Christian woman." He said "She's not a Christian, she's a Confucian!" I replied "She's a better person than many a Christian I know."

Given such a wide experience of religion in its many forms, I decided to write my column for the *Belfast Telegraph* each week with an open mind, and to try to make it relevant to the news of the day. I was mindful of the theologian Karl Barth who advised the clergy to preach with a Bible in one hand and with a good newspaper in the other – in other words to make what they said relevant to everyday life.

That's what I tried to do in my weekly column. For example, if I wanted to discuss redemption I would write about the morality of giving a new liver to George Best. Was it right to give a second chance to a brilliant footballer who had been a helpless drunk, or should a liver transplant be reserved for a person who had never touched alcohol and therefore might have a better chance of recovery?

This in turn raised the whole question of redemption. Was George Best too far gone to be redeemed, and if he was given a liver transplant would he become a reformed character? And if doctors began to base their decisions on personalities rather than medical data, would they refuse transplants to criminals, or people from certain backgrounds, or those of whom they did not approve? It was a subject fraught with difficulty.

There was little space to discuss in depth such controversial issues, but I was clear that if my religion columns were to be widely read, they had to be in non-churchy language that people could understand.

One of the clerics who impressed me in earlier years with his clarity and perception was the American preacher Norman Vincent Peale. He was one of the first self-improvement authors who wrote the huge bestseller titled *The Power of Positive Thinking*, and many other books based on the enabling power of Christianity, properly understood.

Even as an elderly man he remained active and prolific. When I met him in his elegant apartment in uptown New York he was aged ninety, and he had just come back the previous day from a major speaking engagement in Montreal.

He was a gracious and friendly person, and when he told me that he was preparing to embark on a tour in Asia, I asked him "How do you keep this up at ninety?"

He smiled, and replied in his slow American drawl "Ah think work, ah think health, ah think I can, and with God's help I can! Next time you are in Noo York come and see me!"

I thought "Here's a man who practices what he preaches." I also thought that at ninety he was a little ambitious in asking me to visit him next time I was in New York. In fact he lived until he was ninety-six. Obviously I was the man of little faith.

My role as Religion Correspondent of the *Belfast Telegraph* gave me a comprehensive awareness of what people believed and did in the name of religion, in a part of the world where it could be such a contentious subject.

My work confirmed my view that while people from different denominations were willing to work together, and others were not, everyone at heart believed that they were right in their interpretation of Christianity – but I felt that they couldn't all be right. However, that did not seem to worry them.

One day on a visit to the North Coast in Northern Ireland I noticed in a Portstewart gift shop a prominent sign which stated "God Has No Religion". It summed up for me the dangers of too intense denominationalism and at the extreme end, sectarianism. Sometimes the organised churches are so self-serving that they fail to realise that they are not connecting with people who are unable to share their way of looking at this world, or the next.

Sometimes I least find God in large Synods, General Assemblies and other set pieces of organised religion where there is much ecclesiastical wheeler-dealing, grand-standing and, in some cases, sheer bloody-mindedness. On the other hand I have found qualities of 'Christianity' among people who rarely go to church.

The theologian Reinhold Niebuhr once said "Nothing so masks the face of God as religion" and that still applies today. However, from direct experience, I am aware of the enormous amount of goodness among a very large number of people who go to Church regularly and who take seriously the practical implications of their faith in a troubled world.

They rarely are given credit for this by the critics of religion who never darken the doors of the churches, except for weddings, baptisms and funerals, and who criticise them from a position of supreme ignorance. Good news is often less interesting than bad news, so the blameless life of, say, a church organist is rarely commented upon whereas the predatory misbehaviour of a paedophile youth leader attracts major headlines, and rightly so. However the vast majority of news from the churches is wholesome and uplifting, and while some good headlines are welcome at times, the oxygen for the goodness that is found in churches comes from the Bible rather than from publicity.

During my visits to many different churches, before and after my appointment as the *Telegraph's* Religion Correspondent, I was all too aware that each denomination had a long-earned reputation for its own 'speciality' in worship. For the Presbyterians it was the preaching of 'The Word', for Methodists it was their Wesleyan hymns and enthusiastic singing, and for the Roman Catholics and Anglicans it was the theatricality of their liturgies. I also appreciated the spirituality of other smaller groups, including the Society of Friends whom I first encountered in Bessbrook, which had been founded by a Quaker, and the Christian Science Church with its remarkable record of healings, and insights from Mary Baker Eddy.

Quite frequently I met or heard from people with strongly non-Christian views. I have long recognised that it is difficult to change the mind of those who are determined not to believe in religion, so I say to them "If you are right and there is no God, then I am wrong. However if I am right, then we will both find out the truth, sooner or later."

I recall one professional man who laughed disdainfully when I suggested that he might be inherently religious. That did not worry me, because I was mature enough to be comfortable with my own beliefs, but when he died in tragic circumstances several months later, I felt sorry for the turmoil he must have gone through, and the fact that his intellect alone had not given him the comfort and support he needed.

His funeral was without a glimmer of hope, Christian or otherwise. I am not writing this to be judgemental, but rather to record my respect for those who are confirmed non-believers and who have the courage to face life and death on their own terms, and without any religious persuasion.

In the busy world of journalism my 'religion' beat gave me a wide opportunity to report on many fascinating people and events. Some of my assignments were not totally 'religious' as such but they had a 'peg' on which to hang a good story, and I was happy to branch into other areas of reporting, including the world of show business.

One memorable example of this was the wedding of Daniel O'Donnell, the popular singer and entertainer. The ceremony in Donegal was performed by his friend Father Brian D'Arcy, the 'show-biz' priest.

I admired Brian greatly for his independence of mind, and for his courage in standing up against the Vatican who tried to censor some of his comments as a Sunday newspaper columnist. Brian was also a good broadcaster, and if he had chosen to follow a career on radio and television he would undoubtedly have become a top media professional.

I also liked Daniel O'Donnell, whom I had interviewed some time earlier. Over many years he developed a warm rapport with a huge range of his intensely loyal fans, many of whom followed him from concert to concert. Despite his folksy image, Daniel was a shrewd businessman who had built up his career steadily and with a clear focus both at home and abroad.

His marriage to Majella McLennan at his home village in Kincasslagh in Donegal on Monday 4 November 2002 was an unforgettable event. Before the ceremony in St Mary's Church, hundreds of Daniel's fans crowded into the area to get a good view of the wedding.

I arrived well in time to write a descriptive 'colour piece' for the early edition of the *Telegraph*, and I talked to a lady from Coleraine who told me "My heart was beating like a chicken's fist. When Daniel came over to greet us, he called me 'Betty', and that just made my day." When Daniel arrived outside the Chapel I was on hand to record his comments. He told the crowd "I am so happy that Majella has come into my life, and it is wonderful that we can be married in my home church here today."

From my point of view it was all going smoothly, except for one major worry. The bride was late and if she did not arrive soon, I would miss the deadline for the final edition of that day's *Telegraph*.

The news editor Ronan Henry was speaking to me constantly on my mobile phone as I stood on a windy hillside overlooking the scene, and he was asking anxiously when he could expect confirmation that Majella had arrived, and that the wedding was getting under way. It was unthinkable for both of us that the *Telegraph* would miss the biggest story of the day, but if Majella did not appear within a couple of minutes there was nothing I could do about it.

With the seconds to our deadline ticking away, the bride finally arrived, and greeted the cheering crowds. It was the nearest thing you could imagine to a 'Royal' wedding in Donegal. I stood with my mobile phone glued to my ear and talked to my news editor down the line. My wife Hilary, who was beside me, supplied the details of Majella's dress and flowers. I passed these on to Ronan Henry who 'subbed' my copy as we talked, and we eventually made our deadline just in time. Immediately the presses started rolling to print the final edition of the day.

That evening my story appeared on Page One of the *Telegraph*, under the heading "Daniel weds on 'best day of my life'." Without doubt it was one of the best read stories in the paper, but it had been a nerve-wracking experience for me, and also great fun. I had watched with amusement as the Donegal tide wafted in, and seawater crept up higher and higher towards a large BBC Television outside broadcast van which was very nearly marooned by the Atlantic waves because all of us had been kept waiting for so long. After the ceremony a reporter said to Brian D'Arcy "It took you longer to marry Daniel than it took them to bury Pope John Paul II in Rome!" D'Arcy replied cheerily "Sure we got yer man married anyhow!"

Unfortunately most of the stories I reported in those days were not so happy, and I wrote many articles on grim subjects, including the scandal of clerical child sexual abuse which has so disfigured the Roman Catholic Church in Ireland and elsewhere, and which will hang like a dark shadow over its work and witness for years to come.

Of course there were stories about errant clerics and laity from other denominations, as well as the continuing controversies about same-sex relationships and 'gay' marriage. Sometimes I felt that my religion column was mostly about sex in its various forms, or the lack of it. However while there was much else on which to report, the daily news list reminded me of a remark by my old friend Gloria Hunniford, the broadcaster. She said to me a long time ago "There are only a handful of topics which constantly interests the public, and they include sex, violence, money, health, the latest fashion and the pursuit of happiness."

Sadly one of the most difficult stories I had to report was about the near-destruction of Whitehouse Presbyterian Church by arsonists in August 2002. I have been a member of that Church for decades and it was heart-breaking to stand among smoking ruins of the old building where our children had been baptised and where so many people had shared such happy fellowships over so many years.

However, the members of Whitehouse were dedicated and resourceful. The fire had occurred early in the morning, and even before the firemen had left, members of the congregation were arranging the chairs in the Church Hall for the next Sunday service.

That remarkable practicality and refusal to be overwhelmed by events beyond their control was typical of the Whitehouse congregation, and soon the plans were underway to construct a fine new building.

One of the inspiring features of the rebuilding programme was the tremendous financial support for Whitehouse from Protestant and Roman Catholic congregations nearby, and from a wide variety of well-wishers from every denomination and of none. This was typical of the decency of ordinary people which rarely makes major headlines, but which is the social glue which has kept Northern Ireland going, through so many years of trouble.

I remember one particularly sad story about the murder of a young Roman Catholic man by loyalist paramilitaries in the North Belfast area. This received widespread publicity, and there was a further depressing story when Loyalist vandals destroyed his headstone. I found out later that a Presbyterian from a town some distance away had then sent the family some money to buy a new headstone. However, when the expenses had all been paid, they discovered that there was money left over.

So in an act of impressive cross-community generosity, they gave the surplus money to help rebuild Whitehouse Presbyterian Church. The symbolism of a bereaved Catholic family giving a donation to a Protestant church almost destroyed by arson was an inspiring act of goodness in the most appalling of circumstances, and I was tempted to report this in the *Telegraph*.

However the situation was still raw and dangerous, and after talking to the Whitehouse minister the Reverend Liz Hughes, I decided that if the story became well known publicly, this might draw the unwelcome attention of those who might make a point of destroying the new headstone as well.

Sometimes it is better to remain silent for the greater good, and so no story appeared. Unfortunately the public does not always realise the degree of self-censorship within the media, despite the behaviour of a minority of British national newspaper journalists whose alleged phone-hacking and other disgraceful behaviour brings the practice of journalism into disrepute.

My work as a Religion Correspondent, and as the author of several books on religious topics, gave me the opportunity to meet and to interview a number of important church leaders. They included Archbishop Robert Runcie, a gentle and courageous man who wrote the foreword for one of my books titled *Tried by Fire*, which contained reflections from people who been helped greatly by their Christian faith to deal with the bereavement of loved ones.

Significantly, one of the most moving contributions came from Baroness Jane Ewart-Biggs, an agnostic whose husband Christopher Ewart-Biggs, the British Ambassador to Ireland, was killed by a terrorist landmine in 1976. She was left with three young children. She told me "I wanted to bring something out of this act of insanity, so it seemed the right thing to stay on Dublin and to make a bond with Ireland against the enemy of reason and sanity. There is no point in putting blame, it would only bring on a serious depression.

"When I hear that people have made some little contact with each other, or when people do something constructive, groups in England who support community work in Northern Ireland, or if the Press seems to do something constructive, I count up all these things. I really do."

I also met a later Archbishop of Canterbury Dr Rowan Williams, a helpful, charming and impressive man, who gave me a long interview when I was researching for a book on the Church of Ireland Primate Archbishop (now Lord) Eames. Dr Williams in private was not at all like his image of the academic whose public statements as Archbishop of Canterbury were often too convoluted for most members of the public to follow. On a one-to-one basis his answers were concise, and much to the point. If he had maintained this style in public he would have communicated much better to his mass audiences, but perhaps he felt that his public statements were too complex to be reduced to sound-bites. On the other hand, good sound-bites demonstrate an ability to get to the heart of any matter.

I also interviewed Archbishop Desmond Tutu during one of his visits to London. He was not quite as genial as I had expected, and indeed he was a little reserved at first. I sensed that he was under pressure, and I was not surprised when he told me that he would have to cut our scheduled interview of thirty minutes by half. However he told me more in fifteen minutes than many other church leaders in twice that time. I also noted that he asked me to join him in a short prayer before our interview began. Maybe that is why he was such an eloquent and profound interviewee!

§

Back home I never interviewed one of the most significant church leaders in Northern Ireland, the Reverend Dr Ian Paisley who had played such an important role in local politics. He and I had very different views, and Ian Paisley was so incensed by the liberal stance of the *Belfast Telegraph*, where I had received my early training, that he set up his own hardline *Protestant Telegraph*.

I met Ian Paisley in January 2008 near the end of his public career when he stepped down from the Moderatorship of the Free Presbyterian Church after a record tenure of fifty-seven years. The media had been tipped off that an announcement would be made after a special meeting in Dungannon Free Presbyterian Church.

Unfortunately I had already booked a ticket to hear the Welsh bass-baritone singer Bryn Terfel in the Waterfront Hall in Belfast, but my news editor Ronan Henry had indicated that he wanted me in Dungannon to report on any breaking news.

I spent several hours in the car park of the Free Presbyterian Church in Dungannon trying to shelter from the wind and rain on a cold winter's evening. The media was not allowed into the Church, so I had to resort to huddling in the open boot of my car while wearing my all-weather golf gear. I said to myself "What am I doing here? Most other sensible people are warm and comfortable at home, or listening to Bryn Terfel in the Waterfront Hall!"

However my inherent curiosity overcame my discomfort, as always, and just before 10 pm the Church doors opened and out came Ian Paisley and a senior colleague, just in time to make an announcement for the evening television and radio bulletins.

I was standing beside Paisley as he announced that he was indeed standing down as Moderator. He had no idea that I was beside him, because even my wife would not have recognised me in my storm gear.

After Dr Paisley had read his formal statement he took a few questions from the media, and the impromptu press conference livened up considerably. One journalist asked him "Will you miss us Dr Paisley?" He replied good-humouredly "Not at all young man. Any more questions like that and I'll box your ears." Paisley then fielded a question from another journalist, and when he heard his Dublin accent he replied "No editor from a Dublin newspaper will tell Ian Paisley what to do."

Paisley was clearly enjoying his joust with the media, who were also enjoying their joust with him. However he became serious when one reporter asked him "Dr Paisley why did you agree to share power with Sinn Fein?"

Ian Paisley thought for a moment and then said quietly "The Lord works in mysterious ways." The theological dimension to his reply was largely lost on the Press pack, but I thought it was significant. Was Paisley trying to indicate that there had been a divine inspiration and impetus for his extraordinary decision which had totally changed the politics of Northern Ireland, or was he at a loss himself to explain his motive for doing so, which perhaps lay far beyond politics?

Either way I was glad that this political miracle had taken place. Ironically this man who had caused such controversy during most of his career was arguably the only Unionist politician who could deliver an agreement with Sinn Fein, and make it stick. Maybe the Lord did indeed work in mysterious ways.

I met many other church leaders in Ireland, some of them very able, and others who were less so, but the most exotic leader I met from abroad was the Dalai Lama during one of his rare visits to Northern Ireland. I arrived very early for a Press conference he was holding in a centre in University Street and for fifteen minutes there was only him and me in the room, plus an interpreter.

He was a friendly, jolly man who giggled a lot, but behind the humour there was a deep spiritual depth which I found attractive. He was interested in the work of the Corrymeela Community which he was due to visit and to meet Ray Davey, one of my spiritual heroes. So naturally our conversation turned to the subject of forgiveness.

The Dalai Lama told me about a friend of his, a Buddhist monk, who had been imprisoned for twenty years by the Chinese authorities, and badly treated. On his release the Dalai Lama asked him if he felt bitter against the Chinese who had mistreated him. The monk replied "I could feel very bitter, but my bitterness would not hurt the Chinese government. It would only damage me. So I try not to be bitter." It was a message from the Dalai Lama which could have applied to a large number of people in Northern Ireland, and I have never forgotten it.

My encounter with the Dalai Lama had a somewhat comic sequel later than day. He was scheduled to speak in St Anne's Cathedral which was packed to overflowing. When I arrived at the big front door it was locked, with scores of people waiting outside. It was the first time I had ever found a Cathedral closed to the public, but when word went round that the religious media had been locked out, a chink between the great doors appeared, I was 'smuggled' inside, together with my colleague William Scholes from the *Irish News*, by a church official who was also a member of a Loyal Order called the Royal Black Preceptory. It seemed a bit like getting squeezed into heaven!

Years later I met a man who said "Do you remember me? I'm the 'Black Man' who got you into Belfast Cathedral to hear the Dalai Lama!" Indeed he was, and I greeted him warmly. I wondered later, however, if anyone outside Northern Ireland would have understood what he meant when he spoke to me!

Some years later my former *Belfast Telegraph* colleague Robin Morton, sent me an e-mail which contained a most revealing reply by the Dalai Lama who was asked what surprised him most about humanity.

He replied "What surprises me most about humanity is man. Because he sacrifices his health in order to make money. Then he sacrifices money to recuperate his health. And then he is so anxious about the future, that he does not enjoy the present; the result being that he does not live in the present or the future; he lives as if he is never going to die, and then dies having never really lived." I agree with that totally.

My meeting with the Dalai Lama in Belfast was very special, but my most memorable experience of all as a Religion Correspondent was not in Belfast but in Rome, where I reported on one of the greatest religious and historical stories of my lifetime.

CHAPTER TWENTY-TWO

The Pope and the President

O<small>N A BRIGHT</small> Saturday morning in early April 2005, I walked into a travel agency in Belfast and asked the young lady behind the counter to book me a trip to Rome. "When do you want to go?" she asked. "I'm not sure," I replied. There was a silence. Then she continued, "When might you want to return?" Hesitantly, I told her, "I don't know."

There was another silence, during which she gave me that cool gaze of someone who was used to oddballs who did not know whether they were coming or going. Finally I replied, "I'm not sure when I am going to Rome or returning, because I'm waiting for the Pope to die." Being a practical young woman, at this, my interlocutor suggested that I should at least choose provisional dates, and she booked me to fly from Dublin to Rome on the next Wednesday, and returning the following Saturday. She even managed to book a hotel just ten minutes' walk from St Peter's Square. There was the added bonus that I had two days to think it over, before confirming the booking.

I left the travel agency with the satisfying sense of having done a good morning's work. And so it proved. Early the same evening, the Vatican announced that Pope John Paul II had died after a long illness. It was the end of a memorable era in world history. The television coverage later that evening was impressive, and extensive. The BBC's Ten O'Clock News programme from London set the tone with gravitas, highlighting the historical importance and the urgency of this big story. The coverage on RTÉ was even longer and more detailed. Though I was sad about the Pope's long illness and death, I was already looking forward professionally to covering the story for the *Belfast Telegraph*, as its Religion Correspondent. I knew that I was set for one of the most challenging and memorable assignments of my reporting career.

My interest in Pope John Paul II was not just professional. It was also personal because I had covered his historic visit to Ireland back in 1979, and this had left a lasting impression on me. It was also a big story in its day, because it was the first time that a Pope had visited Ireland, and – to paraphrase a later British Prime Minister, Tony Blair – I could feel the hand of history upon all of us.

§

John Paul's visit to Ireland in 1979 had been eagerly anticipated: he had only recently been elected as Pope, and he had a freshness and a handsome charisma that his recent predecessors had lacked. He was also an ecclesiastical showman, and every young and not-so-young journalist with an eye for a good story was keen to be part of that remarkable Papal cavalcade in Ireland.

Fortunately for me, the *Belfast Telegraph* editor, Roy Lilley had had the foresight to make advance plans, and immediately after the Irish visit was confirmed by the Vatican, our deputy editor Jim Gray booked me and two colleagues into a guesthouse in the tiny village of Knock, which was to be one of the key places the Pope would visit. It was indeed a wise move, because within hours, every available room in Knock and the wide surrounding hinterland was booked out.

Two days before John Paul II was due to land in Dublin, I travelled with the *Telegraph* reporter Robin Morton, whom I mentioned earlier, and the photographer Charlie Cockcroft to file scene-setting reports from Knock. The normally sleepy village was a hive of activity as preparations were made for the big day. I recall not only the buzz in and around the Marian Church and shrine, but also the spectacle of a JCB digger removing drink signs for Guinness and Harp from outside local Catholic pubs – in case the Holy Father might spot them during his visit. It reminded me that abstention was not a Christian virtue among Protestants alone.

I was also struck by the number of shops which were selling religious objects of all kinds, and some of them were tacky. A long-buried

Calvinism deep in my soul surfaced for a moment – but I reminded myself that the inner man or woman is more important than what we see on the surface, or the personal qualities we choose to exhibit to the world.

My most exciting memory prior to the Pope's appearance in Knock was that of the live television coverage of his arrival in Dublin. Disembarking from an Aer Lingus jet, he made his triumphant descent down the aircraft's steps, and then he knelt dramatically to kiss Irish soil. It was a moment of history, and I was excited that this figure of world importance was going to be with us in Knock.

As we waited on the Sunday in question for the Pope to arrive from Galway, there was a great deal happening on the ground in Knock. The large basilica was crowded with people, and there were only three places for the Press – one for the Dublin-based *Irish Times*, another for *Le Monde* from Paris and a third which was not yet allocated. So I was allowed to take the vacant Press seat in the Basilica, as the journalist from "the cross-community *Belfast Telegraph*". That's what I told them, and in any case it was true.

In the final event, however, the Pope's appearance was delayed by an enthusiastic and lengthy celebration of Mass earlier in Galway, in the presence of thousands of young people and the Bishop of Galway, Eamon Casey. At that point, Casey was still a high-flying prelate, before indiscretions in his private life later led to his descent into disgrace. As we all waited excitedly in the Church for the Pope to arrive, we weren't disappointed. When John Paul II entered the building, a huge wave of affection and applause swept to him from the assembled crowd, and a group of young seminarians started singing, surprisingly, a catchy pop tune of the day, 'Viva l'Espana'. As the entire congregation joined in the singing, the French reporter beside me murmured, with typically Gallic cynicism, "Aha, I think zis man is ze 'Top of Ze Popes!'" He was right. This was a huge historic ecclesiastical occasion, but it was also ecclesiastical show business.

Soon enough the jollity evaporated, and the Pope and members of the senior hierarchy of the Irish Catholic Church led the solemn liturgy. The main focus of the service was the healing of hundreds of ill people who had been brought by their families and friends into the large Basilica for a blessing. I looked at some them, sitting in wheelchairs or lying on stretchers, and I prayed too that they would find some healing and peace of mind in the presence of the Pope.

When the service was over, John Paul II made his way slowly out of the church, moving outside toward a specially-constructed platform. He was to speak to the thousands of people who had been waiting patiently for many hours to see and hear their Holy Father.

As he passed by where I was standing, I had a close-up view of this man who was making world headlines. He looked fit, handsome and ruddy, but perhaps he was a little tired inside and was unable to show it. Then, as now, it struck me that some of the world's biggest figures about whom I reported at close quarters – including Queen Elizabeth II, the US Presidents Reagan and Clinton, and several other famous people – must have sometimes felt the same way. Once they had embarked on such high-profile journeys, however, it was too late for them to draw back.

I remember, for example, hearing an anecdote about Queen Elizabeth, the Queen Mother, during an official visit to Belfast Harbour in 1958. After a busy day, she had come into what she thought was an empty room, kicked off her shoes and muttered, "Thank God, that's over." The drinks steward, who had heard and seen this from a chink in the bar curtain, behind which he was standing, then politely brought Her Majesty her favourite and well-deserved evening tipple. Neither party batted an eyelid, and carried on as if nothing had happened.

Anyway, back to Knock, and as the Pope had passed by me at a distance of about six feet, I suddenly noticed a good-looking woman who was working as a steward for the organisers. She seemed transfixed by the sight of the Holy Father, and when he stretched out his hand towards her, she dropped to her knees and kissed the Papal ring on his outstretched hand. For some thirty seconds afterwards, she remained on her knees with a beatific expression on her face as if she had caught a glimpse of God Himself. This was no ordinary human being who was at the centre of everyone's attention at Knock.

Meantime the international media were busily hammering out the story at an improvised Press Centre somewhere deep in the complex of the church buildings. Each of the confessional boxes had a telephone and its own special number, and it was strange to hear a voice calling over the intercom, "Johnny Apple, *New York Times* – go to box three! Alf

McCreary, *Belfast Telegraph*, go to box four. Your calls to your newspapers are being put through," and so on.

However I had much to do before filing my own story, so I went out into the rain and sat on the designated Press benches to watch the Pope deliver his homily to the huge crowds which stretched all around the Church. Strictly speaking, I had no need to do so, as the ceremony was being relayed live on television, and the rest of the media were filing their stories in the warmth and comfort of the Church premises. However, it must have been some part of my hair-shirt Presbyterianism that made me go into the wind and rain and sit alone outside for a short period. Yet at the same time, I knew that, just a few yards away from me, thousands of people had been standing all day and any of them would have been glad of a seat. It seemed unfair.

Meanwhile inside the Church complex, the Dublin morning paper reporters, who had tighter deadlines than mine, were already filing their stories about the Pope's triumphant visit to Knock and his journey on his 'Popemobile' amid the cheering crowds – which was by now a familiar aspect of every Papal visit. But there was only one snag: suddenly, it seemed, the 'Popemobile' tour would not be taking place.

There was widespread commotion in the media centre. "Bloody hell!" yelled one Dublin journalist who had been monitoring the television screen. His next words were to change the running story of every reporter in the room. "The Pope's not doing the tour of the people, after all!" he shouted. "His minders are taking him back to Dublin immediately by helicopter. He's already running late, and the pilots are saying that low-based cloud is sweeping in from the Atlantic. They have to take off right now."

And that was that. The Pope was bundled into a large helicopter and simply disappeared into the heavens, like Christ at the Ascension. In doing so, he left the tens of thousands of people now assembled in and around Knock standing there, stunned and dismayed. There was to be no motorcade, no glimpses of His Holiness in the flesh, and later on, no boast that "I saw the Pope at Knock".

It was a disappointing way to end the day for so many thousands of the faithful Catholics who had travelled so far, and had waited for so long to see the Pope. I tried to get a few comments for my paper, but no-one would say a critical word about the Pope, or the Irish hierarchy.

In today's world where people have greater expectations and are not afraid to raise their voices, it would be a very different story.

However, I was one of the privileged people to have seen and heard John Paul II at Knock, and it was with all the more care that I eventually filed my first-person account to the *Belfast Telegraph* newspaper from the media centre. Soon enough it was time to leave the church buildings but on the way out, something occurred, which reminded me once again that this was indeed a special day.

As I passed by the members of the Gardai band, who been on duty all day and were exhausted, I heard them playing gleefully, 'The Sash My Father Wore'. This has always been the unofficial anthem of the Orangemen in the North who would definitely have no truck with "the Pope of Rome". It was indeed a unique occasion!

To end the evening, I went for a drink with my *Belfast Telegraph* colleagues and journalists from the *Irish Press* who were always on good terms personally. Unfortunately, all the pubs in Knock were officially closed. So when one of the *Irish Press* reporters said that he 'knew somebody', all too soon we filtered into a pub through the side door. Once inside I noticed that the place was packed with all kinds of people, including scores of Irish policemen and women who were relaxing after so many long hours on duty. It was a night when no-one took any notice of normal rules and regulations!

The chat at our table was good, but we were getting hungry, after a long day's work. Eventually an *Irish Press* reporter came to our table with a big plate of sandwiches. "Where did you get those?" I asked incredulously. "Oh – they were meant for the ill people still in the Basilica," he replied. At that point I felt that the evening was getting out of hand, so I said my farewells and left for the digs I shared with my two *Telegraph* colleagues.

It had been a remarkable day for Knock, for Ireland and for those of us who had taken part in making history in Holy Catholic Ireland. Most people felt that this was the beginning of a new liberalism in the Catholic Church, and there was a sense of anticipation among reporters and commentators at Knock, that we were going to experience a repeat of the heady days of Pope John XXIII and a possible Vatican Three. At the time I shared that view, but I was taken aback by a report from the BBC's respected religious affairs correspondent, Gerald Priestland. He predicted that John Paul II, who had survived the rigours of Nazism and Communism in his native Poland, would turn out to be an ultra-conservative Pope. All of this was yet to unfold, of course. And neither could I have anticipated, as I left Knock on that grey day after the Pope's visit, that over twenty-five years later, I would be reporting on the funeral of this remarkable man who would in the interim become one of the great ecclesiastical figures of Catholic Church history.

§

Inevitably many of these memories were running through my mind as I left my home in Belfast that early morning of April 2005, to catch a flight from Dublin to Rome. I was keenly aware that I had no accreditation to cover the Pope's funeral from the Vatican Press Office: unfortunately, my online application seemed to have vanished into the ether. I also knew that once I reached Rome, I would be on my own and that I would have to rely on my wits and my long experience as a reporter in order to somehow gather the best stories to send back to my newspaper.

Some sixth sense had prompted me to bring with me an easily recognisable Press Accreditation card, and on my way out of my home on that April morning, I had rushed upstairs to my study and, after some searching, hurriedly grabbed a media pass I had been given back in 1984 to cover the visit of the US President Ronald Reagan to Ballyporeen in Ireland. I had no idea, however, that this piece of thick paper with my picture encased on the front would prove to be a magic wand as soon as I set foot on the streets of Rome for the momentous funeral of Pope John Paul II.

I arrived in the city in the late afternoon of Wednesday 8 April, and after the usual difficulty of getting transport into the city centre, I made my way to my hotel near St Peter's Square. My room was high enough to see the dome of St Peter's Basilica on the skyline. When I opened the window, the evening air wafted in, together with the sounds of solemn music drifting across from loudspeakers in the Square.

The mood in Rome was reverential, and on my way in from the airport, I had noticed the Papal flags of yellow and white fluttering in the gentle breeze. By 7.30 pm that evening I had filed my first 'scene-setter' for the *Belfast Telegraph*, and I then made my way down to one of the beautiful piazzas near St Peter's for a meal. As I dined virtually alone in such majestic surroundings, the thought occurred to me that it might be wise to carry out a reconnoitre of the streets leading into St Peter's Square: I would doubtless need to know their layout thoroughly for the next couple of days.

As I approached St Peter's Square after dinner, I quickly realised that there were thousands of people thronging the main approach road, which was cut off progressively by a series of manned checkpoints. However I had travelled too far that day to be put off by any barrier. Armed only with my long-outdated Press Pass for President Reagan's visit to Ballyporeen, I approached the officials on duty. I was wearing a long flowing black coat, a vivid red scarf and my wide-brimmed black hat, and I was fervently hoping that I looked like a tall Cardinal in non-clerical garb. I held my breath, and swiftly produced my Reagan pass, with my fingers hiding the outdated picture and the giveaway date.

In the dim light, all the officials could make out was the words "Press Accreditation". Looking at my big hat and long dark coat, they simply waved me through, with a polite "Prego", which I assumed was Italian for "Away you go!" I walked on slowly as if it was the most natural thing in the world to do. Inside however, my heart was thumping madly. I was on my way.

The same thing happened several times and eventually, to my amazement, I passed through all the barriers and found myself standing beside well-known television reporters from CNN, the BBC, and other high-profile news stations – right at the barrier on the very edge of St Peter's Square.

The Square itself was empty, apart from a long snaking queue of pilgrims who had been waiting for up to twelve hours to view the Pope's remains inside the Basilica. The atmosphere was sombre; the only sounds came from loudspeakers relaying recorded readings from the New Testament, which were interspersed with music that sounded like chants from Taizé. There was a deeply spiritual atmosphere, of which even the Papacy's arch-critic, the Reverend Dr Paisley, would have approved.

After a few minutes' standing at the barrier, I phoned my wife Hilary, at home in Belfast, to tell her where I was. "Well done," she said, "Now, how about getting in to the Basilica?" "There's no chance of that," I replied. "People have been queuing for hours to get in. I can't go any further without a proper pass. I've done very well to get this far!"

As usual, however, Hilary had set me thinking, and as soon as we finished our call, I approached yet another security man who was guarding the final barrier to St Peter's Square. I tried the same ruse again, but this time the official was not impressed. In broken English, he said to me, "You are media man: you must stay here with reporters." It looked as if my journey had finally been stalled, but my long experience as a journalist had taught me to stand my ground. I knew that security guards regularly take a break from their duties and are replaced by others – I reckoned that I might still slip through, during a changeover of personnel.

This proved to be the case. Within fifteen minutes, a new set of officials arrived, and as they took up their positions, three burly Italian television technicians in dark tracksuits approached the final barrier. I immediately joined them, and in my dark attire, I hoped that I looked like one of them. Without further fuss, one of the new guards checked all four of us through. Once again, I was on my way!

As I walked across the Square and through another unmanned barrier, I could hardly believe my luck. I then joined another long queue of nuns and monks in old-fashioned clerical attire which made me speculate that they might have come from somewhere like the Pope's native Poland. At that moment, however, as we made our way in a solemn procession to the front steps of St Peter's Basilica, it felt like we were all brothers and sisters together. I kept my head bowed under my big hat, pulled my flowing, cloak-like coat around me, and hoped that I looked impressively clerical enough to prevent anyone checking my credentials, which were non-existent of course, given that I only had the outdated Press Pass for Ronald Reagan's 1984 visit to Ireland. I found myself wondering if Reagan would have been amused or annoyed at this minor religious fraud being perpetrated in his name.

Once inside the vast Church, I took up a position some distance from the place where the Pope's body was lying in state. Beside me, an elegant woman pulled a finely-carved wooden box from her neat leather handbag. Inside was a set of rosary beads, which she took out and held carefully before beginning to pray. Her dignified presence, as well as that of the rows of people of all ages who were moving reverentially past the Pope's body on the other side of the Church, served to remind me yet again that this was a Papal wake, and not just an important moment in history.

Nevertheless, my own sense of reverence was quickly disturbed by a persistence and very earthly thought: that I should try to get even closer to the Pope's body. "I can do better than this," I told myself. So, in a dignified manner, I walked up to and around the High Altar of the Basilica, until at last I stood gazing at the Pope's body which was now only about twenty feet away from me.

As I stood silently for several moments, behind the serried ranks of Cardinals from all over the world, I was even crass enough to take a picture of the scene with my small but powerful digital camera – just to prove to myself that I had been this close to the Pope's earthly remains.

All too soon however, a Basilica steward politely moved me on, and I slowly made my way out of the Church and down the steps towards St Peter's Square. I tried to get back to the Press area, but the security there was so tight that I eventually had to join the thousands of people who were still milling about in the side streets of the Vatican. I was content, however, not to push my luck any further at this point. I knew that my unauthorised visit inside the Basilica had been made possible by a bit of poetic licence or Divine Providence, or both.

That night I went back to the hotel and wrote my story in longhand, with the details still fresh in my mind. Early the next morning I phoned my report through to the *Belfast Telegraph* and it was published back home later that day.

However it was only when I eventually returned home to Northern Ireland a few days later and read the cutting of my article that I fully realised how fortunate I had been in getting so near the Pope as he lay in state. The *Belfast Telegraph* had published my story beneath a photograph of the current US President George W Bush and former US Presidents George Bush Sr and Bill Clinton, and the US Foreign Secretary, Condoleezza Rice. All four of these major public figures had been photographed together, standing in the exact spot where I had been earlier that evening after I had made my unauthorised entry into the Basilica!

The next day in Rome was full of activity, as I went about researching and filing more background stories for the *Telegraph*. It seemed that the public's appetite for stories was insatiable – people could just not read or hear enough about the build-up to John Paul's funeral. I spoke to pilgrims from all parts of Northern Ireland who had come to Rome for the occasion, and who shared their thoughts with me.

I also attended a news conference at the Irish College in Rome, which was hosted by the Irish Primate, Cardinal Sean Brady. I also talked to Bishop John Magee, a Newry man who had been John Paul's secretary for several years and who told me of how he had dined nightly with the Pope, who would then request him to sing Irish songs. Bishop Magee also made a point of saying how much the Pope had appreciated his Irish visit, and had deeply regretted being unable to visit Armagh because of security problems in a then very troubled Northern Ireland. I recalled myself how, in a keynote speech in Drogheda, John Paul had appealed "on bended knees" to the Irish Republican movement to lay down their arms.

According to Bishop Magee, in subsequent years, the Pope had often talked about his Irish visit, and had asked what had happened to the huge silver cross that had, for the occasion of his visit, been erected on a hillside just outside Drogheda. In fact, the silver cross is still standing there impressively.

The day of John Paul's funeral dawned bright and clear. Heavy rain was forecast for later on, and I fervently hoped that it would stay away long enough to allow the magnificent ceremony to take place in St Peter's Square and not, as was the standby arrangement, in the Church itself. On my way to the Square, I marvelled at the hordes of people who were trying to cram into the space still available. Some of the pilgrims had camped overnight in the side streets, and were cooking large pots of stew for breakfast, in order to sustain themselves through the long ceremony to come.

This time, I was confident about gaining access to the proceedings: the day before I had finally made fruitful contact with the Vatican Press Office which had finally been able to process my online application. Although the resultant Press Pass was made out in the name of 'Mr Alfred' and not 'Alf McCreary', it was enough to get me through all the barriers that were left.

Once in the media area again – this time legitimately – I had to decide whether I should stay there or move instead among the large crowd assembled in the Square itself. There would be obvious disadvantages to doing the latter – because of the size of the crowd, and also the lack of creature comforts on offer, such as coffee machines, computer connections and, most importantly of all, access to toilets. However, I chose to take my place with the ordinary people because I knew that it would give me a better story to report, and one with much more atmosphere. So I joined a large group of central Europeans, and waited for the funeral service to start.

It began promptly, and the celebrant was Cardinal Joseph Ratzinger, then known as 'The Pope's Enforcer', because, as head of the Department of Doctrine, a key part of his role was to preserve the conservative purity of the Roman Catholic faith. A document entitled "Dominus Jesus" had been produced by Ratzinger's office in 2000, which asserted that the Reformation churches were not churches in the full sense. As a practising Protestant, this piece of arrant Vatican nonsense would have annoyed me greatly, had I taken it seriously, but I had no intention of doing so. And here, at John Paul's funeral, the 'Pope's Enforcer' was right before my eyes.

The stunning architecture of St Peter's was a magnificent backdrop for the funeral ceremony, and it also offered a huge contrast to the simplicity of the plain wooden coffin which sat alone at the centre of this scene on which the eyes of the world were focused. The starkness of this coffin drew every eye, while a gentle breeze ruffled the pages of the volume of the Holy Scriptures which had been placed on top of its wooden lid. For me, it was a vivid reminder that while Popes, Presidents, monarchs and all the rest of us make our fleeting journey across the sands of time, the unchanging challenge of the Scriptures lives on.

As the ceremony progressed in its splendour, Cardinal Ratzinger spoke with emotion about his friend John Paul II. His obvious authority and composure on this momentous occasion was impressive. I recall muttering to myself, "This man is already becoming something bigger. He could well be the next Pope" And so I was not at all surprised when, a couple of weeks or so later, he was elected Pope and became Benedict XVI.

I had little time for day-dreaming, however. My job was to report directly to the *Belfast Telegraph* so that we could process the story as it unfolded and fill the pages for the final edition to be published that afternoon. I needed to write an atmospheric commentary, while the sub-editors and backbench team in the *Telegraph* were collating the words of Cardinal Ratzinger's speech, a transcript of which had been issued in different languages by the Vatican's Press Office, as soon as the service had begun.

My only means of communication with the newspaper was my mobile phone. In those days, iPads had not been invented, and a hand-held computer of any size would have been too unwieldy to use in a crowd. So, at regular intervals, I knelt down among the people as if in prayer – but in fact I was dictating my copy to an extremely efficient copy-taker back in Belfast. It was only later on that I was told that mobile phones sometimes fail to work in the midst of such large crowds. Fortunately I did not know this at the time, nor did I realise how precarious my situation was. If my phone had failed to operate, my story would – literally – have been very different, and perhaps even non-existent!

As the funeral service moved steadily towards its conclusion, I had other matters to contend with. There was little enough space in the huge crowd, but to make matters worse, I could feel someone pressing hard against my right side, trying to push through to the front. I looked around to see a young female photographer wielding a camera with a long lens. She also had, over one arm, what looked to be a small step-ladder. The pressing continued so insistently that I finally hissed impatiently, "You can't get any further. There's a barrier here." She whispered back, "I want to get pictures of President Bush and Tony Blair among the celebrities up there." "You've got absolutely no chance of getting any further," I insisted again. "There's a barrier just in front of us, and they won't let you through."

As I stared at her impatiently, she suddenly broke the deadlock, with words that amazed me: "I know your face. You are Alf McCreary of the *Belfast Telegraph*! I am Bernie Brown of the *News Letter*." Then, smiling cheerily, she went on her way. Knowing her, before the day was out, she probably did get the pictures she wanted. I was dumbfounded: the chances of two Belfast journalists meeting in the middle of a vast crowd in St Peter's Square were almost incalculable. But it was that kind of a day, one on which you felt almost anything could happen.

During the last stages of the funeral, there was an impressive procession of world religious leaders, each of whom paid tribute in turn beside John Paul's coffin. There were clerics from Middle Eastern, Coptic, Orthodox, and other branches of Christianity that I hardly knew existed. The final prayers for the soul of John Paul II invoked blessings from a long line of saints from Roman Catholic theology, many of whom again I had not heard of – although incidentally, I cannot recall St Patrick being on the list.

As the Pope's coffin was borne at last towards the great doors of St Peter's, the pall-bearers turned it around to face the crowd. It was a wonderfully theatrical gesture of which John Paul, a former amateur actor, would have approved. At that point I was expecting floods of tears from the mourners around me, but to my surprise, there was only applause and cheering! I noticed a particularly vivacious young black nun waving her large white scarf and crying passionately, "Adieu, Papa, adieu, adieu!"

Turning the coffin around one last time, the pall-bearers then carried it through the doors, which closed firmly behind them while the great bells tolled outside. The Pope's funeral was over. John Paul II, the man who in his lifetime had so impressed the world, was being taken to his resting place, deep down in the heart of the Basilica.

Slowly I made my way back through the crowd, where young people were still singing hymns, and I returned to my hotel to write my final piece for the next day's edition of the *Belfast Telegraph*. I had seen and experienced so much. Once I had phoned it through, I switched off my mobile and lay down wearily on the bed. Then the rain came. It lashed down with such an intensity that it would have made the earlier funeral service in St Peter's Square impossible. This downpour was a dramatic, and downbeat, finale to such a memorable occasion.

I felt depressed, with that sense of anticlimax that follows the funeral of any relative or friend, when, after days of tension and activity fuelled by nervous energy, it is suddenly all over. The person has gone, and the mourners have to move on also. It was understandable that I felt such personal sadness at the funeral of Pope John Paul II – this was the man I had been standing so close to at Knock so many years earlier, and whose subsequent career I had followed with such a special interest. It was not just another public funeral I had been reporting. Although it was a professional assignment, it was of personal significance for me too.

Once I awoke from a brief nap, the rest of the afternoon passed slowly. My job was finished, but I was not due to fly home until the next day. Rome is one of the most beautiful cities in which to spend an evening, but despite this, my slightly downcast mood persisted as the rain continued to pour down. To lift my spirits, I decided to visit a good restaurant which I remembered well from visiting Rome on previous occasions with rugby friends to attend Ireland v Italy international games.

I took a taxi to the restaurant at about 6 pm, but I had to wait for an hour until the place opened. There was nowhere else to go, and no-one to talk to, so I bought a packet of small cigars and a coffee in a little café along the street. There I was, puffing a slim cigar and sheltering from the pouring rain under a tarpaulin outside the café, while the rain gushed down the gutters. My sense of anticlimax was complete, and even the warmth, good food in the restaurant failed to lift my spirits – though of course I was pleased professionally that the story had gone so well and that my time in Rome had been so productive.

When travelling abroad, I dislike dining alone and having no-one to talk to about the day's events. So I decided to ring my old friend and former editor, Roy Lilley who had shared convivial evenings with me in Rome in that very restaurant, and who knew the ambience it could provide. Roy had read my published pieces about the Pope's funeral and assured me that my time had been well spent. Part of me knew that already, but when you are in full flight reporting abroad, it's difficult to find time to assess all your copy clinically. It was good to have a respected second opinion from my former boss, and the reassurance that all had gone well.

Later that evening, I went back to my hotel, bone-weary from the exertions and excitement of the previous few days. I switched on an Italian television station to relax, and behold, there was a comprehensive tribute to Pope John Paul II, as well as highlights from the funeral which helped to place my busy day in a wider context. The profile of John Paul II (which was in Italian with English subtitles) was particularly illuminating, and it revealed again the charisma and strength of character of that remarkable man. There was one recorded sequence which showed his appearance before thousands of young people in a New Jersey stadium. The crowd gave him a standing ovation, which John Paul milked like a true showman. Then he paused dramatically, and said in his thick Polish accent, "Yonk peepel, I luff yew!" The applause rocked around the stadium. It helped me to understand why the young people at his funeral earlier that day had been so enthusiastic and respectful.

Even then, it seemed to me to be a strange phenomenon, as it still does now. Here was an old man with rigidly conservative views, which were out of keeping with the burgeoning freedom and self-awareness of the younger generations. And yet they all loved him. That night, I felt strongly that his funeral had been a celebration of his life, perhaps more so than the mourning of his death.

That night I slept soundly for the first time for ages. Early the next morning, I was due to return to Dublin, and then on to Belfast. On the way to the airport in Rome, I shared a conversation in the bus with a lady from Liverpool who told me how much John Paul had meant to her and how she had made a huge financial and physical effort to be at his funeral. She confirmed my own feelings about the impact of the life and death of one of the most popular Popes in history.

As the Dublin-bound plane rose from the runway and I finally left Rome, I knew in my bones that I would not report on a bigger or more poignant human story for the rest of my writing career. I was so glad to have been in Rome for those few unforgettable days.

A few days after I returned home, I had a pleasant surprise, in the form of a personal letter from Cardinal Cahal Daly, the former Irish Catholic Primate, whom I knew well and liked. In the letter, he thanked me for my "accurate and appreciative coverage" of the Pope's funeral, and ended jocularly, "You did well for a Northern Irish Protestant!"

I took that as a considerable compliment.

CHAPTER TWENTY-THREE

Brought To Book

THE FUNERAL OF Pope John Paul II in Rome, like the visit of President Ronald Reagan to Ballyporeen, was one of the most memorable episodes of my writing career, but my daily beat in Northern Ireland was reporting on a community at war with itself.

This was the major theme of nearly all my work for the *Belfast Telegraph* and other publications, as well as seeking out the inspiring, touching and sometimes humourous stories which lightened the prevailing gloom in Northern Ireland.

I was also privileged to travel to other places like Vietnam, Cambodia, Sri Lanka, and Rwanda in central Africa – all poor countries where the slaughter and suffering of thousands of people helped to put our own Troubles in Northern Ireland into perspective.

I also wrote a wide range of books which covered the same major themes in much more depth. Some of these, including *Corrymeela*, *Survivors, Tried by Fire*, and *Profiles of Hope* concentrated on the Troubles, but others did not.

One of my favourites was *An Ulster Journey*, published in 1986 and dedicated to my daughter Emma, whom I described as "my faithful companion along the way."

I travelled throughout Ulster to report on the normality which rarely made the headlines, and I was grateful for the help of the photographer Stephen Bradley as well as Bryan McCabe and Roy Baillie who masterminded the publication, which was enhanced by the design of Arnold Gormley.

I was pleased by the tribute from the distinguished Ulster writer

Sam Hanna Bell who wrote "Alf McCreary moves among historic landmarks and familiar sights with a refreshingly light touch; here and there uncovering a new fact or suggesting a novel way of observing the familiar. He encourages you to think that tolerance, compassion and kindly humour are still abroad in Ulster."

Several of my books also dealt with a wide range of social and economic subjects, including the histories of several iconic Ulster institutions, including the Old Bushmills Distillery, the Trustee Savings Bank, Larne Harbour, the Balmoral Show and Queen's University (with Professor Brian Walker, which I mentioned earlier.)

I felt that it was important to capture the stories of these in print, before their circumstances – and therefore their history – changed. For example, when I was writing the history of the TSB, the network was taken over by Allied Irish Banks and re-named the First Trust Bank, with the result that the TSB name receded further into history.

Whatever the subject, I became engrossed in writing every book, because each one took on a life of its own. I still dip into one or other of these publications, often for reference purposes, and I still remember cameos about some of the people I met, and the nuggets of history which gave each publication its unique character.

In my history of the TSB, titled *By All Accounts* and published in 1991, I was moved by the stories of Belfast women in bare feet and black shawls as they queued to place their pennies into the Trustee Banks of the early nineteenth century. I was also amused by a story from the TSB managing director Bryan Johnston who told me about the aftermath of a bomb blast at the Andersonstown branch of the bank during the Troubles.

He said "I went up on the Sunday to inspect the damage, and I was inside the building surveying the shambles when a man poked his head through a broken window and asked me 'Can I get some money out?' And on a Sunday too. You could hardly believe it."

Those were the days when Belfast survived by living out its motto 'Business As Usual', because there was no alternative.

I had a similar sense of being directly involved in local history when I wrote my book about Larne Harbour, titled *A Vintage Port* and published in 2000. I was intrigued by the life of the entrepreneur James Chaine, who bought the Harbour in 1882 for £20,000 and set about making it one of the principal ferry ports in the north of Ireland. However he died from pneumonia three years later, after catching a cold when he was only forty-four.

The Larne Council of the day described his death as "A sad and sudden calamity that the town has suffered." Despite the attention of doctors, Mr Chaine died within a week of developing pneumonia. I could not help thinking that with the benefit of modern medicines, he would probably have survived to continue his work for the benefit of Larne and its people.

I met Archie McGarel whose father William was one of the 133 people who died when the *Princess Victoria* ferry foundered during a fierce storm while on her way from Stranraer to Larne on 31 January 1953. For a brief period I had possession of the late Mr McGarel's pocket watch, which had stopped at 2.13 pm, the time when the vessel was in her last throes. This brought home to me the personal dimensions of the disaster. The figure of 133 dead was hard to grasp, but when I held in my hand the pocket watch of one of the victims, the reality was inescapable.

In another book titled *Business as Usual* and published in 2002, I traced the history of Cochrane's menswear shop in High Street, Belfast. This was the story of an enterprising family who ran one of the best known shops in the city, and also a history of the drapery business from the end of the First World War, through the Second World War and the worst years of the Troubles.

I remember John Cochrane telling me about his father Robert who founded the business in 1926 and who survived the German bombing of Belfast during the Second World War. After the air raids of early Spring in 1941, part of the area around his shop, as well as other parts of Belfast, had been devastated, but for Mr Cochrane it was not the time to give in to violence.

In his ledger he wrote "First Air Raid – Business as Usual". Further down the page is the historic entry "£4 taken on Thursday 16th". It was clear that neither Adolf Hitler nor anyone else was going to put Robert Cochrane out of business. He was typical of the sturdy spirit of Belfast traders through many years of troubles.

Years afterwards, I was about to interview the former Irish Taioseach Dr Garret Fitzgerald in Dublin for another book, on the story of the

International Fund for Ireland. I said "I met you many years ago in the *Belfast Telegraph* when you came to lunch, but I'm sure you don't remember me." He replied, in his cheery manner, "Of course I do. I've just been reading your book on Cochrane's menswear store in Belfast!"

Garrett, as usual, was a fund of stories and he told me about the months leading up to the establishment of the International Fund for Ireland (IFI) in 1986. This followed the controversial Anglo-Irish Agreement of the previous year, which was the beginning of a long and tortured peace process in Northern Ireland.

As far back as 1977, President Jimmy Carter had made an important statement on US policy in Northern Ireland which internationalised the problem for the first time. In a key passage he said "In the event of a (peaceful) settlement, the US government would be prepared to join with others to see how additional job-creating investment could be encouraged for the benefit of all the people of Northern Ireland."

The Anglo-Irish Agreement, though flawed, was the signal for the IFI to swing into operation and in the twenty-one years from 1986, around £600 millions were invested in cross-border projects in Ireland – with contributions from the USA, the European Union and also, to a lesser extent, from Canada, Australia and New Zealand.

However it was not easy to raise the European money. Garret Fitzgerald told me about his efforts in lobbying other leaders for help. He said "On occasions it even reached the point of me dashing round to speak to some of them in the car park after a European Council meeting!" One of his harder tasks was to sell the idea to the British Prime Minister Margaret Thatcher. Garret told me that after they had signed the Anglo-Irish Agreement at Hillsborough, he told the formidable Iron Lady about the proposed European grant to the IFI.

"Margaret said to me 'WHAT? Money for THESE PEOPLE? Look at their roads, look at their schools! I need it for MY people.'" and she cancelled the whole thing. It took us two years to get it back on course. The British Chancellor Geoffrey Howe worked hard at it, and we managed to get some funding, but the scale was far less than it might have been."

I also talked to my friend Geoff Martin, who had been the first EU representative in Northern Ireland from 1979–85 and who had been aware of the implications of a European intervention in Northern

Ireland. He said "It was an unusual step for Europe to hand over funds to an independent body like the IFI, but I believe that it was the right thing to do."

I also heard an intriguing story about Governor Ronald Reagan from Sean Donlan, a former Irish Ambassador in Washington. Donlan said to Reagan "With a name like that, you must have some Irish roots!"

Reagan replied that, as far as he knew, his family had links with London, but he was happy for Donlan and his staff to try to find his connections with Ireland. They did so, and they traced Reagan's roots to Ballyporeen in County Tipperary, which he visited in 1984, as I have noted.

When Reagan became President, he broke new ground by accepting an invitation to lunch at the Irish Embassy in Washington on St Patrick's Day 1979. Donlan told me that on his way into the building, Reagan noted the Irish and American flags flying together, and he said "My great grandfather would be very proud of this!"

This story made me think that I may have been too harsh in describing Reagan's visit to Ballyporeen merely as part of an election campaign. Clearly he had a deeply personal connection with the place where he was able to read details of his great grandfather's baptism in 1829 in the Ballyporeen Baptismal Register.

§

The International Fund for Ireland inspired people of all ages to work together on cross-border and cross-community projects which greatly increased understanding and tolerance. When the book on the IFI was finished it was launched at separate functions in Brussels, London, Dublin, Ottawa and Washington – for which I had a single, transferable speech, with local amendments.

It was a privilege to be the messenger for the good news from Ireland and I said that I had been "moved and deeply impressed by the vision of so many men and women, who tried to achieve the best of things in the worst of times, and who kept alive the light of hope when there seemed to be only darkness on the horizon."

As time progressed that light grew stronger, and one of my most challenging assignments later on was to write the history of Belfast

Harbour. The book was titled *Titanic Port*, and published in 2010. It was funded by the Belfast Harbour Commissioners, and I was grateful for the strong support of the Chairman Dr Len O'Hagan and the CEO Roy Adair, and their colleagues, in producing the book.

It covered the complex story of the 400 years of history at the Harbour and also of the town, and later city, of Belfast which was founded by King James I in 1613. I came to the project with the advantage of having no preconceptions about the Harbour, so I had to begin my research virtually from scratch.

I soon discovered that the growth of the Harbour and of the city were closely intertwined, and that without the vision of the Commissioners over many decades, and the hard work and entrepreneurship of the Harbour managers and workers, the city of Belfast and the Harbour itself would not be as impressive as they are today.

I had not known, for example, that the Harbour had been mudlocked for many decades and that it had required extensive dredging, which took place in the early nineteenth century, before it became a major port open to the world; or that the Commissioners had created the reclaimed land for the establishment of the Harland and Wolff shipyard, and also the reclaimed land which became the site of the Sydenham Airport, and eventually the George Best Belfast City Airport.

My research became a journey of adventure within the extensive archive in the Belfast Harbour Office, and I recall the day when I unexpectedly uncovered a dusty mid-eighteenth century book about Harbour regulations. I found on the flyleaf the pencilled scrawl 'EJH 1875.'

These were the initials of Sir Edward Harland, who with Gustav Wolff and others, had created one of the world's greatest shipbuilding companies Harland and Wolff, which had built some of the greatest ships in maritime history, including the magnificent but ill-fated *Titanic*. When I looked at Harland's initials on that page of a dull-looking Harbour regulations manual, it was like touching history itself.

The book also brought me back in touch with Sheila and Sandra Connell, whom I had known in Newry Grammar School long ago, and whose ancestor Charles Connell had taken over one of the earlier shipyards on the harbour estate in 1824.

In turn they introduced me to their cousin the late Aengus Fanning, who was then the legendary editor of the *Sunday Independent* and who shared with me his vividly expressed thoughts about his shipbuilding ancestors from the North.

My work at Belfast Harbour reminded me of something which I had discovered many times earlier in researching different projects, namely the 'inter-connectedness' of things. I discovered, for example, that the Harbour Commissioners had done so much – collectively and sometimes individually – to help shape the Belfast skyline, not only in expanding the port, but also in creating buildings like the Sinclair Seamen's Presbyterian Church. This had been funded in the 1850s by Thomas Sinclair, a Harbour Commissioner and Chairman, in memory of his brother John, and it remains one of the most distinctive ecclesiastic buildings in Belfast.

I also became aware of the many everyday details of life in Belfast which had a direct connection with the Harbour. Unless people knew the detailed history of the city they would not have been aware, for example, that a 'JP Corry' vehicle driving through the city had a link with a famous Harbour family back to the 19th century; or that a van bearing the name of 'Dargan' had a direct link with William Dargan, the Irish contractor who had made the first 'cuts' in the mudlocked Harbour and opened it up to help develop its subsequent prosperity and prestige.

I spent three years in researching and writing *Titanic Port*, and it was given three splendid launches – in the Harbour Office, at the Houses of Parliament in Westminster, and also in the Metropolitan Club in New York, where the first President was JP Morgan, the US rail magnate who had also helped to fund the *Titanic*.

From my research, I had discovered that Mr Morgan had been sensitive about his bulbous nose. Before I went into dinner with my wife Hilary and other guests at the Metropolitan Club, I noticed a marble bust of its first President, but with a perfectly formed nose. The sculptor obviously had known who was paying for his work of art.

Following the dinner, each guest was given a presentation copy of the book, courtesy of the Belfast Harbour Commissioners. As I walked towards the pile of books beautifully displayed outside the large function room, a young man asked me "Would you like a copy Sir? It's a really good one." I shook my head politely and replied "No, thanks." I didn't have the heart to tell him that I had a written it!

The book had become a labour of love, and I was delighted to work with the book designer Wendy Dunbar, who made the fabulous collection of pictures and documents from the Harbour archives and other sources look so well in a beautiful publication.

My *Titanic Port* remains high on my list of favourite books because it helps to provide a detailed account of the Harbour emerging from the mists of time, and of Belfast itself emerging from the darkness of the Troubles.

However, some other books remain significant for me personally, because they read like a road map through the Troubles, with the stories about the worst and best of humanity during those dreadful years. They include my biography of Lord Eames, and my trilogy about the family of Senator Gordon Wilson who lost his daughter Marie in the Provisional IRA bomb which exploded without warning at the Cenotaph in Enniskillen on Remembrance Sunday in 1987.

These books were like reporting from a war zone, and they recall a Northern Ireland that hopefully has moved on some distance from such dark and dangerous days. However the work of people like Gordon Wilson, Robin Eames and many others must not be overlooked in the long and winding road towards peace in Northern Ireland.

CHAPTER TWENTY-FOUR

War and Peace

I HAD KNOWN Robin Eames for quite a long time, and we were near-contemporaries at Queen's. He had a distinguished career not only in the Church of Ireland, where he was the Primate and Archbishop of Armagh, but also in the Anglican Communion where he had played a leading role and was well known to senior Anglicans throughout the world. Robin had many stories, and I was pleased when he agreed to co-operate with me in writing his biography titled *Nobody's Fool*, and published in 2004.

My research was carried out during extended interviews with Eames himself, and also with well known people with whom he had worked, including his Church colleagues in Ireland and overseas. Robin was most helpful in giving me a great deal of his time, and also in opening doors to gain access to other important people. This in itself told me something about the standing of the man in religious and political circles.

Accordingly, I talked to Sir John Major, the former British Prime Minister, as well as Albert Reynolds, the former Irish Taioseach who did so much groundwork to produce the Downing Street Declaration of 1993, which paved the way for the breakthrough made by the Good Friday Agreement several years later.

Reynolds and Major have not been given enough credit for their work behind the scenes, when there was deadlock in Northern Ireland, and certainly little political capital to be gained from trying to start a dialogue between the power blocks in Northern Ireland.

I met Sir John Major in his London office high over the Thames, not long after he had stepped down as Prime Minister. He was pressed for time, and we exchanged few formalities before we started the interview. I prayed silently that my tape recorder was working properly because I did not have time to check it beforehand.

Major was a more vibrant and impressive figure than his bland television image suggested. He was a little reserved with me at first, but he relaxed visibly when I told him that I had met Reynolds the week before in Dublin and that he had sent him his good wishes.

Major smiled and said "I'm very fond of Albert", and I recalled Reynolds' remark during our interview: "We first met as Finance Ministers in Brussels, and on Major's first day he said 'Maybe you will mark my card!' I replied, 'Every issue here is 11-1 against Britain' because at that time Margaret Thatcher was opposing everything. Later on, however, when it was not against Ireland's interests, I sometimes made that balance 10-2, which might have made John think that this was not just the usual 'Bash the British' campaign."

The personal chemistry between the two men was vital in rolling uphill the huge political boulder of peace-making in Ireland, at a time when most other people saw no signs of any breakthrough.

Despite their closeness, they had some strong disagreements. Reynolds told me that before one meeting in Dublin they suspected that people were 'leaking' to the Press. This was confirmed by Major, who said "Albert thought that I was operating behind his back, and I felt the same. So it was an explosion waiting to happen. We cleared the room and we had an hour on our own. It is extremely fortunate that posterity does not record what was said."

Afterwards, they shook hands and went to lunch where they talked about cricket. Reynolds told me "When we talked to the media and our officials, I looked at Major and he looked at me. We started speaking together and it was word for word, without any rehearsal. We were of one mind."

However they also needed a reliable go-between in Northern Ireland, and they both knew and trusted Robin Eames. Major said "Albert and I squabbled over every dot and comma, but I needed an independent view that the deal would be accepted by Unionists. Robin understood the nuances which an outsider like me, or the Civil Service, might not have known."

Reynolds said "I did not need the ear of Eames to get to Major, but he was an important part of the loop. He was friendly with James Molyneaux who was talking to Major who in turn was talking to Eames. However Robin was important in his own right because he was the authentic voice of Protestantism."

Eames confirmed all of this to me as well, and I found it extraordinary that this senior Irish cleric was so deeply involved at such a high level of Anglo-Irish politics, to the point where part of his drafts for the Downing Street Declaration was contained in the final document, almost word for word. Major told me that Eames was one of the few people who enabled them "to bring the threads together. His name did not appear on any key documents, he made no public speeches, but he had a very significant role. He was part of the engine that made the motor go."

Eames underplayed to me his role in helping to establish this landmark in Anglo-Irish relations, but I was impressed by what he had achieved. He said "We were living in highly unusual and dangerous times when lives were being lost… and I felt that there was no way in which I could stand aside."

However, Eames faced a much more difficult task in trying to bring peace to his own ecclesiastical doorstep at Drumcree. Much has been written about this stand-off between the Orangemen of the Portadown district and the nationalist residents who prevented them from completing their traditional Sunday march down the Garvaghy Road.

The dispute which began in 1995, and remains unresolved, cuts to the heart of the Northern Ireland problems of disputed territory and cultural divisions. As Archbishop of Armagh, Robin Eames and the Church of Ireland were caught in the middle of a dispute which they could not solve on their own. Eames was accused of not moving quickly enough to nip the Orange protest in the bud by demanding that the Drumcree minister the Reverend John Pickering and his Select Vestry should close the Church.

However, the Archbishop chose to take the long and difficult route of attempting to achieve a compromise, rather than trying to close down the church. It cost him dearly. He was criticised by many in his own flock, and particularly by Church of Ireland members and non-members from across the border.

My respected colleague Patsy McGarry, the Religion Correspondent of the *Irish Times*, told me that he had a high respect for Robin Eames' leadership in many other spheres, but he remained critical of his handling of Drumcree.

"He failed to give leadership on Drumcree which had the potential to be disastrous not only for the Church of Ireland, but for the island as a whole. Robin has said that Drumcree was his Calvary, and he was right."

Eames said to me "There was nothing I did through the entire situation that was simply letting something run. I may be judged right or wrong in the light of history, but I did what I thought was right."

It was a difficult situation which would have taxed the diplomacy of anyone, but in my opinion Robin Eames was right. If the Drumcree Church had been forced to close, the Orangemen would have held endless 'Drumhead' services on the hills nearby, and they would have gained even more publicity.

By taking the arduous route of trying to find consensus, Eames managed to hold the Church of Ireland together and try to keep the lid on Drumcree, as far as possible, but he was given little thanks for it.

§

Outside Northern Ireland, Robin Eames had a high profile in the Anglican Communion, and many people tipped him to succeed Dr Robert Runcie as Archbishop of Canterbury. I discovered from my extensive research that his name was indeed high on the list of possible contenders.

I believe that he would have made a good Archbishop of Canterbury, and very different from Dr George Carey who was appointed. However I also think that if Robin had had to survive the bed of nails in Lambeth Palace, the experience would have taken a serious toll on him. Besides, he still had a crucial role to play as the Church of Ireland leader in a troubled Province. So Canterbury's loss was Ireland's gain.

Eames had the intellectual, diplomatic, ecclesiastical and political skills which made him one of the most significant Primates in the history of the Church of Ireland, but he was most of all a pastor.

I recall one winter's morning when he turned up in a Belfast church hall for our regular interview. I made him his usual cup of strong black coffee, switched on my tape-recorder and started talking about the personal toll of the Troubles not only on the victims and their relatives, but also on the clergy who had to break the bad news about the death of a loved one and then conduct the funeral service.

He told me about having to talk to young women who had lost their husbands, and also about having to speak at the funerals. "Sometimes I went to the church the day before, just to absorb the atmosphere. I would see in my mind's eye what would happen the next day – the long snake of the funeral procession, the crunch of feet on the gravel, the rows of grieving faces… the political and community representatives… but every funeral was different."

Some were particularly harrowing. "On one occasion we were burying a policeman, and I was standing by the graveside as they lowered in his coffin. Suddenly I felt a tugging on my stole. I looked down and saw the face of the policeman's four-year-old daughter. She looked up at me and asked 'What are they doing with my Daddy?' That question from an innocent child has haunted me ever since."

As Robin Eames talked to me about this and other painful memories, he was almost in tears, and he seemed to be in another world of tragedy and suffering which he and too many others had experienced much too often.

My book was described by Archbishop Rowan Williams as "the best and most rounded picture we are likely have of Robin Eames for a long time," which reassured me that I had achieved a proper balance in writing about someone I had known so well personally.

Even so, he was hard to pin down completely as the subject of a biography because he is such a very private man at heart. He said to me once "If you ask me 'who is the real Robin Eames?' I could hardly tell you sometimes. The job and I are one. It's absolutely total."

There is no doubt, however, about his contribution to Northern Ireland in very troubled times. This was summed up by a former Presbyterian Moderator Dr John Dunlop, who told me "Robin had to be a moderate voice when it would have been easy to provide a tribal leadership which would have tipped this society into civil war. He was one of those people who helped Northern Ireland back from total anarchy, and he did that well."

One thing which I have not mentioned as yet is Robin's great sense of humour, and his ability to be what John Major described as 'a worldly cleric'. He added "I don't mean to question his religious credentials... but he is a man whose religion is out in the community, and not stuck behind the walls of his church. That is true among the best clerics."

When Robin Eames retired, I had advanced notice of this, and I wrote the story in the *Belfast Telegraph* which appeared early on the first morning of his last General Synod in Armagh. Due to an unfortunate mix-up, it appeared before Robin had made the announcement publicly.

My name was mud as I listened to the complaints from clerics and church administrators who accused me of stealing their Primate's big moment by flagging up his retirement in advance.

I sat through his long speech, and there was no mention of retirement. I thought "Surely Robin's not going to drop me in it by not retiring just yet..." Then he said solemnly "After much prayer, and consultation with my family, and not – I may say – with the *Belfast Telegraph*, I have decided to retire..."

I breathed a sigh of relief, and Joe Lyttle, the Religious Correspondent of RTE, had great fun running a story all day about "the Archbishop who read about his own retirement in the *Belfast Telegraph*." For the next two days I had to run the gauntlet of disaffected Anglicans who felt that I had let Robin Eames down, and he did not help by telling people "Watch what you say to that man."

Finally I took him aside, and asked him "Did my story really annoy you?" He nodded solemnly in the affirmative. My heart sank, for I had not intended to embarrass him. Then his face broke into a big grin and he said "Yes, you did annoy me and hurt me – but only officially!" He told me all I needed to know. Eames understood how the media worked, and he bore no grudge. He was the communicator and politician supreme and also a man of God who was worldly-wise. It was an attractive combination.

§

There was one other man who was also one of the most impressive human beings I met during my entire career. That man was Gordon Wilson who made national and international headlines in November

1987 when a BBC reporter asked him to comment on the death of his daughter Marie, a student nurse, following the no-warning Provisional IRA bomb at the Enniskillen Cenotaph. Marie was one of eleven people killed in the blast, which badly injured scores of others including Gordon Wilson himself, who suffered a dislocated shoulder.

His response to the BBC reporter's question on the evening of the bomb was remarkable by any standards, and it is worth repeating again. He said "I bear no ill-will. I bear no grudge. Dirty sort of talk is not going to bring her back to life. Don't ask me, please, for a purpose. I don't have a purpose. I don't have an answer. But I know there has to be a plan. It's part of a greater plan, and God is good. And we shall meet again."

I listened to the recording as I was having breakfast the next day, and I was transfixed by what he had said. His lack of ill-will was as remarkable as the cohesion of his statement, which had been made without any time to think about what he was going to say.

His words had a profound effect on many people, including the Queen who mentioned him by name in her Christmas broadcast that year. Many other people from all backgrounds were inspired by what he said.

I first met Gordon some time later. The London-based editor of one of my previous books was Christine Smith, who had been in touch with Gordon and had asked him if he would like to write a book about his experience. It was decided later on, however, that he needed professional help, so Christine arranged for us to meet in a hotel in Dungannon, roughly halfway between my home in Belfast and Enniskillen, where Gordon lived.

I discovered that he was a tall, gangly and friendly man, with a bone-crushing handshake. We liked each other immediately and I agreed to help him as best I could.

Our extended interviews took place at his home in Enniskillen where I often stayed the weekend with Gordon and his equally remarkable wife Joan, with whom I also became good friends. Usually Gordon and I would kick-start ourselves with coffee, then talk all morning, share lunch somewhere in Enniskillen, and then resume in the afternoon.

It was an intense experience for both of us. I had to maintain total concentration in trying to ask the right questions which would encourage him to open up to me. Equally it was not easy for Gordon to return in depth to one of the most horrifying experiences which could befall any family, and unfortunately this was an all-too-common experience in Northern Ireland.

Gordon Wilson had a gift for sound-bites, which is why the media quoted him so often. In private he was also a great raconteur with a sharp sense of humour and an abundant charm, but he did not find it easy to talk about the death of Marie and about all the trauma which the family had experienced. He was also conscious of the suffering of many other families, and particularly those whose relatives had been affected by the Provisional IRA bomb in Enniskillen.

One of my challenges was to ask him to explain about the whole subject of forgiveness. Some media headlines had referred to "the forgiving father" but Gordon had not used the word 'forgiveness'. Instead he had referred to bearing no 'ill-will', which was not the same.

I put this to him. He paused for a long time, and then he said "You are right, I did not mention forgiveness. The crime of the people who killed Marie and the others, and who maimed so many people, was too heinous for me to forgive. Only God can forgive them, if they are prepared to repent. I pray for them every night, and I still bear them no ill-will."

It was a typically straight answer from an honest man, and I have always remembered it. So when people say to me "I can't forgive somebody who has hurt and wronged me" I tell them about Gordon Wilson. I urge them not to bear ill-will and to work on this so that it might develop one day into full forgiveness. It is also a message which I try to apply to myself, and I am still grappling with it.

When I was writing about Gordon and his family, I was also conscious to keep alive the memory of Marie, who could not speak for herself. She had written a short prayer, almost a year before she died, and she was wrestling with challenges about her job. She wrote "Lord, my career is up-front in my mind at the moment, with Night Duty. Help me to listen to my patients and act on their problems… I pray for Northern Ireland and the whole world. I pray for the church that I might do my role. Thank you Lord. Give me wisdom."

Her father Gordon said to me "This was the voice of Marie which I would like people to remember when they think of Enniskillen."

I also discovered that Marie's mother Joan was a tower of strength. It was her strong and practical Christian faith which had helped to bring the whole family through their terrible and prolonged crisis.

The book titled *Marie – A Story from Enniskillen* and published in 1990 made a big impact and it received widespread publicity. Gordon was much in demand on television and radio, and I noticed that he was claiming the authorship of the book, though I had written every word. I did not know, at that stage, that this is the fate of most 'ghost-writers' of biographies and other books.

I began to resent this, but I gave myself a good talking to. I said "You must not seek any credit for this book. It belongs to Gordon who has gone through hell, and you are privileged to have been asked to help him write it."

So I 'gave' the book back to Gordon, and immediately it was as if a weight had lifted from my shoulders. I was also glad that I had been able to write the book in such a way that it was not only a tragedy that had befallen an Enniskillen draper and his family. I made it plain that this was a father grieving over a murdered child. It was a universal tragedy that had a universal human message.

I remained close to Gordon, and some time after the Marie book was published, I met him by chance outside the Parliament buildings in Dublin, where he served as an independent Senator, at the invitation of Albert Reynolds. He was in good form, and full of 'craic' about the gossip and interaction of Dublin politics which he was enjoying immensely.

I left feeling that he was at last emerging from the dark tunnel where he had been so long. Then tragedy struck again. Some months later, in December 1994, his adult son Peter died in a car crash, and this virtually broke his heart.

Not long afterwards, Gordon Wilson died peacefully in his home at Enniskillen on a beautiful June day in 1995. He had gone up to his room for a nap that warm morning. He fell asleep, and passed away. It was a huge shock to his family and friends, but it was a peaceful release for a man who had suffered so much.

I first heard about Gordon's death when a BBC colleague Martin O'Brien, who had Fermanagh roots, rang to tell me about it. I wrote a major obituary for the *Belfast Telegraph*, and I was interviewed for the main BBC News bulletin, which my son Mark saw when he was working in Brussels.

Gordon's funeral in Enniskillen was attended by a wide range of people, including a military aide-de-camp of President Mary Robinson, who was a close friend, as well as Albert Reynolds, and many public figures from all parts of the island, including official representatives of the British government.

The minister at the funeral suggested that the story of Gordon Wilson's life had been so rich and full of goodness that it would make a best-seller. However, I was thinking only of the death of Gordon, my good friend. The untimely death of a man who had done so much was an immense tragedy for everyone.

I stayed in touch with Gordon's family, and several months later I had a call from Joan. She asked about me and my family, as she always did, and then she said "A well known Fleet Street journalist who knew Gordon phoned me up yesterday to ask if I would help her with a biography of him. So I said to her "The only person who will write a biography of Gordon Wilson is Alf McCreary."

I was glad she had said that, because I did not want to ask her myself, in case she might not have felt able to return to memories of personal sorrow, as Gordon had done in helping me with the book on Marie.

A couple of years later, Gordon's biography was written and published with the apt title *An Ordinary Hero*. It is one of the books for which I would like to be remembered, for it tells the vivid story of how an ordinary family coped with the immense grief cause by terrorism, and which represent the feelings of so many people on all sides who had suffered through the terrible conflict.

The 'Gordon' book has remained very special to me, for another reason. The offer to write the Marie book had come to me out of the blue. When I had finished it, I wanted to claim ownership of it, but I gave it back totally to Gordon. Then when Gordon died unexpectedly, Joan gave me the opportunity, again out of the blue, to write his biography. I told myself "There's a lesson here for you. Things have their own way of happening, provided your motive is right."

Since those days I kept regularly in touch with Joan and her family. The last time I saw her was on yet another anniversary of the Enniskillen bomb. As she talked to me I noticed the portraits of Gordon and Marie hanging on the wall, and I realised again how quickly the reporters and cameras move on from each tragedy, and the family is left to their lifetime of bereavement. Joan said to me sadly "Sorrow is a frost that settles on your heart." It is an epitaph that applies to so much of Northern Ireland where reconciliation is still so vital on the path to a shared future.

After so many years of writing about the tribulations of Northern Ireland, I felt that I had witnessed enough suffering for a lifetime. However I was to experience, later in my career, a degree of suffering that surpassed anything on the scale that I had written about back home.

In 2011 I was invited by Tearfund, the UK church-based organisation which works with its partners in the developing world, to visit Rwanda with a group from Northern Ireland, and I returned there two years later.

In 1994 the country experienced the most appalling genocide when in an episode of communal madness the majority Hutu population slaughtered over one million of the Tutsi minority in 100 days, while the world's major powers including Britain and the USA did nothing to prevent it.

The roots of this internal conflict had their origin in the complex history of the country, and the details of the genocide are chronicled in a wide range of books, of which Lieutenant-General Romeo Dallaire's *Shake Hands With The Devil* is one of the best. He was UN commander in Rwanda during the genocide period.

During my visit to Rwanda I soon realised that almost everyone with whom I talked had lost relatives during the genocide, and in some cases a shocking number of people in their wider family.

The Director of Tearfund in Rwanda and Burundi, the Reverend Emmanuel Murangira told me that he had lost over ninety relatives. Another man Albert Mabasi, lost twenty-two family members, including his two younger brothers.

Claudette Uwimana, the director of the Moucecoure Centre, also suffered greatly in the genocide during which her father, two sisters and two brothers were murdered.

The Moucecoure organisation works closely with the local churches across the cultural and religious divide to establish and to foster greater community development. It is supported by a range of international donors, including Tearfund. In doing so it is bringing together Hutus and Tutsis in the villages throughout Rwanda, and it is making remarkable progress.

Albert Mabasi, who also works with Moucecoure told me "It is still extremely difficult to make sense of what happened, and to try to come to terms with the suffering. I have learned that violence totally destroys people and infrastructure. It destroys everything. I have also learned that reconciliation is the only way forward. There is no option for all of us. We have to share, and we have to come together to rebuild our country."

These words were spoken to me in a society where most people go hungry for much of the time. I visited the Gikondo Presbyterian Church in Kigali, on an advance mission to help establish a twinning link with my own Whitehouse Presbyterian Church in north Belfast, and also with Moucecoure as part of the Tearfund 'Connected Church' programme. I asked the Clerk of Session "How many people in your church have breakfast or lunch every day?" He replied "None, and although about five percent of people claim to have breakfast, this is little more than a cup of hot tea."

In the poor urban and rural parts of Rwanda, which I visited, people have only one meal a day, and meat only once a year, at Christmas. Yet this society is metaphorically pulling itself up by its bootstraps, even if in reality many Rwandans cannot afford footwear at all.

I was deeply impressed by such people. One evening I interviewed Michael Kayatiba, the former Director of Moucecoure who lost fifty-six members of his family. During the genocide he was on the run from warlike Hutus, who hunted him with dogs and rifles. He was given shelter in several different houses, which also placed his helpers in extreme danger.

In his last house he warned the lady sheltering him that one day there would be a knock on her door and the Hutus would be there to kill him. He said "When the knock comes, don't accompany me because they will kill you too." She replied "You and I are Christians, and if I let you go out to die alone, what will the angels say to me some day about leaving a fellow Christian to die in this way. So I will come with you."

The knock on the door duly came, and they went forward together to open it. However instead of being confronted by Hutu killers, they met French paratroopers who were bringing people to safety.

I thought that I had heard all the stories about suffering in my own country, but here was a new dimension in heroism. Just before our interview ended Michael confided in me "I am a Tutsi but you need to know that all the people who gave me shelter were moderate Hutus. Therefore I cannot say that all Hutus are bad people."

The parallel with my own tribal Northern Ireland was inescapable. So too was Michael's next comment. He said "We are all children of God, and we need to come out from our ethnic mindsets, and to repent and to forgive, in order to transform our society."

I had travelled a long way to hear such wisdom from a man who had miraculously survived in the cauldron of madness and murder that had engulfed his country. Sadly, however, I knew in my heart that his message was still badly needed in my own country, where many blind and bigoted people on both sides still wanted a victory and not a solution to our own tribal warfare.

However, reconciliation does not come easily anywhere. Claudette, the new Director of Moucecoure, is an elegant, thoughtful and deeply Christian young woman who told me about her struggle to forgive those who had murdered her father, her two sisters and her two brothers, and had also assaulted her.

She said "As a Christian, I have to try to forgive. I believe that the people who killed members of my family were Hutus, but I cannot hate all Hutus. Perhaps if I met the killers, I might be able to judge my forgiveness better.

"I make a distinction between tolerance and forgiveness. You can learn to tolerate someone who has harmed you, but forgiveness touches the heart. Forgiveness means that 'I also have to love you.' I feel that God has kept me alive, and that I am living for a purpose. So I do try to forgive, but it's not easy."

I came back home from Rwanda with deep questions on my mind, and deep emotions within my heart. I knew that our reconciliation process in Northern Ireland was only still in its infancy despite the efforts of so many good people to outline a shared path forward for everyone.

I also knew that I still had a long journey of reconciliation for myself, as I tried to come to terms with my attitude to my own father and mother, and to try to heal the wounds that had been inflicted so long ago.

CHAPTER TWENTY-FIVE

Relative Values

W HEN I CAUGHT up with my father Norman Leitch for the last time, in March 2010, it was too late to heal our broken relationship. Norman was dead.

I attended his funeral in Bessbrook where he had expressed a wish to be buried. The story of his funeral was as strange as my attempts to get to know him during the previous twenty-four years.

Back in 1976 when my mother Lena told me that my father was in Bessbrook Presbyterian Church for the funerals of the men murdered in the Kingsmills Massacre, I decided that I would set out to find him, in my own good time.

I had heard so much about this man who was my natural father, and I had a strong impulse to know more about him, and why he had chosen to ignore me during all those years since my childhood.

The attitude of society has changed drastically since 1940 when I was born, and some people may find it difficult to understand why anyone who had experienced the pain of being stigmatised as 'illegitimate' would wish to revisit that experience.

However I have met people with a background similar to mine who desperately wanted to meet their natural father or mother. There were others who did not care, and they were the fortunate ones. Nevertheless anyone with the compulsion to meet a parent who deserted them in childhood will understand my inner need to meet my father.

In doing so I was aware that he might not want to see me, and also that if we did meet, it might be an unhappy outcome. So I took a deep breath as I set out to find Norman Leitch and to try to discover who he really was.

I had heard a number of things about him. I knew that he had gone to England and had prospered in business to the extent that he had become very rich. I also knew that he had married a woman called Doreen, who had been a secretary to the Governor of the Bank of England.

I was also aware that in mid-life he was involved in a serious motor accident. He had spent a long time in hospital, and a great deal of it in traction. I also knew that he had written two self-published books about his life, titled *Paddy's Progress*. Most important of all, I knew that he and Doreen were childless, either by intent or because they were unable to have a baby. That meant that I was Norman's only child.

When I was confident enough in my own identity, I asked my mother Lena to tell me more about him, even though it was not easy for her to do so. She said that he was good looking, and that he was fond of me as a child.

Lena also told me that during the years long after my birth she sometimes met Norman by accident in the main street of Bessbrook, which he often visited from his base in Watford, England. She said to me each time "I met your father the other day, and I told him that I wanted him to look after you financially in his will. He said "Lena, don't you worry about Alf. He will be provided for."

It was a touching, but unrealistic, gesture on Lena's part. I knew that Norman was fobbing her off, and that he would not leave me a penny. That's the way it turned out, but I was not after his money. All I wanted was his recognition of me as his son, and also to try to build up a relationship in the years that were left to us.

However in the mid-Seventies my problem was how to find him. I discovered that he and Doreen had left England and were living in Mourne Hall, a rather grand house at Rostrevor. So I wrote to him.

My letter was polite, but to the point. I stated, in effect "I would like to meet you, but if you find that difficult to do, I will respect your decision." Crucially I did not mention our father–son relationship, and it was only later that I realised why this omission was so important.

To my surprise Norman agreed to meet me and my wife Hilary and our children Emma, Mark and Matthew. He invited us to lunch at Mourne Hall, and one afternoon we set off for Rostrevor.

Our meeting was cordial. I noticed that Norman was indeed a handsome big man. He and I shared the inconsequential conversation of people who have baggage between them, but are deciding not to mention it. His wife Doreen was charming, but in a slightly reserved English way.

Norman was proud of Mourne Hall, and he told me that his neighbours included the well known British jazz musician Chris Barber and his then wife Ottilie Patterson. Inevitably we were given a tour of Norman's large house and the outbuildings.

Our lunch was quite formal, and it seemed that Norman was putting on a show to impress us. We were served by a waitress wearing a white pinafore and lace cap while she dished out a meal of mince meat and potatoes. I thought to myself "Oh dear, Norman may be exhibiting delusions of grandeur."

After lunch Doreen took Hilary and the children for a tour of the gardens, and I went to Norman's study for a chat. I had decided deliberately not to confront him. I wanted to build a relationship of trust where the discussion of any painful matters would come naturally.

He talked several times about "Your 'father' Tommy McCreary", even though he knew that he was my real father. Clearly Norman was in denial even after all these years, and our journey of mutual discovery was not going to be easy.

I was aware, however, that our meeting may have been emotionally difficult for him also. Yet I could not understand why he had agreed to meet me, and then had made a point of denying our true relationship.

I also wondered what he had told his wife Doreen about me. Did he try to pass me off merely as a journalist from Bessbrook who wanted to talk to him? I am certain that Norman had not told her that I was his son, and that he had bluffed his way, as usual.

However, Doreen was a clever person with a woman's instinct, and I suspect that she had worked out for herself why I was there. The trouble with Norman was that he thought that he could outsmart everyone else. Sadly the only person he outsmarted in the end was himself.

Nevertheless I decided that after our Rostrevor meeting I would stay in contact with him. Initially things went well. We exchanged Christmas cards for several years, and wrote briefly to tell each other our news.

When I was appointed Director of Information at Queen's University late in 1984, I told Norman about it, and he seemed pleased. He wrote to me offering advice on how to make a success of it.

This relationship continued for some time, and then I made a mistake – though I did not find out that it was a mistake until afterwards.

A group of people who had left the village to make their career elsewhere were asked to contribute to a special updated edition of the book which the Bessbrook Spinning Company had published in 1945 to mark the centenary of the village.

The contributors included my friend Geoff Martin, my cousin Gywnneth Jones, who was making a highly-regarded name for herself in television journalism, Billy Kennedy a *News Letter* journalist and the author of several books on Ulster emigrants to America, his brother Danny, who became a Unionist minister at Stormont, and several others.

It was a handsome publication, and we gave it a special send-off at a reception in Bessbrook Town Hall. I felt instinctively that it would make a good present for Norman, so I sent him a copy, having signed it "To my Father, with best wishes."

This was my big mistake. Once I had posted the book to him, the line of communication between us went dead. There was no more contact. I had crossed a line in the sand of his make-believe by signing myself as his 'son'. He could handle a relationship with "Alf McCreary the journalist" but not the "Alf McCreary my son" who had just signed a book for him and had defined our blood relationship by addressing him as 'father'.

After that I was left in limbo, but as a journalist I knew how to find people. Norman owed me an explanation, and I was not going to give up on him, even though once again he was giving up on me.

I had one stroke of luck, and a breakthrough was provided unwittingly by my mother Lena. She told me that she had heard about the death of Norman's sister Edith and she suggested that I write a letter of sympathy to her daughter Arlene and the family.

I did so willingly, and in return I received a warm reply. Arlene and I arranged to meet, and soon we were like old friends. Arlene knew her 'Uncle Norman' well, and despite his eccentricities and bombast, she was fond of him.

She also knew the wider history of the Leitch family, and she confirmed that my lifelong friend Geoff Martin, who had connections on the Leitch side, was indeed my second cousin, which pleased me greatly.

Arlene also remembered me as a younger pupil at Newry Grammar, which brought back memories of a blonde girl at school who was kind to me, though I never knew why. That was Arlene.

Her English teacher was the same Miss Meneely who had befriended me as a young pupil, and had given me the confidence to believe in myself and to work hard at my writing. I was also delighted to discover that Arlene had a flair for English, that she had become a teacher, and that she had spent many years setting the English Literature questions for the GCSE and Senior Certificate examinations, as well as writing poetry in her spare time.

Miss Meneely had spotted the talent for writing in both of us, but she would have had no idea about the complex family connection we shared, and about which I knew nothing at that time.

Now that my father Norman had chosen not to communicate with me, there was little I could do, but Arlene kept me in touch with developments on that side of my family.

I knew that Norman was suffering from ill health, and a few years later Arlene told me that he was terminally ill with cancer. He was in his early eighties, and time was running out for both of us.

I thought about going to see him, but I had no idea as to how I would be received by him, if at all. So I wrote him a warm farewell, without making the "Good-bye" too obvious to a dying man.

I told him that I respected him for what he had achieved, and that I would have liked to have known him better. I expressed regret that we had not been able to develop our relationship further, after we had met in Rostrevor. In short I did everything I could in that letter to build a final bridge to him, but there was no reply. However I was told later by someone else that he smiled when he read my letter and that he had kept it, which surprised me.

Some time afterwards, in the year 2000, Arlene told me that he had died and that his remains would be cremated. I decided to tell my mother Lena myself before she heard from anyone else. She said "He was so handsome", and I realised that after all those years and what he had not done for her, or me, she still had a flicker of regard for him. She also told me, as she had done previously, that he had been fond of me as a baby.

I decided not to attend the cremation service in England, but Arlene still kept me in touch. I discovered that when Norman and Doreen had left Rostrevor to live in England again, they had become friendly with a young woman whom I shall call Mary, though that is not her real name.

She had been one of their tenants in England, and she later became one of their legal executors. I wrote to Mary but there was no reply. Again the trail went dead, and it remained that way for several years. I knew, however, that Doreen's health had deteriorated, and that she was suffering from dementia.

Then early in February 2010, Arlene told me that Doreen had died some time previously and had been cremated. She also told me that Mary was bringing the ashes of Norman and Doreen for burial in Bessbrook the next week, to fulfil Norman's dying wish of several years previously.

On Sunday 28 February I attended the christening in Belfast of our grandaughter Cara Rose McCreary. Our son Mark, who was in a senior editorial post in the *Sydney Morning Herald*, and one of Cara's godparents, came home for the ceremony.

On the next day 1 March 2010 my father Norman and his wife Doreen were scheduled to be buried in Bessbrook. I asked Mark to accompany me there, partly because our other son Matthew, who was a journalist in the *Belfast Telegraph*, was extremely busy at work. So Mark and I travelled to Bessbrook, and I noted that he was wearing his one and only good suit on successive days, even though people of his generation were not 'into' wearing suits. Those were memorable times indeed!

The morning of the funeral was crisp, sunny and bright, and before we went up to the Church of Ireland's Christ Church in Bessbrook we dropped in to see Auntie Jean. She took everything in her stride, and expressed no great emotion, when we told her that we were going to Norman Leitch's funeral. However she made us fresh tea, and produced her famous freshly baked scones. Jean was a woman who always had her priorities right.

As we approached the church, where I had attended services as a Boy Scout so long ago, I said to Mark "I'm not sure what will happen here, and whether this woman Mary will want me here or not."

I parked my car at the church, and the first person I met was Arlene. She then introduced me to a young woman who walked across the car park. This was Mary. She was younger that I had expected, and friendly, and we shook hands before going in to the church.

Because Norman was so elderly, and at that stage virtually unknown in Bessbrook, there was only a handful of other people present. I sat down beside Mark and Arlene in a seat near the front, while Mary went into the room of the rector, Archdeacon Raymond Hoey, whom I knew from my work as Religion Correspondent of the *Belfast Telegraph*.

Up at the front I could see the two small but handsome wooden caskets bearing the ashes of Norman and Doreen. The strong winter sun which flooded through the stained glass windows shone over the brass name plates on the caskets. It seemed like a surreal movie. I could not believe that after searching for my father for most of my life, his remains were resting just in front of me.

The funeral service was short. Halfway through, the minister said "We will now proceed to the graveside for the interment. I would like to ask Alf to carry Norman's ashes, and Mary to carry those of Doreen."

I could not believe my ears, and remained motionless, but Mark gave me a sharp elbow in the ribs. His expression was non-committal, but he had immediately recognised what this situation meant to me.

So I went to the front of the church, lifted the small casket containing my father's ashes and carried it down the aisle, while Mary carried Doreen's ashes beside me.

We moved slowly out of the church and into the strong sunshine, and then we walked towards the graveside. I talked to myself, and also to my father, as I walked. I said "I don't really believe this is happening Norman. You ran away from me all your life, and now I am carrying your ashes to your grave!"

On the way to the graveside I said to Mary "Just over that hedge, in the Presbyterian cemetery, is my mother's grave, where she is buried with her husband John. Norman is being buried only a few yards away from her in this graveyard with his wife. This is like a chapter from a novel."

The graveside service was also brief. I noticed that when Mary said "Goodbye Norman" she had a smile on her face, and I knew that she and my father must have been good friends.

There was little time to talk, following the interment, as we all had agreed to have lunch at an hotel in Banbridge where Mary was staying, close to Arlene's home.

As we drove to Banbridge, Mark and I tried to come to terms with the unexpected developments of that morning. I said to him "At the lunch will you please try to shield me from people, because I want to talk privately to Mary, and we have very little time available."

Mark did just that, and over lunch Mary and I had time to talk. She told me that she had no idea of my existence until she had read my last letter to Norman, who – not surprisingly – had never told her about me.

It transpired that she had been one of his tenants in Watford and she had become close to Doreen and Norman, who even gave her away at her wedding.

Mary had not had an easy time after Norman's death. He had owed a huge sum of money to the Inland Revenue in unpaid taxes and it had taken her a long time to unravel his complex financial affairs, with expensive professional help. She also had to look after Doreen who was in ailing health.

Mary and I got on reasonably well, for two people who were virtual strangers but who had only one thing in common – my father Norman. It was clear to me that Mary had become the surrogate daughter that Norman and Doreen had never had, and I was the natural-born son whom he had chosen to ignore for nearly all of my existence. However none of us could change the past, and we all had to move on from where we were.

Before we said our farewells, Arlene's husband David, who was an accomplished wit, uttered the best comment of the day. He paraphrased Shakespeare's Julius Caesar and said "We came to bury Norman, not to praise him…" That summed it up.

§

By that time my mother was also dead. As I noted earlier, she had learned about Norman's death from me, but during the long delay in burying his ashes, she had also passed away. If she had been alive I think that she might have gone to Norman's funeral, but equally she may well have decided not to do so. She was always embarrassed by the memory of her relationship with him, and she was worried about "What will the neighbours say?" Tragically for both of them, there were hardly any neighbours of their age left to care about what had happened.

In her later years my mother had various illnesses which she bore with fortitude, and I admired her for that. We maintained a fairly good relationship, and we rarely mentioned the 'elephant in the room' which had dominated both of us for so long.

On a few occasions we got on particularly well, but it was never the normal mother–son relationship. She was proud of me, but she could never get over what had happened to her so long ago. I don't think it was deliberate, but she always made me feel not quite the same as her other children, namely my half-brothers and half-sisters Margaret, Hilary, Richard, Harry and Pauline. To be fair to them, they did not share my mother's hang-up with the past, nor mine.

Lena was a complex person. She could be the life and soul of a party, but she could also 'turn on a sixpence', and she had an edge that could slice through steel. In contrast, her sister Jean was invariably positive, caring and encouraging, and my Uncle Bill was always like a big brother to me.

Lena's last years were difficult for her. She had had a successful heart bypass operation but in the end she developed cancer. I drove from Belfast to see her at least once a week, and I usually arrived in mid-morning when she was still in bed.

One morning our conversation drifted back to the past. She told me again how frightened she had been when she discovered she was pregnant.

I realised yet again how difficult it had been for her, but I said "Lena, did you ever realise how hard it was for me too?" At that point I think that she was beginning to understand the depths of my misery and sense of loss when she walked off and left me at the age of five.

And then she abruptly changed the subject. Even on her deathbed, she had made me feel different. We were never going to square that circle, and we both knew it. We were marooned in an emotional wasteland, and that made me sad. I think that deep down she must have been very sad too.

In the end she passed away quickly. I was on my way to a writing assignment in Enniskillen when Pauline phoned me and told me to get back to the Newry hospice as quickly as possible.

I set off for Newry but she had died just before I reached the hospice. I entered the room. I noticed that on my mother's bedside locker she had placed one of my recently-published books which she had been reading. Both of us were now beyond words.

Any bereavement is difficult for a family, and people react to death in their own different ways. The next day I returned to Enniskillen to finish my writing assignment. My family in Bessbrook were coping more than well with the funeral arrangements, and there was little I could do to help them in a practical way.

However they had requested me to say a few words at the funeral, and although I knew it would not be easy, I appreciated them asking me. On the day of the funeral we all said our farewells individually in her home.

Then I drove up to the Presbyterian Church and delivered one of the best eulogies that any mother could have wished for. Maybe that was my way, unconsciously, of squaring the circle that had hemmed both of us in, for all of our lives.

My father and mother are long gone, but I still think of them often. I have more sympathy for Lena. Some of my women friends empathise with her, but those people who have gone through a similar experience to mine almost without exception understand exactly how I feel.

A small child is powerless and vulnerable, and what happens to it in the first few years of its existence can sustain or scar that new human being for a lifetime.

I have little sympathy for Norman who ran from me, and from Lena, all his life and thought that he had outsmarted us. Sadly he was not smart enough to realise that he had a grown-up son and family who did not need him, but who were prepared to give him all the recognition he craved, and he was too afraid to accept. That was his loss. Despite all his outward show of achievement and worldly success, I felt that inside Norman there was a hollow man, and I resented his attempts to bluff even me, right to the very end.

I can understand the terrible predicament they were in, at a young age, and at a time when an unwanted pregnancy was such a social disgrace. However they had more than half a century to make amends to me, and neither of them measured up fully to their responsibilities.

All I wanted was their unconditional recognition of me as the child of their union. I wanted equality, fairness and justice, but I never received it. So I had to follow my own path, and – sadly – I learned not to need their recognition any more. You cannot chose your parents, yet Norman, Lena and I were all bound together in a unique human bond which provided the gift of life itself.

For that gift I am grateful, and although our journey was long, complicated and often painful, it developed in me the qualities of insight, confidence and strength which helped me along the way.

As I close this difficult chapter of my life, I have come to realise, at last, that somewhere within me, the three of us can be finally at peace. That will be the only kind of closure worth having.

Now it is time to move on…

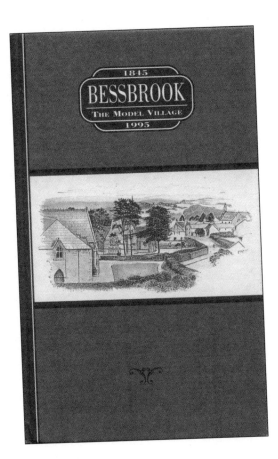

The Bessbrook Commemorative book which was published in 1995. My father was buried from the Church of Ireland building, centre. The Presbyterian Church which I attended as a boy and teenager, sometimes with my mother, is on the left.

CHAPTER TWENTY-SIX

Digging...

"Between my finger and thumb
The squat pen rests
I'll dig with it."

THESE WORDS FROM Seamus Heaney's poem 'Digging' in his *Death of a Naturalist* encapsulate the dream of every writer at every age.

They have always been important to me throughout my professional life, partly because they summarise my attitude to writing, and also because they were written by a very special human being. Seamus was one of my contemporaries at Queen's University, and we met several times later when our paths crossed during our different careers.

His untimely death on 30 August 2013 marked the end of a remarkable career as one of the best-loved and best-known poets in the English language. I was honoured to write a tribute to him in the *Belfast Telegraph,* and it was this newspaper which had published one of his first poems, in 1962. This was something which he greatly appreciated.

I wrote that "He was a charming and unassuming man who carried his poetic genius lightly", and I have fond memories of his kindness and courtesy to me, just like the many other people who had similarly warm memories of this exceptional man.

However his poem 'Digging' has always resonated with me for another reason. In these words, Heaney also implicitly acknowledged the historic breakthrough in the provision of education in the late Forties which allowed people of our generation to gain access to third-level education, and which spared us the drudgery of working on the land, or perhaps in my case, in the local linen mill.

So I have always been aware that I was privileged to follow my career of 'digging' with my pen, and by this means unearthing all kinds of rich treasures, as well as scraping along the bedrock of hard disappointments, along my life's journey.

Someone once wrote that "Life cannot be lived backwards, but only forwards." There is much truth in this, but not totally so. The present has its roots in the past, and it also has a bearing on the future.

However misguided it is to dwell too much on the past, it is tempting in the final chapter of my autobiography to take a broad view of the patterns which emerged during my life, although I had no idea what they were at the time.

When I went to Queen's University I wanted to study English, but I could not do so because I did not have the correct subjects for matriculation. Instead I read for a degree in Modern History, and then followed this with a Diploma in Education. However I soon discovered that I did not want to teach, so in one sense my university education did not seem to have had any practical outcome.

Yet much later in my career my training in historical scholarship was important, and most significantly for my book on the history of Belfast Harbour which required much detailed research.

Another new departure for me, when I left Queen's in 1998, was to hold classes for prospective authors. These took place at the University as well as in the Irish Writers School in Dublin, and also during residential weekends at the homely atmosphere of Arnold's Hotel in Donegal. I soon realised that I actually enjoyed teaching people who wanted to learn about writing.

I also discovered that many people have an inherent talent for this, and that all they need is the confidence and encouragement to express themselves. Nearly everyone has his or her story to tell, including the people in my classes who had done something worth writing about.

I am delighted every time that one of my pupils produces a book or a collection of short stories. Unfortunately, some people do not get their work published, but the real failure lies in not having the courage to try, and then spending the rest of your life wondering if you might have been a successful writer.

So in tutoring classes, and in writing historical and other books, my earlier training in academic research and in teaching was not in vain. Indeed, I believe that no experience in life is wasted, if you apply the lessons it teaches you.

However it is tempting at this stage of my life to reflect on the "What if?" questions. For example what if... my mother and her parents had given me away for adoption...? What if... I had not had a fierce primary school headmaster who literally hammered English grammar and composition into me, or a perceptive English teacher at Newry Grammar who had encouraged me to imagine, and to dream, and to build on the solid foundation for a writing career which she had gifted to me?

What if I had not passed the Eleven plus examination and perhaps ended up working in the linen factory in Bessbrook – what if I had not got the high grades required for a university scholarship?

What if... Jack Sayers, my first editor, had not given me my big break in journalism so early on... What if... I had not met Hilary at a 'hop' in the City Hospital in Belfast at the end of an unpredictable midsummer night after the results of the medical finals had been announced...?

What if... I had not been given the opportunities to visit the developing world and to report on stories of suffering and also inspiration in these deprived places, and to share them with a wider audience back home to help relieve some of that suffering?... And so it goes on.

Of course it is pointless to ask any of these questions, because they have no rational answers. You try to live your life as fully as possible at the time, and when you are young, you don't worry much about the future.

It is only when you are older that you look back on developments which seemed due to good luck, but you realise that they were not all coincidental. I have learned the hard way that some doors do not open, no matter how much you want them to do so. I am also aware that if you push too hard, the doors might burst open, but they could prove to be the wrong doors.

However I now realise that some of the best things that have happened to me – like meeting the most memorable people, or travelling to the most exciting places and being offered the most fulfilling assignments – were often unexpected. You never know when Fate is knocking kindly on your door, but it is important to recognise the opportunity being offered to you, and having the initiative to make the best of it.

So without being immodest, I might conclude that the Bessbrook boy who was born in a war-torn Europe and placed in a drawer because nobody could afford a cot for him, has travelled a long way since then.

However, somewhere in the back of my mind that same small boy who felt abandoned by his mother and father is still alive. Sometimes he talks to me, especially when I am being over-sensitive, or because I realise that he may be insecure too.

However I remind him about how far we have journeyed together, and I reassure him that he can rely on me to look after both of us, to the very end. I know that he trusts me, and that he then goes back happily to where he rests securely at the back of my head. I have also noticed that in recent years we have not needed to talk to each other so often, and I think that he, too, is beginning to forget the bad times, and that he is now much more secure within himself.

This also gives me more time and confidence to deal with my life, and to look back with more equanimity than I might have done earlier.

There is a danger, of course, that older people often think that the summers of their youth were sunnier than now, that they had the best sports teams, that they belonged to the best classes at university, and that all their geese were swans. That was not necessarily so.

Yet allowing for the danger of looking at the past through tinted spectacles, I believe that my contemporaries had the best of times, as well as some of the worst. We were the first working-class generation who had free university education, provided we could make the grades. We went to a much smaller Queen's University, which was intimate and exciting, and at a time when a university degree was a passport to a choice of different careers, unlike now when most young graduates find it hard to get the job they want.

We also avoided the two World Wars which had killed millions of the previous generations in the flower of their youth. Those of us who stayed in Northern Ireland had to deal with the horrors of the Troubles, but there was also the consolation that those who devoted their talents to bridge-building could claim the satisfaction of being part of the solution.

In a period of self-reflection it is also tempting to ask myself what were some of the best moments in my life's journey.

They have included the births of our three children Emma, Mark and Matthew and watching them grow up into such fine adults. Our daughter Emma is one of the most loving people I know, and she has wonderful gifts as a wood sculptor and weaver with the Camphill Community, and an enduring love for animals.

Our sons Matthew and Mark are both very good journalists, and I am proud that they have followed me into a tough but fascinating profession. However I am sorry that written journalism today is even less decently paid, than it was when I was their age.

I also worry about the way modern communications are developing. With such an unending coverage of world events as well as local news, there is little time to take it all in. We are a society which craves instant information, instant explanation, instant gratification, and instant 'celebrity' and success. We live in an age of greater technical communication than the world has ever known, but we seem to be even less able than our ancestors to communicate as human beings.

Journalism throughout my career was no easier than it is today, but with more outlets, more commentators, instant experts, and inter-active interlopers who often exhibit more bias than expertise, the results are often taken less seriously. People seem to have less time to read or listen carefully, and to reflect, and our society is the poorer for it.

Nevertheless journalism continues to play a vital role in our society, and it is the life-blood of democracy. It is not just a job, but a way of life, and I have always enjoyed being a part of it. I still enjoy writing, and also carrying on a long tradition in the *Belfast Telegraph* where I have worked for some fifty years under no fewer than six editors – Jack Sayers, Eugene Wason, Roy Lilley, Edmund Curran, Martin Lindsay, and Mike Gilson.

Many people have asked me how their child can get into journalism, which is regarded by many bright young people as a 'glamorous' profession. My reply is simple, but challenging: "If a person does not have the talent, determination and ability to break into journalism, he or she will not make a good journalist anyway."

Sometimes people ask me about the most important newspaper report I have written. Several of these have been described already in this book, but probably the most extraordinary story I have ever covered, in a long list of worthy contenders for this personal choice, was about the funeral of Pope John Paul II in Rome.

I face the same difficulties in choosing the favourite book I have written. Some have been mentioned earlier, but all of them were important to me in their time and context, and each remains a treasured part of my own literary family.

§

Some people choose the song 'My Way' for their retirement party, and in some cases for their funeral, but the lyrics have always seemed to me to be self-serving. I know people who have done it 'my way' and some of them have left a trail of heartbreak and chaos in their wake.

Because of the nature of my profession and the need for an individual writing style, I have often done it 'my way', but I am also aware of the large number of editors, sub-editors, designers, publishers, interviewees and other people who have contributed to the articles and books for which I am given the credit – and sometimes the blame!

Most of all I am aware of the constant support and encouragement of my wife Hilary who made so many things possible, and who never complained about my extended travels at home or abroad, and the hours spent writing in my study when I should have been trying to bring some order to the comparative chaos in our roofspace or assisting her more to keep our large garden so beautiful, or helping her in so many other ways.

Watching her with our young grandchildren Molly, Thomas, Annie and Cara, (and happily at this time of writing, another grandchild on the way!) I am reminded of what priceless treasures they all are. You really need to be a grandparent to experience the joy of sharing in these precious young lives, and of seeing the world through the eyes of a child. These are magic moments, tempered by the realisation that time passes so quickly, and that you have to cherish every good moment which is given to you.

My concentration on writing has meant that I have had less time than some other people to pursue hobbies. However I have achieved most of my minor ambitions, such as scoring a 'hole in one' on my favourite golf course at Massereene in Antrim where I still enjoy the fresh air – though not the 'air' shots!

I always wanted to catch a big fish, and I did so once on a fishing expedition with my brother-in-law Alastair Campbell, on a visit to

South Africa together with my sister-in-law Rosemary Campbell and my wife Hilary. As soon as I had caught it, however, I felt sorry for the poor thing, and I have never fished again.

I take great solace and pleasure in classical music, and I am indebted to the Ulster Orchestra for its continued excellence throughout all the decades of the Troubles and beyond. I still 'collect' some of the world's major orchestras and I go to hear them at the BBC London Proms and the National Concert Hall in Dublin, and elsewhere, as often as I can. I also like beautiful gardens, and my wife and family are great supporters of the National Trust.

However my greatest 'hobby' of all is writing itself. One of the advantages of my calling is that I can continue to write for as long as I retain my faculties, and the compulsion to put my ideas into print, and already I have a number of new projects on the horizon.

I have always enjoyed birthdays, and we are a family which celebrates each one, but my most difficult birthday was when I was thirty. I thought then that I was getting old, but after that, the steady march of time did not matter so much.

People sometimes ask me for my philosophy, and this can vary according to my mood, or the circumstances in which the question is asked, or by whom. I recall, however, a card which Hilary gave me on my fortieth birthday. It had a quotation from Goethe which stated "Nothing is more highly to be prized than the value of each day." This seems to me to be an admirable philosophy for each day of our lives.

I continue to find strength and comfort from the Scriptures, and I believe that Psalm 23 and the Lord's Prayer are admirable guidelines for life and death – in the poetic beauty of the King James' Version, of course. I am also greatly drawn to the message known as 'Desiderata' and which was reputedly found in Old Saint Paul's Church in Baltimore, dated 1692.

I hang this in my study, where I can see it every time I am writing, as I do now, and I love the final words: "Therefore be at peace with God, whatever you conceive Him to be, and whatever your labours and aspirations, in the noisy confusion of life, keep peace with your soul. With all its sham, drudgery and broken dreams, it is still a beautiful world. Strive to be happy."

The past has gone and the future remains unknown. I am grateful that I have been able to travel for so long and so far, and for much of that journey with such special companions, and not forgetting the few people who really annoyed me as much as I no doubt annoyed them!

I am by no means a saint, as my family and friends will tell you, and I retain some healthy prejudices, and doubtlessly irritating traits. I am known to yell regularly at politicians on the television, but everybody does that now and again. However I am deeply aware that we are all bound together in the bundle of life, and that we are all travelling the same road to our inevitable final human destination, and hopefully beyond that.

Of course I have regrets about people and situations which I should have handled better, and I have made mistakes and misjudgements which prompt me to ask myself "How on earth could you have done that?" On the other hand I have been continually reminded of the quiet and often unexpected goodness, decency and generosity of so many ordinary people I have met along my journey.

Sadly, I have a deep regret that peace is not yet complete in Northern Ireland. Despite all the suffering that we have been through, and despite the efforts of so many good people inside and outside Northern Ireland to make peace a reality – and not without a commendable degree of success – there is still a poisonous sectarianism in our society which has to be drained from the body politic. I have worked hard for many years with a wide range of people to build bridges, and it is now up to the younger generation to continue that vital work of healing in our wider community. I wish them well.

My story is not yet finished and I will continue writing until just before the very last chapter, if my timing is right.

In the meantime I am buoyed and chastened each day by a quote from the American newspaper editor and satirist HL Menken who was once asked for a job by a hopeful would-be journalist. Menken said to him "Young man, journalism will kill you in the end, but it will keep you alive while you are at it."

And to that I say, "Amen!"

ACKNOWLEDGEMENTS

I WOULD LIKE to thank many people for making this book possible. They include my wife Hilary, Susan and Paul Feldstein of The Feldstein Agency, Roy Lilley, Phil Coulter, and Malcolm Johnston, Jacky Hawkes, Tom Dunwoody and Rachel Irwin of Colourpoint Books.

The author and publisher would also like to thank the Belfast Development Company Ltd, Harrison Photography, Pacemaker, the *Belfast Telegraph*, Faber and Faber, the Belfast Harbour Commissioners, Ursula Mitchel and Martyn Boyd of Queen's University, and all the editors and publishers of material duly noted in this publication.

Every attempt has been made to ensure that the material in this book is correct at the time of going to press. Any significant omissions or inaccuracies will be rectified in subsequent editions.

INDEX

ALSO BY ALF MCCREARY

The Troubles:

Corrymeela
Survivors
Profiles of Hope
Tried by Fire
Marie – A Story from Enniskillen
An Ordinary Hero – The Biography of Senator Gordon Wilson
All Shall be Well (with Joan Wilson)
In War and Peace: The Story of Corrymeela
A Fund of Goodwill – The History of the International Fund for Ireland

Travelogues:

An Ulster Journey
This Northern Land
Northern Ireland – A Journey

Third World:

Up with People
Peace in Our Time

Biographical:

Nobody's Fool – The Life of Archbishop Robin Eames

Corporate and Institutional History:

The Story of the Royal Belfast Hospital for Sick Children
Spirit of the Age – The History of Old Bushmills
By All Accounts – The Story of the TSB
Degrees of Excellence – Queen's University of 1845-1995 (with
    Professor Brian Walker)
Making a Difference – The History of the Ulster Garden Villages

On With The Show – The Centenary History of the Royal Ulster
   Agricultural Society
The Story of Fleming Fulton School
A Vintage Port – Larne and its People
A Passion for Success – The Story of Coca-Cola
St. Patrick's City – The Story of Armagh
Business as Usual – Cochrane's of Belfast
Titanic Port – An Illustrated History of Belfast Harbour

Essays and Collected Journalism:

Princes, Presidents and Punters
The Good, the Bad and the Barmy
The Canary that did not Sing – Short Stories (Editor)

Autobiographical:

Remember When

Sport:

Going for Goal
Blue is the Colour

REVIEWS FOR PREVIOUS PUBLICATIONS

Titanic Port – An Illustrated History of Belfast Harbour

"It's a history not just of the port, but of the city itself and,
in many ways, a history of Ireland."
Belfast Telegraph

"a book to be proud of"
Irish News

"Alf McCreary has done a marvellous expose in giving us
such a wonderful tapestry of the history of one of the world's
great ports, and its people."
Irish Arts Review

Remember When

"To write about life one has to be a shrewd observer,
while the observer has to be able to write well to make use
of what he sees – Alf McCreary is able to do both."
Belfast Telegraph

"Evocative and entertaining, shrewd and perceptive by turns."
Irish News